Cabals and Satires

Cabals and Satires

Mozart's Comic Operas in Vienna

IAN WOODFIELD

OXFORD
UNIVERSITY PRESS

OXFORD

UNIVERSITY PRESS

Oxford University Press is a department of the University of Oxford. It furthers
the University's objective of excellence in research, scholarship, and education
by publishing worldwide. Oxford is a registered trade mark of Oxford University
Press in the UK and certain other countries.

Published in the United States of America by Oxford University Press
198 Madison Avenue, New York, NY 10016, United States of America.

CIP data is on file at the Library of Congress
ISBN 978-0-19-069263-6

This volume is published with the generous support of the Gustave Reese
Endowment of the American Musicological Society, funded in part by the National
Endowment for the Humanities and the Andrew W. Mellon Foundation.

1 3 5 7 9 8 6 4 2

Printed by Sheridan Books, Inc., United States of America

In memory of Alison Dunlop

Contents

Figures

Tables

Sources

THE DIGITIZATION OF eighteenth-century newspapers has progressed so rapidly that it is now possible to call up on screen in minutes an extraordinary range of titles.[1] Even a few years ago, systematic research coverage of this major resource would have been unrealistically time-consuming, impossible for all practical purposes. This study makes use of the reporting of current affairs in the following journals, which are listed here, rather than in the bibliography, to dramatize the extent to which the source-base for the study of eighteenth-century music has been transformed:

Amsterdamsche Courant
Annalen [Bonn]
Augspurgische Ordinari Postzeitung
Auszug aller europäischen Zeitungen [Vienna][2]
Bayreuther Zeitung
Brünner Zeitung
Budissinische Wöchentliche Nachrichten [Bautzen]
Carslruher Zeitung
Courier de l'Europe [London and Boulogne-sur-Mer]
Courier du Bas-Rhin [Cleves]
Der Baierische Landbote [Munich]
Der Wiener bothe
Dörptsche Zeitung [Tartu]
Erlanger Real Zeitung
Freiburger Zeitung

---

1. For the record, I needed to consult sources in the traditional way—in person—in only four locations: Leipzig, Salzburg, Graz, and Linz. I acknowledge with gratitude the friendly assistance I received during these library visits.

2. This journal provided an abstracting service, which sometimes reprinted items of musical news now difficult to access in the original location or even lost altogether.

Gülich und Bergische Wöchentliche Nachrichten [Düsseldorf]

Gazette de Berne

Gazette de Bonn

Gazette de Cologne

Gazette de France

Gazette van Gend

Gazzetta di Mantova

Gazzetta Toscana

Gazzetta di Weimar

Gazzetta bolognesi

Gazzetta universale [Florence]

Gothaische gelerte Zeitungen

Grätzer [Gräzer] Zeitung

Hochfürstlich Bambergisches Wochenblatt

Journal Historique et Litteraire [Luxemburg]

Journal politique de Bruxelles

Journal Politique, ou Gazette des Gazettes [Paris]

Kaiserl. Königl. Prager Oberpostamts-zeitung

Königlich privilegirte Stettinische Zeitung

Kroatischer Korrespondent

Kurfürstlich gnädigst privilegirte Münchner Zeitung

Kurfürstlich gnädigst privilegirte Wochen Blat [Munich]

Laibacher Zeitung [Ljubljana]

Langensalzisches Wochenblatt

Leipziger Zeitungen

Linzer [ordinari] Zeitung

Magazin der Sächsischen Geschichte [Dresden]

Mannheimer Zeitung

Münsterisches Intelligenzblatt

Notizie del Mondo [Florence]

Oberdeutsche Staatszeitung [Salzburg]

Paderbörnisches Intelligenzblatt

Prager interessante Nachrichten

Preßburger Zeitung

Provinzialnachrichten [Vienna]

Regensburgisches Diarium

Schlesische privilegirte Zeitung [Breslau]

Schlesische Provinzialblätter [Breslau]

Staats-Relation der neuesten europäischen Nachrichten und Begebenheiten
   [Regensburg]

Staats- und gelehrte Zeitung des Hamburgischen unpartheyischen Correspondenten
Stralsundische Zeitung
Strasburgische privilegirte Zeitung
Ungarische Staats- und Gelehrte Nachrichten [Ofen]
Weimarische Wöchentlich Anzeigen
Wienerblättchen
Wiener Zeitung
Zweibrücker Zeitung

These sixty or so titles represent a selection from the impressive number of newspapers published in Saxony, Bavaria, France, and the wider Austrian Monarchy.[3] Dutch-language journals, despite the increasingly turbulent course of events in the Low Countries, paid little attention to Viennese culture. In Prussia, there was an almost studied indifference to the literary, theatrical, and musical life of its main German-speaking rival in southern Europe, exemplified by the lack of coverage in the *Allgemeine deutsche Bibliothek*.[4] This lacuna was brought out into the open in an anonymous piece published in 1766 titled "Von dem wienerischen Geschmack in der Musik" that explicitly criticized the Berlin literary journal for failings in its coverage of Vienna.[5] The *Courier du Bas-Rhin*, published in Cleves, a Prussian exclave in the Rhinelands, reported from Vienna in an independent fashion, at times tailoring its coverage to reflect attitudes prevalent in Berlin. In the weeks leading up to the marriage of Maria Theresia and Anton, the *Courier du Bas-Rhin* consistently refused to believe that there would be any worthwhile festivities, musical or otherwise. Further north along the Baltic coast, some cities in Mecklenburg and Pomerania received musical news from Austria. One would not have anticipated that the newspaper published in Stralsund, a small town located in the eastern right-angle where Denmark abuts Germany, would be so useful a source for Viennese theater.[6]

3. Not included in this list is the sector of the press that focused exclusively on local affairs, commercial announcements, and personal advertisements, obviously of limited value in the study of international politics.

4. Bauman, "Music Reviews."

5. *Wiener Diarium* (18 October 1766), no. 84. Heartz, *Haydn, Mozart and the Viennese School*, 444, argues that the author was Dittersdorf: "On the basis of the data cited, we can conclude that the only professional composer with an inside knowledge of the imperial musical establishment and sufficient literary acumen to have written such a polemic was Ditters."

6. Blanning, *Joseph II*, 168, notes how German writers and journalists flocked to Vienna in the wake of the liberalization of censorship regulations. Some of these influential individuals, such as Joseph Friedrich von Keppler from Stralsund, may well have acted as a conduit for the transfer of information northward to their home cities.

It goes without saying that the digitization of sources is set to transform the scholarly recreation of the past. New documents relating to Mozart are appearing more rapidly than ever before.[7] Much more significant, though, is the ease with which contextual material can now be accessed. Even the best known sources are suddenly starting to appear in a new light. An example is the short notice in the *Wiener Zeitung* concerning the first performance of *Le nozze di Figaro*. The passage relating to Mozart's opera is widely cited, but the digitized version immediately reveals that the report in question covered three performances, an Italian opera, a play, and a Singspiel. It is the relative enthusiasm (or lack of it) that conveys how each work was felt to have been received. The failure to include contextual material should not of course be construed as any kind of criticism of the documentary biography project, for which strict criteria relating to the naming of the composer or his works were (and remain) the only practical means of controlling the volume of information.

Valuable though newspaper evidence is, it must be approached with caution. Press coverage tended to mix well-attested fact with conjecture, and it is often very hard to tell the one from the other. Joseph II was notoriously reluctant to divulge his intentions, and newspapers often had to resort to analysing aspects of life impossible to disguise, such as the movement of horses and equipment or the refurbishment of accommodation. In the case of the much-traveled Habsburgs, speculative travel plans were a godsend to the political commentator. If a new foreign policy or marriage treaty was thought to be imminent, itineraries for the main players would be adduced with confidence. When the predicted arrivals and departures failed to materialize, the commentator would imaginatively conjure with plausible reasons for the delay rather than admit defeat. The gray area between mere speculation and the dissemination of hard fact was often indicated by the well-worn "we hear": "man sagt" in German, "dit on" in French, "come si disse" in Italian. This mode of commentary acknowledged the leakage of snippets of information from officials who knew what was going on.

In the cultural field, foreign journals constitute an underused source of evidence. In any individual title, opera reporting may amount to little more than a series of isolated stories, but when the full spectrum of press coverage of the National Court Theater during Mozart's years in Vienna is pieced together, a significant enrichment of the existing picture takes shape. The major documentary study, Dorothea Link's indispensable work *The National Court Theatre in*

---

7. A new internet resource has been made available. *Mozart: New Documents*, a database maintained by Dexter Edge and David Black, will provide supplements to the Deutsch-Eisen documentary biography project, in the main deriving from searchable digitized sources. Michael Lorenz's long-running blog *Musical Trifles and Biographical Paralipomena* remains indispensable.

Mozart's Vienna: Sources and Documents 1783–1792 (Oxford, 1998), is based on financial records, theater posters, and Count Zinzendorf's diary. It also takes into account any pertinent information in the *Wiener Zeitung* and similar sources, but the Viennese newspaper coverage of music and theater in the 1780s is disappointing. As a matter of policy, concerts and plays were announced but not usually reviewed, and almost entirely absent is the vitriolic but revealing mudslinging that is characteristic of artistic rivalries as played out in the anarchic London papers. Even so basic a component of operatic news as the cast list is usually missing in all printed sources. In marked contrast, foreign titles made much use of unsigned private communications, a recognized channel for the dissemination of gossip. A large number of informal letters emanating from Vienna must have been in circulation; published extracts from them were typically headed "aus Privatbriefen"; "Schreiben aus Wien"; or "aus Privatnachrichten."

External coverage of the world of Viennese opera supplied human interest stories on the activities of singers, composers, poets, and theater directors and patrons. Tales of unfortunate deaths, large salaries, unusual illnesses, and unexpected occurrences were invariably appealing. News that the English composer Stephen Storace had been arrested in Vienna following an altercation at a dance was simply irresistible.[8] A proud English gentleman suffering the indignities of a rough Viennese police jail was the angle usually taken.[9] Then, as now, the press was fascinated by the life and times of any singer with the superstar status of Storace/Storacci/Sturazzo/Sturazze—everyone knew who she was, however her name was spelt. At her peak, more column inches were devoted to her in the European press than any other singer, excepting Marchesi and Gertrude Mara. Her ability to generate publicity was astonishing. Long after her departure from Vienna, stories with a byline from that city continued to appear, such as a false rumor that she had been injured in a coaching accident in England.[10]

---

8. *Kurfürstlich gnädigst privilegirte Münchner Zeitung* (2 March 1787), no. 35, 141: "Mademoiselle Storace . . . tanzte auf lezter Redoute mit einem engländischen Kavalier. Als Zuschauer stand da ein Uhlanenoffizier. Sie tratt ihm auf einen Fuß empfindlich auf. Dieser betrachtete die That als eine vorsezliche Unhöflichkeit, und machte ihr einige Vorwürfe. Sie erbitterte darüber: ihr Bruder kam hinzu, und hob einen Arm auf den Offizier bedrohend. Der Wache habende Lieutenant erblikte es, nahm den Bruder der Sängerin in Arrest, und führte ihn auf die Hauptwach."

9. *Oberdeutsche Staatszeitung* (6 March 1787), no. 47, 186: "Der Bruder der von hier abgereiseten Sängerinn Storaci (oder Sturazzo) ist 3 Täge in Eisen gesessen, hat 3 Nächte auf einer Pritsche gelegen."

10. *Strasburgische privilegirte Zeitung* (16 January 1788), no. 7, 51: Wien, den 6. Jan: "Nach Briefen aus England soll die Madame Sturazzo durch einen Sturz aus dem Wagen eines Kavaliers den Hals gebrochen haben."

Famous individuals invariably featured in anecdotes, which pithily describe a colorful incident or a neat verbal exchange. Even if the detail was embellished in the telling, these stories often contained a core of truth, and they were thus regularly reprinted in serious journals, resulting in what appears, to the modern eye, an odd mixture of fact and part-fiction. The star *buffo* singer in Joseph's troupe, Francesco Benucci, was of sufficient status to attract stories, such as a lighthearted account of a failed attempt to claim 30 ducats left in the box office.[11] The emperor himself generated a wealth of anecdotes, largely because he made a point of meeting people from all walks of life. These encounters—their number astonished contemporaries—allowed him to demonstrate his wit in conversation, and his desire to have the last word is much in evidence. When the weather made it necessary to switch rooms during a session of music-making at Laxenburg in 1786, the behavior of an unnamed musician attracted Joseph's censure.[12] Irrespective of its accuracy, the anecdote illustrated a core aspect of his credo: his lack of respect for formal rank and his instinctive urge to challenge hierarchical behavior, whenever he encountered it.

The emperor created a powerful impression with every aspect of his lifestyle: as military commander, as traveler, as administrator, as would-be man of the people, and eventually as suffering patient. Harder to discern, though, is the image of his representational role as head of state, an absence made all the more conspicuous by his modest style of dress, his desire for informality, and his eventual rejection of formal obeisance of any kind. Yet for all that he loathed static spectacle, the elaborate etiquette of courtly ritual, the emperor fully comprehended the value of visibility. His most significant concession to the need for public state ceremonial was his practice of riding out from Vienna to meet and formally accompany family members back to the Hofburg. Opera was very much part of the package. Upon arrival, distinguished visitors would appear in the theater with their host to receive the customary ovation.[13] Whether by accident or design, the distance covered by the escorting

---

11. *Bayreuther Zeitung* (13 March 1784), no. 32, 225–26: "Als der Kayser in diese Oper kam, stand Benucci neben dem Entrepnenneur bey der Casse. Der Kayser, der ihn kannte, sagte zu ihm: Vi saluto, Benucci! und legte zugleich 30 Ducaten auf den cassatisch. Benucci glaubte das Geld für sich bestimmt und wollte es einstreichen; Allein der Entrepnenneur kam ihm mit den Worten zuvor: il Complimento era per Voi, ma gli Zechini sono per me."

12. *Stralsundische Zeitung* (29 June 1786), no. 77: Wien, den 17 Junii. This anecdote refers to a recent "academy," probably the performance of Sarti's *Miserere* on Whitsunday (4 June), the only day on which there was no theatrical performance. Eleanore Liechtenstein, who thought the work beautiful, noted a "dreadful storm." Beales, *Against the World 1780–1790*, 443.

13. On 11 January 1786, Albert and Marie Christine, hours after their arrival in Vienna, went to see *Il burbero di buon cuore*. *Provinzialnachrichten* (14 January 1786), no. 4, 50.

party seemed to match the significance of the occasion. In 1785, Albert and Marie Christine were greeted in Purkersdorf in the Vienna Woods, as was Ferdinand in 1786, perhaps because Joseph himself had only just returned from a grueling journey. For his younger brother Maximilian Franz, the emperor went out much further to St. Pölten, a fact reported with pride in the Bonn press. It was a well-rehearsed and effective sequence: a meeting in one of the Austrian provinces; a formal escort; a reception at the Hofburg; and an immediate appearance in the theater.

Prominent among the emperor's "state" visits to the theater were the occasions of his own formal departures and returns. Descriptions are highly standardized and focus on the public demonstration of his role as sovereign.[14] The typical report depicts a packed auditorium into which Joseph enters to receive the acknowledgment of a brilliant company, through formal cheers or spontaneous handclapping.[15] It was noted that Austrian practice differed from that in Paris and London, where the appearance of the sovereign was marked with a verbal salutation.[16] That these occasions were fundamentally political in nature is evident from the strength of their correlation with operatic premieres. As Joseph's long-serving theater director, Count Rosenberg had to take account of this significant symbolic function when arranging the schedules.[17]

---

14. An early biographer summed up the main elements from which the descriptions derived: his preference for comic opera; his habitual occupation of an ordinary (but highly visible) box; his tendency not to remain for the full performance; and the tradition of applause to mark his return to Vienna. *Leben und Geschichte Kaiser Josephs der Zweiten*, 130.

15. Other members of the Habsburg family were saluted in similar fashion, especially during periods when the emperor was away from Vienna. *Ungarische Staats- und Gelehrte Nachrichten* (28 April 1787), no. 33, 290–91: "Den 19ten April wurde der Geburtstag der Durchl. *Prinzessin* von Würtenberg gefeyert, wo im Theater beym Kärthner Thor ein vortrefliches Concert gegeben wurde, dabey hat sich die Madame *Morichelli* und ein Virtuose auf dem Violoncelle, welcher in Russisch-kaiserl. Diensten steht, vorzüglich ausgezeichnet. Als die Durchl. Prinzessin im Theater erschien, wurde sie von allen Anwesenden mit 3maligen Händeklatschen empfangen."

16. *Oberdeutsche Staatszeitung* (29 December 1788), no. 256, 1031: Wien, den 20sten Dezember: "Der Franzose ruft, wenn der Monarch erscheint: Es lebe der König! Der Engländer ruft, wenn sich Sein König im Theater zeigt: Es lebe der König!" A rare exception was reported in October 1785, when Joseph entered the box of Elisabeth von Württemberg, hoping for once to remain unseen. A comic incident in the parterre caused him to peer over the balcony, whereupon he was greeted with a "vivat." *Carlsruher Zeitung* (17 October 1785), no. 124, 579: Wien, vom 8 Oct.

17. Such a relationship is also implied in some press reporting, at least through the juxtaposition of stories. *Gazzetta universale* (7 October 1786), no. 80, 637: VIENNA 25. Settembre. "L'Imperial M. S. dicesi, che sarà quì di ritorno verso i primi del prossimo mese, e jeri giunse d[a]lle sue Terre nella Carintia il Conte Orsini di Rosemberg Gran Ciamberlano. Frattanto si stà quì preparando il Dramma giocoso intitolato il *Mondo della Luna*."

Name day celebrations were also political occasions, to be marked with a first performance, if one was available.[18] Salieri's long-delayed *La grotta di Trofonio* was eventually given on the name day of Maximilian Franz, the emperor's youngest brother, who was Elector of Cologne.[19] Particularly significant was the first performance of *Una cosa rara*, which took place on the name day of Elisabeth von Württemberg. A charming gesture on the part of Franz, her betrothed, was applauded in the theater and taken by one press commentator as a signal that the long-awaited union was now imminent. The influence of name day observance in the operatic calendar is seen in the practice (after death) of leaving the theaters silent as a mark of respect. When added to the religious festival days—the Annunciation, Pentecost, Corpus Christi, the Nativity of the Virgin, and Christmas—as well as death-day commemorations—Franz I (17 August), Maria Theresia (28 and 29 November) and then Joseph (20 and 21 February)—name days were contributing to a gradual but inexorable increase in the number of occasions upon which the stage at the National Theater was expected to fall silent. But premieres on the name days of the living, in conjunction with festive commissions, had a beneficial effect: promoting the growth of a small canon of operas, distinctive as recipients of formal imperial patronage and frequently repeated on those grounds as well as those of their intrinsic merit.

The foreign press fully recognized the significance of these occasions of state theater and reported them with consistency. Rarely was the musical performance on such an evening allowed to have been a failure, yet there is no evidence of direct news management; rather, there seems to have been a consensus as to which attendances were worthy of note. Especial interest would be shown in the monarch's appearance in his box after a long absence; all would be well if he seemed to be in a good state of health. During the dark days of Joseph's final illness, the question was whether he could remain for the whole evening.[20]

---

18. Every now and then, a conundrum arose. In 1791, the name day of Maria Theresia, Archduke Franz's second wife, was celebrated with a gala, while the theaters remained closed as a mark of respect to the empress who shared the same name. *Bayreuther Zeitung* (21 October 1791), no. 125, Anhang, 977: Wien. vom 15 October.

19. The applause he received was typical for such an occasion. As a popular figure in Vienna, his entry was invariably "noticed" in this way by the audience. *Carlsruher Zeitung* (24 October 1785), no. 127, 591: Wien, vom 8 October: "Dieser von den Wienern noch eben so, wie vorher geliebte Fürst beehrte scither die Opern Ré Theodoro [5 October], und la Fiera di Venezia [7 October] mit seiner hohen Gegenwart und wurde jedesmal von dem zahlreichst versammelten Volk mit dem freudigsten Händeklatschen empfangen."

20. *Laibacher Zeitung* (1 December 1789), no. 49: Wien, den 25. Winterm.: "Se. Maj. befinden sich zur allgemeinen Freude jetzt so gut, daß Sie nicht nur öffentlich erscheinen, sondern auch den Theater-Vorstellungen bis an's Ende beywohnen."

It would be no exaggeration to say that the sovereign's opera attendance was everywhere used as a completely reliable litmus test for political significance. In early December 1784, Joseph was awaiting a response from Paris to his proposal for a Bavarian swap. When dispatches arrived on 3 December, he was "not at leisure," as a London newspaper put it, "to assist at the opera as he had intended."[21] On this occasion, Cimarosa's *Giannina e Bernadone* coincided with a critical juncture in state affairs. The press did not elaborate on the political question at issue (which had yet to be divulged) but took the emperor's absence from the opera house as an indisputable signal that events were afoot of sufficient importance to merit international news coverage.

On a less ceremonial level, the opera house itself often functioned as a venue for the transaction of state business. On the evening of 22 January 1787 at a performance of Sarti's *Fra i due litiganti*, Joseph was observed having a long conversation with Graf Lodovico di Belgiojoso, his representative in the Austrian Low Countries.[22] Radical reform of the seminaries and the abolition of the Council of Brabant had made it necessary to issue a proclamation on 1 January concerning the new administration and its judicial structures.[23] If Joseph received unwelcome news from Belgiojoso at the opera house as to the likely strength of the opposition, he disguised his anger well. The reporter knew nothing of the context and could offer no explanation. Later that year, Marie Christine was said to have been in the emperor's box at the theater when news of the failed attempt to seize Belgrade was delivered by a messenger.[24] By its very nature, the audience for Italian opera in Vienna was politically aware, and on one occasion the emperor received applause for a perceived success for the Austrian Monarchy. Following the arrival of two messengers from Paris with news of a resolution of a dispute over the Scheldt, he appeared at the opera on 30 September 1785 in a cheerful frame

---

21. *Daily Universal Register* (1 January 1785). On the exchanges between Vienna and Paris, see Blanning, *Joseph II*, 143–46.

22. *Bayreuther Zeitung* (29 January 1787), no. 12, Anhang, 79: Wien, vom 22. Jan.: "Graf Belgiogoso ist hier angekommen, und Sr. Maj. begegneten ihm in der Wälschen Opera außerordentlich gnädig, sprachen sehr viel mit ihm, und schienen diesen Abend sehr munter zu seyn. Die wahre Ursache seines Hierseyns weiß sich niemand zu erklären."

23. Mayer, "Price of Austria's Security," pt. 2, 475.

24. Wolf, *Marie Christine*, vol. 1, 263: "Eines Tages brachte man ihm in's Theater die Nachricht von einer mißlungenen Expedition gegen Belgrad; er erzählte das Faktum seiner Schwester und fügte hinzu: 'Ich sehe wohl, daß ich in allem, was ich unternehme, unglücklich bin.'" The emperor's reported comment is a variant of his own epitaph on his failure as he perceived it.

of mind. Everyone knew why.[25] Political discussions also took place at private concerts. Shortly after the emperor left for the front line at the end of
February 1788, the Venetian ambassador sponsored a private soirée, followed
by a reception at the Russian embassy, at which access rights to the Adriatic
for the Russian fleet were agreed.[26]

The established picture of the National Theater in Josephinian Vienna is
greatly enriched by the two German-language newspapers that consistently
analyzed the fortunes of the city's competing companies: the *Bayreuther
Zeitung* and the *Kurfürstlich gnädigst privilegirte Münchner Zeitung*. The
Bayreuther Zeitung in particular was far better informed about the Vienna
stage than any title published in Austria. Its coverage was so consistent and
distinctive that it seems reasonable to infer that it employed the services of a
regular correspondent.[27] When Joseph decided to re-form the Singspiel in the
autumn of 1785, these two newspapers were in no doubt that competition with
Italian opera was in prospect, and they followed the struggle for supremacy
as it developed. From an outside perspective, the internal pecking order of an
individual ensemble, understandably the focus of witnesses such as Da Ponte,
Kelly, Dittersdorf, and the Mozarts, was less newsworthy than the vicissitudes
of intercompany rivalry. The press also analyzed the effects of the challenge
from the commercial theater in Leopoldstadt when it decided to compete with
the repertoire of the National Theater. The ensuing rivalry between different
modes of theater, state and suburban, subsidized and commercial, was also
conducted through the medium of anonymous pamphlet exchanges, adding
to the deluge of such literature (the "Broschurenflut") that followed Joseph's
easing of restrictions.

In a study based on press reporting, it is a pity to have to admit that we
know very little about Mozart's habits as a regular newspaper reader, if he was

---

25. Beales, *Against the World 1780–1790*, 396–97; *Carlsruher Zeitung* (12 October 1785),
no. 122, 570: Wien, vom 30 Sept.: "Zwey aus Paris eingetroffne Eilboten überbrachten die
angenehme Nachricht von den mit Holland geschlossnen Friedens-Präliminarien. Des
Kaysers Majestät waren bey dieser Nachricht sehr heiter, begaben sich am Abend in die
Oper und als Sie sich mit der Prinzessinn Elisabeth von Würtemberg in der Loge befanden,
fieng das Publikum zu applaudieren an."

26. *Strasburgische privilegirte Zeitung* (11 April 1788), no. 44, 351: Wien, den 3 April: "Heute ist
Koncert beym Venetianischen Gesandten, und Souper beym russischen. Politisch! . . . Alle
Mistöne haben sich nun in den harmonischsten Akkord aufgelöset. Venedig hat sich für die
Kayserhöfe erklärt. Seine Flotte agiert nun gegen die Pforte, und das adriatische Meer steht
der russischen Flotte offen."

27. The *Bayreuther Zeitung* (14 February 1792), no. 20, 130, refers to "einen unserer Wiener
Hrn. Correspondenten."

one at all.[28] Some of the few direct references to the press in his letters come during periods when he was away from Vienna. On 18 July 1778, he mentions current gossip in Paris at the start of the War of Bavarian Succession.[29] All kinds of seismic events were supposedly under way: the emperor had invaded Saxony with 40,000 men; Baron Ernst Gideon von Laudon had been shot dead. None of this was true, and Mozart was aware that it was rumor. At the same time, he credited an unnamed newspaper with a story much more characteristic of this war of diplomatic shuttling and skirmishing: the death of a Saxon officer named Hopfgarten, a former acquaintance of his. This incident was indeed reported in the press.[30] But Leopold Mozart regularly looked through the German-language newspapers. In the autumn of 1785, for example, he alludes on 16–17 September to an anecdote about Joseph Lange that he had read in the "Wienner Currant." On 25 September, he comments on the illness of Aloysia Lange reported in the "Regensp:[urg] Zeitung von Wienn." Then on 16 December he mentions the "Erlanger Zeitung."[31]

28. Pezzl, *Skizze*, vol. 4, 558, listed the most-read foreign titles in Vienna: "Von andern Zeitungen werden am meisten gelesen die Brünner, Erlanger, Hamburger, Frankfurter, Augsburger, Regensburger, die französische von Koln, Leiden, Courrier du Bas Rhin; die wälsche von Florenz, das London Chronicle, das politische Journal . . . die allgemeine Litteraturzeitung."

29. Anderson, *Letters*, vol. 3, 851–52.

30. *London Chronicle* (2–4 July 1778): Leipsic, June 19: "A number of Imperialists were made prisoners on the above occasion, and conducted to Dresden. On our side, a Captain of grenadiers and the Chamberlain Van Hopfgarten an officer of great merit were slain."

31. *Mozart: Briefe und Aufzeichnungen*, vol. 3, 412, 416, 472; Anderson, *Letters*, vol. 3, 1330.

Introduction

ACCORDING TO THE traditional narrative of Mozart's life in Vienna, the year 1786 marked a turning point in his fortunes. He "was in continual demand as a performer and teacher, he composed a popular Singspiel, and he earned a great deal of money. Then, about the time of *Le nozze di Figaro* in 1786, things began to go sour . . . his popularity declined precipitously: his music went out of fashion, invitations to perform disappeared, and his income plummeted."[32] This image of a great composer experiencing the humiliation of undeserved professional decline, reinforced by the hauntingly autumnal qualities discerned in the music of his final years, has come under sustained attack.[33] My study of his three late Italian comedies, the Da Ponte operas, joins the ranks of revisionist works by pointing to the repeated good fortune Mozart enjoyed as a writer for the stage. Despite the mixed reception accorded to *Figaro* during its first performance run, new opportunities soon opened up: the award of a commission for *Don Giovanni* to celebrate the arrival of Maria Theresia in Prague (1787); Joseph II's last-minute choice of *Figaro* as its replacement (1787); the transfer of *Don Giovanni* to Vienna (1788); the restaging of *Figaro* as part of a retrospective for the ailing emperor (1789); and finally the decision to give *Così fan tutte* in the period of euphoria after the capture of Belgrade (1790).

Politics at every level influenced the reception of these works.[34] The contexts include: (1) Habsburg foreign policy, notably the war with the Ottoman Empire

---

32. Edge, "Mozart's Reception in Vienna," 66, summarizing the prevailing orthodoxy. An overly neat musical metaphor for the composer's rise and fall was Landon's analogy with a hairpin dynamic: five and a half years crescendo, five and a half decrescendo. Landon, *Mozart in Vienna*, 192.

33. Wolff, *Mozart at the Gateway*, 2.

34. My primary source of information about Habsburg policy in the 1780s has been the magisterial second volume, *Against the World 1780–1790*, of Beales's biography *Joseph II*. A shorter but very helpful guide is Blanning, *Joseph II*. I have benefited from Matthew Z. Mayer's lucid exposition of the shifting military and political alliances with which Joseph II and Leopold had to contend when formulating foreign policy: "The Price for Austria's Security," pts. 1 and 2. The best account of music in the Austrian Monarchy in the period leading up to the 1780s is Heartz, *Haydn, Mozart and the Viennese School 1740–1780*.

and two dynastic marriages; (2) the management of the National Theater and the effect of its repeated reorganization on the commercial stage; (3) interest groups and their activities in support of the competing national genres, opera buffa and Singspiel; and (4) individual relationships. This last category has always loomed large in the popular story of the composer's decline. Thanks to the film *Amadeus*, the image of Salieri as a devious plotter, an instigator of cabals, a master of the dark arts of theater politics, seems well-nigh indelible. Such a formidable adversary might have been expected to figure prominently in this study, yet he does not appear center stage. The spotlight falls instead on a very different character: the urbane but calculating Ditters von Dittersdorf, who was in sharp contention with Mozart in 1786 but left Vienna in the spring of 1787. The continuing rivalry (on his part) was conducted from distant Silesia, its most memorable manifestation a satirical setting of *Die Hochzeit des Figaro*.

The late 1780s were fraught years for opera in Vienna. The highly charged atmosphere stemmed from an unexpected volte-face on the part of Joseph II: his decision to reinstate the Singspiel troupe, disbanded when the opera buffa was recruited in the spring of 1783. This change of mind may have been provoked by the failure of his attempt to acquire Bavaria in exchange for the Austrian Low Countries, the so-called swap (Vertauschung). With his image as Holy Roman Emperor somewhat tarnished by the revelation of this scheme, cultural policy was an area in which he could take immediate action to improve his standing in the German-speaking world. Accordingly, he marked the reestablishment of the Singspiel troupe with a flamboyance wholly uncharacteristic of the reign. A festive evening in the Schönbrunn Orangerie, reported far and wide, constituted a cultural publicity coup without parallel in the late-eighteenth century Austrian Monarchy. Typically, Joseph staged the event as a competition, on this occasion between the opera buffa and Singspiel companies. This was a lighthearted contest, but it inaugurated two years of fierce operatic rivalry at the National Theater.

With careers on the line, cabals in support of the competing genres sprang into action. As the flagship work for the Italians, *Figaro* was targeted by the rival claque, and Mozart suffered significant damage to his reputation when anonymous correspondents attacked his new opera in the press. The first review to appear, published in a leading Munich newspaper, thought it boring ("langweilig"). In marked contrast, Dittersdorf, champion of the Singspiel troupe, achieved a resounding triumph with *Der Apotheker und der Doktor*, the scale of which suggested that the allegiance of high society to Italian opera might itself be under threat. In response, a new work by Martín y Soler, *Una cosa rara*, was brought to the stage in some haste. Explicitly designed to appeal to the tastes of women with its strong emphasis on fashion, it was an immediate success. With both troupes attracting crowds to must-see works, Mozart's opera quietly disappeared from view.

The reappearance of Singspiel at the National Theater had an immediate impact on the commercial stage. The leading suburban theater in Leopoldstadt, once again facing a state-sponsored rival performing German opera as well as one devoted to theater, staged a counterattack by commissioning its own version of *Una cosa rara*, opportunistically presented during a lengthy hiatus in performances of the original. Ferdinand Eberl's translation, *Der seltene Fall*, was an instant hit, successful enough to alarm both troupes at the National Theater: the opera buffa company because its most popular commission had been usurped; the Singspiel ensemble because it feared (rightly) that it would struggle to match the impact of this work. The theatrical world was in some ferment, and pamphleteers became very active, debating the merits of the musical genres and competing troupes.

At the start of the new season in the spring of 1787, Joseph traveled to the Crimea for a long-planned meeting with Catherine II of Russia. Upon his return to Vienna, he was confronted with a political crisis, as simmering opposition to his reform program in the Low Countries broke out into open revolt. His reaction was to dispatch an army northward, but before all the arrangements for this were in place, the prospect of a more serious external conflict caused them to be revoked. The Austrian Monarchy had bound itself by treaty to respond to any declaration of war on Russia with full-scale military assistance. As the Ottoman Empire had now taken such a step, there could be little doubt that the front line to the southeast of Vienna was about to become a major theater of war. In view of this, two dynastic marriages, pending for some time, had to be scheduled in some haste. Much the more important was the long-planned union between Franz, eldest son of Joseph's brother and nominated successor, Leopold, Grand Duke of Tuscany, and Elisabeth von Württemberg, protégée of Catherine II of Russia. The second was between Anton, younger brother of the Elector of Saxony, and Maria Theresia, Leopold's eldest daughter.

The upshot of these fast-moving political events was that three composers, Martín y Soler, Mozart, and Salieri, each received a festive commission. As the senior figure, Salieri was awarded the contract for a work to celebrate the marriage between Franz and Elisabeth (*Axur*), while Martín y Soler, now at the peak of his popularity, was the obvious choice for Maria Theresia's arrival in Vienna (*L'arbore di Diana*). Mozart's circumstances are less clear. Tradition, stemming from Franz Niemetschek's reference to a contract, has it that *Don Giovanni* originated as a commission from the Prague opera troupe, anxious to build upon the success of *Le nozze di Figaro*, but in one of his letters, Mozart hints that the opera may originally have been intended for Vienna. If such a plan ever existed, it was soon dropped. Instead, he was given the chance to provide a work for a gala evening in the Bohemian capital. Festive status was highly prized because opportunities to establish a permanent link between a composer's name and an occasion of state were as infrequent as the rewards could be great. Of more lasting value than a one-off special payment was career preferment, with its obvious correlation with the receipt of a commission. Mozart's failure to have *Don Giovanni* ready in time could have been a serious setback, but in a dramatic twist of fate, Joseph II's Hofkammerfourier, Leopold Lenoble von Edlersberg, announced a new plan: if the new opera was not ready, then *Figaro* would have to be given! ("Wenn die Neue Oper nichtgegeben werden könne, Figaro gegeben werden müsse!")[35] Its Vienna performance run having come to a rather undistinguished end, the opera unexpectedly acquired festive status and with it an altogether brighter future.

The sharp competition between German and Italian opera in 1786 placed Dittersdorf in opposition to Mozart; in effect, each was taking on a figurehead role for the ensemble for which he was currently writing. (Salieri, the obvious choice for the opera buffa faction, was away in Paris.) To judge by the public response, Dittersdorf emerged the clear victor in this contest, but it did not lead to the offer of a position. Once back in Austrian Silesia, he began work on three new Singspiels reportedly on the basis of a commission from the German troupe at the National Theater, where his standing was now at an all-time high.[36] His decision to prepare a version of *La folle journée*, entitled *Die Hochzeit des Figaro*, stemmed from the desire to fashion an attack on members of the opera buffa ensemble, a payback for the failure of his *Democritto corretto*, attributed in some quarters to the actions of leading Italian singers. Irrespective of its composer's personal motivation, the libretto affords many insights into the early reception of Mozart's opera. In transforming Beaumarchais's play into a satire, Dittersdorf was offering a commentary on *Le nozze di Figaro*: identifying, at least implicitly, what he regarded as its shortcomings. It is clear that he wrote it for Joseph II, as opposition to the emperor's political credo is lampooned in a series of vignettes. In caricaturing the star singers of the opera buffa troupe, Dittersdorf would have been well aware that the emperor relished personal parody in the theater. Mozart is cast

---

35. Leopold Lenoble von Edlersberg, usually identified in the press as Le Noble, was listed as "Kammerfourier und Quartiermeister" at the time of the coronation of Leopold II in 1791. *Urkunde über die vollzogene Krönung*, Anhang, 21.

36. *Musik*, July 1789, 51.

as Cherubino: a slight figure with abundant hair and a pale countenance, exhibiting an obsessive desire to attend the evening dance.

If Dittersdorf was hoping for an early return to Vienna, he was to be disappointed. With war approaching and cutbacks in state expenditure urgently required, Joseph decided to close the Singspiel, bringing to an end the two-year contest between the rival troupes. Before leaving Vienna, he made sure that every singer in the discontinued ensemble was offered an alternative position or financial compensation. Mozart, newly appointed to imperial service, was asked to revise *Don Giovanni* for the surviving Italian troupe, but the work's reception was adversely affected by a military crisis that came to a head in the summer of 1788. After an early success, the Austrian forces appeared to be becalmed. Low in spirits and suffering from a debilitating respiratory ailment, Joseph faced a deteriorating situation on the front line as well as unrest in Vienna. A few days after a small riot over the price and availability of bread, Salieri's *Axur* became enmeshed in war propaganda when a widely circulated story claimed that a claque had intervened in the stage action to demand that the aging hero Baron Ernst Gideon von Laudon be offered command of the imperial forces, now suddenly on the defensive following major Turkish incursions into the Banat.[37] So bad had the situation become that the emperor decided to disband the opera buffa troupe at the end of the season. The prospect that there would be no more opera at the National Theater suggested to the backers of the commercial stages that the time was right for expansion. Accordingly, the established theater at Leopoldstadt and its new rival, the Theater auf der Wieden, laid plans to enhance their existing programs of Singspiel.

But early in 1789, another volte-face on Joseph's part transformed the situation. He was persuaded to grant the opera buffa a reprieve, the decision perhaps owing something to the lighter political mood abroad in the city, following the arrival of news of Potemkin's victory at Ochakiv. A pasticcio entitled *L'ape musicale*, put together by Da Ponte as a collective benefit, saluted the change of mind. The start of the new season coincided with Mozart's journey to Berlin, undertaken in the hope of establishing a profitable relationship with Frederick William II, the music-loving king of Prussia. He was followed—doubtless the timing was fortuitous—by Dittersdorf, who in August 1788

---

37. Another political inference drawn from the plot of *Axur* came when Count Ferdinand Trauttmansdorff, Joseph's minister for the Austrian Low Countries (Belgiojoso's replacement), cited two lines from its libretto on the subject of mercy, when writing to persuade the emperor to show leniency to the rebels. Rice, *Antonio Salieri*, 417–18: Trauttmansdorf to Joseph, 3 March 1789. Schlitter, *Geheime Correspondenz*, 215.

had lost one of his two administrative posts in Silesia. With no prospect now of being asked to provide further works for the National Theater in Vienna, he had to find other ways of developing his international profile. During his weeks in Berlin, he gave a masterclass in how to manage an exploratory visit, although he was not offered a post.

Not much is known about how the reprieved troupe was managed. With the backing of fourteen aristocratic aficionados of opera buffa, led by Prince Alois Joseph Liechtenstein, Da Ponte appears to have assumed a position as a semiindependent impresario, free to promote his own dramas and ensure that his mistress, Adriana Ferrarese del Bene, remained the star attraction.[38] The new arrangement, unsurprisingly, got off to a shaky start because no recruitment had been possible during the previous six months. In time, though, it began to work in Mozart's favor. He received an immediate commission to revise *Le nozze di Figaro*, which, second time around and crucially now as a festive work, quickly established a position as a favored repertoire opera. In circumstances that remain unclear, he was also offered the chance to set *La scuola degli amanti*, an original libretto by Da Ponte for Salieri, who had soon abandoned work on it. Under its new title, *Così fan tutte* was prepared for performance during the months following the announcement of the fall of Belgrade on 14 October 1789. Although this opera enjoyed several full houses, it was adversely affected by the closure of the National Theater. Interest in it dwindled so quickly that only a single duet went on sale, a notable low for an opera given its premiere on the Vienna stage.

The death of Joseph II in February 1790, shortly before the start of the new season, might have signaled an immediate end to his operatic regime, but such was the scale of the crisis facing Leopold that he had no time to implement changes in theatrical policy or personnel. As a result, Da Ponte was left in control for a third and final year. Only in March 1791 did his dismissal signal the end of the old order. With his strongly Italianate background, the new emperor knew he had to be seen to be supportive of German theatrical culture, and the two leading suburban stages, the Leopoldstadttheater and the Theater auf der Wieden, thrived during his short reign. Leopold's interest in German opera, especially manifest at the end of 1790, suggests that Mozart's decision to join Schikaneder at the Theater auf der Wieden was in every respect a timely one.

---

38. Rice, *Antonio Salieri*, 427, gives some striking examples of this dominance; for example, during Carnival 1790, all but two of the twenty-three performances were settings of librettos by Da Ponte.

DURING THE EARLY stages of work on this study, the news of the untimely death of Dr. Alison Dunlop on 18 July 2013 came as a shock to all her friends at Queen's. A recent PhD graduate, Alison had been working at the Don Juan Archiv in Vienna, where her *Documentary Biography of Muffat* had just been advertised on the webpages of the Hollitzer Verlag. In only a few years in Vienna, she developed an extraordinary mastery of the imperial archives and was set to make a major contribution to the history of music in the city in the late eighteenth century. Our last meeting was at Sezzate Castle in Tuscany on 3 February 2013 during an informal conference hosted by Dr. Hans Ernst Weidinger.[39] During the return car-journey to the Pisa airport, Dr. Weidinger and I reviewed the events leading up to the betrothal of Maria Theresia, a conversation that provided the direct impetus for this study.[40]

---

39. She presented a paper titled "The 'Kaisersammlung': Franz II/I as Musician and Collector." This was subsequently published as Dunlop, "The 'Kaisersammlung.'"

40. The political events of the summer of 1787, explored in chapter 2 here, received a groundbreaking analysis in Dr. Weidinger's thesis, "Il dissoluto punito": section VI: "Hochszeitpläne—Reisepläne—Festpläne."

I

Intertroupe Rivalries

THE RECEPTION OF *FIGARO*

JOSEPH'S DIPLOMATIC CAMPAIGN to acquire Bavaria was conducted in secret.[1] When news of the proposal broke at the end of 1784, it dominated the headlines for a considerable period.[2] The immediate political consequence of this revelation was the formation of the Fürstenbund, a league of northern German states strongly opposed to any reconfiguration of Europe in the Habsburg interest. In the longer term, this group looked well set to establish a dominant position in the Holy Roman Empire, but a promising way of curtailing its influence would be to conclude an alliance between Austria and Saxony, on the grounds that if Dresden could be detached altogether from the northern group or at least rendered a less wholehearted member, some of the ground in the core German territories might retain a degree of neutrality. That was the view widely taken by commentators. As 1785 drew to a close, speculation about a marriage between Maria Theresia and Anton to seal this union reached fever pitch. Travel plans for the various parties were laid out with confidence; Leopold and his daughter Maria Theresia would come to Vienna, while Anton was believed to be making his way to Prague in preparation for the marriage

---

1. Zinzendorf learnt of the plan only on 17 November 1784. Beales, *Against the World 1780–1790*, 394.

2. Long after the idea had been abandoned, the exchange remained a topic for lively discussion, as can be seen in the letters of Leopold Mozart, who several times alluded to it. On 3 November 1785, he was stimulated by what he had read in the "Salzb: Zeitung." Mozart: *Briefe und Aufzeichnungen*, vol. 3, 439. In early 1786, he was convinced that the swap was still being actively sought: "wer glaubt, daß der Kayser den gedanken der *Vertauschung Bayern* aufgiebt, der irret sich sehr." *Mozart: Briefe und Aufzeichnungen*, vol. 3, 482. As a resident of Salzburg, he might have been affected personally had his city been ensnared in Joseph's grand scheme. Beales, *Against the World 1780–1790*, 394.

ceremony.[3] Divorced from reality though the anticipated conclave was, it provided a context for the evaluation of Habsburg opera attendance. The appearance of Maximilian Franz (fig. 1.1) at the National Theater was linked by one commentator to the idea that he had been lobbying the Elector of Trier; clearly this had to be the reason for the enthusiasm with which he was received at a performance of Giovanni Paisiello's *Il re Teodoro*.[4] The unknown writer executed a seamless segue from the opera report to the political question. As the weeks went by and the anticipated arrivals did not materialize, it was obvious that the diplomatic initiative had stalled. It was not difficult to come up with an explanation: opposition from Berlin.[5]

The idea that Joseph's decision early in 1785 to order the re-formation of the Singspiel troupe—even by his standards a notable volte-face—was an emergency measure, aimed at enhancing his image in the German-speaking world, deserves attention. A recommitment to the idea of a German National Theater, presenting sung repertoire as well as spoken, would demonstrate his determination to establish cultural parity with Berlin and provide some reassurance for the inhabitants of Bavaria. But the initial announcement of the new program of Singspiel provoked some sharp responses abroad. Having noted the decision, a Bayreuth commentator remarked with apparent sarcasm: "Hail to the German Caesar, who is actually going to allow the language of the land to be sung on stage."[6] Yet in time the

3. *Gazette de Leyde* (25 October 1785), no. 85, 7: De VIENNE, le 12. Octobre. "Du moins l'on assure ici, que le Mariage entre le Prince *Antoine* de *Saxe* & l'aînée des Princesses de *Toscane* est une Alliance conclüe; que, pour y mettre la dernière main, le Grand-Duc & la Grand Duchesse de *Toscane* sont attendus ici le 17. de ce mois, avec l'Archi-Duchesse *Marie-Thérèse*; & que dans l'intervalle le Prince *Antoine* de *Saxe* se rendra à *Prague*, où se sera la Cérémonie du Mariage. Si ces assertions se vérifient, le projet d'échange de la *Bavière*, auquel l'Empereur semble ne pas avoir renoncé pour tousjours, rencontreroit moins d'obstacles."

4. *Münsterisches Intelligenzblatt* (21 October 1785), no. 84: Wien, vom 5 Oct.: "Sr. Kuhrfürstl. Durchlaucht zu Ehren, wird heute das vortrefliche Singspiel: il Re Theodoro, von Päsiello, mit großem Pracht aufgeführt. Der freundschaftlichen Unterhandlung dieses liebenswürdigsten Fürsten mit Sr. Kuhrfürstl. Durchlaucht von Trier wird auch der gänzliche Abschluß wegen der Vermählung des Prinzen von Sachsen mit der Toskanischen Prinzeßinn Theresia zugeschrieben."

5. *Gazette de Leyde* (8 November 1785), no. 86, 1: De VIENNE, le 22. Octobre: "Comme le Mariage de Madame l'Archiduchesse avec le Prince *Antoine* de *Saxe*, Frère de l'Electeur, ne pourroit que réfroidir le zèle de la Cour de *Dresde* pour la Confédération *Germanique*, & faciliter au contraire le projet de l'échange des Etats *Bavarois*, l'on n'ignore pas, que la Cour de *Berlin* verroit cette Alliance de Famille avec déplaisir, & qu'elle agit en conséquence."

6. *Bayreuther Zeitung* (11 February 1785), no. 18, Anhang, 119: Wien, vom 4 Februar: "Heil dem deutschen Kayser, der auf deutschen Boden doch seine Landessprache singen läßt." Situated to the north of Bavaria, Bayreuth was a far from disinterested party, as its political future appeared to lie with Prussia, the Margrave having no male heir and the line of succession passing directly to Frederick the Great.

FIGURE 1.1 Archduke Maximilian Franz of Austria (1756–1801); portrait miniature (c. 1785), unknown artist.
Courtesy of Bildarchiv, Vienna

message got through. A correspondent in Frankfurt, musing on the prospects for a new alliance between the houses of Austria and Saxony and the consequential defection of the Dresden court from the "Ligue Germanique," prefaced the discussion by pointing out that Joseph II had acted to ensure that the entertainments ("divertissements") and pleasures ("plaisirs"), suspended in recent times, would soon become more brilliant.[7]

---

7. *Gazette de Leyde* (25 October 1785), no. 85, 8: "De FRANCOFORT, le 18. Octobre. "La Cour de *Vienne*, où les divertissemens & les plaisirs avoient été suspensus pendant les différands avec les *Hollandois*, va devenir bien brillante." The recent "differences" with the Dutch had been provoked by Joseph II's attempt to reopen the Scheldt (long closed to traffic from the Austrian Low Countries) by ordering a ship to sail downstream from Antwerp. Dutch artillery fire had forced a retreat. Blanning, *Joseph II*, 136–43.

An important source of evidence for Joseph's policy on opera in the mid-1780s is a briefing document prepared by Count Rosenberg.[8] It is unsigned, but the author identifies himself through the use of "ich" in reference to his own appointment. Although the report is undated, mention of "an outcome after almost two years" ("ein fast zweyjähriger Erfolg") in relation to the Singspiel troupe, which was restored on 16 October 1785, suggests a date in August or September 1787. The purpose of the document is thus clear; it is to provide a review of recent theatrical history in Vienna, to inform the emperor's decision as to which of the two opera troupes should be disbanded, as the Austrian Monarchy prepared for war. In compiling it, Rosenberg adopted the objective tone necessary in any official briefing for Joseph II, but his own preference for Italian opera is clear enough.

In order to give some background, Rosenberg outlined the basic rationale for theater, which, not surprisingly, emphasized the reformation of morals.[9] He described the success enjoyed by the first Singspiel troupe, showing a degree of tact when it came to coverage of its closure, which he blamed on personnel problems, notably the "excessive and insolent demands of the bass singer Fischer" ("übertriebenen groben Forderungen des Bassisten Fischer"). Turning to the Italian troupe, he explained with clarity why the considerable expense of its formation in 1783 had been entertained; its function, in significant measure political, had been to provide the community of diplomats and other foreigners, resident in Vienna, with theatrical entertainment in a language that they could understand.[10] Commenting next on what he termed "a new experiment with German opera," Rosenberg was economical with the truth. He outlined the argument that another class of inhabitants in Vienna were, although not well versed in Italian, nonetheless lovers of opera, but was

---

8. Hassmann, *Quellen und Regesten*, Doc. 487 (Bericht zu den Veränderungen bei den k. k. Hoftheatern in der Zeit von 1765 bis 1787), 310–11. This was one of a series of such reports.

9. Hassmann, *Quellen und Regesten*, 310–11: "Bey erwehnter übernahme des Theater erging zugleich der allerhöchste Befehl, daß, da die Schau-Bühne in einer volckreichen Stadt nicht bloß ein Belustigungs Orth ist, sondern vielmehr zu Einführung einer reineren Mundarth und Besserung der Sitten, überhaupt zum moralischen Nutzen dienen muß, der Bedacht genohmen werden solle, nur regelmässige, sprachrichtige und gute Sitten erzielende Stücke aufführen zu lassen."

10. Hassmann, *Quellen und Regesten*, 310–11: "1783 . . . um die vielen fremden Ministern, und anderen Ausländern, die hier seyn müssen, mit Unterhaltung auf der Bühne, die sie verstehen, zu verschaffen."

notably unforthcoming as to why this self-evident truth had not been taken into account when the first German troupe was closed in 1783.[11]

Having decided to reestablish the Singspiel, Joseph issued instructions that the new German troupe should be set up as soon as possible, with a view to starting its program in the autumn, halfway through the theatrical year; the speed is indicative of the urgency.[12] A decisive gesture was needed immediately, and for this purpose Schönbrunn was brought back into use as an artistic venue. The return to this magnificent building, effectively mothballed since the great fête on 25 November 1781 for Grand Duke Paul, spoke volumes.[13] Joseph's idea was to stage a high-profile festive competition in which German culture would compete on equal terms with Italian, a symbolic gesture certain to be widely noted. The works presented on 6 February 1785 were act 2 of Gotthold Ephraim Lessing's *Emilia Galotti*, Paisiello's *La finta amante*, and Friedrich Ludwig Wilhelm Meyer's *Der seltne Freyer*. The second of these, an Italian chamber opera, had been performed at the meeting between Joseph II and Catherine on 5 June 1780, prompting Dorothea Link to suggest that by ordering this repetition the emperor may have been hoping "to underscore his political alliance with Russia."[14] (On 2 May the previous year, Joseph had celebrated the birthday of Catherine II with music.)[15] As was the intention, the evening generated abundant publicity.[16] The following year, there would be a still grander occasion, once the two opera troupes were ready to go head-to-head in festive rivalry.

---

11. Hassmann, *Quellen und Regesten*, 310–11: "1785 wurde im Kärnthner Thor Theater abermals hauptsächlich darum ein neuer Versuch mit teutschen Opern gemacht, weil bemerckt worden ist, daß eine zweyte Classe hiesiger Einwohner, welche der wälschen Sprache nicht kundig ist, dennoch ein grosses Verlangen nach Singspielern habe."

12. So recent had been the disbandment of the original German troupe that there were sufficient performers still in Vienna to stage two Singspiels on 29 March and 1 April 1785, when the illness of a leading Italian singer prevented the opera buffa from starting its new season on schedule. The personal indisposition of a member of the rival troupe was timely, as these performances served as a declaration of intent.

13. Beales, *Against the World 1780–1790*, 127 and 447.

14. Link, *National Court Theatre*, 240. It may also have been intended as an acknowledgment of Catherine's support for his Bavarian dream.

15. *Augspurgische Ordinari Postzeitung* (17 May 1784), no. 118: Wien, den 10. May: "Am 2ten dieses wurde in dem Kayserliche Lustschlosse im Augarten, unter Anstimmung einer prächtigen Musik, das Geburtsfest Ihrer Majestät der Kayserin aller Reußen gefeyert."

16. An entire column was devoted to it in the *Staats-Relation* (13 February 1785), no. 19, which noted that there had been a "rare entertainment" ("seltene Unterhaltung") at Schönbrunn.

The Vienna public, knowing Joseph's fondness for artistic contests, was well aware that a competition between rival national genres was in prospect. Quite apart from the wider political context, the new arrangements would provide an opportunity for the leading stars of the two companies to strive for public acclaim. Mozart alluded to this in his famous letter of 21 March 1785, one of his very few statements on nationalism in music:

> My sister-in-law, Madme Lange, is the only singer permitted to join the German Opera,—Cavallieri, Adamberger, Teüber, all of them Germans of whom Germany can be proud, are obliged to stay with the Italian theater—and will be made to compete against singers from their own country! . . . If we had only one director with a sense of patriotism— everything would acquire a different face!—But it might also mean that the *National Theater*, which began to sprout so handsomely, would actually bear some fruit; and it would certainly be an everlasting embarrassment for Germany if we Germans had the audacity to act as Germans—think as Germans— speak in German, and perhaps even Sing in German!!![17]

As Link has observed, the split along national lines between the personnel of the two troupes was more pronounced now than it had been after the dissolution of the original Singspiel troupe in 1783, when thirteen of its members were transferred to the new opera buffa.[18]

In addition to the festive display in Schönbrunn and the order to reinstate the Singspiel troupe, Joseph took a third step, one at such variance with his personal taste that a political purpose seems all but certain. Notwithstanding his dislike of opera seria, he decided to recruit a leading castrato as soon as possible. A star singer would be brought to Vienna to appear in a series of special performances over the course of a month or so. The purpose behind this unexpected initiative was probably to send a cultural signal to Munich, where castrati were routinely employed, that the proposed incorporation of Bavaria into the Austrian Monarchy would not adversely affect established tastes in music there. As the featured singer would have to be newsworthy, Joseph sought his man among the most prestigious performers in Europe. His first choice was Gasparo Pacchierotti, an operatic star of the brightest magnitude, who was currently coming toward the end of a season in Trieste. An invitation

17. Spaethling, *Mozart's Letters*, 174.

18. Link, *National Court Theatre*, 12.

must have been sent very early in 1785, as the singer referred to it in a letter to Charles Burney dated 16 February: "My present engagement will end at Passion's week. The Emperor desired I would make an *Excursion* to Vienna as soon as it is over, to sing three or four times at Court. Were I to go I must spend there a month, before I return to Venice, in which neighbourhood I propose to set quiet and if I can, brase up my health during the spring and summer."[19] Such was Pacchierotti's status that he felt able to turn down a mere emperor. As he wrote to Burney on 2 May 1785, "you will immagine by what I related, that I gave up Vienna and its inhabitants, as well as many other proposals."

Having failed with Pacchierotti, Joseph tried again and was soon successful with Pacchierotti's great rival, Luigi Marchesi, recruited in person during an unscheduled visit to Italy. In spring 1785, the press was anticipating that the Neapolitan royal family would be guests at Laxenburg during Joseph's annual early summer sojourn there; the program of entertainment was to include comedy, opera, hunting, and fireworks.[20] The emperor was expected there on 27 May, where in due course he would attend the premiere of Salieri's *La grotta di Trofonio*.[21] Instead, he left without warning for Mantua, leading to speculation that the king of Naples and Maria Carolina had changed their minds about traveling northward to the Austrian Monarchy. If Joseph wished to see them, he would have to go to Italy. So abrupt was the change of plan and precipitous the departure that when he left Vienna around 5:00 a.m., everyone assumed that Laxenburg was still his destination.[22] Rosenberg suddenly found himself having to reschedule everything.[23] By traveling at exceptional speed, Joseph was able to reach Mantua in time to greet the king and his wife. The following

---

19. Beinecke Library, Yale University, Osborn Mss 3, box 13, folder 984. Pacchierotti had previously passed through Munich when returning to Italy from a London engagement. In a letter to Burney from the city dated 20 September 1784, he apologizes for not having wished Fanny "adieu." The controversial exhumation of his remains by Italian scientists in 2013 afforded many insights into the precarious state of his health, and why periods of rest would have been essential to sustaining his international career.

20. *Bayreuther Zeitung* (13 June 1785), no. 69, Anhang, 569: Wien, vom 5 Juni.

21. *Bayreuther Zeitung* (18 May 1785), no. 63, 522: Aus Oesterreich, vom 18 May. A libretto for the premiere in Laxenburg had already been printed. After the cancelation of that year's Laxenburg sojourn, Salieri's opera was not given until the autumn. It may or may not be a coincidence that Paisiello selected this subject for an opera at the Teatro di Fiorentini in Naples. *Gazetta universale* (31 December 1785), no. 105, 840: Napoli 20. Dicembre.

22. *Gazzetta universale* (11 June 1785), no. 47, 371: VIENNA 30 Maggio.

23. *Gazzetta universale* (28 June 1785), no. 52, 412: VIENNA 16 Giugno. "Il medesimo ha recato l'ordine a questo gran Ciamberlano Conte di Rosemberg di sospendere tutti i preparativi, e gli spettacoli Teatrali già ordinati per la villeggiatura al R. Castello di Luxemburgo."

day, together with his brother Ferdinand, the titular head of Lombardy, Joseph accompanied the visitors to a performance by Marchesi. Upon learning that the singer was planning to travel to Russia, Joseph seized his chance, offering him a contract for six performances of *Giulio Sabino*.[24] When the celebrated castrato appeared in the Kärntnertortheater in August, he was greeted with adulation by the Vienna audience, as the quality of his voice seized the imagination of habitual operagoers like Zinzendorf. Joseph himself seems to have been won over, to judge by his acknowledgment of the singer's virtues in a letter to Count Ludwig Cobenzl, his ambassador at St. Petersburg.[25] While it is unlikely that the emperor's impetuous dash to Italy had the recruitment of Marchesi as one of its primary objectives, it at least enabled him to realize his plan to stage a high-profile demonstration of his willingness to sponsor top-quality opera seria, notwithstanding his personal antipathy to the genre.

The reconstituted Singspiel troupe was scheduled to give its first performance on 16 October 1785. In late September, it was reported that three new singers, two men and one woman, had been recruited.[26] Although it was not yet at full strength, the company presented a German version of Monsigny's *Felix*, but critics were unimpressed, and one reviewer implied that the audience had been sent to sleep, with only Emanuel Schikaneder managing to raise a few laughs.[27] Now that Singspiel and opera buffa were once again in direct competition at the National Theater, the time was right for public discussion of the merits of the rival genres. A journal specializing in lighthearted character pieces on the foibles of the Viennese ran a short skit titled "Ein Beytrag zum Patriotismus und Theatergeschmack der Wiener." In this entertaining debate, a young lady, her mother, and an unnamed connoisseur ("Kenner"), proclaim the merits of opera buffa, while Herr von Z., who has been to the Singspiel, defends the German genre. The connoisseur agrees

24. He wrote to Rosenberg on 8 June 1785: "Il y a ici Marchesini qui passera au mois de Juillet par Vienne pour aller en Russie, il est reellement étonnant." Payer von Thurn, *Joseph II. als Theaterdirektor*, 69–70.

25. Beer and Friedler, *Joseph II. und Graf Ludwig Cobenzl*, 50: Joseph an Cobenzl: Vienne ce 26 Juillet 1785: "cet homme est un prodige pour l'étendue de sa voix et les cordes de basse qu'il a, de même que pour l'art de la musique, qu'il possède, et pour l'exécution et la variété de son chant, ayant formé de son gosier un vrai instrument dont il joue à plaisir; outre celà il est d'une très jolie figure, fort bon acteur, et il récite bien."

26. *Bayreuther Zeitung* (27 September 1785), no. 116, 917: Wien, vom 26 Sept.

27. *Bayreuther Zeitung* (27 October 1785), no. 129, 1005: Wien, vom 21 October: "Der einzige Herr Schikaneder erzwang durch seine buffonische Spaße zuweilen ein Lächeln, sonsten wäre das ganze Publikum eingeschlafen." Zinzendorf, who went with Rosenberg, thought the inaugural work "detestablement executé." Link, *National Court Theatre*, 255.

with the mother's brusque dismissal of German nonsense, pointing out that Italians possess more skill in singing. The response is that Germans are able to express the truth of emotions through a balance of acting and singing skills.[28] Z. makes the mistake of introducing "technical" terminology ("Triller und Gurgeleyen") into the debate and is promptly put down on the grounds of his self-confessed ignorance about music.[29] The argument starts to become heated when he asserts that only the Germans, only the Viennese, are stupid enough to saddle themselves with Italian drivel, rejecting the tasteful homegrown product.[30] At this point, the landlord intervenes to suggest that Z. should leave; it turns out that he, too, is a great admirer of Italian opera.[31]

Any doubt that what Joseph had in mind was a direct competition between the two opera troupes was dispelled when the weekly calendar was rejigged to incorporate the third ensemble in a carefully constructed timetable (Table 1.1). Occasionally, as at the start of the 1786 season, the sequence would for some reason depart from its normal pattern, with performances by the various troupes a day out, but the usual pattern was resumed before the premiere of *Le nozze di Figaro*. A "silent" night at the National Theater on the

Table 1.1 The weekly schedule at the National Theater (1785–86)

	Sun	Mon	Tue	Wed	Thu	Fri	Sat
2 troupes	P	O	P	O	P	O	P
3 troupes	P, S	O	P, S	O	P	O, S	P

P = play; O = Italian opera; S = Singspiel

28. *Der wienerische Zuschauer*, no. 5, 13: *Ein Musikkenner.* "Da haben Euer Gnaden wohl recht. Die wälsche Sprache ist viel sonorer; auch besitzen die Wälschen mehr Geschicklichkeit im Singen." *Herr v. Z.* "Und ich kann Sie versichern, daß ich mehrere deutsche Sängerinen hörte, die mit dem gehörigen Ausdruck und wahren Gefühle sangen, und auch richtiges Spiel mit Gesang verbanden."

29. *Der wienerische Zuschauer*, no. 5, 13: *Herr v. Z:* "Sie meinen doch nicht Triller und Gurgeleyen?" *Musikkenner.* "Gurgeleyen! Gurgeleyen! Verziehen Sie mir, Herr v. Z. —, aber von der Musik können Sie unmöglich urtheilen, da Sie, wie Sie mir erst gestern gestanden, nicht eine Note kennen." This amusing exchange was cited by Hunter, *Culture of Opera Buffa*, 43.

30. *Der wienerische Zuschauer*, no. 5, 13: *Herr v. Z.* "Nur der Deutsche . . . nur Wiener sind thöricht genug, sich wälschen Unsinn aufbürden zu lassen, und geschmackvolle Landesproduckte zu verwerfen."

31. *Der wienerische Zuschauer*, no. 5, 13: *Der Herr von Haus.* "Ich bin selbst ein ungleich grösserer Liebhaber von der wälschen Opera als von der Deutschen."

occasion of a religious festival or name day observance would not disrupt the schedules; the company affected would simply lose the revenue. Under the new arrangements, the German theater company and Italian opera each retained two nights when they could perform unopposed. The new Singspiel ensemble would not usually play without competition but would challenge the actors on two nights and their fellow singers once a week. Friday nights would thus be opera nights, head-to-head competitions between the two languages, pitting singer against singer, exactly as predicted by Mozart. At this once-a-week confrontation, public (and indeed imperial) preferences would be hard to disguise.

This rivalry would come at a cost, as a second theater would be required to service three troupes. The Burgtheater remained the venue for theater and opera buffa, while the Kärntnertortheater was designated as the home of the restored Singspiel. A news item in Bayreuth interpreted the imminent opening of the Kärntnertortheater as an outright triumph for German culture in Vienna, over-egging the story in startling fashion. Reporting that the auditorium was nearly ready, the item claimed that the building was set to take over the title of National Theater, as the Burgtheater was about to be taken down![32] Table 1.2 summarizes the total salary bill in gulden for the three ensembles using figures provided by Link. The years before and after the competition are included for comparison.

In addition to the expense of running a second theater, some 20,000 gulden (in a full year) would be required for the personnel of the third company, to add to the 80,000 for the existing troupes. Some form of financial guarantee would be required. Link summarizes the situation, noting that in the setup year for the Singspiel Joseph provided 12,000 gulden and in the following years 10,000 and 12,000.[33] On the balance sheet, this was an accumulating liability, to be paid back over time or else written off. Press reports early in 1786 demonstrate awareness of not just the new troupe but the additional funding. There was no political sense in making these resources available if the wider world did not know about them. To offset higher expenditure, an increase in box office takings could be expected, at least in the short term. Over a longer period, the effect of increasing the number of weekly opera performances from three to five and the scheduling of four on successive nights (Sunday to Wednesday) was harder to predict.

As a further step to demonstrate support for German theatrical culture, there were several well-publicized Habsburg visits to the commercial theater in

---

32. *Bayreuther Zeitung* (16 June 1785), no. 71, 577: Wien, vom 10 Junii: "Das Kärntner Thortheater wird nun bald in fertigen Stande seyn. Es sieht ganz allerliebst aus, und soll künftig das Nationaltheater genennet werden, weil das Burgtheater eingerissen werden soll."

33. Link, *National Court Theatre*, 302.

Table 1.2 Salary costs at the National Theater (1784–89)

	1784–85			1785–86			1786–87			1787–88			1788–89		
	T	O	S	T	O	S	T	O	S	T	O	S	T	O	S
	35,547	36,278		32,526	38,171	5,776	32,221	38,910	14,933	32,455	36,651	14,918	32,164	37,110	
		11,674			11,924	2,587		12,186	5,174		11,159	4,742		12,340	

T = theater; O = Italian opera; S = Singspiel

Sums in the second row are payments to orchestral musicians.

Leopoldstadt. A party including Maximilian Franz went to see Johann Baptist Schenk's *Die Weinlese* on 23 October 1785.[34] Albert, Duke of Sachsen-Teschen, husband of Joseph II's sister Marie Christine (see fig. 1.2), also attended a performance on 24 January 1786.[35] These visits acknowledged the considerable success of this Singspiel, which, according to one report, drew a link between its title (the grape harvest) and the failure of the crop that year. *Die Weinlese* generated 9,000 gulden from its first twenty performances, an average of 450 gulden a night.[36] A further sign of its success is that in 1786 Hieronymus Löschenkohl included a "Weinlese" fan in his collection, advertised in a fashion magazine.[37]

What was starting to look like a trend was reinforced by an unequivocal gesture that generated widespread international coverage: a full Habsburg party consisting of Joseph, Franz, Albert, and Marie Christine went to a Kasperl performance, an acknowledgment of the much-loved but lowbrow German comic figure by the high-minded emperor rightly seen as significant. The language used to describe the comedy—"notorious" ("berüchtigen") in one German source, "ridiculous" ("ridicola") in an Italian—points to the surprise occasioned by his choice.[38] Another notice revealingly reports Joseph at the performance by "our" Kasperl, the implication being that this was not "his" Kasperl.[39] According

---

34. *Bayreuther Zeitung* (31 October 1785), no. 130, Anhang, 1016: Wien, vom 25. October: "Sonntags Abends geruheten Se. Majestät der Kayser, Se. K. H. der Churfürst von Cölln, der Großherzogliche Prinz Franz und die Princeßin Elisabeth in der Leopoldstadt der nun zum 10ten mal aufgeführten Opera, betittelt die Weinlese, bey dem sogennanten Kasperl beyzuwohnen." Angermüller, *Wenzel Müller*, 165: 23 October [1785]: "Joseph II und Erzherzog Maximilian Franz schauen sich das Singspiel 'Die Weinlese' an."

35. *Kurfürstlich gnädigst privilegirte Münchner Zeitung* (31 January 1786), no. 18, 69: Aus Privatbriefen vom 25 Jäner: "Gestern beehrt der Herzog Albert das komische Theater des sogenannten Kasperl in der Leopoldstadt mit seiner Gegenwart, wo die teutsche Oper die Weinlese aufgeführt ward." Angermüller, *Wenzel Müller*, 167, records another visit by Joseph II to *Die Weinlese* on 21 November 1786.

36. *Laibacher Zeitung* (22 December 1785), no. 51: Wien, den 21. Nov.: "Die allgemeine Weinlese ist traurig ausgefallen.—wenig, und schlecht. Dafür hat des hiesigen Kasperle seine Opera, die Weinlese betittelt, welche 20 mal aufgeführet worden, bereits dem Impresario (Entrepreneur) baare Neuntausend Gulden eintragen."

37. *Intelligenz Blatt des Journals der Moden* (June 1786) [catalogue of fans available from Löschenkohl in Vienna], no. 12: "Die Weinlese; Auf diesem Fächer befindet sich der 7 Auftritt des 3 Aufzugs, aus Kasperls Weinlese."

38. *Zweibrücker Zeitung* (26 February 1786), no. 25. *Gazzetta universale* (28 February 1786), no. 17, 131. In his *Tagebuch*, Wenzel Müller mentioned only Marie Christine and Albert, possibly because they were guests of honor in Vienna. Angermüller, *Wenzel Müller*, 167.

39. *Bayreuther Zeitung* (24 February 1786), no. 24, Anhang, 153: Wien, vom 17 Febr.: "Vorgestern verfügte sich der Kayserl. Hof nach der Leopoldstadt, um den luftigen Schuster-Feyerabend unseres Casperl anzusehen."

FIGURE I.2 Duke Albert of Sachsen-Teschen (1738–1822) and Archduchess Marie Christine of Austria (1742–1789); portrait miniature (c. 1790), unknown artist. Courtesy of Bildarchiv, Vienna

to Dittersdorf, however, he enjoyed the evening sufficiently to ask for a score of a bass aria to sing with his Kammermusik.[40] The sheer incongruity of Joseph in the role of Kasperl generated an anecdote in which a simple-minded musician blurts out praise for the accuracy of the emperor's portrayal.[41] If the idea of

40. Dittersdorf, *Lebensbeschreibung*, 240: "Der Kaiser gieng eines Abends ins Marinellische Theater in der Leopoldstadt. Kasperl sang, als Nachwächter, eine Arie außerordentlich komisch. Der Kaiser, dem sie sehr gefiel, ließ sie sich abschreiben und, da er eine gute Baßstimme hatte, so sang er sie bey seiner Kammermusik."

41. *Der neue deutsche Zuschauer*, (1790), vol. 4, pt. 10, 32: Skizzirte Lebensgeschichte Joseph II: "Oft hatte er Abends seine Kammermusick bei sich und da sang er gewöhnlich selbst einige Arien aus komischen Opern. . . . Aus dem marinlischen Theater, wo der beliebte Wienerkasperl spielt, ließ sich Kaiser Joseph die Weinlese, der Musick nach ein niedliches Singspiel, bringen, und sang davon die Liederchen von Kasperl. Ein simpler einfältiger Musikus ward darüber so entzückt, daß er in seiner Einfalt entzückt ausrufte: Euer Majestät der akurate Kasperl!" Dittersdorf identified this unnamed individual as a rather more substantial figure: Joseph's valet and chamber player, Franz Kreibich.

patronizing the theater in Leopoldstadt was intended to encourage publicity in the wider German-language press, it was a complete success.[42]

As a curtain-raiser for the forthcoming season of competition between opera buffa and Singspiel, a second high-profile festive night was staged at Schönbrunn.[43] The new German troupe and the established Italian opera ensemble were each instructed to prepare a one-act comedy.[44] Although both are well-known works, it will be useful to summarize their plots here, as this distinctive style of in-house satire was emulated several times during the following five years, on the assumption that Joseph II appreciated the genre's potential for sharp personal caricature. *Prima la musica poi le parole* concerns a new opera to be made ready in four days. The score has been completed, but the poet is having such trouble with the verse that he has to resort to adapting previously written material. The prima donna Eleanora enters to perform a scene from Giuseppe Sarti's *Giulio Sabino*, a comic parody of a serious moment. Tonina, the *buffa* soprano, is next. She demands an aria and is hastily supplied with one, but the two singers quarrel over which piece should come first. The solution is simultaneous performance. The humor comes from the fact that individuals are readily identifiable: Giovanni Battista Casti and Da Ponte as rival poets; Storace (Eleanora) and Celeste Coltellini (Tonina) as rival sopranos.

After an interval, a new comedy followed with music by Mozart: *Der Schauspieldirektor*, a one-act play with elaborate arias and ensembles. Two singers, also readily identifiable as competitors in real life, are auditioned for a new company. Madame Herz (Aloysia Lange) is the first to have her salary settled, at 16 thalers a week. In another reflection of reality, Madame Silberklang (Cavalieri) then turns up for her audition. Lange was already an established member of the new German ensemble, having transferred in the autumn of 1785, but Cavalieri had remained with the opera buffa. For the purpose of the Schönbrunn skit, she now returned to the Singspiel

---

42. As Link, *National Court Theatre*, 200, has pointed out, German drama was also presented to Albert and Marie Christine when they visited one of Johann Eszterházy's *comédies de société*, a gesture with potential symbolism: "The hosts may simply have been showing off the local culture, but it might be worth considering that these choices were symbolic."

43. A traditional view of the Schönbrunn festival is that it was, if slightly unexpected, a conventional "dynastische Faschingsfest" to honor the visit of Albert and Marie Christine. Greisenegger, "Höfische Theaterfeste in Wien," 74.

44. Early reports were not specific. *Carlsruher Zeitung* (1 February 1786), no. 14, 64: Wien, vom 18 Jan.: "die neusten Sing- und Schauspiele."

(her original ensemble) to join Lange in the fictional auditions for the proposed troupe. She, too, is successful, but her rival is not happy that she has been offered the same salary. At the climax of this operatic trifle, the two singers debate the question as to who is most fit to assume the title of "first" singer. A compromise is reached when both are awarded top billing.

Joseph was not only responsible for devising the overall plan of the evening; he was also widely credited with having come up with the outline of the plot of *Der Schauspieldirektor* himself.[45] Whether or not this was so, it drew the public's attention to the extent of his personal involvement with the newly re-formed troupe. By mid-January, Stephanie had developed this synopsis into a drama.[46] After the contest was over, a Vienna journal gave the verdict to the Singspiel: "But it is most certainly not due to national partiality, nor to base flattery, if we say that the German piece infinitely surpassed the Italian one in intrinsic value."[47] The rewards offered to the participants were carefully calibrated, with Mozart famously receiving only half Salieri's fee because of the smaller amount of work required.[48] In some press reports, however, the two composers are on an equal footing, receiving 100 ducats each: information that was on message politically, even if not true.[49]

Artistic rivalry, the theme of the Schönbrunn evening, inaugurated the two seasons of the opera contest. The double bill was repeated three times in the Kärntnertortheater on the following Saturdays—in effect as extra events.

---

45. *Brünner Zeitung* (8 February 1786), no. 11, 86. Oesterreich, vom 3 Februar: "Zu der Oper, die man daselbst aufführen will, soll der Monarch selbst den Plan hergegeben haben."

46. *Budissinische Wöchentliche Nachrichten* (4 February 1786), no. 5, 20: Wien, den 18. Jan.: "Der berühmte Schauspieler Stephani allhier, der die Gnade des Monarchen besitzt, bearbeitet nach einem vom Kayser selbst vorgelegten Plan ein theatralisches Stück."

47. Deutsch, *Mozart: A Documentary Biography*, 266, citing *Allgemeine Wiener Bücher-Nachrichten oder Verzeichnis Neuer und Alter Bücher für das Jahr 1786* (22 February 1786). Schwob, "Partner oder Rivalen?," 79, characterizes the outcome of the contest as to a degree predetermined: "der Sieg Salieris war mehr oder weniger vorprogrammiert." There is no evidence, however, to suggest a formal determination of the outcome, a "regelrechten Urteil einer Jury oder des Kaisers."

48. The tiny remuneration awarded to each of the prompters, 10 gulden for the Italian assistant, 6 gulden for the German, also took account of the greater duties undertaken by the former. *Gazzetta universale* (21 February 1786), no. 15, 115: VIENNA 9. Febbrajo.

49. *Bayreuther Zeitung* (15 February 1786), no. 21, 131: Wien, vom 10. Febr.: "Die Italiänischen und deutschen Sänger erhielten bey dem Festin zu Schönbrunn jeder 50 Ducaten, das Orchester 100, und die Compositeurs jeder 100 Stück Ducaten."

Such was the level of interest in Vienna that the police had to be called to
restore order at the first performance, as the numbers wanting to get in
exceeded even the crowds who had flocked to hear the celebrated castrato
Marchesi.[50] Now that a direct choice between opera and Singspiel was available, Joseph's theater attendance was keenly observed, but a report relating to
the evening of 27 February 1786, the first operatic clash after the third public
performance of the Schönbrunn double bill, fails to specify whether he chose
to go to Salieri's *La grotta di Trofonio* or Gluck's *Die Pilgrimme von Mecca*. As
it happened, the main news story was the flare-up of an eye infection that
forced him to leave early.[51]

In the weeks leading up to the first full season of intercompany rivalry,
there was speculation as to how the appearance of a third troupe might affect
the management of the National Theater. A significant realignment of duties
was predicted, with some foreign press notices indicating that Rosenberg
was about to relinquish his position altogether. According to Grand Duke
Leopold's *Relazione*, observations on his time in Vienna written in secret
during a visit to his brother in 1784, Joseph's theater director enjoyed a position of unequaled access, as his duty was to attend Joseph daily when he rose
at 6:00 a.m.[52] An unusually detailed news item in Bayreuth summarized
the theatrical rumors circulating before the start of the new season. Its author acknowledged that his information was merely the current word on the
street, although it is clear that he thought the changes significant enough to
mark a new beginning.[53] It was reasonable to predict that the addition of a
second opera company to Rosenberg's portfolio would increase its vexatious
elements, but in the light of his attempt to refuse Mozart the use of dancers
in *Figaro*, the rumor that he was discontented with his troublesome post and

50. *Carslruher Zeitung* (3 March 1786), no. 27, 123: Wien, vom 18 Febr.: "Bey den ersten
Vorstellung war die Menge der Zuschauer so stark, daß sie jene, welche herbeygeeilt war,
den berühmten Marchesini zu hören überstieg. Es fiel einige Unordnung vor, welcher aber
die Thätigkeit der Polizey sogleich vorbeugte."

51. *Journal Historique et Litteraire* (1 April 1786), 533: VIENNE (le 10 Mars): "L'Empereur est
attaqué de nouveau d'une fluxion sur les yeux depuis le 25 Février, & quoique Sa M. assistât
encore le 27 au spectacle, le mal empira tellement tout-à-coup qu'elle fut obligée de se re-
tirer." Joseph had struggled with serious eye problems since the early 1780s. Beales, *Against
the World 1780–1790*, 225.

52. Beales, *Against the World 1780–1790*, 425.

53. *Bayreuther Zeitung* (15 February 1786), no. 21, 131: Wien: vom 10. Febr: "Mit unserm
National-Theater soll eine neue Schöpfung vor sich gehen. Ich muß ihnen doch alles wieder
erzählen, was man hier öffentlich spricht."

that overall theatrical direction might pass to Baron Gottfried van Swieten is fascinating.[54] Rosenberg's attitude to German opera at this period is uncertain, although it is telling that in his briefing paper on theater he passed over Dittersdorf's achievements in silence. A few years later he was thought to be a sworn enemy of the genre.[55] The realignment of duties did not happen, yet that did not stop it from being reported as fact.[56] In a preecho of modern times, rumors of cabinet reshuffles often escalated into an open season for febrile speculation.

In a preview of the 1786 season, another commentator (very much on message) praised the efforts Joseph was making to ensure that his newly constituted Singspiel troupe would be the finest in Germany.[57] He, too, presented the start of the new season as a relaunch of opera in Vienna, with the clear, if unspoken, implication that a bid was under way to outdo the city's main cultural rival, Berlin. Some of the predictions of increased expenditure were unfounded. The reported offer of a contract to the celebrated balletmaster Jean Georges Noverre to form an ensemble of dancers for the new Singspiel, for example, was mere rumor, fueled, perhaps, by the presence in Vienna of the dancer Auguste Vestris.[58]

The decision by Storace to remain for the 1786 season was encouraging news for the Italian troupe as it prepared to face competition from its German rival. Her future had been in some doubt after she lost her voice during a

---

54. *Bayreuther Zeitung* (15 February 1786), no. 21, 131: "Die Ober-Direction über das ganze Theater erhielte der Freyherr von Suieten weil der Graf Rosenberg diesen mühsamen Posten nicht länger zu begleiten wünsche." Van Swieten was regarded as a safe pair of hands but was heartily disliked. Even one of his supporters could not understand "how such a man could hide so much graciousness and goodness behind such a disagreeable exterior, and such a frosty manner." Beales, *Against the World 1780–1790*, 310–11.

55. Hassmann, *Quellen und Regesten*, 310–11. *Berlinische musikalische Zeitung* (1793) 141: 12 October: "Fürst Rosenberg . . . der ein abgesagter Feind der Deutschen ist und durchaus nichts hören kann, was nicht Italienisch ist." Cited in Rice, *Antonio Salieri*, 562.

56. *Oberdeutsche Staatszeitung* (21 February 1786), no. 37, 145: Wien, den 20. Febr.: "Baron Swieten wird auf des Kaysers Verlangen seine Stellen als Oberhaupt der Studienkommission, und Direktor der kayserl. königl. Bibliothek an einen andern überlassen, und [unclear] Directeurs des Plaisirs (Oberaussehers der Belustigungen) welche Stelle bisher der Oberkammerherr Graf von Rosenberg bekleidete, nebst der Aussicht und Censur über sämmtliche Theater übernehmen."

57. *Erlanger Real Zeitung* (10 February 1786), no. 12, 103: Wiener Nachrichten: "Auf die neue deutsche Oper werden von dem Monarchen grosse Kosten verwendet, um sie zur ersten in Deutschland zu erheben . . . Hr. Noverre soll ersucht worden seyn, für das deutsche Operntheater ein Ballet zu formiren."

58. *Mannheimer Zeitung* (7 December 1785), no. 147, 602.

performance of her brother's opera *Gli sposi malcontenti*.[59] The cantata *Per la ricuperata salute di Ofelia*, an unusual musical accolade composed jointly by Salieri, Mozart, and Cornetti to celebrate Storace's return on 19 September 1785, could be read as an expression of relief on the part of the opera buffa troupe as a whole, their most bankable star having returned from illness. It may also have been intended as a public relations exercise, timed to appear a few weeks before the Singspiel ensemble was due to enter the fray. In the light of the forthcoming contest, her retention for the new season was a priority, and she was able to negotiate a large salary increase to 1,000 ducats.[60] With two new women singers also expected soon, the future of Italian opera appeared healthy. In an exact mirror of what was predicted for the Singspiel, Vienna could now hope to hear the best Italian opera in all Germany—a telling choice of geography by a reporter in Bayreuth.[61]

It is not known when the idea of an opera on *La folle journée* was first mooted. The extended review article devoted to a German translation of the play in three issues of the *Wienerblättchen* between 28 February and 2 March 1785 could certainly have provided the initial impetus. From the outset, the authors would have been in no doubt that imperial approval would be essential in view of the recent ban on *Der närrische Tag*. Da Ponte took it upon himself to seek what in effect was an exemption.[62] On 11 November 1785, Leopold Mozart told his daughter that he had received a note from her brother in which he apologized for its brevity on the grounds that he had been working flat out on the new opera.[63] Leopold surmised that Count Rosenberg was badgering Wolfgang to finish: "nun muß er einmahl mit Ernst daran, weil es vom Gr: Rosenberg getrieben wird." Mozart's rush suggests that he felt

---

59. In the context of Storace's ongoing illnesses, Link questions whether Kelly's recollection that she lost her voice completely is accurate. Link, "Nancy Storace's *Annus Horribilis*," 4.

60. *Oberdeutsche Staatszeitung* (22 February 1786), no. 38, 149: Wien, den 18ten Febr.: "Storazzo aber wurde ihr Gehalt noch mit 200 Dukaten vermehrt, daß sie also jährliche 1000 Dukaten ihrer Kehle zu verdanken hat." Link, *National Court Theatre*, 415 and 421, confirms the increase was from 4071.20 gulden to 4,500 gulden.

61. *Bayreuther Zeitung* (13 January 1786), no. 6, Anhang, 34: Wien, vom 6 Januar: "Madame Sturazzo, unsere beliebte Opera-Sängerin bleibt nun wiederum bey uns. Sie hat in etwas von ihrem weiblichen Eigensinn nachgelassen, und dafür eine Zulage erhalten. Es sind auch zwey neue Sängerinnen verschrieben worden, und wir dürfen uns schmeicheln, in ganz Deutschland die beste Italiänische Oper zu besitzen."

62. Woodfield, "Trouble with Cherubino," 168.

63. *Mozart: Briefe und Aufzeichnungen*, vol. 3, 443–44: "weil er über Hals und Kopf die opera, *le Nozze di Figaro*, fertig machen muß."

under pressure to complete the opera as soon as possible. It is by no means out of the question that the intertroupe rivalry, as yet only a few weeks old, contributed to the sense of urgency. From the perspective of the Italian party and their champion Rosenberg, a premiere in January or February would allow the opera buffa to end the season with a work based on Europe's most universally popular play. For some reason—the unexpected appearance of a contract for *Der Schauspieldirektor* may well have caused some delay—*Figaro* was not ready in time, and the Italian program came to an end on an unfortunate note with Giuseppe Gazzaniga's *Il finto cieco*, a feeble effort that was performed a mere three times. By way of an excuse, Da Ponte pointed out that he had been instructed to prioritize it.[64] As much of the music for act 2 was missing, he had been obliged to commandeer scores from elsewhere. An uncomfortable demonstration of what could happen when an opera was flung together at the last moment, it neatly inverted Casti's satire in which texts have to be located for preexisting music. As a reviewer in the *Realzeitung* drily observed, "too often one was reminded of arias and choruses in other operas."[65]

In December 1785, with the first phase of work on *Figaro* complete, Mozart's reputation as a composer of opera buffa received a significant boost when his contributions to Francesco Bianchi's *La villanella rapita* (25 November) received publicity abroad. One wonders who was responsible for the notice that appeared in the Florentine journal *Gazzetta universale* as part of an end-of-year summary.[66] Although his name was mangled, "Moshard" was mentioned for his contribution, the ensembles "Dite almeno" and "Mandina amabile."[67] The

---

64. The choice of a Gazzaniga work may have been a consequence of Joseph II's visit to La Scala in Milan with his brother Ferdinand to hear that composer's *Il serraglio di Osmano*. *Gazzetta universale* (28 June 1785), no. 52, 415: MILANO 22. Giugno. An unidentified "Gazaniga" was present at a dinner given by the French ambassador in Vienna on 13 March 1785. Link, *National Court Theatre*, 241.

65. Michtner, *Das alte Burgtheater*, 201–2; cited in Heartz, *Mozart, Haydn and Early Beethoven*, 127.

66. *Gazzetta universale* (10 December 1785), no. 99, 788: VIENNA 28. Novembre: "E' noto a tutta l'Italia quale scelta Compagnia di Comici abbiamo in questa Dominante, e sono cognite non meno le Opere buffe, la di cui musica è scritta per questi valenti Soggetti, e che difficilmente può riescire gradevole se viene cantata da Compagnie di minor merito. Fra le altre rappresentanze sorprende quella che ha per titolo *la Villanella rapita* con terzetti, e quartetti nuovi del Maestro Moshard." Edge, "Report on the Viennese Premiere of *La villanella rapita*," in Edge and Black, *Mozart*.

67. Interestingly, in his first reference to Mozart, Zinzendorf, noting his attendance at *La villanella rapita* on 30 November, also uses the spelling "Moshart." Link, *National Court Theatre*, 258.

Vienna troupe was praised for its ability to stage works that would challenge
"less meritorious ensembles" ("compagnie di minor merito"). To the average
Italian reader, this comment would probably have come across as generic
praise, but anyone aware of current theatrical developments in Vienna might
have read it as coded disparagement of the Singspiel troupe. In a subsequent
notice, Mozart's enrichment of Bianchi's score was singled out a second time;
the repetition provides a whiff of some form of news management.[68]
    Further encouragement for Mozart came with the selection of *Idomeneo*
for a private series at the Auersperg Palace. In the wake of Marchesi's tri-
umphant passage through Vienna in the summer of 1785, the attraction of
the figure of the castrato to women had elicited humorous comment.[69] The
world of Viennese fashion was quick to exploit this fascination. In June 1786, a
Parisian journal reported that ear pendants "à la Marchesini," long enough to
reach an appropriate part of the female anatomy, were popular in Vienna; they
even sported a favorite aria of the singer in readable golden notes.[70] It seems
probable, therefore, that the short Auersperg season of works was driven by
women's taste, a follow-up to the success of *Giulio Sabino*. But even though
a castrato named Viganoni was expected in Vienna, according to a news item
in April 1786, it is unlikely that he took part.[71] The three unnamed operas
mentioned in the report were presumably *Idomeneo* and Gluck's *Alceste* in the

---

68. *Gazzetta universale* (24 January 1786), no. 7, 52: VIENNA 12. Gennajo: "La Musica di
essa è del Sig. Maestro Bianchi di Cremona . . . e solo ora arricchita di un Terzetto, ed un
Quartetto dal celebre Maestro Sig. Mozart." Edge, "*La villanelle rapita* in Vienna," in Edge
and Black, *Mozart*.

69. *Der wienerische Zuschauer*, no. 1, 59: Oeffentliche Spektakel: "Dieser Sänger hat sich auch
die allgemeine Bewunderung erworben, und die Damen gestehen sich einhellig (wiewohl
mit einigen Lächeln), daß sie noch nie so einen Helden gesehen haben." The Marchesi effect
was still a talking point in 1789. Reitzenstein, *Reise nach Wien*, 246, recorded the following
envious comment: "Wenn ich singen könnte wie Marchesini . . . so würde ich die Eroberung
aller schönen Weiber von Wien machen." Reitzenstein's account of his year in Vienna is
discussed in Keefe, *Mozart in Vienna*, 2.

70. *Der Journal der Moden* (June 1786), 224: "In Wien trägt man Ohren-Gehänge von Gold *à
la Marchesini*. Sie sind sehr lang, so daß sie fast auf den Busen herabhängen, und bestehen
aus lauter kleinen aneinander hängenden goldnen Noten-Blättern, auf denen eine Lieblings-
Arie des berühmten und in Wien so beliebten Sängers *Marchesini*, gravirt ist, so daß man sie
davon absingen kann."

71. *Oberdeutsche Staatszeitung* (18 April 1786), no. 76, 301: Wien, den 12ten April: "Die
allerwichtigste Neuigkeit . . . welche unsre Schöne Welt so sehr entzückt, ist . . . daß ein
Castrat Viganoni genannt, hier angekommen ist, welcher sich in 3 Opern hören lassen
wird." Whether this singer was related to the well-known tenor Giuseppe Vigagnoni, who
was employed by the opera buffa troupe during the 1784–85 season, is not known. A singer
identified as "Hr. Vigarano, Operist" passed through Regensburg en route to Nuremberg on
28 July 1786. Haberl, *Das Regensburgische Diarium*, 235.

Auersperg series and *Orfeo*, given as an academy at the Kärntnertortheater on 11 March.[72] The nonappearance of an expected castrato might account for some of the late changes to the voice types required for the Auersperg *Idomeneo*, as well as the fact that no beneficiary is named for the Kärntnertortheater benefit, the only occasion during the season when this happened.[73]

In the early weeks of the season, the advantage went to the Singspiel troupe, who gave a double bill of premieres on their opening night. It featured Friedrich Karl Lippert, a performer with pulling power whose star quality was immediately recognized in an anecdote describing the manner in which he acknowledged his applause; he compared his joy to that of the deserter upon receiving his pardon.[74] His was a first appearance of sufficient interest to merit a substantial report ("Debüt des Hrn. Lippert"). The reviewer praised his "charming, light-toned, manly, beautiful voice" ("reizende, helltönende, männlich schöne Stimme") and his "fine, unaffected acting" ("edle und ungezwungene Aktion").[75] Because commentary on operatic performances (reviewing) was restricted to the assessment of new singers, this evaluation of Lippert's first appearance had to act as a proxy for the Singspiel troupe as a whole as it set out its stall for the new season. However they were read, though, reports of his debut in *Der Deserteur* gave notice that the Italian singers were facing a formidable rival. The Italian opera company had to wait until 1 May for its first new work (*Le nozze di Figaro*), with a short delay in the arrival of Luisa Laschi and Dorotea Sardi (Bussani) contributing to the slow start. Among supporters of opera buffa, hopes were high for Laschi, who had been well liked during an earlier eight-month contract in Vienna and had since attracted favorable notice in Italy.[76]

---

72. Zinzendorf was unimpressed: "La musique d'Orfée ne fit pas tres grand effect." Link, *National Court Theatre*, 267.

73. A year later, another visiting castrato, Giovanni Carlo Conciliani, was awarded a benefit academy in the Kärntnertortheater.

74. *Erlanger Real Zeitung* (28 April 1786), no. 33, 281: Aus den kaiserl. königlichen Staaten: "Als am 21. [April] Hr. Lippert, der ehmals bei der Großmannischen Gesellschaft war, im k. k. Hoftheater am Kärnthner-Thor in dem Singspiel: der Deserteur, in Gegenwart des Hofes debütirte, erhielt er so allgemeinen Beifall, daß er am Ende des Stücks hervorgerufen wurde, er erschien und sagte ganz gerührt: der wirkliche Deserteur kann über seine Begnadigung nicht fröhlicher seyn, als ich es bei diesem überausgnädigen und schmeichelhaften Beifall bin." When he passed through Regensburg on his way to Vienna on 18 March, he was described as a Court singer, probably by mistake: "Herr[n] Lippert, Hofsänger bey Sr. k. k. Majestät." Haberl, *Das Regensburgische Diarium*, 230.

75. *Provinzialnachrichten* (22 April 1786), no. 11, 103.

76. *Gazzetta di Toscana* (1785), no. 31, 123: FIRENZE 30 Luglio: "Tutti gli Attori si distinguono con la bravura nel canto, e sorprende la Sig. Laschi con un aria specialmente che con gran maestria canta nel secondo Atto."

The opposing factions opened their campaigns in boisterous fashion. In its preview, the Salzburg pamphlet *Pfeffer und Salz* anticipated that *Figaro* would encounter opposition. It expected Mozart's new work to surpass other operas recently staged in Vienna but ominously used a satirical skit to posit the existence of a cabal. Leopold Kozeluch, it was alleged, had written an opera for Celeste Coltellini that had run into difficulty, perhaps owing to a scheduling problem. Should a similar fate await Mozart, what then was to be said about native talent? An ironic salutation—long live Salieri and Casti!—ends the piece. This is all rather obscure, probably a make-believe scenario; its point, though, was that Mozart as a German composer was about to face opposition from the Italian party—in other words, from some members of the very troupe for whom he was currently writing.[77]

The term "cabal" implies an interest group, acting sometimes in secret, usually with hostile intent. When Joseph placed his two opera troupes in direct opposition, he guaranteed the emergence of factions, divided along national lines. The struggle was not just between two ensembles but between two genres and even two languages. At the height of the contest in 1786, a widespread perception on both sides was that the opposition was resorting to the dark arts of theater politics in an effort to gain the upper hand: the organization of claques primed to hiss or applaud as appropriate; the deliberate circulation of malicious rumors; and attempts to influence reception in published sources. The sense of paranoia fed by the intertroupe contest added to the in-house rivalries that so often bedeviled personal relationships, as librettists and composers competed for commissions and singers for roles.[78] In one respect, however, the sharpness of this contest should not come as a surprise, as it reflected the uncertainty inherent in working for an individual as unpredictable as Joseph II. There was no guarantee that the rich theatrical program to

---

77. *Pfeffer und Salz*, Salzburg, 1786: Wien: am 5 April: "Man freuet sich auf eine Opera, die Hr. Mozart für das Theater gemacht haben soll, sie kann leicht die wälsche Opern, die Zeit her gegeben wurden, übertreffen. Auch Hr. Kozeluch sollte eine schreiben, er schrieb sie für M. Coldolini, und man wollte sie dann erst geben, da M. Coldelini nicht mehr zu Wien sein würde. Kozeluch übersah den wälschen Plan der Ro+gischen Lieblinge und blieb aus. Wenn es Hr. Mozarten eben so geht, ha, welche Unterstützung für einheimische! Künstler. Es leben Salieri und Casti!" Deutsch, *Mozart: Die Dokumente*, 236.

78. A case in point was an "Italian" dispute, which Da Ponte frames in the context of his rivalry with Giovanni Battista Casti. When Francesco Bussani informed the theater management that there was to be a dance in act 3 of *Le nozze di Figaro* in apparent contravention of the emperor's policy, there was a concerted attempt to have it removed. The famous scene in which Rosenberg is seen tearing out the offending pages from the libretto is followed by the counter-coup staged by Da Ponte in which Joseph rescinds the prohibition, to the obvious chagrin of Casti.

be presented during 1786 for a very specific purpose would be sustained, and a significant number of livelihoods and reputations would be at stake if either company had to close. Insecurity was made worse by constant speculation in the press (no doubt sometimes planted) that one or other troupe was on the verge of being disbanded. Even before the start of the season, the Italian performers saw their futures up for discussion, although for the time being they were deemed to have security because the political situation was stable, a view reinforced by the comforting observation that Joseph was a connoisseur of music who was hardly likely to act against his own tastes.[79]

In the weeks before *Figaro* came to the stage, Mozart found himself in an especially awkward situation. As composer of *Die Entführung*, the most successful Singspiel by far in the repertoire of the German troupe, and as their recent champion (and victor as some saw it) in the Schönbrunn contest, he was crossing the national dividing line with his new opera buffa at a particularly contentious moment. It is little wonder that Leopold Mozart, perhaps taking his cue from the skit in *Pfeffer und Salz* as well as Josefa and Franz Xaver Duschek, alluded to the strength of the cabals (plural) ranged against his son.[80] Mozart, it seems, was facing opposition both from elements in the Singspiel faction (as composer of the new Italian opera) and from some Italians (as a German). Rightly or wrongly, Leopold laid the blame squarely at Salieri's door. He failed to see—or perhaps he did not know enough of the background—that the more dangerous threat to his son's work came from the German party. In fairness to Salieri, who by then was on the verge of leaving Vienna for Paris, it should be pointed out that he was away for more than a year, exactly the period during which *Figaro* struggled to make an impact. Moreover, when the dust settled at the end of the season, there were dark hints that Mozart had suffered more from the actions of false friends (Germans) than declared enemies (Italians).

---

79. *Kurfürstlich gnädigst privilegirte Münchner Zeitung* (9 January 1786), no. 5, 18: Wien, vom 31 Dezbr. (aus Privatbriefen): "Es hatte sich das Gerücht verbreitet, daß Seine Majestät die italiänische Opernsänger abdanken wollten; aber so lange Friedenshofnung ist, wird es wohl nicht geschehen, denn der Kaiser [unclear] die Tonkunst, ist Kenner, und ergözt sich selbst in den Stunden Seiner Musse auf verschiedenen Instrumente."

80. "Heute den 28ten gehet deines Bruders Opera, *le Nozze di Figaro*, das erste mal in Scena. Es wird viel seyn, wenn er reußiert, denn ich weis, daß er erstaunliche starke Cabalen wider sich hat. *Salieri* mit seinem ganzen Anhang wird wieder Himmel und Erden in Bewegung zu bringen sich alle Mühe geben. H: und Mdem Duschek sagten mir es schon, daß dein Bruder eben desswegen so sehr viele Cabalen gegen sich habe, weil er wegen seinem besonderen Talent und Geschicklichkeit in so grossem Ansehen stehe." *Mozart: Briefe und Aufzeichnungen*, vol. 3, 536; Anderson, *Letters*, vol. 3, 1336.

While the immediate fortunes of Italian opera depended to no small extent upon the reception accorded to *Figaro*, the Singspiel troupe could look forward to Dittersdorf's new commission to provide the highlight of its season.[81] The two composers thus found themselves (willingly or not) preparing to be cast as temporary champions of the two troupes.[82] A contentious matter soon arose: the scheduling of Dittersdorf's concert in the Augarten, offered to him in recognition of his generosity in providing the Tonkünstler-Societät with an oratorio.[83] He intended to make use of the occasion to introduce his innovative symphonies on subjects selected from Ovid's *Metamorphoses*.[84] It is clear that this performance was to have been scheduled around the time of the second night of *Figaro* on 3 May, although the plan was thwarted by the weather. On 30 April, Vienna was basking in warm spring sunshine with a temperature of seventy degrees. The following day, with a northerly wind established, temperatures plummeted toward freezing. The weather was unusual enough to attract attention abroad.[85] By 10:00 p.m., with *Figaro* still presumably in progress, 45 degrees fahrenheit was recorded, and the next

81. The precise timing of his commission for *Der Apotheker* is unclear. In his autobiography, he was inconsistent, recollecting that Stephanie had come to ask about a new work as he was preparing to leave after his symphony concert in the Augarten (i.e., mid-May). But this is immediately followed by the statement that he took about six months to compose it, placing the contract nearer to the start of the year. Dittersdorf's *Lebensbeschreibung* was constructed from materials dictated late in life to his son; the text was completed two days before his death on 24 October 1799. Although the composer played no part in the editorial process of bringing the work to fruition, historians and musicologists concede that in matters of factual detail his recollections appear to be quite reliable. An earlier version of the celebrated passage in which Dittersdorf gave his views on Mozart was published in the *Allgemeine musikalische Zeitung*, March 1799, 382. Some material (omitted in the final text) is of significant interest.

82. The idea that Dittersdorf was a significant competitor for Mozart around the time of *Figaro* is not a new one. See Schenk, *Mozart and His Times*, 367–69.

83. On behalf of the society, Giuseppe Bonno had written to inform him that his oratorio *Hiob* would be given on 7 and 9 April, with rehearsals the previous week. Unverricht, *Carl von Dittersdorf: Briefe*, 49: Vienna, 24 February. The letter offers some interesting advice; the performance should be no longer than an hour and a half (excluding any concert items)— this presumably meant per night—and Dittersdorf would do well to restrict the amount of simple recitative, Viennese tastes having recently changed. In the 1780s, older oratorios, or new settings of older texts, were routinely abbreviated in Vienna to take account of overall length. Black, "Mozart's Association with the Tonkünstler-Societät," 55–75.

84. Rice, "New Light on Dittersdorf's Ovid Symphonies," 453–98, discusses the Vienna performances of these works.

85. *Kurfürstlich gnädigst privilegirte Münchner Zeitung* (9 May 1786), no. 73, 290: Wien vom 5ten Mai. (aus Wienerzeitung.): "Den 1 Mai Nachmittags erhob sich ein so kalter Nordwind, daß das Reaum. Thermometer, welches den 30 April um 5 Uhr Nachmittags eine Wärme von 17 Grade ober [zero] angezeigt hatte, den 1.Mai um die nämliche Stunde nur 8 Gr. und um 10 Uhr Abends gar nur auf 6 Gr. gewiesen hat."

morning heavy falls of snow were observed on the mountains to the south around Semmering, where the Alps give way to the Hungarian Plain.[86] In his autobiography, Dittersdorf recalled that a number of subscribers asked him to postpone the event, owing to the severity of the cold snap. A change of date would require permission, and in seeking it he had his famous encounter with Joseph II. In view of the emperor's imminent departure for his sojourn at Laxenburg, it was important to secure a date when he could attend, and in this aim Dittersdorf was successful.[87] The program went down so well that it was immediately transferred to the Kärntnertortheater.[88] Dittersdorf did not remember the dates of these two performances except that they had been eight days apart, but John Rice points out that the phrase "acht Tage" can signify a week. In the light of a notice in the *Brünner Zeitung* that gave 20 May as the date of the theater performance, it was reasonable to conclude that the Augarten event probably took place on 13 May (a play night). A press reference to a Thursday, however, implies that the previous play night (11 May) was actually the date.[89]

Whether Dittersdorf's original plan to schedule his concert close to the premiere of *Figaro* would have been seen as the work of a cabal is hard to say. Had the early May weather been more typically balmy, an evening performance in the Augarten might well have had sufficient pulling power to diminish attendance at the Burgtheater on surrounding nights—the availability of outdoor entertainment was indeed the main reason why theater and opera receipts generally declined during the summer months—but it would not have been in his interests, even if allowed to do so, to stage a direct clash with

---

86. *Kurfürstlich gnädigst privilegirte Münchner Zeitung* (16 May 1786), no. 77, 305: Wien vom 10 Mai. "Der Schnee, der den 2 Mai gefallen, ist auf dem Gebirge durch drei Täge liegen geblieben; der Himmel war auch beständig mit Wolken überzogen." *Journal Politique, ou Gazette des Gazettes*, Juin 1786, Seconde Quinzaine, 18: VIENNE (le 25 Mai): "Les voyageurs rapportent qu'il y a 3 à 4 pieds de neige dans les montagnes de la Stirie & de la Carinthie, ainsi que sur le mont Simmering."

87. *Kurfürstlich gnädigst privilegirte Münchner Zeitung* (19 May 1786), no. 129, 314: [13 May] "Se. Majestät der Kaiser und die ansehnlichsten Kavaliers und Damen beehrten solche mit ihrer Gegenwart."

88. As often happened, a significant occasion spawned a charming anecdote. As impressive as Dittersdorf's frog impressions (in Symphony no. 5) were, such sounds were to be heard in the country every day. *Laibacher Zeitung* (1 June 1786), no. 22. Anecdote or not, the story was taken seriously and republished in a musical journal. Forkel, *Musikalischer Almanach*, 1789, 128–29.

89. Rice, "New Light on Dittersdorf's Ovid Symphonies," 469. The report in the *Brünner Zeitung* was published by Edge in his review of Morrow, *Concert Life*, 151. The *Carlsruher Zeitung* (26 May 1786), no. 63, 293, confirms that it was "last Thursday."

either opera troupe, as that would have significantly reduced the number and quality of musicians available for hire. This left him the choice of a Thursday or a Saturday night. The original date was therefore most likely Thursday, 4 May, the night following the second performance of *Figaro*. There was nothing particularly sinister in this choice, as his objective was simply to schedule his concert so that the emperor could hear his new symphonies. Confusion in the press (and perhaps in reality) about the date on which Joseph was intending to leave for Laxenburg added to the urgency. All sources reported that it would be a Monday, but there was uncertainty as to which one. In Laibach it was suggested that he would adjourn on 1 May with the intention that Franz and Elisabeth should follow later.[90] In Munich a report mentioned 8 May.[91] The majority of sources, however, correctly recorded that the emperor attended the first performance of Pasquale Anfossi's *Il trionfo delle donne* on 15 May before leaving the same night.[92]

There is no incontrovertible evidence that Joseph II was present on the first night of *Figaro*.[93] Around 1 May, he was resident in the Augarten, coming into the city for his regular audiences.[94] In the normal course of events, he would certainly have been there, yet it cannot be ruled out that for some reason he was unable to come, especially as in 1780s Vienna, a premiere was deemed to consist of the first three performances. The emperor's nonappearance on the first night would not necessarily have been a bad sign; it might, indeed, have had some advantages, allowing for problems in a complex production to be ironed out before he saw the work. It is possible that the final choice of date for the premiere followed a short postponement, as on 28 April, Leopold Mozart was expecting his son's new work to be given that night, a regular Friday opera

---

90. *Laibacher Zeitung* (18 May 1786), no. 20: Wien: "Der Kaiser wird schon am 1sten das Lustschloß Laxenburg bezogen haben, und in wenigen Tagen wird der Erzherzog Franz und die Prinzessin Elisabeth von Würtemberg dahin nachfolgen."

91. *Kurfürstlich gnädigst privilegirte Münchner Zeitung* (25 April 1786), no. 65, 259: Wien, vom 19 April (aus Privatnachrichten): "so wird derselbe sich gegen den 8 Mai nach Laxenburg erheben." *Carslruher Zeitung* (3 May 1786), no. 53, 246: "um den 8. Mai."

92. *Gazzetta universale* (30 May 1786), no. 43, 339: VIENNA 18. Maggio: "Lunedì sera dopo l'Opera buffa Italiana, S. M. l'Imperatore si trasferì a Laxemburgo."

93. Niemetschek's later account of the first performance in which he reports claims that some Italian singers deliberately sabotaged the occasion—and that Mozart had to have recourse to the emperor to insist that they did their duty—implies that Joseph II was present. Mauntner, *Life of Mozart*, 34.

94. *Bayreuther Zeitung* (8 May 1786), no. 55, Anhang, 359: Wien, vom 1 May: "Des Kaisers Majestät, welche den Pavillon im Augarten bezogen haben . . . kommen täglich in die Stadt um Audienzen zu ertheilen."

slot. The replacement opera, Pietro Alessandro Guglielmi's *Le vicende d'amor,* had a free run without competition from the Singspiel, a decision conceivably made when the premiere of *Figaro* was still in the schedule. A complicating factor, noted by Zinzendorf in his diary on 26 April, was that fire had briefly taken hold on one of the "decorations" (sets) at the performance of Sarti's *Fra i due litiganti.* It does not seem to have been serious, yet it could have caused sufficient damage to necessitate a change of opera three days later. Joseph attended a rehearsal of *Figaro* on 29 April, which was almost certainly the oc-casion on which permission to use dancers was given.[95] Michael Kelly, mistak-enly associating the new work with an earlier race to complete in the spring of 1785 involving Salieri's *La grotta di Trofonio,* recalled a dramatic intervention by the emperor: "The mighty contest was put an end to by His Majesty issuing a mandate for Mozart's *Nozze di Figaro,* to be instantly put into rehearsal."[96] One wonders whether this element of the story stemmed from a demand that a full rehearsal be scheduled immediately so that the emperor could attend, because a departure for Laxenburg on 1 May had yet to be ruled out. On the other hand a late decision by the emperor to remain in Vienna a week or two longer than expected may itself have facilitated the putting back of the premiere from 28 April to 1 May.

The first performance of *Figaro* was recorded in the *Wiener Zeitung* without comment, other than that it marked the debut performances of Luisa Laschi and Dorotea Bussani.[97] Theater reports in this newspaper sometimes grouped several events together in a single story, working chronologically backward. The cele-brated entry on *Figaro* was followed directly by an account of *Der Deserteur,* given its first performance in a new run ten days earlier. Reading the runes of this typ-ically brief paragraph, one is struck by the fact that Lippert's reception was the only one to elicit positive comment.[98] The inference was that the two new Italian singers in *Figaro* had not enjoyed a comparable ovation.[99] The next singer to make

95. Link, *National Court Theatre,* 270: "29 Avril: Apres 11h je cherchois l'Empereur *a l'Augarten,* il etoit *en ville,* il etoit a la repetition del'opera."

96. Kelly, *Reminiscences,* vol. 1, 258.

97. Deutsch, *Mozart: A Documentary Biography,* 275.

98. *Wiener Zeitung* (3 May 1786), 1018, no. 35: K. K. Hoftheater: [*Figaro* report] followed by: "Im Theater nächst dem Kärntnerthor ward gegeben Freytag den 21. April das bekannte Singspiel, Der Deserteur, welchen Herr Lippert, ein neuangenommener Sänger, vorstellte, und eine sehr glückliche Aufnahme damit fand."

99. The *Wiener Zeitung*'s identification of the roles performed by the debutants Laschi and Bussani ("als Gräfin und Page") reflects Rautenstrauch's avoidance of the name of Cherubino in his translation *Der närrische Tag.* Woodfield, "Trouble with Cherubino," 176.

his debut was Domenico Mombelli on 12 May.[100] The *Wiener Zeitung* was mark-
edly more favorable to him than it had been to the new singers in *Figaro*.[101] This
might simply reflect the writer's perception of the event, yet the determinedly neutral tone adopted in this newspaper's coverage of opera and theater also implies
that multiple cabal-generated encores of the kind apparently enjoyed by Mozart's
opera were understood for what they were and discounted. A favorable notice
seems to have been reserved for those works accorded general approval.

The first published review of *Le nozze di Figaro* would have come as a blow
to Mozart, all the more galling in that it did not appear in some provincial
backwater but in Munich. Citing as its source a private communication dated
3 May, that is, before or immediately after the second performance, the notice
is painfully to the point.[102] The opera had not had the success anticipated for
it because its music was thought too "artificial" ("gekünstelt") and in consequence boring to listen to. This put-down marked the moment when the perception that Mozart's style, for all its manifest originality, asked too much of
its listeners, began to come sharply into focus. Dittersdorf associated himself
with this critique, articulating it in his celebrated encounter with Joseph II.

This conversation, as recalled many years later by Dittersdorf, began with
a discussion about leading violinists, but then the emperor changed the subject, asking Dittersdorf repeatedly for his views on Mozart. Influenced by
the magnitude of the composer's reputation two hundred years on, modern
interpretations miss the fact that Joseph's persistence in pursuing this topic
is slightly surprising, notwithstanding that it took place around the time of

---

100. Notwithstanding his reputation, Mombelli's contribution to the season was a curiously
low-profile one for a singer in receipt of such a large salary. He was still receiving 4,500
gulden the following year, even though a list of Italian opera personnel drawn up shortly
before 13 March 1787 omits his name, otherwise presenting an accurate snapshot of the ensemble between the departure of Storace and the arrival of Morichelli. *Wiens gegenwärtiger
Zustand*, 367–68: "Italienische Hofoperisten: Benucci. Bussani. Bussani. (Madam) Cavesi
[*sic*]. Cavesi. (Madam) Cavallieri. (Madame) Aschi [Laschi]. (Madame) Lolli. Mandini.
Mandini. (Madame) Molinelli. (Madame) Okelli."

101. *Wiener Zeitung* (20 May 1786), no. 40, 1198: "Den Freytag voher am 12. May kamen das
erstemal zum Vorschein bey der Italienerin in London ein Paar neue Sänger, Hr. Mombelli,
und Hr. Lolli, welche man gut aufnahm, vorzüglich aber wurde der erstere mit ungemein
viel Beyfall von dem sämtlichen Publikum beehrt." Zinzendorf confirms that Mombelli had
been "prodigieusement applaudi." Link, *National Court Theatre*, 271.

102. *Kurfürstlich gnädigst privilegirte Münchner Zeitung* (9 May 1786), no. 73, 291: Wien vom
3ten Mai. (aus Privatnachrichten): "Am Mondtage ward die neue Oper le Nozze di Figaro,
Musik von Motzart, zum erstenmale aufgeführt. Das Stük gefiel nicht so allgemein, als man
es wohl hätte erwarten sollen; denn man sezte daran aus, daß die Musik zu gekünstelt, und
folglich langweilig anzuhören seie." Edge, "Report on the Premiere of *Le nozze di Figaro*
(*Münchner Zeitung*)," in Edge and Black, *Mozart*.

the premiere of *Le nozze di Figaro*; he is implicitly credited with a degree of prescience. Faced with a friendly but persistent inquisition, Dittersdorf had no difficulty in ranking Mozart above Clementi as a performer—Clementi had merely "art" ("Kunst"), Mozart both "art and taste" ("Kunst und Geschmack")—but in evaluating his rival's compositional merit, he chose his words carefully and damningly. He acknowledged Mozart's "wealth of ideas" ("Reichthum von Gedanken") but wished that he would deploy them less profusely.[103] The emperor, appearing to agree, observed that a common complaint among singers was that Mozart's orchestral accompaniments were too full. Dittersdorf, never one to neglect a chance to set himself up for a compliment, feigned surprise: rich scoring need not obscure a "cantilena," surely? On cue, Joseph responded by expressing admiration for this quality in Dittersdorf's oratorios *Esther* and *Hiob*. Next, the emperor asked about chamber music. He let slip (deliberately) that he had had occasion to formulate a comparison between the works of Haydn and Mozart, but before revealing it, he would be interested to hear whether Dittersdorf could come up with one. The composer's spur-of-the-moment analogy with the works of the poets Friedrich Gottlieb Klopstock and Christian Furchtgott Gellert was understood: the beauties of the one require repeated hearing, while those of the other are immediately apparent.[104] In turn, Dittersdorf, with due deference, wondered what the emperor's comparative formula was. His response—that Mozart's chamber works might be compared with a snuffbox made in Paris, Haydn's with one made in London—has sometimes been seen as a rather trite analogy, but in the text as first published in the *Allgemeine musikalische Zeitung*, Dittersdorf presents his argument with greater sophistication: Mozart's works are beautiful because of their "many tasteful ornaments," Haydn's because of their "simplicity and exceedingly beautiful polish."[105] Or, to put it another way, the baroque and galant idioms both have their assets.

As the meeting drew to a close, Joseph offered a telling if highly provocative comment. He informed Dittersdorf that he had a reputation as an egotist who begrudged the smallest recognition to any virtuoso or to any other

---

103. Dittersdorf, *Lebensbeschreibung*, 237.

104. The emperor did not come up with the poetic comparison himself. Beales, *Against the World 1780–1790*, 455, seems to imply that it was Joseph's own idea, though the exchange is correctly reported in *Enlightenment and Reform*, 96.

105. *Allgemeine musikalische Zeitung* (March 1799), 382: "Beyde sind schön, die erste ihrer vielen geschmackvollen Verzierungen, die zweyte ihrer Simplicität und ausnehmend schönen Politur wegen."

composer.[106] In the first published version of the text, the criticism was even harsher; he is described as "generally proud and puffed up."[107] Rather than bother with a rebuttal, his son or an editor removed the reported slander before the publication of the final text. Joseph greatly relished hearing about and stirring up artistic bitching. It is clear from his conversation with Dittersdorf that he was well aware of the potential for personal conflict in the structural contest between the troupes he had set up.[108] Rather cunningly, he had prefaced the discussion by reminding Dittersdorf that he prized direct speech and would not tolerate flattery of any kind. What he elicited from this masterful performance in which he reeled the composer in and let him out like a skilled fly fisherman was a spectrum of commentary on Mozart's music that was taking hold around the time of *Figaro*. Negative in tone, it turned the composer's positive qualities against him, whether fertility of imagination (too many themes), richness of orchestration (too many instruments), or level of ornamental detail (too many notes). As the Munich reviewer bluntly implied, the high level of artifice was proving something of a hindrance for the general audience, at least some of whom—famously including Zinzendorf—had been bored at the premiere of the new opera.

The next notice to appear in Germany was in the *Bayreuther Zeitung*. Brief and dismissive, it was dated 16 May and was thus able to take account of the three performances that constituted the full official premiere on 1, 3, and 8 May. Claiming that the work had only half pleased, its author questioned Mozart's competence by pointing out that connoisseurs had identified some matters in need of improvement. It appeared that the composer had agreed to make the necessary alterations.[109] From his study of the original orchestral parts of *Le nozze di Figaro*, Dexter Edge concluded that significant changes to

106. Dittersdorf, *Lebensbeschreibung*, 239: "Man hat mir gesagt, daß Sie ein Egoist wären, der weder einem Virtuosen noch einem Komponisten die mindeste Ehre gönnte."

107. *Allgemeine musikalische Zeitung* (March 1799), 382: "dass Sie überhaupt stolz und aufgeblasen seyen."

108. Dittersdorf, *Lebensbeschreibung*, 201, describes another example of imperial stirring, naturally to his advantage, in his recollection of Joseph's comment on his oratorio *Esther*: "Gaßmann hat dem Ditters eine Nase drehen wollen, Ditters aber hat ihm dafür eine tüchtige gedreht, denn ich ziehe sein Oratorium dem Hassischen und dem Gaßmannischen weit vor."

109. *Bayreuther Zeitung* (22 May 1786), no. 61, Anhang, 400: Wien, vom 16. May: "Die zur Oper gemachte Nozza del Figaro von Hrn. Mozzart, gefällt nur halb, und die Kenner haben verschiedenes daran ausgesezt, welches der geschickte Herr Compositor zu verbessern sich vorgenommen hat." Edge, "Report on the Reception of *Le nozze di Figaro* (*Bayreuther Zeitung*)," in Edge and Black, *Mozart*.

the score were indeed made during the first performance run.[110] The Bayreuth notice implies that some of these revisions had to be implemented almost immediately, although the nature of the problem is unclear. If overabundance of musical invention was the perceived difficulty, it is hard to see how this could have been easily remedied. The work (with encores) may simply have been thought too long, yet identifying selective cuts after a premiere was commonplace, hardly unusual enough to warrant special news coverage.[111]

The comment that the work had pleased only half ("nur halb") may have had a literal dimension—that Mozart was reconsidering aspects of acts 3 and 4 in particular. If this was the case, then one possible problem could have been that the self-censorship of the plot was thought not to have been rigorous enough. There is an abundance of evidence that the portrayal of Cherubino remained contentious. Some of his scenes in act 2 were toned down, but other issues had seemingly arisen, notably the impropriety of the Count's behavior toward Barbarina.[112] The version of *Figaro* performed in 1787 for Joseph's brother Ferdinand in Monza incorporates a systematic reconsideration of acts 3 and 4, which removes the character of the maid from the plot altogether.[113] For reasons that remain unclear, Angelo Tarchi was commissioned to provide replacement music for the whole of acts 3 and 4, resulting in a rare instance of dual authorship in an opera buffa. The damage to Mozart's reputation was compounded by the fact that this reshaping of his work received international coverage in almanacs, which gave no explanation as to the reason: "LE NOZZE DI FIGARO, avec des choeurs, le premier et le deuxième acte, musique del Signor Wolfgango *Mozart*; le troisième et le quatrième, musique nouvelle del Sig. Ang. Tarchi."[114] While aria substitution was commonplace, the rewriting of two complete acts, however glossed, could hardly have been taken as a vote of confidence in the original composer, only half of whose new opera apparently deserved to survive.

---

110. Edge, "Mozart's Viennese Copyists," 1461–741.

111. Link, "Fandango Scene," 92, points out that the dancers required for the Fandango in act 3 were paid for only three performances and that this feature of the score then probably had to be rethought.

112. Woodfield, "Trouble with Cherubino," 180–96.

113. For the record, Beales regards the rumor that Joseph II visited his gardener's daughter every day—the assumption being for sexual relief—as "not very likely." Beales, *Against the World 1780–1790,* 430. Were there any truth (or perceived truth) in this story, the onstage representation of the Count's behavior toward Barbarina could have been awkward. But the episode could just as easily have been censored on general grounds.

114. *Calendrier musical universel,* vol. 10 (1789), 168.

The disappointing reaction in Bayreuth must also be seen in the context of this newspaper's enthusiastic reception of the Ovid symphonies. Dittersdorf was unusually "brazen" (to use Rice's term) as a self-publicist, making much use of ostensibly anonymous submissions to the press that were highly flattering of his oeuvre.[115] Whether on the occasion of the 1786 Vienna premiere of his symphonies, innovative and attractive works without question, he personally oversaw the dispatch of a favorable evaluation is impossible to establish, but the clear impression left by the published record is that the premiere of *Figaro* coincided with a peak in publicity on Dittersdorf's behalf. On 4 May, a news item in Bayreuth, dated 28 April and thus perhaps circulated by design on the day originally selected for the opera's premiere, noted that his forthcoming symphonies were being spoken of as the "first" (i.e. of this programmatic type) in the world.[116]

As more and more newspapers are digitized, it is becoming possible to identify press releases that received general circulation. The Dittersdorf report took a week longer to appear in Karlsruhe, but its wording and source date are identical.[117] Two weeks later, Bayreuth readers were given further details of the memorable academy in the Augarten at which the symphonies were performed.[118] A very large crowd had attended, and the gardens looked beautiful. (They perhaps still hosted some of the nightingales that Joseph had had released.) The music was so full of spirit and expression that connoisseurs and amateurs alike were delighted. In the second of the cycle, the Fall of Phaethon, there is a musical depiction of a storm, which the heavens obligingly threatened to supply, a scene that was described memorably by the reporter, whose theme was the price and availability of transport.[119] Another

---

115. Rice, "New Light on Dittersdorf's Ovid Symphonies," 458.

116. *Bayreuther Zeitung* (4 May 1786), no. 53, 349: Wien, vom 28. April: "Herr von Dieters giebt einige Synfonien heraus, die die ersten in der Welt seyn sollen, und worinnen die unglaublichsten Dinge ausgedruckt sind."

117. *Carlsruher Zeitung* (10 May 1786), no. 56, 261.

118. *Bayreuther Zeitung* (18 May 1786), no. 60, 389: Wien, vom 12. May.

119. *Bayreuther Zeitung* (18 May 1786), no. 60, 389: "Um 7 Uhr zeigte sich wiederum am Firmament eine schwere sinstere Gewitterwolke, und erhub sich ein so mächtiger Wind, daß den schöngeputzten Frauenzimmern sehr warm ums Herz ward, und manche überlegten, ob, und wie sie mit den Fiakres wegen des Species Ducatens Fuhrlohns aus dem Handel kommen mögten. Es war eine schmerzliche Freude, die jungen Mädgen in den Alleen galopiren, die alten Matronen trottiren und die steifen Fräuleins an den Heckengängen traversiren zu sehen. . . . Endlich legte sich der Wind, die Sonne gieng beschämt feuerroth unter, und die Fiakres fuhren um den gewöhnlichen Preiß, und murrten über die Veränderlichkeit der Witterung."

review politicized the occasion, hailing Dittersdorf's achievement as a new triumph for Germany ("ein neuer Triumph für Deutschland").[120] But for an apparent factual inaccuracy—the notice implies that the same six symphonies were performed at both concerts—the language employed might well be taken as unrestrained self-publicity.[121] The delay in the appearance of this nationalistic "take" on the event also suggests that it was being circulated to prepare the ground for the premiere of the Singspiel. The geographical reach of this publicity drive was remarkable. In distant Stralsund, the local newspaper followed the general line in commending the symphonies.[122]

A two-pronged campaign appeared to be under way, aimed at ensuring that Dittersdorf's symphonies received unstinting praise but *Figaro* grudging recognition at best. In Vienna, the verdict on the opera seems to have been reached quite quickly, to judge by Zinzendorf's comment after attending on 4 July, describing Mozart's music as "odd" ("singulière").[123] The lack of balance in the press coverage could hardly go unanswered, and the response came on 11 July in the celebrated apologia published in the *Wiener Realzeitung*. Only rarely did this weekly journal carry a discursive piece about Italian opera, a fact that points to an unusual situation. The article offers an explanation for the mixed success of *Figaro*, but its main point is a direct rebuttal of the aesthetic complaint espoused by Dittersdorf:

> Already at the first performance the music by Herr Mozart was generally admired by connoisseurs, excepting those who out of self-love and pride cannot admit to finding good something that they themselves have not made.
>
> Indeed on the first day the *public* (and one often finds this with the public) hardly knew what to think. Many Bravos were heard from impartial connoisseurs, but impetuous lads in the uppermost balconies burst their hired lungs as best they could, in order to over-power the singers and the listeners with their St! and Pst!; and consequently opinions were divided at the end of the piece.

---

120. *Brünner Zeitung* (23 June 1786), no. 50, 397.

121. Rice, "New Light on Dittersdorf's Ovid Symphonies," 469, citing Edge, Review of Morrow, *Concert Life*, 151–52.

122. *Stralsundische Zeitung* (24 May 1786), no. 62: Wien, den 10 May: "Herr von Ditters giebt einige Synfonien heraus, welche die ersten in ihrer Art seyn sollen."

123. Link, *National Court Theatre*, 276: "A l'opera. *Le nozze di Figaro*. La musique de Mozart singulière, des [mains?] sans tête."

Moreover it must be admitted that the first performance did not make the best impression, because the composition is very difficult.

Now after repeated performances, however, one would, obviously admit either to a *cabal* or to *tastelessness*, if one maintained any other opinion than that the music of Herr Mozart is a masterpiece of art.

It contains so many beauties and such a wealth of ideas that it could only have been created from the spring of innate genius.

Some newspaper writers have liked to claim that Herr Mozart's opera did not please at all. One can only imagine what sort of correspondents these must have been, who could let such outright lies see the light of day. I believe it is sufficiently well known that it was the third performance of this opera and the encores that were so frequently demanded in it that were the reason why, on the following day, by *highest decree*, it was made publicly known that *it would henceforth be forbidden in the opera to encore any piece that included more than one voice.*[124]

The timing of this notice, the very day of the premiere of Dittersdorf's *Der Apotheker*, was no accident; an attempt was being made to ensure that members of the audience knew some of the background before they entered the theater. The unknown author observes that Mozart's opera has been well received by connoisseurs but not by those whose self-esteem debars them from finding good in anything they have not created themselves. The critique is thus addressed to composers or perhaps, in the light of the jaundiced view of Dittersdorf's reputation articulated by Joseph II, to one in particular. The aesthetic judgment is confronted head-on. Mozart's score contains "so many beauties" ("so viele Schönheiten") and "such a wealth of ideas" ("einen solchen Reichthum von Gedanken")—these were the very words Dittersdorf recalled having used in his conversation with Joseph—that innate genius could be the only explanation. Refusal to concede this was a sign either of tastelessness or a cynical cabal. A final shaft is directed against anonymous correspondents in the German press. Not only had they demonstrated their lack of discernment; they were also accused of submitting misinformation, exaggerating the opera's failure.

The identity of this articulate supporter of Mozart is not known, but a case can be made for Johann Rautenstrauch, who had better reason than most to offer his thoughts on a new production of a dramatic work on the Figaro

---

124. Deutsch, *Mozart: A Documentary Biography*, 278.

story.[125] The piece begins not with the account of the reception of *Le nozze di Figaro* but with a backward glance at the last-minute refusal of the censor, early in 1785, to allow the staging of Rautenstrauch's translation *Der närrische Tag*. Later that year, Rautenstrauch published a fable entitled *Das neue Wien*, based on the conceit that he has just awoken from a twenty-year sleep and is now in a position to compare the "new" Vienna of 1805 with the year in which he is actually writing. Naturally, some things have changed, others not. The commentary offered by an unnamed "Freund" ("Fr."), the imaginary interlocutor with whom he debates in his dream, is in effect making predictions. The early demise of the hated "Ausschuβ" (the committee responsible for the selection of plays at the National Theater) is correctly foreseen.[126] Given his recent trouble with the censor, Rautenstrauch has some fun at his own expense, reacting to news that this office has been shut down with the single word "impossible!"[127]

Readers of this entertaining "dream" might have associated the "Fr." at the foot of the *Realzeitung* piece with Rautenstrauch's imaginary friend. If this was the intended connection, it might help to explain the curiously mixed attitude toward historical accuracy in the opening remarks of what is otherwise a factual report. The author begins by adapting Figaro's observation in *Le Barbier de Séville* (act 1, scene 2)—"Aujourd'hui, ce qui ne vaut pas la peine d'être dit, on le chante'—to the debacle over *Der närrische Tag*: "what is not worth saying, these days, is sung" becomes "what is not allowed to be said, these days, is sung." The allusion to the banning of translations, good or bad, similarly, with a touch of wry humor, references Rautenstrauch's recent experience. Clearly inaccurate, though, is the unqualified statement that *Figaro* was banned in Paris. The failure to acknowledge its subsequent great success there allows the depiction of Vienna, with its recent staging of an opera on the subject, ahead of the game, so to speak, with respect to the reception of works on the theme. This approach, blending fact and fiction in the service of satirical commentary, is akin to that adopted in *Das neue Wien*, whose title page cites Horace's dictum "Ficta voluptatis causa, sint proxima veris"—fictions intended to please should approximate truths. (The Figaro play was at first banned in Paris, and the opera had since been permitted in Vienna.) Many of the developments reported by "Fr." from his vantage point in 1805 could not easily have been predicted in 1785, and this was clearly the case with Joseph

125. Lütteken, "Depoliticized Drama," suggests Johann Friedel as a possible author, on the grounds of the signature "Fr."

126. Rautenstrauch, *Das neue Wien*, 69.

127. Rautenstrauch, *Das neue Wien*, 59: Fr.: "wir keine Censur mehr haben." Ich: "unmöglich!"

II's decision to allow the staging of *Le nozze di Figaro*. If not Rautenstrauch himself, then one of his supporters was perhaps the individual who came out in support of Mozart, as the campaign of denigration, which the substance of the piece describes, got under way.

Although broadly favorable to Mozart, the piece in the *Wiener Realzeitung* did not seek to deny that the first two performances had not been particularly successful, and the early dissemination of this news could itself explain some of the ambivalence in the German press. While no correspondent went so far as to suggest a complete flop, there is no hint of the cheering reported at the time by Leopold Mozart and many years later by Kelly. Supporters of Mozart could at least point to one hard fact: Joseph II's response to the problem of multiple encores, evidently a matter of concern by the time of its third per-formance on 8 May.[128] In Mannheim, a news item dated 10 May suggested that the prohibition of excessive applause stemmed directly from a personal request for assistance from Storace.[129] According to Leopold Mozart, presum-ably passing on details sent by his son, there were five encores on 3 May and seven on 8 May, perhaps implying that there had been none on 1 May. One in-terpretation of this seemingly rapid climb in approval ratings is that it reflects the activities of a counter-cabal organized by the supporters of opera buffa, who, having been caught unprepared at the first performance, had started to escalate the number of demands for encores, thereby prolonging the operatic night unreasonably. The emperor's solution was tailored neatly to Storace's complaint that her voice was becoming overtired.[130] As Susanna, she had to sing in every ensemble: all six duettinos, both terzettos, and the sestetto. If

---

128. Deutsch, *Mozart: A Documentary Biography*, 275.

129. *Mannheimer Zeitung* (22 May 1786), no. 61, 253: Wien, den 10 Wonnem: "Unsere vortrefliche Sängerin Madame Storace beschwerte sich jüngst bei dem Monarchen, daß sie zu sehr strapazirt werde, indem sie meistens die schwersten Bravourarien durch das anhaltende Klatschen gezwungen 2. 3 auch 4 mal wiederholen müsse. Sr. Majestät haben daher Dero Theatral Direktion befohlen, öffentlich bekannt machen zu lassen, daß Niemand mehr unter Strafe der öffentlichen Hinwegschaffung aus dem Theater, oder Arretirung durch die Wache, sich unter stehen soll, durch anhaltendes Händeklatschen oder Stamfen sich sittenwidrig auszuzeichnen." Edge, "Report on the Limitation of Encores in the Viennese Court Theatres (*Mannheimer Zeitung*)," in Edge and Black, *Mozart*. The same report, with minor variants, appeared in the *Carlsruher Zeitung* (24 May 1786), no. 62, 288, dated 9 May, the day following the third performance of *Figaro*. The imperial command is said to have been directed to the "Oberaufsehern des Theaters."

130. The decree was publicized on the Theaterzettel for *L'Italiana in Londra* on 12 May: "Es wird hiemit jederman zu wissen gemacht, daß von nun an, um die für die Singspiele bestimmte Dauerzeit nicht zu überschreitten, kein aus mehr als einer Singstimme bestehendes Stück, mehr wird wiederholet werden." Link, *National Court Theatre*, 83.

members of the audience were starting to demand repeats of these, she might indeed have found multiple encores of her arias too much.

Assuming that Leopold Mozart was correctly informed, *Figaro* was originally slated to receive its premiere on 28 April, a Friday night. As a result of its late postponement, it was given on Monday, 1 May, unopposed, as was its second performance on Wednesday, 3 May. On Friday, 5 May, however, those responsible for the schedule decided that Martín y Soler's *Il burbero* should compete with Paisiello's *Die engebildeten philosophen*. The third performance of *Figaro* thus fell on Monday, 8 May, a normal approach to scheduling a new work but one that had the effect of shielding Mozart's opera from direct competition. On Wednesday, 10 May, there was a surprise; instead of opera buffa, a performance of *Die Entführung* is recorded, despite the fact that it had been given on 7 May. The reason is not clear, for if an Italian opera could not be given at short notice, it was usual to substitute a play by the troupe sharing the theater.[131] The Bayreuth review of *Figaro*, published after the three performances of the premiere, implied that revisions to the opera were already under way. It is conceivable that, with a short delay now anticipated before the fourth performance, Joseph II ordered Mozart's Singspiel to be given so that he could receive the box office, often awarded to the composer on the occasion of a fourth performance. Arbitrary imperial interventions, switching a night or a theater on behalf of a composer, were rare but not unknown. Joseph decided that Dittersdorf's benefit performance of *Der Apotheker* should take place on a Saturday when it would be unopposed by the opera buffa, and on 27 October 1787, he authorized a performance of *L'arbore di Diana* in the Kärntnertortheater as a benefit for Martín y Soler, who was about to leave.[132] Some such consideration for Mozart is not out of the question, even though there is no hint of it in any source.

The *Gazzetta universale*, following its positive coverage of Mozart's contributions to Bianchi's *La villanella rapita*, continued to express approval of Mozart's music.[133] Referring to the universal approbation with which "du"

---

131. The logistics of a last-minute switch of production between theaters apparently posed no insuperable obstacle. *Una cosa rara* was twice transferred to the Kärntnertortheater for a single performance.

132. The performance of his festive opera netted him the handsome sum of 565 gulden. Edge, "Mozart's Fee," 229.

133. *Gazzetta universale* (16 May 1786), no. 39, 310: VIENNA 7. Maggio: "Andò in scena lunedì sera per la prima volta nel Teatro presso la Corte il Dramma giocoso *le Nozze di Figaro* con Musica del celebre Maestro di Cappella Sig. Wolfango [*sic*] Mozart. Se l'originale di tal Commedia meritò molti applausi, questo ridotto a Dramma dal Sig. Abate du [*sic*] Ponte, ha incontrata l'universale approvazione." Edge, "Report on the Premiere of *Le nozze di Figaro* (*Gazzetta universale*)," in Edge and Black, *Mozart*.

Ponte's drama had been received, the *Gazzetta universale*'s account might have been describing an entirely different occasion. A sharp difference of opinion was starting to open up between the German press, supplied with a slanted account in private letters emanating from the Singspiel cabal in Vienna, and this international Italian journal, which took a more favorable line. Yet confirmation of the German view of events was to come several years later in Pressburg, where a report on the premiere of the second run of *Figaro* noted that the audience had expressed its satisfaction more than on the occasion of the original first performance.[134]

With his own operatic premiere imminent, Dittersdorf demonstrated outstanding skills as a self-publicist. Good public relations were no substitute for quality, but they could certainly smooth the way for a favorable reception. Building on the success of his performance in the Augarten, he volunteered to direct the series of open-air summer concerts in the garden of the Belvedere, the first of which fell on 26 June.[135] The thinking was clear: aristocratic music lovers, offered free or inexpensive entertainment, might be well disposed to support the forthcoming theatrical premiere, an event always running the risk in high summer of falling foul of hot weather.[136] An added advantage was that Elisabeth von Württemberg (fig. 1.3), now in her summer apartments in the Salesian convent next to the Belvedere, was on the spot to act as a delightfully informal patron. The venture seems to have been a great success. Elisabeth was enthusiastic, and from her perspective the showery weather only added to the fun.[137] Her high profile at the Belvedere series amounted to another significant endorsement for Dittersdorf. All told, the garden concerts made an excellent public relations precursor to the premiere of his Singspiel.

---

134. *Preßburger Zeitung* (2 September 1789), no. 70, 634: Wien, den 31sten August: "Das Publikum war damit sehr zufrieden, und legte seine Zufriedenheit mehr an Tag, als vor 3 Jahren, wie das Stück zum erstenmal erschien."

135. *Brünner Zeitung* (7 July 1786), no. 54, 429: Oesterreich, vom 4 July.

136. Schirlbauer, "Belvedere-Sommerkonzerte im Josephinischen Wien," 189–211. Morrow, *Concert Life in Haydn's Vienna*, 61–62, gives notices of the three series published in the *Wiener Zeitung*. The *Kurfürstlich gnädigst privilegirte Münchner Zeitung* (14 July 1786), no. 109, 434, noted: Wien, vom 8. July. (aus Privatnachrichten): "Vorgestern frühe um 7 Uhr war im Belvedere zu Ehren der Herzogin von Würtemberg, eine sehr schön Musik."

137. Weyda, "Briefe an Erzherzog Franz," 6: Vienne, ce 26 de Juin 1786: "Aujourd'hui il y a eu pour la première fois musique au jardin, mais comme il pleuvait à chaque instant, on s'est promené en parapluie, ce qu'il était assez drôle, d'autant plus que la musique se tenait dans le salon."

FIGURE 1.3 Princess Elisabeth of Württemberg (1767–1790); Portrait miniature (before 1790), unknown artist.
Courtesy of Bildarchiv, Vienna

The summer vacation period for the German theater company began on 30 June, at which point the Singspiel troupe was able to perform unopposed for an extended period. Until mid-August, Italian and German opera would be given on alternate nights in the same venue. This was Dittersdorf's opportunity, and he scored a personal triumph with *Der Apotheker* on the evening of 11 July. Zinzendorf, who attended the second performance on 13 July, thought the music detestable but noted that one air had to be performed nine times.[138] The musical rivalry extended to Dittersdorf's first essay in the genre of the large-scale finale. Numerous writers have seen in the manner in which act 1 of *Der Apotheker* ends a response to the magnificent imbroglio at the climax of act 2 of *Le nozze di Figaro*. As John Warrack put it:"Dittersdorf's most ambitious

---

138. Link, *National Court Theatre*, 276. By the following year, even he had been won round: "La musique est belle de Dieters"; 297. For an appraisal of this opera, see Joubert, "Dittersdorf's Doktor und Apotheker."

contribution to this new approach to the conventions is the long Act I finale. There can be little doubt that the immediate example of the *Figaro* Act II finale was not lost on this sharply observant composer."[139] With this compositional decision, Dittersdorf was submitting himself for comparison with his rival while at the same time demonstrating his political acumen. His line of attack remained Mozart's prolixity (as he saw it), but there were situations in which sustained writing was needed to build an effective climax.

The impact of *Der Apotheker* was felt at the highest levels of Viennese society. Elisabeth von Württemberg, at heart an Italian opera lover, was entranced.[140] From this point, the German press followed Dittersdorf's career with close attention. Mozart had been warned how fickle the Viennese public could be. In 1784, he had been the one in the limelight, attracting long lists of aristocratic subscribers, but now it was his rival's moment in the sun, with a Salzburg newspaper describing him as the darling of Vienna ("Wiens Liebling").[141]

In Bayreuth, the premiere of *Der Apotheker* was viewed favorably, albeit with a pointed aside: not so much a criticism of Dittersdorf as a lightly coded comment on the relative financial resources available to the two troupes to hire singers.[142] An especially thought-provoking notice was published in Erlangen, where a correspondent demonstrated a clear awareness of the current trial of strength between the two national operatic genres. The preference for Italian opera seen hitherto in Vienna appeared to the writer to be on the wane, and henceforth German music would take deserved pride of place in the "first city."[143] Although not mentioned by name, *Figaro* could take some of

---

139. Warrack, *German Opera*, 142.

140. Weyda, "Briefe an Erzherzog Franz," 12: Vienne, ce 14 juillet 1786: "Je fus l'autre jour [11 or 13 July] au théâtre pour voir un nouvel opéra qu'on représentait et donc la musique est de Mr. Ditters de Dittersdorf. On peut dire que la musique en est de toute beauté; il y a fait la plus grande sensation ici, quoique ce soit un opéra allemand et il est à mourir de rire. J'en ai été vraiment enchantée. Il s'appelle 'Der Apotheker und der Doctor.'"

141. *Oberdeutsche Staatszeitung* (16 October 1786), no. 203, 809: Wien, den 11ten Okt. The day after the premiere, Löschenköhl advertised Dittersdorf's portrait. *Wiener Zeitung* (12 July 1786), no. 55, 1649.

142. *Bayreuther Zeitung* (29 July 1786), no. 91, 599: Schreiben aus Wien, vom 22. July. "Herr von Ditters hat eine Composition zu der Opera comica: der Doctor und der Apotheker, gemacht, die alle bisherigen an Eigenheit übertrift. Sie wurde schon sechsmal aufgeführt, und man kann sie nicht statt hören. Schade daß wir nicht lauter gute Sänger und Sängerinnen haben."

143. This comes across as a calculated snub to Berlin. Early in the reign of Frederick the Great, the *Erlanger Real Zeitung* had adopted a stridently anti-Prussian position, although this extreme stance had since moderated. In December 1791, Erlangen was sold by its abdicating "owner" to Prussia, ending up, after the chaos of the subsequent decades, as part of Bavaria.

the credit for this. The claim that *Der Apotheker* had been granted the accolade of being a "non plus ultra" of composition, even by the Italian establishment, is a striking one.[144] The identity of the recent Italian work said to have been hissed is not clear. Vincenzo Righini's *Il Demogorgone* suffered the misfortune of being the filling in a sandwich with Dittersdorf's hit success, with its premiere on 12 July falling between the second and third performances of *Der Apotheker*.[145] *Il Demogorgone*'s next two hearings were unusually delayed (22 July and 21 August). While Elisabeth derived some enjoyment from it, Zinzendorf remarked acidly that Righini's music was, as usual, "derivative" ("pillée").[146] Yet no firm indication has come to light of an adverse reception, nor was Anfossi's *Il trionfo delle donne* received with obvious hostility.[147] The allusion, therefore, seems to be to the fate of *Figaro*, which even the supportive piece in the *Wiener Realzeitung* admitted was hissed, by implication

---

144. *Erlanger Real Zeitung* (28 July 1786), no. 58, 499: Aus den kaiserl. königlichen Staaten: "Der grosse Hang zum italienischen Singspiel scheint sich in Wien zu vermindern, und deutsche Musik wird nun in Deutschlands erster Stadt zum ersten Rang erhoben. Die neue Oper des Herrn Ditters von Dittersdorf: der Apotheker und der Doktor, erregt allgemeine Bewunderung und wurde dreimal vor der zahlreichsten Menge aufgeführt. . . . Selbst die Italiener sagen: diese Musik des deutschen Ditters ist das non plus ultra der Komposition. Als kürzlich eine neue italienische Oper der deutschen zum Trotz aufgeführt wurde, soll sie ausgepfiffen worden seyn."

145. A few days earlier, the intention had been to schedule *Il Demogorgone* before *Der Apotheker*, as reported in the *Wiener Zeitung* on 8 July. Link, *National Court Theatre*, 87. A libretto for *Il Demogorgone* refers to a performance at Laxenburg, implying that a significantly earlier date had been under consideration: "Da rappresentarsi nell'Imperial Villeggiatura di Laxemburg L'anno 1786"; 88, citing Robinson, "Paisiello, Mozart and Casti." If there was a kernel of truth in Kelly's muddled recollections of the cabals surrounding *Figaro*, then Righini's *Demogorgone* could have been in competition with Mozart's new opera and *Il trionfo delle donne* for the first available slot. It seems clear that the three operas were originally due to receive their premieres in quick succession: *Figaro* (1 May); *Il trionfo delle donne* (15 May); *Il Demogorgone* (before 12 June). The reason for the urgency was the emperor's imminent departure on a journey from which he would not return until late October; a work received modestly in the interim might well find itself discontinued long before Joseph could hear it, although a direct imperial request would never be ignored. In view of the closer proximity between *Figaro* and *Il Demogorgone* that was originally envisaged, it is interesting that Da Ponte incorporated the abandoned text of Susanna's rondò "Non tardar amato bene" into Righini's opera. Platoff, "Non tardar amato bene," 557–60. Ultimately, Kelly's confusion may have stemmed from a memory lapse: both *La grotta di Trofonio* (1785) and *Il Demogorgone* (1786) were scheduled for Laxenburg before being transferred at the last moment, after the libretto had been printed.

146. Weyda, "Briefe an Erzherzog Franz," 11: Vienne, ce 14 juillet 1786: "Je fus hier [12 July] à l'opéra de Righini qui sans être un des tous beaux est cependant assez joli." Link, *National Court Theatre*, 276.

147. It caught the attention of Zinzendorf, who reported on it at greater length than usual. He evidently enjoyed the finales. Link, *National Court Theatre*, 272–73.

in an organized fashion. What was meant by the comment that it had been performed in defiance of the Germans ("der Deutschen zum Trotz") is not altogether clear, but the correspondent seemed to be hinting that its premiere was a gesture, if an unsuccessful one, in the ongoing rivalry between national genres.

A striking indicator of *Der Apotheker*'s impact is the report published in the *Gazzetta universale*, which tended to ignore German stage works unless especially newsworthy. The piece is dated 17 July, following the fourth performance.[148] The comparison with same paper's good if slightly routine write-up of Mozart's opera is instructive. Dittersdorf receives several glowing commendations; his work is rated original and tasteful. For a quotable phrase, "superb music" could hardly be bettered. It would not have taken much reading between the lines to see *Figaro* as a run-of-the-mill success and *Der Apotheker* as an exceptional one.

In the immediate aftermath of Dittersdorf's triumph, an anonymous pamphlet was published that lavishes extravagant praise on the composer's achievement. Daniel Heartz tentatively suggested that Dittersdorf might have written *Über das deutsche Singspiel den Apotheker* himself, given his penchant for concocting highly favorable self-evaluations attributed to unnamed friends.[149] On the face of it, its main purpose was to salute a signal victory for the Singspiel party in the ongoing contest. A flavor of its rhetorical style is conveyed in Cliff Eisen's translation of a section that discusses the sense of inferiority felt by the German party before Dittersdorf came to the rescue:

> It is almost unbelievable and truly vexing, how the German Singspiel, and those who are interested in it, are treated in the German capital. Until now there remained but a glimmer of hope—in spite of a conspiracy by the aristocracy and some influential musical scholars—of some time seeing fulfilled the wishes of our monarch, himself the founder of it. For the basic principle of this sect has been to find nothing good that has not been wafted to us by a foreign breeze. And those scholars have gone to so much trouble to decry every honourable man as an idiot, that everyone . . . must agree with them in finding everything so

---

148. *Gazzetta Universale* (29 July 1786), no. 60, 477: Vienna, 17. Luglio: "Il celebre Professore Sig. Ditters de Dittersdorf ha quì posto in musica un Dramma Comico in Lingua Nazionale, tanto originale, e di buon gusto, che per 4. sere è stato sempre pieno il Teatro grande in Porta d'Italia. Tutti hanno commendato il di lui stile, e la superba musica. Soddisfattissima la Cesarea Regia Direzione Teatrale gli mandò il doppo della paga fissata per la composizione del Dramma, che è intitolato il *Medico*, e lo *Speziale*."

149. Heartz, *Haydn, Mozart and the Viennese School*, 449–50.

magnificent and beautiful (and in fact must surely know that nothing the common man finds pleasurable can be good—or indeed that he is perhaps capable of judging), because they are—scholars.[150]

But there is a personal agenda as well; as a result of his triumph with *Der Apotheker*, Dittersdorf is now to be regarded as Gluck's legitimate heir. In this respect, the pamphlet could be read as a marker for a future application for employment. Incapacitated after several strokes, Gluck was ailing, and it was clear that his death was not likely to be long delayed, at which point, so far as anyone at the time knew, a prestigious position might become available.[151] In the account of his conversation with Joseph II, Dittersdorf revealed that the emperor was aware that others regarded him as something of a narcissist, a man who had little good to say of any rival. Perhaps stung by this, and probably realizing that it was impolitic to be overly critical of competitors when advancing one's own claim for preferment—Mozart, for example, was scrupulous to give Salieri his (operatic) due when claiming special expertise in church music—Dittersdorf (or his mouthpiece) credits Mozart's contribution in the struggle to promote native talent:

> For this reason it came to the point that—the poor German muse, hunted from the stage in order to tyrannize our taste with foreign nations (and there have been significant wagers with which the gloating foreign partisans jeered at so many native lovers of the art)—it was unlikely ever again to find a German opera at the National Theater . . . [or] to hear good music for an Italian Singspiel by a German master. [But] they have completely lost their bet, for Mozart's *Nozze di Figaro*, and the subsequently reintroduced German opera, have put to shame the ridiculous pride of this fashionable sect.[152]

---

150. *Über das deutsche Singspiel den Apotheker*; Eisen, *New Mozart Documents*, 45.

151. This may well have been a motivating factor for composers like Mozart and Dittersdorf who were striving for public esteem in 1786 with particular determination. When Gluck's position finally fell vacant, there was an abundance of speculation. One commentator linked his death with the advancement of the virtuoso Mozart and that of another unnamed "Musikus." *Königlich privilegirte Stettinische Zeitung* (25 January 1788), no. 7, Beylage: Wien, vom 26. December. Other sources surmised that Martín y Soler would fill Gluck's place, a reasonable assumption in view of the scale of his triumph with *Una cosa rara*. The *Vaterlandschronik* awarded the Spaniard this imperial appointment in its obituary of Gluck in December 1787, no. 25, 355: "An Glucks Stelle tritt Martin ein, dem die Jake des Modegeschmaks besser anpaßt, als dem gigantischen Körper eines Gluks."

152. *Über das deutsche Singspiel den Apotheker*; Eisen, *New Mozart Documents*, 45.

This passage reflects the fact that the complex interlocking strands of partisan-ship could sometimes cast rivals on the same side of a particular issue; Mozart was a German writing for a top-flight opera buffa troupe, and Dittersdorf was shortly to attempt the same feat.

Having made clear his view on the political issue, the author moves on to discuss Dittersdorf as Gluck's natural successor. Before embarking upon an appraisal of *Der Apotheker* as a work in the tradition of the ailing master, he acknowledges that credit must be given to Stephanie for his libretto but, thanks having been duly and briefly recorded, the main topic must now be addressed: the masterpiece of our "great Ditters."[153] Truth in expression was the single-minded goal of the immortal Gluck, and it is now once again to be found—you guessed it!—in the music of Dittersdorf.[154] Detailed attention to word setting is another inherited characteristic, as is the praiseworthy simplicity of the vocal writing, achieved without depriving performers of the chance to enrapture their listeners. All in all, a glowing testimonial is fleshed out. In its final pages, the pamphlet returns briefly to the subject of the contest. Through his triumph, Dittersdorf has overcome the main problem facing German opera: that the fashionable world has been reluc-tant to embrace it. Now, faced with *Der Apotheker*, arbiters of taste are being driven to applaud it as immoderately as they would a *Grotta di Trofonio* or a *Re Teodoro*, whose authors are naturally worthy of respect.[155] While tech-nical justifications for the superiority of opera buffa advanced by experts (scholars)—the supposed inferiority of the German language for singing; the better professional training of Italian singers—greatly irked supporters of Singspiel, the trump card of the opposition remained its seemingly unas-sailable cachet in the beau monde.

---

153. *Über das deutsche Singspiel*, 8: "Und nun ein Wort—von der Meisterarbeit unseres (so wünscht ihn bald das Publikum für immer nennen zu können) großen Ditters."

154. *Über das deutsche Singspiel*, 10: "Die Wahrheit des Audrucks schien des unsterblichen Glukes einziges Ziel zu seyn, er wuste uns aus durch jeden Ton eine Empfindung aus unserem Herzen zu stehlen, ohne das wir bemerken konnten, wer eigentlich von diesem Zauberspiel der Schöpfer sey—und sieh! wem es daran liegen mag Gluks Genie—von neuem unter uns wieder aufblühen zu sehen—der höre—der fühle—die Musik von dem Geiste Ditters!"

155. *Über das deutsche Singspiel*, 14: "und er hat uns das Problem das unsere Stutzer und Tongebende Damen so unbegreiflich fanden—wie es denn möglich sey eine deutsche Oper auszuhalten—so triumphirend ausgelöset—daß diese Mode Hähne—nun eben so genöthiget sind ihm ihren Beyfall par bon ton zuzukrähen als sich bey einer Grotta—oder il Re Theodoro—par mode die Hände wund zu schlagen, um darüber den wahren Beyfall den diese beyde italiänischen Meisterstücke verdienten, zu vergessen."

A telling commentary on the state of play in Viennese theater in the wake of *Der Apotheker* appeared in the second (and last) issue of *Pfeffer und Salz*.[156] By then, Dittersdorf's Singspiel had achieved the unusual accolade of having had five straight performances, with the unbroken run coming to an end only on 21 July. Such had been the impact of his new work that a comparison with the reception of *Il re Teodoro* seemed not unreasonable.[157] While its poetry was poor, its music was incontestably excellent, and its composer was now to be regarded as "preeminent among the Germans" ("der erste unter den Deutschen").[158] On the other hand the writer considered the Italian troupe to be in a far from robust state, as Rosenberg, although a good manager, was insufficiently well versed in the art of dramaturgy.

In the high summer of 1786, Dittersdorf was in the ascendant. Publicity on his behalf continued unabated, including exaggerated claims about the number of performances accumulated by *Der Apotheker*.[159] Yet the public adulation masked a personal crisis. His period of leave was up, and he needed to find ways of extending his stay in order to reap the benefits that seemed his for the taking, while at the same time retaining the right to return to his administrative positions in Silesia. In all, three letters from him to Baron von Kaschnitz have survived. Dittersdorf was well aware that by requesting an extension he might place the financial security of his family in Johannisberg in

---

156. The Vienna censor took action against this satirical publication, reportedly placing a penalty of 50 gulden per copy on its sale. *Erlanger Real-Zeitung* (11 August 1786), no. 62, 535: "Auf den Verkauf einer andern Piece: Pfeffer und Salz, ist für jedes Exemplar eine Strafe von 50 fl. gesetzt."

157. Pezzl, *Skizze*, vol. 3, 422, listed this work among the top five performed Italian operas along with *Il barbiere, Fra i due litiganti, La grotta di Trofonio* and *Una cosa rara.*

158. *Pfeffer und Salz* (1786), no. 2, 35–36: Wien den 23ten July 1786: "Auf dem hiesigen Theater macht gegenwärtig, die neue Opera: der Doktor und der Apotheker, wozu Herr von Dittersdorf die Musik machte, grossen Lärm. So schlecht die Poesie ist, so schön ist die Musik, und man treibt es damit beinahe so, wie vorm Jahr mit Re Teodoro. Sie wird sehr oft, und immer mit dem nemlichen Beifall, wiederholt. Auch hat Hr. v. Dittersdorf der erste unter den Deutschen 100 Dukaten dafür bekommen. Sonst zahlte man für die deutschen Operetten nur 30 Dukaten, und für wälsche 100. So wie man auch einen elenden italienischen Theater Dichter mit 800 fl. besoldet, und vermuthlich darum nur, weil der Stephanie noch immer seine 5 rüstigen Finger bewegen kann, eines deutschem Theater Dichters auf dem National Theater nicht zu bedürfen glaubt. Wenn die wälsche Opera nicht viel taugt, so taugt das deutsche National Theater vollends gar nichts. Graf Rosenberg scheint nicht viel Dramaturgie studirt zu haben, und so exzellent übrigens seine Theaterdirecktion seyn mag, so wenig kann dennoch ein gutes Stück nunmehr besetzt werden."

159. *Kurfürstlich gnädigst privilegirte Münchner Zeitung* (1 August 1786), no. 119, 474: "Die neue Oper der Doktor und Apotheker, Musik von Ditters, wird heute schon zum 11ten male aufgeführt, und erhält noch immer den bisherigen Zulauf, und ungetheilten Beifall."

jeopardy. Much less spontaneous a writer than Mozart, he outlined his woes as though compiling a memorandum. At one point in the second letter, he claimed that he had written a paragraph with tears in his eyes.[160] Despite its brevity, this correspondence contains useful insights into the sometimes unpredictable managerial style of Joseph and Rosenberg.

The first letter is dated 19 July, the day of the fifth performance of *Der Apotheker*, by which time the scale of its splendid reception must have been fully apparent. Dittersdorf expresses the wish to remain in Vienna so that he can take charge of a performance for Joseph II, as it seemed to him that the work might suffer some form of disfigurement in his absence.[161] He begs for a speedy reply, promising to redouble his administrative efforts after his leave is up. But by the end of the summer, a serious crisis had arisen, as events in Johannisberg did not seem to match assurances he had received by post. In a letter dated (in another hand) 26 October but written probably toward the end of September, to judge by the reference to the premiere of *Betrug durch Aberglauben* (3 October) "next week" and Joseph's continued absence, Dittersdorf expresses concern over his salary.

In reviewing the circumstances in which he accepted a contract for further operas, he gives interesting glimpses of Rosenberg. On 16 July, the day after the third performance of *Der Apotheker*, the alert impresario instructed Baron Rienmayer, his deputy, to ask Dittersdorf if he would be willing to write two more operas, one German and one Italian—an even-handed decision in the context of the ongoing contest.[162] The composer responded that he could not accept the commission until he had been granted an extension of his leave. Having (as he thought) received the go-ahead, he agreed to the contract.[163] But now, facing the possibility that he might have to leave before the premiere of his second

---

160. Unverricht, *Carl von Dittersdorf: Briefe*, 54: "Mit Thränen in den Augen hab ich diesen Paragraph geschrieben."

161. Unverricht, *Carl von Dittersdorf: Briefe*, 51: "zweytens: möchte ich gerne meine hier verfertigte *opera*, welche ziemlichen Beyfall erhalten, unter meiner eigenen *Direction* vor seiner Mayestätt aufführen, um sicher zu seyn, daß sie mir in meiner Abwesenheit nicht verunstaltet wird."

162. Unverricht, *Carl von Dittersdorf: Briefe*, 53: "Am 16t *July* sagte mir Hl: *Baron Rienmayer* im Nahmen seiner *Excell: Graf Rosenberg*, daß lezterer gerne sähe, wenn ich so geschwind als möglich nebst der schon aufgeführten *Oper* noch 2 nemlich noch eine deutsche und noch eine wällsche schriebe."

163. Unverricht, *Carl von Dittersdorf: Briefe*, 53: "Mit dieser Zusicherung gedekt ließ ich mich *engagiren* und *contra[c]trirte* noch 2 *Opern* so schleinig als möglich zu *componiren* und die eine ist bereits fertig und wird die künftige Woche aufgeführet; die zweyte soll ich noch anfangen."

Singspiel, he claimed that Joseph had requested to hear both this work and *Der Apotheker* upon his return from Bohemia, citing the librettist Stephanie as his witness.[164] In pleading his case for an extension, Dittersdorf noted the financial outcome of his recent opera; *Der Apotheker* had already (after about thirteen performances) made 7,000 gulden in profit. (It is unclear whether this amount was simply a tally of box office receipts; if so, it would imply an average nightly take of over 500 gulden, a splendid result without doubt.) He had received further assurances that his next two operas would make 30,000 gulden.[165] This is a huge sum. It would imply that the forthcoming operas were expected each to make double the amount *Der Apotheker* had so far taken. Whether Baron von Kaschnitz would have believed this must be open to doubt.[166]

Upon his return to Vienna, the emperor put in an immediate appearance at the theater. His choice of genre was keenly awaited. As it was a Friday night contest between opera buffa and Singspiel, it would send out a signal of imperial preference. The *Realzeitung*, which had carried a piece on behalf of Mozart's new opera on the day of the premiere of *Der Apotheker*, now gave its support to Dittersdorf: "Of all new German operas, this is the one that receives the most approval and that deserves it. The music, containing the most beautiful thoughts, is richly original: a true masterpiece of art."[167] This last phrase, without the qualifier "true," had been applied to *Le nozze di Figaro* in the 11 July report; its addition now could have been taken as a dig against Mozart. The emperor, obliged to make a very public choice, went to the premiere of Paisiello's *Il mondo della luna* on 20 October rather than *Der Apotheker*. Having nailed his colors to the Italian mast, he was then scrupulous in demonstrating even-handedness; on the next available occasion (22 October) he attended Dittersdorf's opera.[168] He rewarded the composer and several members of the

---

164. Unverricht, *Carl von Dittersdorf: Briefe*, 53: "Seine May[es]tätt der Kayser sind nicht nur allein davon *informirt*, sondern haben es auch mit Wohlgefallen genehmiget, und durch Hl: *Stephanie* dem Jüngren auf welchen ich mich als Zeugen berufe ist mir im Namen des Monarchen bedeutet worden: daß *Allerhöchst Dieselbe* bey *Ihrer Zurükkunft* aus Böhmen alle beyde bald zu hören Verlangen haben."

165. Unverricht, *Carl von Dittersdorf: Briefe*, 54: "um so mehr als meine erste *Opera* bereits über 7000 fl: klaren Nuzen gebracht, und mich die hiesige *Theatral=Ober*direction versichert daß meine 2 neue *Opern* dem höchsten *cerario* [*cerarium*: a fee for sealing a document] über 30,000 fl: Nuzen bringen werden."

166. He was Oberadministrator of the Brünn theater. *Theaterspiegel*, [7].

167. Joubert, "Dittersdorf's Doktor und Apotheker," 190–201.

168. *Kurfürstlich gnädigst privilegirte Münchner Zeitung* (27 October 1786), no. 169, 678: Wien vom 21. Oktob.: "Gestern Abends jedoch wohnte Höchstderselbe der ersten Vorstellung der neuen wälschen Oper, il Mondo Della Luna, bei, die mit ausgezeichnetem Beifalle aufgenommen ward."

cast with an ostentatious signal of imperial approval.[169] For close observers of the emperor's demeanor, the warmth of his acclamation of Dittersdorf as he entered the orchestra was such that only one conclusion was possible: he was in line for a permanent position in imperial service.[170] Whether such an outcome was likely is almost beside the point; the mere fact that a newspaper was willing to print the story would have been enough to send a very discouraging message to Mozart, who was keenly aware of the relative standing of composers in line for preferment.

The immediate impact of *Figaro* had been relatively modest, and matters did not improve during the months of Dittersdorf's triumph in the summer of 1786. *Figaro*'s declining profile, clearly one factor in the reduced standing of the opera buffa troupe, can be seen in the calendar of its performances. As Edge pointed out in his study of opera and theater receipts, the size of the box office as well as the frequency of performances must be taken into account in any overall evaluation of a work's success, but for the 1786–87 season this information is unavailable.[171] The trajectory of *Figaro*'s reception, however, is essentially a negative one, with a dwindling number of performances: May 1, 3, 8, and 24; July 4; August 28; September 28; November 15; December 18.

After its fourth performance on 24 May, a full three months elapsed with only a single hearing on 4 July. As a result, the opera failed to derive any benefit from the annual summer vacation of the competitor ensembles: the Singspiel troupe (13 June to 1 July) and the German theater company (1 July to 15 August). Moreover, three of the five later performances (4 July, 15 November, and 18 December) were scheduled in conjunction with *Il barbiere di Siviglia*. If coattails played a part in this policy, they belonged to Paisiello's widely admired work. It is especially striking that during the high summer for Dittersdorf, weeks during which the German opera troupe had relocated to the Burgtheater, allowing very direct comparisons with the Italians, *Figaro*

---

169. *Erlanger Real Zeitung* (3 November 1786), no. 86, 751: Aus der österreichischen Monarchie: "Als der Komponist Hr. Ditters von Dittersdorf ins Orchester tratt, applaudirte ihm der Monarch öffentlich, so wie auch die trefliche Sängerin Cavalieri, und die Herren Adamberger, Rhode, Lippert und Dauer den lauten Beifall des Hofes erhielten." Lippert had been away from Vienna for a time. Cutting it fine, he is recorded as having left Regensburg for Vienna on 15 October. Haberl, *Das Regensburgische Diarium*, 236: "schicket ein Gemsel nach Wien, damit Hr. Lippert, Operist bey dem k. k. Theater in Wien."

170. *Kurfürstlich gnädigst privilegirte Münchner Zeitung* (31 October 1786), no. 171, 687: Wien, vom 21 Oktob. (aus Privatnachrichten): "Se Majestät geruheten dem Tonsezer Herrn v. Dittersdorf bei dem Eintritt ins Orchester ihren Beifall zu bezeigen. Man glaubt, Se. Majestät werde nächsten Tagen ihn in k. k. Hofdienste anstellen."

171. Edge, "Mozart's Reception in Vienna."

was scheduled but once. It would not come as a surprise to discover that the correspondent who wrote on behalf of the opera on 11 July was provoked into doing so by news that it was to be set aside. Around this time, the press reported an incident that demonstrated how heated the contest was becoming, and how easily partisan behavior could get out of hand. At a performance of *Die eingebildeten philosophen*, a few days before Dittersdorf's premiere, a stone was said to have been lobbed from one of the upper galleries down onto the parterre noble. No one had been hurt, but the miscreant had yet to be identified.[172] While in no way attributable to any of the musicians involved, the incident coincided exactly with a difficult period for the opera buffa.

Symptomatic of *Figaro*'s declining public profile was Zinzendorf's failure to attend the performance in Laxenburg on 3 June.[173] In his diary, he recorded every other work given during that summer's sojourn, even when, as on 20, 23, and 27 May, he arrived back from a day in Vienna in time to see only part of the entertainment.[174] On 3 June, however, he did not return to Laxenburg until 10:00 p.m., by which time supper was already in progress. As a result, *Le nozze di Figaro* is the only work in the published list that he does not confirm. That *Il re Teodoro* (26 May) did not finish until 11:00 p.m. and *Il barbiere* (10 June) 11:15 p.m. implies that Mozart's opera may have been abbreviated, and it is far from certain that Joseph II was even present, as on 3 June he returned to Vienna to take part in a deer hunt in the Prater, where he met the Russian ambassador, Prince Galitzin.[175] It is not recorded when Joseph arrived back in Laxenburg or whether he was able to attend part of the opera, assuming it was given at all.

Perhaps the best evidence that *Figaro* could not (yet) be relied upon to attract large audiences comes from analysing the Friday night head-to-head confrontations between opera buffa and Singspiel.[176] Table 1.3 presents a summary of these evenings.

---

172. *Stralsundische Zeitung* (29 July 1786), no. 90: Wien, den 15 Julii: "Am 9ten dieses wurde von einer der Gallerien im Nationaltheater ein Stein auf das Parterre Noble herabgeschleudert, ohne daß jedoch jemand dabey beschädigt wäre. Noch hat man aber nicht entdecken können, wer diese Bosheit verübt hat."

173. Link, "*Le nozze di Figaro* in Laxenburg," in Edge and Black, *Mozart*.

174. The quality of that summer's opera program at Laxenburg was linked to speculation that Joseph's brother Ferdinand might be about to arrive back in Vienna from his travels in England. *Kurfürstlich gnädigst privilegirte Münchner Zeitung* (21 July 1786), no. 113, 449.

175. *Carlsruher Zeitung* (21 June 1786), no. 74: Wien, vom 9 Juny: "Se. Majestät erhoben sich am Samstag von Laxenburg in den hiesigen Prater und hielten da eine grose Hirschjagd."

176. It is interesting that many years later Da Ponte recalled that *Figaro* "had to make head against a host of intriguers, both before and *after* [my italics] the representation of the piece." This implies a continuing struggle for full recognition. Da Ponte, *Extract*, 14.

Table 1.3 Friday opera clashes in Vienna (1786–87)

	Burgtheater	Kärntnertortheater	Comments
May 5	Il burbero	Die eingebildeten philosophen	Le nozze di Figaro is not scheduled head-to-head.
May 12	L'italiana in Londra	(no performance)	Mombelli makes his debut unopposed.
	Laxenburg recess followed by summer vacation periods for the two German troupes		
Aug 18	L'italiana in Londra	Die Entführung aus dem Serail	Mozart's Singspiel is chosen for the first postrecess clash.
Aug 25	Il trionfo delle donne	Die schöne Arsene	
Sep 1	Le gare generose	Zémire und Azor	
Sep 8	Closed	Closed	
Sep 15	Gli sposi malcontenti	Der Apotheker	
Sep 22	Le nozze di Figaro	Das Irrlicht	The night of Le nozze di Figaro's only appearance in a head-to-head clash.
Sep 29	La grotta di Trofonio	(No performance)	
Oct 6	L'italiana in Londra	Betrug durch Aberglauben	Dittersdorf's new opera receives its second performance.
Oct 13	L'italiana in Londra	Der Apotheker	
Oct 20	Il mondo della luna	Der Apotheker	Upon his return from Bohemia, Joseph II chooses opera buffa for his first appearance in the theater.
Oct 27	I finti eredi	Robert und Hannchen	
Nov 3	Il re Teodoro	Das Irrlicht	
Nov 10	La grotta di Trofonio	Die eingebildeten Philosophen	
Nov 17	Una cosa rara	(No performance)	
Nov 24		Una cosa rara	Una cosa rara is transferred to the Kärntnertortheater for its second performance.
Dec 1	Gli sposi malcontenti	Die Entführung aus dem Serail	
Dec 8	I finti eredi	Betrug durch Aberglauben	
	No contests during Christmas and the New Year		
Jan 12	Una cosa rara	Zémire und Azor	

Table 1.3   Continued

	Burgtheater	Kärntnertortheater	Comments
Jan 19	*Il re Teodoro*	*Die glücklichen Jäger*	
Jan 26	*Democritto corretto*	*Der Apotheker*	The second abbreviated performance of *Democritto corretto* results in an all-Dittersdorf evening.
Feb 2	*Le gare generose*	*Der Deserteur*	
Feb 9	*Una cosa rara*	(No performance)	
Feb 16	*La grotta di Trofonio*	*Der Apotheker*	Dittersdorf's benefit performance of *Der Apotheker* is scheduled to allow him to avoid a heavyweight contest with *Una cosa rara*.

Insights into the politics of the ongoing contest can be gleaned from the scheduling choices made on particular nights, but the overall message of Table 1.3 is that both troupes tended to bring out their most reliable successes to bolster their position in the weekly Friday confrontation with the opposition. During the year as a whole, there were three sequences of operatic head-to-heads: a brief period at the start of the season; the autumn months from October to December; and Carnival 1787. No regular competition took place during the Laxenburg recess or the summer holiday periods for the two German troupes, and there was also a break around Christmas and the New Year. Only one of *Figaro*'s nine performances in the Burgtheater (22 September) was on a competitive Friday.

During the summer months, the Italian cause was further damaged by Vincenzo Righini's *Il Demogorgone*, a total flop, after which recourse was had to older favorites such as Salieri's *La grotta di Trofonio* and Martín y Soler's *Il burbero*. In an attempt to address an increasingly difficult situation, *I finti eredi*, a Sarti opera new to Vienna, was brought into production, evidently in the hope that it might match the abiding popularity of *Fra i due litiganti*. A report in the *Wiener Zeitung* was short and factual. A longer review noted, without going into any detail, "the lack of three good personnages" ("la mancanza di tre bravi Personaggi").[177] The Vienna version of *I finti eredi* incorporates a

177. *Gazzetta universale* (15 August 1786), no. 65, 518. VIENNA 3 Agosto. When he attended the opera on 20 September, Zinzendorf was surprised by the absence from the cast of Benucci, Storace, and Mombelli. Link, *National Court Theatre*, 279: "20 Septembre. A l'opera. *I finti Eredi de Sarti*. Ni Benucci, ni la Storace, ni Monbelli, la Laschi et Mandini rendent cet opera un peu tolerable."

substitute aria for Benucci ("Or comprendo"), written by Francesco Antonio
Piticchio, in which "Se vuol ballare" is quoted ostentatiously. Mary Hunter
suggests that the use of Figaro's very recognizable tune "in a situation of raw
class confrontation" implies an awareness on Piticchio's part of the wider political connotations of the source text.[178] Librettists writing for the National
Theater during the period of the intertroupe contest obviously thought that
the onstage representation of equality between the classes—not in itself an
unusual topic for an opera buffa—might be a useful ploy to win imperial approval; it was, after all, one of Joseph's core political beliefs.

In the summer of 1786, the question of where the next popular success for
the opera buffa troupe was going to be found became steadily more urgent.
The possibility of commissioning a sequel to a very popular work was raised
by the librettist Casti. Even before the premiere of *Le nozze di Figaro*, itself a
sequel, he was considering such a project. In a letter to Paolo Greppi dated 26
April 1786, he announced his intention to spend the coming winter in Naples,
where he proposed to work on a companion piece to *Il re Teodoro*, a prequel
rather than a sequel, and to ask Paisiello to set it to music.[179] This proposal may
well have been the subject of a letter from Casti to Rosenberg that was seen
by Joseph II and that was shown to Zinzendorf on 5 June 1786.[180] The reply
has not survived, but it encouraged Casti to submit material for evaluation.
Zinzendorf was present when Rosenberg read the first scenes of Casti's new libretto *Il re Teodoro in Corsica*, expressing the view—it is not clear whether this
was his personal opinion or the collective response—that they were nothing
like as amusing as the original.[181] Nonetheless, the proposal for a new opera
from Paisiello, expressly written for Vienna, would surely have appealed to
Joseph, and when Casti arrived in Naples early in 1787 with his traveling companion Graf Joseph Fries, he was reportedly in possession of a contract.[182]

178. Hunter, "'Se vuol ballare,'" 464–67.

179. Link, *National Court Theatre*, 277: "A Naples, où je passerai une bonne partie de l'hiver
prochain, je pense à faire mettre en musique par Paisiello la 2e, ou plutôt la 1e partie du
Teodoro, à laquelle je travaille."

180. Link, *National Court Theatre*, 274.

181. Link, *National Court Theatre*, 277: "il [le grand Chambelan] nous lut le nouvel *Opera de
Casti*. *Teodoro in Corsica*, il n'est pas a beaucoup pres aussi amusant que l'autre."

182. *Oberdeutsche Staatszeitung* (28 February 1787), no. 43, 171: "In Neapel ist Graf Fries
in Gesellschaft seines Reisegefährten Abate Casti in den ersten Tagen des Februars
angekommen. Lezterer hat vom Kaiser den Auftrag mitgebracht, eine neue komische Oper
von seiner Arbeit für das Nationaltheater zu Wien vom berühmten Paisiello in Musik setzen
zu lassen."

A sequel could not solve the immediate difficulties facing the opera buffa troupe, but a better idea soon emerged, one that directly addressed the problem: alarming indications that women of fashion were starting to transfer their loyalty to German opera. Elisabeth von Württemberg, by virtue of her status an influential arbiter of taste, attended the newly fashionable Singspiel troupe a second time to see a performance of *Der Apotheker* on 31 July.[183] The issue came out into the open following the premiere of Dittersdorf's new opera *Betrug durch Aberglauben*, for which expectations were understandably very high.[184] In view of the importance the German troupe attached to winning Joseph's approval, Eberl had developed a libretto in which a stupid, treasure-seeking aristocrat is easily duped through his superstitious beliefs, a composite of two of the emperor's bêtes noires.[185] With the publication of the first volume of Joseph's new legal codex imminent, a notary is featured with timely satire. In every way a stock character, he spouts legal Latin in the manner espoused by Despina in *Così fan tutte*: "Meine Kanonen / sind Millionen / Distinctionen / Exceptionen / Ich streit in forma, / Und auch per dilemma / Die Jura Romana [Joseph II, of course, was the Holy Roman Emperor] / Sind meine Arcana." If the forthcoming compendium was being referenced directly, it was to be vast in scale and meticulous in character. There is a passing mention of Hugo Grotius, an early advocate of natural law, freed from the constraints of super-stition, a name well worth dropping in Joseph's presence. Dittersdorf took the opportunity to reinforce his admiration for his old friend and mentor Gluck, recently and very openly invoked in *Über das deutsche Singspiel*, by making ref-erence to the Furies scene in *Orfeo*.[186] Although ignored by Zinzendorf, the

---

183. Weyda, "Briefe an Erzherzog Franz," 15: 1 août: "Hier je fus au théâtre."

184. *Bayreuther Zeitung* (28 September 1786), no. 115, Anhang, 807: Wien, vom 18. September: "Der berühmte Compositor Hr. von Dittersdorf, wird uns bald wieder mit einer neuen Oper: Die Schatzgräber betittelt, regaliren, die noch kunstreicher und cantabler seyn soll, als die Oper: Doctor und Apotheker."

185. In the summer of 1786, Vienna was obsessed with the case of Freiherr von Székely, convicted of large-scale theft. In the pamphlet war that erupted over the validity of the ver-dict and the severity of Joseph's punishment, Székely was depicted as a would-be alchemist, attempting to produce gold to reduce his debts. *Szekelys Vertheidigter Strafbarer*, 7: "Jener hat in der Hoffnung, Gold zu machen." Although not a direct satire on this *cause célèbre*, Dittersdorf's Baron is obsessed with gold. In his sleep he mutters: "Gold!—pures Gold! O wie herrlich—wie—Sie klingen—die herrlichen Dukaten."

186. Buch, *Enchanted Forests*, 175. This allusion might well have been recognized. Georg Wilhelm's troupe had included *Orfeo* in its summer season at Baden in 1786. *Theater-Kalendar auf das Jahr 1787*, 223: "Orpheo e Euridice von Hrn. Gluck."

new opera was reviewed everywhere, with glowing reports of packed houses and prolonged applause.[187]

Dittersdorf's second major success was in itself a worrying development for supporters of Italian opera, but more alarming still was a report that drew attention to his music's growing appeal to women, linking the crush at *Betrug durch Aberglauben* with the abandonment of the fashion for hoop skirts ("Bouffanten"). The beneficial effects of this change in attendance patterns would be seen at the end of the financial year.[188] The unqualified allegiance of the fashionable world to Italian opera—the "dandies" ("Stutzer"), the "women arbiters of taste" ("Tongebende Damen") and the "cocks" ("Hähne"), as the author of *Über das deutsche Singspiel* rather contemptuously described that world's leading lights—now seemed to be in question. If the perception was that women in Vienna were abandoning their space-consuming outfits in order to crowd in to see Dittersdorf's latest Singspiel, the time was clearly right for the opera buffa troupe to reply in kind. There is no direct evidence that Da Ponte himself came up with the plan to play the fashion card in so blatant a manner, but it seems quite likely, given his recognition of the "importance and centrality of women to the health and vitality of the opera in Vienna."[189]

The link between fashion and theater had never been closer, thanks to the impact of Beaumarchais on Parisian high society. Advertisements for costumes, hats, and accessories "à la Figaro," "à la Susanne," "à la Cherubin," and "à la Basile" were everywhere, especially in two new fashion magazines, the first such magazines ever published. The *Cabinet des Modes* was founded in Paris in late 1785; after one year of publication it became the *Magasin des modes nouvelles, Françoises et Angloises*. The Weimar *Journal der Moden* commenced in 1786, also adopting a new title in its second year, the celebrated *Journal des Luxus und der Moden*. Both had strong connections with Vienna. Löschenkohl republished the *Cabinet des Modes* from the start of 1786,

---

187. *Laibacher Zeitung* (19 October 1786), no. 42: Wien, den 10. Okt.: "Am 2ten dieses ist die neue vom Hrn. Ditters von Dittersdorf verfertigte Opera: Betrug durch Aberglauben, betitelt, aufgeführt, und am Ende so lang geklatscht worden, bis Hr. Ditters auf dem Theater sich zeigte, dann aber war gar der Bravos kein Ende."

188. *Bayreuther Zeitung* (7 October 1786), no. 121, 843: Wien, vom 30. Sept.: "Ditters neue Opera: Die Schatzgräber, hat den verdienten Beyfall erhalten. Gestern war das Schauspielhaus so gesteckt voll, daß man sich kaum rühren konnte. Und seit dem das schöne Geschlecht die Boufanten abgelegt hat, faßt das Theater den sechsten Theil mehr Zuschauer, welches in Jahresfrist bey der Cassa einen merklichen Ueberschuß machen wird."

189. He made full use of this influential constituency when it came to lobbying to save the Italian opera troupe from closure at the start of 1789. Clark, "Reading and Listening," 146.

and in June he advertised his collection of fashionable fans in the *Journal der Moden*.[190] Although Viennese fashion was derivative, a conservative version of Parisian taste, both journals carried periodic reports from Vienna. From the descriptions given in these exquisitely illustrated magazines, readers could easily see how opera functioned as a generator of new fashion. The "pouf à la Grande-Prêtresse"—a monstrous creation, as damaging to sight lines as any theatrical pillar—came from Gluck's opera, and it soon became known as the "pouf à la Iphigénie." In 1787, an operatic contest was waged on the heads of Parisian beauties between two contenders. Although *Tarare* had not had quite the impact predicted for a new work by Beaumarchais, it nonetheless inspired a "Huth à la Tarare."[191] Its rival was a "Huth à la Theodor," representing Paisiello's *Le Roi Théodore à Venise*.[192] The fashion journals reported fully on this contest, which reached its zenith at the end of 1787.[193] With a largely female readership in mind, the editor of the *Cabinet des Modes* complained about the tendency to adopt masculine nomenclature for women's hats.[194] As *Tarare* established its brand in the world of fashion, an example soon cropped up. There was a complaint about the naming of a cap "à la Calpigi" (after the male slave played by a castrato) when it would more aptly have been known as a cap "à la Spinette" (after the woman slave).[195]

Having worked on *La folle journée*, Da Ponte would have been very well aware of its links with Parisian fashion. In the first duettino of *Le nozze di Figaro*, he chose to make a feature of Susanna's hat. In Beaumarchais, she is seen in front of a mirror adjusting her headdress: "Suzanne attach à sa tête, devant une glace, le petit bocquet de fleurs d'orange appèlé chapeau de la mariée."[196]

---

190. *Intelligenz Blatt des Journals der Moden* (June 1786).

191. *Cabinet des Modes*, Vingt-septième Cahier (10 August 1787): "Il eût été très-étonnant que *Tarare* n'eût pas donné lieu à quelque mode nouvelle."

192. *Cabinet des Modes*, Trente-troisième Cahier (10 October 1787) 259: "Le Roi Théodore à Venise devoit payer le tribut à la Mode."

193. *Journal des Luxus und der Moden* (December 1787), 416: Paris, den 4ten Novemb.: "Zum Huthe à la Tarare, hat sich ein neuer Modes Huth, à la Theodor . . . gesellet. Er hat seinen Nahmen von einer neuen sehr beliebten komischen Oper, *Le Roi Theodor à Venise*, die man seit einiger Zeit hier spielt; und theilt dermalen mit seinem Bruder à la Tarare, den Thron des Reichs der Mode auf den Köpfen unserer Schönen."

194. *Cabinet des Modes*, Vingt-septième Cahier (10 August 1787).

195. *Cabinet des Modes*, Trentième Cahier (10 September 1787), 236: "un bonnet *à la Calpigi*" . . . (1) "Personnage de l'Opéra de Tarare. Si on eût fait un bonnet *à la Spinette*, on ne seroit point tombé dans le défaut que nous avons reproché."

196. Heartz, "Susanna's Hat."

Preoccupied with his calculations, Figaro acknowledges her "joli boquet vir-ginal" in response to her question, but then the conversation turns to the bed chamber. In Da Ponte's opening scene, Susanna has to persist in her attempts to attract his attention ("Guarda un po', mio caro Figaro, / Guarda adesso il mio cappello"), and the climax of the duettino is their mutual expression of delight in this homemade piece of millinery ("Questo bel cappellino vezzoso / Che Susanna ella stessa à fè"). As Heartz pointed out, Löschenkohl's silhou-ette of Storace could represent her headgear from *Figaro*.[197] (It would also have been seen as an example of the more natural, understated English fashion, the main rival to Parisian taste.) The silhouettes of other women members of the cast, Luisa Laschi, Maria Mandini, and Dorotea Bussani, show them without headdress. If the production of *Le nozze di Figaro* followed the costume advice given in the preface to *La folle journée*, the Countess would have appeared in the opera with "nul ornament sur la tête" and only when dressing up as her maid would have been able to adopt her servant's "haute coiffure." To add to the sensitivities in allocating the two leading women's roles, there lay in the background the specter of their rival looks on stage.

The choice of Spanish fashion to feature in a new opera buffa, aimed at reclaiming the loyalty of women operagoers, was very likely prompted by the arrival of a new Spanish ambassador in Vienna at the start of September, Marquis José Augustin de Llano, whose wife, Isabel, made an immediate impression. Zinzendorf was un-galant in summing up her appearance: "Le visage rude, malgre les yeux noirs, les dents blanches et le pié beau."[198] But she undeniably cut a striking figure, and on 18 September was seen ostentatiously chatting throughout a performance of *La grotta di Trofonio*. In many ways, she was a typical representative of the class of fashionable women, whose behavior at opera, flirting and nattering incessantly, was starting to cause annoyance and provoke calls of "Psst" (shut up please!). An engraving published in 1785 captures their "performance" as they disport themselves in their very visible seats. The denizens of the upper tiers are following the drama on stage in-tently, but the society women in the lowest boxes, prominently displaying their fashionable attire, ignore it completely.[199] While it is unlikely that Isabel played any role in the award of a commission to her compatriot Martín y Soler, her high profile was seized upon by the authors of *Una cosa rara* as they developed

---

197. Heartz, "Susanna's Hat," 585. On Löschenkohl, see Hubmayer, "Hieronymus Löschenkohl."

198. Link, *National Court Theatre*, 279.

199. Clark, "Reading and Listening," 146.

its colorful evocation of Spain. She gave her seal of approval to the new opera by providing the costumes, which Zinzendorf described as "pretty."[200]

The new work was conceived and brought to the stage in unprecedented haste. Da Ponte recalled that it took him thirty days and that the composer completed his work not long thereafter.[201] Da Ponte's description of the premiere of *Una cosa rara* focused on a conspiracy of his own making: his attempt to humiliate singers in the Italian troupe. What he felt he had to gain from this is a mystery. It occurred to him that he could play a trick on his "Zoiluses"—Zoilus was a literary commentator famed for harsh and unjustified critiques—by concealing his role in the new opera and observing the consequences. After starting work on the libretto for Martín y Soler, he received a request from Stephen Storace for a new work. As it was supported by Joseph II, he had no option but to comply, but, banking on the fact that no one would believe that he was working on two books at once, he asked the Spaniard to pretend he had decided to set another libretto instead. In secret, meanwhile, he completed *Una cosa rara* himself. To his great satisfaction, the singers praised the beauty of the poetry, the quality of the characterizations, and the originality of the plot, at the same time complaining bitterly about the way the composer had fashioned their roles.[202] Joseph himself had to intervene. Fortuitously opening the libretto at the page on which Da Ponte's version of the Spanish "che sera, sera" appeared, he instructed Rosenberg to use this aphorism to silence the singers.

On the first night, Da Ponte noted the presence of a large claque in the audience primed to hiss. He was jubilant when it remained silent in the face of the new work's reception: an unusual degree of rapt attention followed by

---

200. Link, *National Court Theatre*, 282: "17 Novembre: A l'opera. *Una cosa rara, o sia bellezza ed onestà*. Il represent des gens de la campagne Espagnols, les habillemens en partie dirigés, en partie donnés par l'ambassadrice d'Espagne, etoient jolis."

201. In the light of its speedy conception, accusations of plagiarism proved hard to shake off. In the satire *Anti-da Ponte*, the librettist (accused in a mock trial) responded to a complaint from Martín y Soler that he had stolen the text of *Una cosa rara* with the pointed riposte that the pot should not call the kettle black; if he was a plagiarist, then so was the composer, whose borrowings could be read about in the issue of the *Wienerbothen* dated 18 March 1789. De Alwis, *Anti-Da Ponte*, 60: "Habe ich den Text von der *Cosa rara* gestohlen, so hat Er die Musik dazu geplündert, worüber man ausführlich nachlesen kann, in den Wienerbothen vom 18 März 1789."

202. There is no independent confirmation of Da Ponte's account of strife between the composer and his singers, although the day after the premiere of *Una cosa rara*, Zinzendorf did record that Laschi was complaining about her role in Storace's forthcoming *Gli equivoci*. Link, *National Court Theatre*, 282: "18. Novembre . . . La *Laschi* vint se plaindre du rôle qu'elle doit prendre dans l'opera de Storace."

storms of applause. Unable to see beyond slights, real or imagined, he failed to entertain the possibility that some of those predisposed to dislike the new work were members of the German party, who had much to lose at that juncture from an Italian success. If it was present, the Singspiel claque was wise to keep silent, because the premiere of *Una cosa rara* was the occasion for a display of Habsburg symbolic theater: a public gesture of recognition for Elisabeth von Württemberg. Joseph II seems to have been at one with the Viennese in regarding Franz's betrothed as the embodiment of the "bellezza ed onestà" (beauty and virtue) of the opera's alternative title. The first performance of Martín y Soler's opera was scheduled for Elisabeth's name day on 17 November. In the theater, Franz enacted a brief scene in which a young man surprises his beloved in her opera box, echoing the onstage drama. A news report in the *Carlsruher Zeitung* drew the conclusion—as was surely the intention—that the date for her marriage was now approaching.[203] The time when public opinion could all but impose a much-forecast royal wedding on a couple, who left to themselves might have had second thoughts, lay far in the future, but in the case of Franz and Elisabeth, a vox populi expressing "surprise" at the length of time being taken to make an announcement was becoming steadily more insistent. In late 1786 and throughout 1787, a growing crescendo of stories in the press followed the grooming of Elisabeth for her role as Habsburg empress. This public salutation at the new opera buffa, following several months during which her patronage of German opera had been the subject of comment, could hardly have come at a more helpful juncture for the Italian party.

On a personal level, Franz's surprise visit was a response to Elisabeth's musical celebration of his own name day the previous month in her summer accommodation in the Salesian convent, where she received religious instruction while at the same time developing a high public profile in the Belvedere.[204] This was the latest in a carefully planned sequence of

203. *Carlsruher Zeitung* (6 December 1786), no. 146, 691: Wien, vom 25 Nov.: "An dem Tag der heil. Elisabeth wohnte die erhabne Prinzeßinn, welche diesen Namen trägt, der Vorstellung einer neuen komischen Oper in dem Nationaltheater bey. Der Erzherzog Franz überraschte Sie auf das angenehmste durch seinen Besuch in ihrer Loge, worüber die Zuschauer ihren Beyfall durch ein allgemeines Händeklatschen zu erkennen gaben. Das Publikum kann kaum den Augenblick erwarten, wo diese beyde hohe Personen durch das heil. Band der Ehe auf ewig miteinander vereinigt werden und dieser Augenblick scheint, wie sich aus manchen Veranstaltungen vermuthen läßt, nicht so gar weit mehr entfernt zu seyn."

204. Beales, *Against the World 1780–1790*, 125–26. In 1786, she took up residence there in May, around the time of the Laxenburg recess. *Augspurgische Ordinari Postzeitung* (19 May 1786), no. 119: Wien, den 13 May.

public engagements, leading, step by step, toward their coming union, and the press interpreted the choreography with relish. At the start of the year, for example, a sleigh ride had been organized during a cold snap. One reporter took the angle that this was the first time that Franz had "driven" Elisabeth, an activity not without risk.[205] Her celebration of his name day at her place of residence—press reports fail to say whether he was present or not—marked a further step. It was a news story of obvious significance, and some details were reported. Following the dinner, there was a performance of *Harmoniemusik.*[206] Another notice described the music as "predominantly" for wind instruments.[207] Franz's return compliment at the first performance of *Una cosa rara* rounded off the exchange, a charming episode of musical courtship.

The premiere of *Una cosa rara*, a pivotal moment in the struggle between the Italian and German genres, effectively secured the position of the opera buffa and all associated with it. It was given unopposed on 17 November, the night of its first performance, and the Singspiel troupe also chose (or was instructed) not to contest the second Friday performance, which was transferred to the Kärntnertortheater.[208] Crowds flocked to see it, and three to four hundred would-be spectators were turned away every evening.[209] On 20 February 1787, the final night of the season, an additional performance was staged, again in the Kärntnertortheater.[210] Zinzendorf was beguiled by the music, albeit observing that the plot lacked common sense, but few others were worried by this supposed defect.[211]

---

205. *Kurfürstlich gnädigst privilegirte Münchner Zeitung* (13 January 1786), no. 8, 30: Wien, vom 7 Jäner.

206. *Stralsundische Zeitung* (2 November 1786), no. 131: Wien, den 18 October: "Die Prinzeßin Elisabeth hat, zu Ehren des Erzherzogs Franz, am 4ten dieses, als an dem Namenstage desselben, im Belvedere große Tafel und dann Concert von Blasé-Instrumenten gegeben."

207. *Kurfürstlich gnädigst privilegirte Münchner Zeitung* (13 October 1786), no. 161, 647: Wien, vom 7 Oktob.: "ein prächtiges Konzert meistens von blasenden Instrumenten gegeben." With its double bass part, K.364 might qualify as an ensemble "mostly" for wind instruments, if that was the sense intended.

208. Link, *National Court Theatre*, 487.

209. Pezzl, *Skizze*, vol. 3, 423: "Diese war es aber welche die Stadt beinahe in Raserei gebracht hätte, und bei deren jeder Vorstellung 3–400 Personen aus Mangel an Plaz wieder vergebens nach Hause gehn mußten."

210. Link, *National Court Theatre*, 99.

211. Link, *National Court Theatre*, 283: "20. Novembre: Le soir a l'*opera* una cosa rara . . . le Duo de Mandini avec la Lilla (la Storace) au seconde acte est charmant. mais la marche de la piéce n'a pas le sens commun."

The wind band version of the new opera proved a good indicator of its popularity. The ensemble employed by Prince Johann Schwarzenberg performed it on 29 March, 15 April, and 5 May 1787.[212] On 2 March 1787, the "Kaisers Harmoniemusik" presented a mixed-genre program at its traditional benefit concert: (1) a Dittersdorf symphony; (2) pieces from *Una cosa rara*; (3) an unnamed symphony; (4) more pieces from *Una cosa rara*; (5) Dittersdorf's symphony (overture) to *Der Apotheker*; (6) pieces from *Der Apotheker*; and (7) an unnamed symphony.[213] Whether this politically well-balanced club sandwich was given on the instructions of the emperor or represented only the desire to present arrangements of the hottest favorites of the moment is unclear, but the following year, with the closure of the Singspiel imminent, the wind band ignored Dittersdorf in favor of Martín y Soler's *L'arbore di Diana*, music from the winning side.

The *Bayreuther Zeitung* noted a marked upturn in the fortunes of Italian opera in a piece published the day after the fourth performance of *Una cosa rara*. The company was commended for its staging of new pieces, and it had established a reputation for good stage action, heavenly voices, and harmony.[214] This was a significant endorsement, as the paper had been following the success of the German troupe with evident approval. An informed reader would have had no difficulty in reaching the conclusion that the effects of Martín y Soler's triumph were being described.[215]

As was clearly the hope, the reception of the opera was greatly assisted by its successful inauguration of a new fashion.[216] The *Journal des Luxus* devoted a long report to the impact of *Una cosa rara* on Viennese style: fabrics and color schemes based on the costumes of the leading characters (red and black)

---

212. Link, "Vienna's Private Theatrical and Musical Life," 246–47.

213. Link, *National Court Theatre*, 100; Morrow, *Concert Life*, 264.

214. *Bayreuther Zeitung* (12 December 1786), no. 149, 1047: Wien, vom 5. Dec.: "Die italienische Oper bietet alles auf, um das Publikum recht sehr zu unterhalten. Immer neue Stücke, gute Actionen, himmlische Stimmen, Harmonie unter einander, und ein beständiges Wetteifern, immer neu zu seyn, ist das Bestreben dieser Gesellschafft."

215. The gift to the composer of a golden snuffbox and 600 gulden was widely reported. *Gräzer Zeitung* (30 January 1787), no. 9: Wien: "Alles läuft izt in die Cosa rara eine wälsche Oper vom Kapelmeister Martini in Musik gesetzt, dieweil sie in spanischem Geschmak ist, ihrer Neuheit wegen allgemeinen Beyfall erhält ." Edge, "Mozart's Fee," 230, cites a similar report to this effect in the *Brünner Zeitung* (12 January 1787), no. 4, 30.

216. *Bayreuther Zeitung* (20 January 1792), no. 9, Anhang, 54: "Diese beliebte Opera hat in Wien eine gleiche Revolution in Moden, und Sitten hervorgebracht, denn alles muß à la cosa rara seyn."

and fans depicting the reconciliation scene.[217] The following year, men's watch chains "à la Cosa rara" were deemed passé.[218] The vogue for Spanish costume inspired by *Una cosa rara* replicated in Vienna the intensity of the Parisian relationship between theater and fashion; a more effective strategy to win back women, in danger of being tempted away from Italian opera by Dittersdorf's triumph, is hard to imagine.

In the wake of Martín y Soler's triumph, Mozart's opera all but disappeared from the schedules, but his evergreen German work was the trump card deployed by the Singspiel troupe in its attempt to compete with *Una cosa rara*. Table 1.4 lists operas scheduled in the two weeks following 17 November.

The scheduling of a short run of *Die Entführung aus dem Serail* at this critical juncture is testament to its durability.[219] A letter from Vienna dated 20 December, the day after the fourth performance, evaluated Lippert as an actor,

Table 1.4 Operas scheduled after the premiere of *Una cosa rara*

	Italian	German
Nov 17	*Una cosa rara* (1)	
Nov 19		*Die Entführung aus dem Serail*
Nov 20	*Una cosa rara* (2)	
Nov 21		*Die Entführung aus dem Serail*
Nov 22	*Il re Teodoro*	
Nov 24	*Una cosa rara* (3)	
Nov 26		*Der Apotheker*
Nov 27	*La scuola de'gelosi*	
Dec 1	*Gli sposi malcontenti*	*Die Entführung aus dem Serail*

---

217. *Journal des Luxus und der Moden* (October 1787), 351: Mode-Neuigkeiten Wien den 30sten August 1787: "einen Flor oder Dünntuch *à la Cosa Rara*, das Schwarz und mit durchgehenden rothen schmalen Seidenstreifen, nach der Farbe des Auszugs der beyden Hauptpersonen des Stückes, ist . . . Uhrketten *à la Cosa Rara* . . . die Fächer à *la Cosa Rara*, worauf die Scene, wie sich beyde Liebende wieder vereinigen, auf der einen Seite desselben, auf der anderen Seite aber das hier so allgemein beliebte und nun sogar zum Volkslied gewordene Duetto Amoroso: *Pace caro mio sposo* etc. das sie dabey singen." This duet was even arranged for two automata. *Bayreuther Zeitung* (12 June 1788), no. 83, 562.

218. *Journal des Luxus und der Moden* (June 1788), 227: "Die Uhrketten *à la Cosa rara* sind ganz paßirt."

219. Given this longevity, it is curious that Mozart seems not to have been approached to write another work for the German troupe.

noting in passing that his reception in the Singspiel had been "quite exceptional" ("ganz ausnehmend").[220] On the critical night of 19 November, in its
first response to the newest Italian sensation, the German ensemble was also
able to offer a *débutée*, Thekla Podleska, who was engaged initially for four
months on a salary (pro rata) of 1,400 gulden, which made her the second best
paid woman performer in the troupe after Aloysia Lange.[221]

The *Wiener Zeitung*'s coverage of *Una cosa rara* is astonishingly low-
key. It begins with a bald statement—that the opera was given on 17
November—and leaves it at that; there is no hint that the evening might
have been anything out of the ordinary. The report moves on to consider
other recent performances, noting the return of the actress Johanna Sacco
in Lessing's *Minna von Barhelm*, in which she had received "honorable applause" ("ehrenvollen Beyfall"). Podleska, making her debut as Constanze in
Die Entführung aus dem Serail, received only "applause."[222] As usual, these
brief evaluations of new members of the cast substituted for a review of the
event itself. There was nothing to be said about the premiere of *Una cosa
rara*, one of the most significant operatic occasions in eighteenth-century
Vienna, simply because all the principal performers had appeared previously
in other works.

Dittersdorf's third letter to Baron von Kaschnitz is dated 20 November
1786. Having been given permission to remain in Vienna, he was now in
the embarrassing position of having to request a further extension, owing
to the fact that his new Italian opera *Democritto corretto* had run into
scheduling difficulties. It was ready, but Rosenberg had directed that it
should not be given before January, despite being told that his period of
leave would be over at the end of November.[223] Dittersdorf had no alternative other than to ask the emperor to overrule this.[224] At the end of his

---

220. *Provinzialnachrichten* (23 December 1786), no. 102, 385: "Brief aus Wien, den 20.
Dezember."

221. Link, *National Court Theatre*, 421 and 426.

222. *Wiener Zeitung* (22 November 1786), no. 93, 2837.

223. Unverricht, *Carl von Dittersdorf: Briefe*, 55. "Da Seine *Excell*: Graf *Rosenberg* meine
bereits fertige wällsche *Opera* nicht in diesem gegenwärtigen Monat, sondern erst im
Januario, ungeachtet der Einwendung die ich ihm machte: so nemlich daß ich von *Eyer
Hochwohlgebohrn* nicht länger als bis Ende *November* Urlaub hätte:."

224. Unverricht, *Carl von Dittersdorf: Briefe*, "so war mir kein ander Mittel übrig, als zu seiner
K: K: Mayestätt selbst zu gehen, und um eine allerhöchste *ordre* zu bitten, daß meine *Opera*
noch diesen Monat aufgeführt werde. S.M. befahlen also bald, daß meine *Opera* aufgeführt
werden sollte."

meeting with Joseph in May, he had been encouraged to come again for further musical discussions, and he evidently now made use of this open invitation.[225] A rehearsal was arranged, but a new order appeared out of the blue, countermanding the recently obtained permission to go ahead. Because an unnamed Italian composer had an engagement in London that necessitated his prompt departure, it had been decided that Dittersdorf's new work should not be given until Christmas. The "Italian" was in fact the Englishman Stephen Storace, whose *Gli equivoci* took precedence.[226] Now facing an acute dilemma, Dittersdorf sought a further audience with the emperor. He claimed to report part of the conversation verbatim, stressing that the underlined words were as spoken by Joseph II.[227] The emperor had addressed the problem with pragmatism, enquiring whether there was anyone in Freiwaldau who could act as a substitute. Upon hearing that such a man was already in place as a result of the first extension, Joseph wanted to know whether he was qualified ("tauglich"). Once reassured on this point, he granted permission for Dittersdorf to remain until Lent.[228]

---

225. *Allgemeine musikalische Zeitung* (March 1799), 382: "auch wird es mich freuen, Sie während Ihres hiesigen Aufenthaltes noch öfters zu sprechen, und Sie werden mich um dieselbe Stunde, wie heute, immer finden." This information was cut from the final version of the autobiography.

226. Unverricht, *Carl von Dittersdorf: Briefe*, 55: "Es wurde auch also gleich die Anstalt zur ersten *Probe* gemacht. Allein, da der Umstand entzwischen kam, daß ein *Italiener* welcher nach Aufführung seiner *Opera* gleich nach *London impegnirt* so kam eine neue *Ordre*, daß ich mit meiner *Opera* bis nach Weynachten warten sollte."

227. Unverricht, *Carl von Dittersdorf: Briefe*, 56: "Hochgebietender *Chef!* Daß die unterstrichenen Worte wirklich die Worte des Monarchen sind, dafür ist mein ehrlicher Name Bürge, und es würde das schwärzeste Verbrechen seyn den Namen und die Worte des mächtigstens *Souverains* zu mis brauchen."

228. Unverricht, *Carl von Dittersdorf: Briefe*, 55. "In dieser Verlegenheit gieng ich den 18t dieses noch einmal zum Monarchen, und stellte allerhöchst denen selben vor, daß ich durch diese Verzögerung in der grösten Verlegenheit wäre, zumahlen ich von *Eyer Hochwohlgebohrn* nicht länger Urlaub hätte, als bis am Ende *Novembris.* S: M: antworteten folgende Worte: *Was haben sie für eine Bedienstung?* ich antwortete: Ich bin Oberamtmann in Freuwaldau. *Haben Sie dann Niemand, welcher während ihres Hierseyns ihre Stelle vertritt?* ich sagte hierauf: O ja Eyer Mayestätt! *Baron Kaschnitz* hat seit dem *August* als bis wohinn sich mein erster Urlaub erstrekte aus seinen Untergeordneten einen Mann nach *Frewaldau* gestellt, welchen ich aus meinen dortigen Einkünften zu bezahlen mich gerne verbunden habe. Der Monarch erwiederte: *Ist er auch tauglich?* ich sagte: Wenn er nicht tauglich wäre, würde ihn *Baron Kaschnitz* nicht selbst gewählt haben. Der Kayser sagte: *So ist es schon recht. Schreiben Sie also dem Bar: Kaschnitz daß ich ihnen die Erlaubniß gebe noch bis über dem künftigen Fasching hier zu bleiben, ohne daß ihnen in ihrer dorten Bedienstung ein Nachtheil geschehe.*"

The same day, Rosenberg, quick to seize a new opportunity, asked Dittersdorf whether he would have time to write yet another opera.[229]

In most respects, this was a routine scheduling problem. In November 1786, two composers of a new Italian opera were in competition for the first slot after *Una cosa rara*, each for valid personal reasons.[230] If Dittersdorf recorded the sequence of events correctly, Rosenberg decided in favor of Storace but was overruled by the emperor. At this point, the Italian lobby made its full strength felt, and this decision was in turn reversed. Following the dispute, the Storace claque did little to support *Democritto corretto* when it finally received its premiere on 24 January. Significantly, as Zinzendorf observed, it was "sans Storace."[231] The second performance was drastically abbreviated.[232] The poster made abundantly clear how severe the pruning had had to be, but even this could not save it.[233] It can hardly be a coincidence that *Der Apotheker* provided the opposition, the only occasion that year when two operas by a single composer resident in the city were scheduled on the same night. The clash could have been staged by the Singspiel faction, but equally it could have been a cynical ploy by the Italian party, in effect obliging Dittersdorf to be seen to execute the coup de grâce upon his own work. There are indications that the poor reception accorded to *Democritto corretto* rankled with him, and it is easy to see why.[234] If his long-term aspiration was a permanent position in the service of Joseph II, this was an undeniable setback, as the emperor rarely pulled his punches when relishing an artistic debacle.

The failure of *Democritto corretto* featured in Joachim Perinet's account of the state of hostilities between the two troupes shortly after the temporary closure of

---

229. Unverricht, *Carl von Dittersdorf: Briefe*, 56: "Und noch den selben Tag erhielt ich von Graf *Rosenberg* den Antrag, daß man es gerne sehen würde wenn ich ohnehinn müssig wäre, noch eine *Opera* wenn es anders möglich wäre schriebe."

230. In the Indice de' teatrali spettacoli, *Democritto corretto* was not listed as one of the operas in Vienna given "IN TUTTO L'ANNO 1786." Corneilson, "Mozart in l'indice de'teatrali spettacoli," 7–8.

231. Link, *National Court Theatre*, 286. Link has noted how frequently Storace replaced pieces with substitutes provided by lesser known composers, notably by her brother Stephen. When it came to his career, she was evidently someone whom it was unwise to cross. Link, *Arias for Nancy Storace*, viii.

232. Link, *National Court Theatre*, 286: 26 Janvier: "Au Spectacle. *Democrito corretto* quoique beaucoup abregé, ne plut pas."

233. Link, *National Court Theatre*, 97: "Um dieses Singspiel kürzer zu machen, werden fürs Künftige viele Stücke wegbleiben."

234. The failure of the Italian original in Vienna did not prevent Singspiel versions from becoming very popular in northern Germany.

the Burgtheater on 21 February 1787.[235] In a piece entitled "Das Nationaltheater," he began with general remarks.[236] For all his self-avowed patriotism, he had to acknowledge the Italian troupe's tireless endeavors to please the public. The opera *Una cosa rara* had conquered his own heart, yet there was a dark side to the comic ensemble. Indeed, secret treachery lay at its core; an opera by a "friend" (Italian), be it ever so poor, would succeed through the concerted efforts of the singers, while an opera by a "nonfriend" (German) would almost always be ruined.[237] A recent victim had been Dittersdorf, whose *Democritto corretto* would certainly have been one of the more popular works had it not been sabotaged by cabals.[238] The famous singer Storace was the driving force behind its failure; things might have gone better had she not insultingly sent back the music composed for her, necessitating the recasting of roles.[239] Perinet's diatribe is a classic example of how easy it was to magnify routine infighting, the hurly-burly of stage life, into something altogether more sinister: a full-fledged conspiracy with strong nationalist overtones. He seemed in no doubt that an Italian cabal was set on undermining any work by a German.[240]

---

235. For an account of Perinet, see Edge, "Joachim Perinet Refers to 'Mozarts Fortepiano,'" in Edge and Black, *Mozart*. In stressing the activities of cabals, it should never be forgotten that a work's intrinsic merit (or lack of it) was also a significant factor in its reception. Brown, "*Lo specchio francese*," described the libretto as insipid.

236. Perinet, *30 Annehmlichkeiten*, 50.

237. Perinet, *30 Annehmlichkeiten*, 53: "Freilich hat die Gesellschaft auch ihre heimlichen Tücke, denn eine Oper von ihren Freunden mag noch so schlecht seyn, so gewinnt sie durch den zusammgestimmten Fleiß der Operisten, wie im Gegentheile die Oper eines Nicht-Freundes oder eines Teutschen fast immer von der Unteutschen Bande gestürzet wird."

238. Perinet, *30 Annehmlichkeiten*, 53–54: "Ditters war uns ein trauriger Beweiß meiner Rede, denn seine italiänische Oper. . . . würde doch sicher eine der beliebteren seyn, wenn man sie nicht aus Kabale unterdrücket, und mit einigen Heulern und Heulerinnen besezzet hätte, die zu schlecht sind, in einer Hütten Komödie zu singen."

239. Perinet, *30 Annehmlichkeiten*, 54: "Die berühmte Madame Storazze Fischer . . . war sicher die Triebfeder zum Falle der Ditter'schen Oper. Hätte sie den für sie gesezten Sang nicht beleidigend zurückgesandt, wären durch eben diese Verweigerung nicht die meisten Rollen verwechselt, folglich vergeben und verdorben worden, so steh' ich dafür, daß das Singspiel eine ungleich bessere Wirkung hervorgebracht hätte." Passages are cited in Link, *National Court Theatre*, 286–87.

240. In *Anekdoten und Bemerkungen*, 31, published at the start of 1787, another commentator, while most impressed with the current quality of the singing and acting in the opera buffa troupe, observed darkly that many a "Kapellmeister" was seeking to suppress the operas of better men, in order to ensure that mediocrity could shine the more brightly: "So gut das deutsche Schauspiel besetzt ist, so vortreflich ist die wälsche Oper mit ausgesuchten Leuten versehen, die sich um die Wette bestreben, das hiesige Publikum durch ihren Gesang sowohl, als durch aufgeweckte Scherze meisterhaft zu unterhalten, wenn gleich mancher Kapellmeister der Queere daher kommt, und die Opern berühmter Männer zu unterdrücken sucht, damit seine mittelmäßigen desto mehr glänzen sollen." This is rather obscure, but it could have been read as a comment on the deferral of *Democritto corretto*, as allegedly engineered by the Storace faction.

Several years later, this debacle featured in the satirical trial *Anti-da Ponte*. Dittersdorf, cast as a German composer suffering discrimination, complains to Da Ponte about the wretched text foisted on him. He is depicted as being still bitter about the actions taken by some members of the opera buffa troupe.[241] As a character, Dittersdorf defends the German position, claiming that musicians of his nationality can demonstrate good taste as much as any Italian maestro. In response, Da Ponte blames him for accepting a poor text and asks how he could possibly imagine that Italian singers would advance the cause of a German musician.[242] Just such a point was subsequently advanced to explain Mozart's relative lack of success in Vienna. The idea that Mozart, too, had fallen victim to an Italian cabal was seized on by Niemetschek, who even suggested that the emperor had had to intervene to insist that the singers did their duty. That relations between Mozart and his cast were not easy in the runup to the premiere of *Figaro* is evident from Francesco Bussani's action in informing Rosenberg that a fandango was to be performed in act 3, a betrayal that led Mozart (allegedly) to threaten to punch him on the nose. Attempts at sabotage behind the scenes—such as rejecting a composer's music outright, as Storace, it was claimed, had done with Dittersdorf's *Democritto corretto*—were one thing, but highly paid opera stars would have been playing a much riskier game by giving less than their best onstage; their careers depended on the success of those who wrote for them of whatever nationality. Niemetschek was obviously aware of difficulties around the time of *Figaro*, but in personalizing his account, he missed the inter-company strife that was the primary structural context for the outbreak of tribal loyalties.

Despite the failure of *Democritto corretto*, Dittersdorf left Vienna on a high note, having been awarded a special benefit performance of *Der Apotheker*.[243] His reported windfall of 960 gulden is broadly accurate; the theater records show that a sum of 687 gulden was taken, and Joseph added a personal gift of 50 ducats (225 gulden).[244] Even the *Theater-Kalendar*, which that year listed the works performed during the past season without comment, made an exception for this piece, noting its unusual success.[245] For the moment, Dittersdorf could do no wrong, at least in the genre of Singspiel, and he was held up as

---

241. De Alwis, *Anti-Da Ponte*, 50 and 56. The original title page is *Anti-da Ponte*.

242. De Alwis, *Anti-Da Ponte*, 56.

243. *Oberdeutsche Staatszeitung* (1 March 1787), no. 44, 173: Oesterreich.

244. Edge, "Mozart's Fee," 229.

245. *Theater-Kalendar auf das Jahr 1787*, 220: "Der Apotheker und der Doktor . . . Musik von Ditters Edlen von Dittersdorf (erhielt ausserordentlichen Beyfall)."

an ideal musician.[246] He attempted to reestablish good relations with Baron von Kaschnitz by dedicating the keyboard arrangement of *Der Apotheker* to his wife, in recognition of her "schönes Talent zur Musik."[247]

Early in 1787, there was gossip that Storace intended to sing each of her main roles one last time before her departure, so that Vienna could properly appreciate what it was about to miss.[248] This was a characteristic act of self-dramatization; she and her supporters were very adept at managing the news agenda. In addition to works currently enjoying a run, *Il burbero* and *Una cosa rara*, Storace reprised her other major roles in *Il re Teodoro* (5 February) and *La grotta di Trofonio* (16 February). A willingness to accommodate her wishes may account for an apparent late change of work. On 12 February, *Il burbero* was listed, but a bill for *Gli equivoci* also survives for that date.[249] There is no sign, however, that a final performance of *Figaro*, last given on 18 December, was considered for inclusion in this informal retrospective.

There was speculation that the failure of negotiations over Storace's salary had been the cause of her departure.[250] The *Bayreuther Zeitung*, as usual taking a rather jaundiced view of Italian stars, criticized what it saw as her mercenary attitude.[251] Her final academy on 23 February was inevitably an occasion with strong political overtones. A central factor in the success of the opera buffa troupe, she was now offered the use of the Kärntnertortheater, the rival house during the past year, for a benefit concert, the first of that year's Lenten series.

---

246. The author of *Philosophische Fragmente über die praktische Musik*, 54, discussing how rarely the skills of a virtuoso and a music director coincide, saw Dittersdorf as an exception who thus deserved to be highly treasured: "daß es eine Seltenheit ist, und daß so ein Mann, wie z. B. Herr von Dittersdorf ist, deßwegen sehr zu schätzen sei."

247. Unverricht, *Carl von Dittersdorf: Briefe*, 70. It was advertised in the *Wiener Zeitung* (24 February 1787), no. 16, 433.

248. *Bayreuther Zeitung* (27 January 1787), no. 12, 75: Wien, vom 20 Jan.: "Bevor sie von hier abreist, soll sie noch in allen Opern einmal auftreten, und uns fühlen lassen, wie viel wir an ihr verlieren werden."

249. Link, *National Court Theatre*, 98.

250. In some quarters, it was noted that her London engagement was for one year only, with the unspoken assumption that she might return. *Oberdeutsche Staatszeitung* (28 February 1787), no. 45: Wien, den 24sten Feb.: "Madame Storazzo, erste Opernsängerinn, geht auf Ein Jahr nach Aengelland."

251. *Bayreuther Zeitung* (7 October 1786), no. 121, 843: Wien, vom 30. Sept.: "Unsere beliebte Madame Sturazzo hat ihren Abschied begehrt und erhalten. Sie wollte einer neuverschriebenen Sängerin welche noch besser, als sie seyn soll, und um deswillen 200 Ducaten mehr Gehalt bekommt, nicht nachstehen, und will deshalb lieber 1000 Ducaten entbehren, als 200 weniger, als eine andere haben."

This enabled her to reap the rewards of singing in a building with greater capacity; it boasted 1,700–1,800 places, as opposed to the Burgtheater's 1,300–1,350.[252] Although it was the regular venue for academies in 1786 and 1787, her presence was nonetheless potentially sensitive. She offered a linguistic gesture—whether conciliatory or provocative is hard to say—by singing an aria from *Gli equivoci* with a German text expressing her regret at having to leave Vienna.[253] Her pronunciation amused Joseph II, yet such was her grip on public opinion that she was excused her shortcomings, as even a German speaker, so the writer claimed, could not have brought out the ambiguity of the text to such good effect![254] In the few years of her ascendancy, she made an indelible impression, recognized in Johann Pezzl's *Skizze*.[255] Wishful thinking of a reengagement appeared sporadically for several years thereafter.[256]

THROUGHOUT 1786, MUSICAL politics in Vienna focused on the rivalry between the competing troupes. It was inevitable that *Figaro*, the first major commission of the new season, would become entangled in the contest. By the time of its third performance, the opposing factions appear to have been out in force, with one cabal encouraging people to hiss and the other calling vociferously for multiple encores. The boisterous opening nights would have been accepted by Mozart as part of the usual operatic rough-and-tumble, but the complaint that his music was too complex, too full of ideas for listeners

---

252. Link, *National Court Theatre*, 14.

253. The farewell aria was "Potessi di piangere." Link, *Arias for Nancy Storace*, xi–xii and xxiii. Zinzendorf noted: "Son compliment allemand tiré des Equivoci fesoit un joli air." Link, *National Court Theatre*, 288.

254. *Kurfürstlich gnädigst privilegirte Münchner Zeitung* (9 March 1787), no. 39, 158. "Demoiselle Storace hatte die lezte Vorstellung im Karneval zu ihren Gewinn. Sie sang eine teutsche Abschiedsarie. Sie stroppierte die teutschen Ausdrücke des Liedes so glüklich aber in einem so verkehrten Sinne, daß der Monarch herzlich darüber lachte, und Leute von Verstand sagten; ein Teutscher hätte das Zweideutige nicht glüklicher herausbringen können. Dieser Tag brachter ihr 1500 fl."

255. Pezzl, *Skizze*, vol. 3, 425: "Der Wahrheit zur Steuer muß man bekennen, daß sie sehr gut singt; aber ihre Figur ist nicht vortheilhaft: ein kleines dickes Geschöpf, ohne irgend einem weiblichen körperlichen Reiz, ein paar grosse wenig sprechende Augen ausgenommen."

256. *Gräzer Zeitung* (25 December 1787), no. 103: "Die bekannte Sängerinn Storazzo ist auf dem künftigen Sommer für das hiesige Hoftheater wieder engagirt." Link, "Anna Morichelli," 10, in connection with the general desire that the soprano Brigida Giorgi Banti be offered a contract, reports a notice in the *Wienerblättchen* (30 June 1787), which observed that if Banti were to be recruited, it would be possible to do without Storace ("und dann könnten wir die Madame Storace entbehren"). In March 1788, she was in salary negotiations, and in the summer of 1789, there was further speculation that she was considering a return.

to grasp, was worrying. As this campaign of denigration started to take hold, there was a clear danger that he would lose the publicity battle in the German press without a shot being fired.[257]

When Mozart returned from Prague, the *Wiener Zeitung* (21 and 28 February, 3 and 7 March) was full of advertisements for instrumental arrangements of Italian operas by Paisiello, Martín y Soler, and Salieri. It must have been very evident to Mozart that little more than half a year after its premiere, *Figaro* was no longer deemed profitable in the market for commercial spinoffs. The disappointing outcome could hardly be denied, but it usually paid to counter bad news with a more positive story. In timely fashion, a notice appeared reporting the success of his end-of-season academy, which had netted a good (if unspecified) amount.[258] It is possible that Franz was present, as his accounts record patronage of three concerts during February 1787.[259] Another report of this academy published in Graz reads distinctly like an exercise in public relations.[260] Mozart's prospective London trip is linked to news of Haydn's English plans—or more accurately English plans for Haydn—which by 1787 were being announced (prematurely) in the London press in order to boost the

---

257. At this point, Leopold Mozart may have taken action on behalf of his son by submitting details of *Figaro*'s enthusiastic reception in Prague to the local Salzburg newspaper. *Oberdeutsche Staatszeitung* (18 January 1787), no. 14, 54: Deutschland: "Zu Prag ist die von dem berühmten Tonsetzer, und Kapellmeister Herrn Mozart (Sohne) in Musik gesetzte neue Oper 'Le Nozze di Figaro' oder die Hochzeit des Figaro mit ungetheiltem Beyfall aufgeführt worden. Eine zahlreiche Gesellschaft von Musikfreunden hat hierauf Herrn Mozart zum Zeichen ihrer innigsten Verehrung ein gedrucktes deutsches Gedicht, nebst 2 Briefen vom sämmtlichen Prager Orchester, und von ansehnlichen Freunden der Tonkunst, nach Wien zugesandt, und den Wunsch geäußert, ihn persönlich zu sehen. Mozart ist bereits dahin abgereiset ." His authorship of this report is not certain, but the details given closely match those in a passage in his letter to Nannerl of 12 January 1787. Anderson, *Letters*, vol. 3, 1343; *Mozart: Briefe und Aufzeichnungen*, vol. 4, 7.

258. *Bayreuther Zeitung* (12 March 1787), no. 30, Anhang, 112: Wien, vom 1 März (Fortsetzung). Black, "Mozart Benefit Concert in the Kärntnertortheater," in Edge and Black, *Mozart*. The academy on 28 February provides a possible occasion on which the young Beethoven, now known to have been in Vienna during this period, could have heard Mozart in public. Woodfield, "Christian Gottlob Neefe," 308–10; Haberl, "Beethovens erste Reise," 215–55.

259. Dunlop, "'Kaisersammlung,'" 53. The only time an individual academy is identified is in February 1788, when Franz attended Anton Stadler's benefit.

260. *Gräzer Zeitung* (27 March 1787), no. 25: Wien, den 23ten März: "Herr Mozzart hat kürzlich eine musikalische Akademie zu seinem Vortheile gegeben, wobei er eine gute Einnahme gehabt hat. Noch diesen Monat reist er mit seiner Frau nach London, wohin er von dem Sohne des königl. Kapellmeisters eingeladen worden, und dieser so sehr beliebte Tonkünstler darf sich gewis versprechen, von den Britten so bewundert zu werden, als es in Deutschland geschieht. Er ist der Zweite Seiner Kunst, der dieses Jahr nach England reist, und beide, Herr Haiden, und Er werden den Ruhm deutscher Talente sicher befestigen."

prospects for the coming season's orchestral subscription concerts at Hanover Square. The two composers are portrayed as standard-bearers of German musical talent in England.[261]

As the season came to an end, Mozart's bruising experience with the reception of *Figaro* found expression in a number of coded comments. Ludwig Fischer's entry in the composer's album, dated 1 April 1787, refers darkly to the fire of envy ("des Neides Feuer") behind honeyed words and to the paucity of friends who bear the mark of truth and integrity.[262] Some of the composer's supporters appeared to feel that a degree of duplicity on the part of his colleagues had characterized the reception of *Figaro*. A poem by Anton Daniel Breicha, printed on behalf of a numerous society of friends of music on the occasion of the performance of *Le nozze di Figaro* in Prague, is more overtly political.[263] Its final stanza offers a pointed if veiled commentary on the Vienna reception of the opera. Germany, the Fatherland, is urged to break the bond of friendship with strangers and acknowledge Mozart as the German Apollo, once squinting envy ("schielenden Neides") has defeated itself.[264] Josefa and Franz Xaver Duschek, too, attributed Mozart's difficulties to envy of his obvious talent.

The final verdict can be left to Rosenberg. In his briefing document on opera, compiled for Joseph II in the summer of 1787, he offered his opinion that the Italian ensemble had provided the best theatrical entertainment in recent times, naming "Paisiello, Martin, Sarti & Salieri etc." as the "great masters" upon whose new operas this splendid era had been founded.[265] Nothing in the reception accorded to *Le nozze di Figaro* qualified Mozart to be anything other than an "etc."

---

261. In view of Mozart's purported plans for a London visit, it is interesting to see that Gottfried van Swieten was being tipped to take up the position of ambassador there as part of a reshuffle, with Cobenzl moving from St. Petersburg to Brussels and the London ambassador in turn moving to Russia. *Courier du Rhin-Bas* (4 August 1787), no. 62, 515: EXTRAIT *d'une lettre de* Vienne, *du 21 Juillet:* "le Baron de *Swieten* ira en Angleterre, & sa place de bibliothécaire sera, dit on, occupée par le Baron Martini."

262. Deutsch, *Mozart: Die Dokumente*, 254: "doch oft ist Herz und Mund verstimmt; dort singen Lippen Hönig, wo doch des Neides Feuer glimmt; glaub mir, es gebe wenig Freünde, die den Stempel tragen ächter Treu, Rechtschaffenkeit."

263. Nedbal, *Prague's Estates Theater*, 5 and 12.

264. Deutsch, *Mozart: Die Dokumente*, 248–49.

265. Hassmann, *Quellen und Regesten*, 310–11: "Diese Singspiele . . . haben bis itzt die gröste Epoche gemacht, und werden, da grosse Meister, als Paisiello, Martin, Sarti, Salieri etc. für ihre neuen Opern reichliche Belohnung erhalten, sehr zahlreich besucht."

2

Dynastic Alliances

THE GENESIS OF *DON GIOVANNI*

AT THE START of the new season, the German and Italian troupes embarked upon a second year of rivalry, and it was quickly clear that the press had by no means lost interest in the contest. There was speculation as to whether the new prima donna, Anna Morichelli, would match up to her predecessor.[1] Her debut on the first night of the season came as Joseph prepared to depart on his long-awaited journey to meet Catherine II in the Crimea.[2] First reactions to Morichelli's performance, sold out well before the event, were keenly awaited, but she did not appeal to Zinzendorf, who commented on 9 April that she could act but had a weak voice with no high notes ("les cordes hautes lui manquent absolument").[3] In published reviews, however, she was usually given the benefit of the doubt.[4]

---

1. *Bayreuther Zeitung* (13 April 1787), no. 44, Anhang, 310: Wien, vom 7. April: "Die neue Sängerin, welche unsere Madame Sturazzo ersetzen soll, ist vorgestern eingetroffen, und wird künftigen Ostermontage debutiren, oder zum erstenmal sich hören lassen. Es ist schon kein Platz mehr zu haben."

2. The occasion warranted a rare opera-related item in a Dutch-language newspaper. *Amsterdamsche Courant* (24 April 1787), no. 49: WEENEN den 11 April. Paasch Maandag . . . "eene niewe Opera."

3. Link, *National Court Theatre*, 291. Her lack of volume is confirmed in a later review: *Musikalische Real-Zeitung* (7 October 1789), no. 40, 314: Neapel, vom 15ten Jun: "Die Prima Donna, Signora Morichelli . . . Ihre Stimme ist für ein so großes Theater nicht stark genug."

4. *Bayreuther Zeitung* (17 April 1787), no. 46, 322: Schreiben aus Wien, vom 11. April. "die neue Sängerin Mad. Morichelli zuerst als Prima Donna sich hören ließ, und allgemein gefiel; man hört seitdem nichts als Morichelli und überall tönt der Widerhall Morichelli."

The general verdict on the current state of play in the operatic world was that the Italian company was sustaining its advantage.[5] Alarmed by this, the German troupe played the Dittersdorf card for all it was worth, featuring his works on six out of the first seven Friday night operatic contests. In the month of April, nine out of ten Singspiel nights were devoted to the three operas he had written for Vienna. The premiere of the third work, *Die Liebe im Narrenhause*, took place on 12 April 1787, only after he had returned to Silesia.[6] A favorable review of Johann Friederich Jünger's *Das Kleid aus Lyon*, subsequently selected as a gala work for Maria Theresia in Laxenburg, provided an overview of the current standings of the three companies. The play had been a big success, but the German opera was no longer attracting large audiences, notwithstanding the excellent performances of Aloysia Lange.[7] The reputation of Morichelli was becoming a significant asset for the Italians; she was establishing her dominance like a quiet stream slowly conquering the terrain.[8]

Notwithstanding the growing ascendancy of Italian opera at the National Theater, the Singspiel troupe remained a significant competitor for the commercial stage. In the light of this, the management of the Leopoldstadttheater made a decision with far-reaching consequences: to accelerate the commissioning of German translations of any works in the repertoire of the opera buffa that seemed destined to be popular successes. After an initial performance run, stage works of all kinds circulated freely; what provoked a great deal of comment in the case of *Una cosa rara* was the sheer speed at which Martín y Soler's hit opera transferred to its nearest commercial competitor. A visitor to Vienna in the spring of 1787 was struck by how quickly the Leopoldstadttheater had been able to put on a German version.[9] Another

5. *Bayreuther Zeitung* (17 April 1787), no. 48, 337: Schreiben aus Wien, vom. 15 April. "Unser Italienischen Theater wird mit jedem Tage besser, und das deutsche Nationaltheater sinkt."

6. In the emperor's absence, Franz may have gone to see it, as on that day he purchased an unidentified German opera libretto. Dunlop, "'Kaisersammlung,'" 57.

7. *Bayreuther Zeitung* (17 May 1787), no. 59, 422: Wien, vom 9. May: "Im Rosenfest von Salenci hat man 2/3tel mehr Stühle, als Menschen gesehen, ohngeacht unsere Madame Langin meisterhaft gesungen. Dafür ist in die Welsche Oper nicht hineinzukommen." Zinzendorf heard Lange on 14 March but was not impressed: "la voix de Mlle Nani ni celle de Me Lang ne me plurent gueres." Link, *National Court Theatre*, 289.

8. *Bayreuther Zeitung* (17 May 1787), no. 59, 422: "Die Madame Morichell gleicht einem stillen Bach, der nach und nach das ganze Terrein einnimmt." Link, "Anna Morichelli," 6–11, argues that, as an opera seria singer, Morichelli enjoyed strong aristocratic support.

9. *Musik*, July 1789, 48–49: "Kasperl aber benutzte diesen Umstand zu seinem Vortheil, ließ in Geschwindigkeit eine deutsche Parodie davon verfertigen, und brachte sie in dieser neuen Gestalt auf sein Theater in der Leopoldvorstadt."

commentator went further, discerning a covert, almost underhand aspect to the staging of *Der seltene Fall*, Eberl's translation.[10] There was also speculation about the surprising decision to discontinue performances at the National Theater. Of obvious benefit to the German production, this development was assumed to be connected in some way to the departure of Storace.[11]

The Leopoldstadttheater scored a runaway success with its newly acquired work, which was given over fifty times within a year of its premiere on 26 June.[12] Critical responses were favorable, including comment on the composer's use of wind instruments.[13] The Wilhelminische Gesellschaft, which presented a summer season in the spa town of Baden to the south of Vienna, was also quick to seize its chance, staging the opera in a translation titled *Die seltne Sache*.[14] Notwithstanding the sensation caused by *Una cosa rara*, the delay before performances of the Italian original resumed at the National Theater was a protracted one.[15] The *Wienerblättchen* advertised a restart on 4 July, suggesting an immediate response to the premiere of *Der seltene Fall* on 26 June, but it did not happen until 20 August, perhaps a consequence of Laschi's failed pregnancy. Zinzendorf reported that she gave birth to a stillborn child on 2 July.[16]

The emperor was away from Vienna from 10 April until late on 30 June, traveling incognito as "Count Falkenstein" with a modest party to meet

---

10. *Dramaturgische Monate* (1790), vol. 1, 210: "Er [Ferdinand Eberl] begann also die beliebtesten italienischen Opern des Wiener Hoftheaters für sein Publikum in der Leopoldstadt in sein Deutsch zu übersezzen, um so sich und seine adoptirten Kinder unter dem Strahlenmantel der Paisello, Salieri und Martini—wenn auch als Contrebande—in den Tempel des Beyfalls einschwärzen zu lassen."

11. *Musik*, July 1789, 48–49: "Die berühmte Sängerinn Storace mußte wegen gewisser Verdrießlichkeiten plötzlich von Wien weg, und damit hatte auch die Aufführung dieser Operette ein Ende." See also *Journal des Luxus und der Moden* (October 1787), 351.

12. *Etwas für Alle*, 4: "Die glückliche Aufführung der seltnen Sache auf dem Leopoldstädter Theater, die bereits drey und fünfzigmal das Theater gefüllt hatte."

13. *Musik*, July 1789, 49–50: "theils aber der Gebrauch der Blasinstrumente, welche im ganzen Stück prädominiren. Die Flöten, Clarinetten, Hoboen, Fagotten, Hörner, thun Alles, und die Saiteninstrumente haben wenig."

14. The fourth performance was advertised for 29 July in the *Wiener Zeitung* (25 July 1787), Anhang, 1792.

15. Platoff, "A New History," 90, suggests that it was a consequence of the number of new roles that the incoming prima donna Anna Morichelli had to learn. Link, "Anna Morichelli," 8, observes that Morichelli, while establishing her reputation in Vienna, preferred to avoid roles closely associated with Storace.

16. Link, *National Court Theatre*, 107 and 297.

Catherine II in the Crimea.[17] On his way back, Joseph was informed of the severity of the revolt in the Low Countries, and it was clear that he faced a major political crisis. There is no record of a visit to the theater immediately upon his return, and his nonappearance quickly became a news story, as it indicated a critical situation for the Austrian Monarchy.[18] A week later on 8 July, when he finally went to see Guglielmi's *L'inganno amoroso*, he experienced what Zinzendorf took to be a snub from the audience. Entering his box just as Morichelli came on stage, Joseph received no applause, which was instead directed pointedly at the singer.[19] On the basis of this striking suspension of the usual etiquette, Link considers it possible that she had in some way been adopted by an aristocratic claque who made use of her timely entry to express their displeasure at recent political developments.[20]

Zinzendorf hints at another embarrassment for the emperor, noting that Joseph had instructed Rosenberg to purchase a copy of the recently published pamphlet *Warum wird Kaiser Joseph von seinem Volke nicht geliebt?* ("Why is Emperor Joseph not loved by his People?"). This makes use of litany as a rhetorical device, each succinctly stated point leading to the refrain "und doch liebt ihn Sein Volk nicht" ("and yet his people do not love him"). Some entries in this catalogue are uncontroversial: Joseph has opened the magnificent Prater and the tasteful Augarten to the public, where he mixes with them without police guard—and yet is still not loved.[21] The section relating to his frugal lifestyle has more bite; like other princes, he *could* fritter away state income on

17. As usual during his travels, he attended theatrical and musical performances whenever these were available. On 11 April he saw August Wilhelm Iffland's *Die Jäger* in Brünn, and during an extended stay at Lemberg (now Lvov in western Ukraine), he went to a concert at an unidentified casino. *Wiener Zeitung* (18 April 1787), no. 31, 393.

18. *Carlsruhe Zeitung* (18 July 1787), no. 86, 408: Wien, vom 6 July: "Seit der Ankunft ist der Kaiser noch nicht in Theater erschienen."

19. Link, *National Court Theatre*, 297: 9 July: "hier au spectacle, on ne l'a point applaudi, mais bien la Morichelli qui sortoit en même tems."

20. Link, "Anna Morichelli," 10, also refers to a document cited by Fuchs, "Nuevas fuentes," 262, the report of a medical student: "Yesterday [29 August] I was at the opera Cosa rara: Madame Morichelli performed in it for the first time in the place of Storace. The crowding of the masses was such that all of us, soaked in sweat, could barely get our breath. She sang well, was much applauded because she had a large following in the noble parterre and the second parterre. It is from such followings that the fate and fame of persons of the theatre usually depends."

21. *Warum wird Kaiser Joseph*, 22: "Joseph eröffnete ihm den herrlichen Prater, den geschmackvollen Augarten. Hier mischt er sich oft selbst, ohne Wache, ohne Begleiter in das Gewimmel Seiner Bürger, zeigt ihnen, daß er keine andere Wache verlange, als ihre Liebe—und doch liebt ihn Sein Volk nicht."

mistresses, impose taxes in order to reward a pimp, pay for a new (woman) singer, build a new opera house—but how differently Joseph thinks![22] The emperor routinely spent significant sums hiring top women singers as well as on the periodic refurbishment of theaters; the (necessarily oblique) corollary was that he might perhaps also squander income on pimps and prostitutes. Whether he slept with women (paid or not) during his long years as a single man is uncertain, but while opera houses across Europe were renowned as places for high-class procurement and indeed as amenable locations where romantics like Zinzendorf could prosecute their dalliances, no one ever so much as hinted that Joseph overstepped the bounds of propriety with his own *prime donne.* Nonetheless, the author of the pamphlet was risking an innuendo that would have been hard to miss.[23] Pamphlets in support of Joseph soon appeared but understandably left the issue well alone. The author of *Kaiser Joseph wird doch geliebt* referred uncontroversially (albeit with an oblique reference to German music) to the general wish of the nobility that Joseph would pay more attention to the arts and sciences.[24] Perhaps stung by the criticism, he decided to make a public appearance on 2 August, in company with Albert and Marie Christine, at one of Vienna's most popular summer entertainments: Johann Georg Stuwer's firework displays in the Prater.[25]

The emperor's return to Vienna on 30 June coincided with the start of the annual vacation for the theater troupe, a circumstance that threw the competition for imperial favor into sharp relief. The Singspiel troupe scheduled three of its most popular works, *Der Apotheker* (9 July), *Zémire und Azor* (11 July), and *Die Entführung aus dem Serail* (13 July), followed by a premiere: *Die Trofonius-Höhle* (15 July). This choice had a competitive dimension: a German

---

22. *Warum wird Kaiser Joseph*, 25: "Joseph könnte, wie so viele Fürsten es thaten, und noch thun, der Wollust opfern, die Einkünfte des Staats mit Mätressen versplittern, Steuern ausschreiben um einen Kuppler zu belohnen, eine neue Sängerin zu bezahlen, ein neues Opernhaus zu bauen—Wie ganz anders denkt Joseph!"

23. Leopold, incidentally, was ready to believe that his brother employed pimps and even named one of them as Püchler in a private document written in code, in which he claimed that women were routinely procured for the emperor from the throng awaiting an audience in the Controleurgang. Beales, *Against the World 1780–1790*, 429–30, cautions that the strength of Leopold's antipathy to his brother should be taken into account when evaluating this statement.

24. *Kaiser Joseph wird doch geliebt*, 31: "Endlich wünschen die Edlen, daß er den Künsten und Wissenschaften mehr Achtung schenke. Das is überhaupt ein Wunsch, den die deutschen Musen den deutschen Fürsten schon lange gethan haben, der aber blos bey der einzigen Musik erhört wurde." There is a briefer reference in *Meine Gedanken über die Broschüre*, 45: "Joseph achtet Künste und Wissenschaften, in soferne sie Nuzen bringen, hoch."

25. Woodfield, "Fireworks and Wind Bands."

translation of Paisiello's setting of the libretto was certain to be compared with Salieri's still very popular score. But the work proved unattractive to audiences and was given only five times. More successful was the Singspiel troupe's production of a translation of Sarti's *Fra i due litiganti*, which was soon to play a part in the festivities staged for Maria Theresia. It seems clear that an attempt was being made to emulate the runaway success of *Una cosa rara* at the Leopoldstadttheater, but the current reliance on translations and new settings of popular Italian works was a partial admission of defeat from an ensemble tasked with developing a German musical repertoire at the National Theater.

For the Italian troupe, it made sense to offer Joseph performances of the three operas introduced during his absence. Accordingly, Bianchi's *Lo stravagante inglese* (premiere 25 May) was given on 2 July, Domenico Cimarosa's *Le trame deluse* (premiere 7 May) on 4 July, and Francesco Antonio Piticchio's *Il Bertoldo* (premiere 22 June) on 6 July, the only locally produced work of the three.[26] Da Ponte's plot dramatizes the theme of class equality, represented by the relationship between a king and a shepherd who claims parity of esteem: "[king] ich bin ein König. [shepherd] Und ich bin ein Mensch; was ist denn für ein Unterschied?"[27] The timing and strength (rather than the fact) of this staging of the emperor's core political belief is significant, but the ploy failed spectacularly. Joseph's response after seeing the work, probably on 12 July, was a brutal put-down. He advised Da Ponte never again to write for "Potacci, Petecchi, Pitocchi, Peticchi, or whatever he calls himself"—a comment that itself parodies an operatic cliché: lack of linguistic fluency.

Well before his arrival back in Vienna, it was clear to Joseph that the revolt in the Low Countries would necessitate changes to the wedding plans for Maria Theresia, eldest daughter of Grand Duke Leopold. An agreement on her marriage to Anton, younger brother of the Elector of Saxony, had been reached only weeks earlier, after protracted negotiations. It was immediately recognized as a coup with the potential to change the political landscape of

---

26. Zinzendorf thought it overlong but found it comical and the music agreeable. Link, *National Court Theatre*, 297: "22 Juin. A l'opera *Il Bertoldo*. Il est fort long, mais assez drole et la musique de Piticchio agréable. Il dura jusqu'a 10h ½." In 1791, Da Ponte described Piticchio as "the first liar in all of Sicily, slanderous, ungrateful and vicious" ("il primo bugiardo, maldicende, ingrato, e vizioso di tutta da Sicilia"). Michtner, "Der Fall," 201.

27. Bertoldo / ein / lustiges Singspiel / in / zwey Aufzügen. / Aufgeführt im k. k. Hoftheater / Wien, 1787. The sentiment takes up Figaro's verse in the concluding vaudeville of *La folle journée:* "Par le sort de naissance, / l'un est roi, l'autre est berger; / le hasard fit leur distance; / l'esprit seul peut tout changer!"

Europe.[28] Joseph's original choice of the Bohemian capital as the venue for the ceremony was a pragmatic one, as Prague lay directly on the quickest route between Tuscany and Saxony. Moreover, a visit to the city was already in his diary of engagements, part of a planned review of military building in the region: a chain of fortresses from Teresienstadt (Terezin) to the north of Prague, through Königgrätz (Hradec Králové) to the east, as far as Pless (Pszczyńskie) in Silesia. But by 16 June, he was already starting to realize that the unrest in the Low Countries might be serious enough to put his participation in doubt.[29] A week later on 23 June, the gravity of the situation had become clearer, leaving Joseph incandescent with rage at the news that many of the demands of the rebels had already been conceded.[30] He informed Leopold on 6 July that it was now impossible for him to consider attending the wedding, as he had countermanded all the camps and would no longer be able to come to Prague.[31] The idea of a proxy marriage, at which neither the emperor nor the groom would need to be present, now entered the discussions. The ceremony could take place in Florence, and Joseph even wondered whether Maria Theresia should undertake the journey to Saxony in private, rather than as a public progress. Leopold soon realized that he had no choice but to accept his brother's reasons for abandoning Prague.[32]

While these discussions were taking place in private, there was growing frustration in the public domain at the lack of a firm announcement. The amorphous but potent "voice" of newspaper readerships was starting to make itself heard.[33] That the emperor's preference was for a ceremony in

---

28. *Oberdeutsche Staatszeitung* (15 August 1787), no. 160, 637: Wien, den 11ten August: "Diese neue Allianz mit Kursachsen ist ein Werk der feinsten Politik. Deutschland gewinnt dadurch eine ganz veränderte Gestalt."

29. Arneth, *Joseph II. und Leopold*, 82: "Si les fâcheuses histoires des Pays-Bas ne l'empêchent, je serais charmé que même l'automne le mariage puisse se célébrer."

30. Arneth, *Joseph II. und Leopold*, 82: "Mais j'ai été bien étonné des nouvelles inconcevables que j'ai trouvées ici des Pays-Bas."

31. Arneth, *Joseph II. und Leopold*, 84: Vienne, le 6 juillet 1787: "J'ai aussi contremandé tous les camps, et par conséquent il faut changer le projet du mariage de votre fille à faire à Prague, car je ne pourrais en être, et si vous ne venez pas non plus, cela serait impossible; il faudra donc faire le mariage par procuration à Florence."

32. Arneth, *Joseph II. und Leopold*, 94: "Vos raisons sont trop justes pour ne plus faire le mariage à Prague, surtout si vous n'y étiez pas."

33. *Oberdeutsche Staatszeitung* (4 May 1787), no. 89, 353: Wien: "Das Publikum ist inzwischen sehr erstaunt, daß es nichts zuverläßiges mehr von der Vermählung des Prinzen von Sachsen mit ihrer ältesten Schwester reden hört, die man jedoch für ganz sicher und nahe bevorstehend angegeben hatte."

Prague started to leak out in early July, but only after this plan had been abandoned.[34] A dissenting voice in the *Courier du Bas-Rhin* poured contempt on the German press for falling for what it regarded as a series of fabricated stories emanating from Vienna, each as silly as the other. While the paper's claim that there had never been any intention to celebrate the marriage in Bohemia was not true, its reading of the current state of play was more accurate than that of its rivals.[35] For the moment, though, Prague remained firmly the center of attention, and commentators were quick to sketch out how the happy event would be staged. It was accepted that Joseph was going to accompany Maria Theresia to Bohemia and participate in the ceremony.[36] When news broke that the city was not to host the wedding after all, an alternative scenario was worked up: that the "consignation," the ceremonial handover of Maria Theresia and her dowry, would take place there. Within days, this, too, was taken to be an established fact.[37] No details were forthcoming, but Prague remained on course to host festive events in honor of the occasion, whatever it might turn out to be.

In late August, weeks of speculation came to an end with firm news that Maria Theresia was about to embark upon her arduous journey. Following a proxy ceremony in Florence, she would travel northward to Austrian Lombardy, to be greeted by Ferdinand in Mantua. The route across the Alps would take her through Bolzano, Bruneck, and Greifenburg to Klagenfurt and then north to Mürzzuschlag in Styria. After the festivities in Laxenburg and Vienna, she would follow the direct route northward, bypassing Brno in

---

34. *Kurfürstlich gnädigst privilegirte Münchner Zeitung* (10 July 1787), no. 106, p.427: Wien, vom 4 July: "Die Ankunft des Großherzogs von Toskana k. H. mit der ältesten Prinzeßin Tochter Theresia, so wie die nahe Vermählung des Prinzen Anton von Sachsen mit diser Prinzeßin braucht nun keine Bestättigung mehr; das Beilager soll in Prag sein."

35. *Courier du Bas-Rhin* (28 July 1787), no. 60, 498: EXTRAIT *d'une lettre de* Vienne, *du* 14 *Juillet*: "Les papiers publics d'*Allemagne* contiennent beaucoup de nouvelles sous la date de *Vienne* qui sont toutes controuvées & les unes plus ridicules que les autres: Entr'autres il n'a jamais été question de célébrer à *Prague* le mariage du prince *Antoine* de *Saxe* avec l'archiduchesse *Marie-Thérèse* de *Toscane*, lequel probablement sera célébré à *Dresde*."

36. *Gazette de Berne* (1 September 1787), no. 70: De Vienne, le 21 Août: "Elle n'y séjournera que 4 jours, devant se rendre d'abord à *Prague*, où se trouvera le Prince son futur époux, & où le mariage sera béni. On fait déja dans cette derniere ville, des préparatifs pour cette fête. L'Empereur y accompagnera la Princesse, & assistera à ses noces."

37. [Bonn] *Annalen* (28 August 1787), no. 35, 138: Oestreichische Monarchie: "nach 14 Tagen aber weiter bis Prag gebracht und daselbst der ihr entgegen zu schickenden Sächsischen Hofstaat übergeben werden."

Moravia to the east, arriving in Prague toward mid-October.[38] The *Courier du Bas-Rhin*, which had assumed that, owing to the emergency in the Low Countries and Joseph's anticipated departure for Bonn, there was to be no fête in Vienna, now conceded that orders had gone out to make the necessary preparations.[39]

For the final leg of her progress through the Austrian Monarchy, Maria Theresia would follow the Elbe to the border. There was an announcement that Aussig (Ústí nad labem), the last major town in Bohemia on the route northward, was to stage her formal handing over to the Saxon entourage.[40] Earlier press reports that Prague would host the ceremony were now seen to be false, and it was becoming clearer by the week that the city's official role was diminishing.[41] The organizers of the festive entertainment now had to cope with a series of contradictory messages. On 1 September, Lenoble von Edlersberg, who was responsible for checking the arrangements at Aussig, arrived in Prague.[42] Despite the loss of its formal function, the city was still expected to mark Maria Theresia's passage, and the Hofkammerfourier was reported to have authorized a ball and the customary free access to theater. In the local press, there was no mention of an opera, although the arrival of the Italian troupe was noted, as well as its intention to commence its program

---

38. *Leipziger Zeitungen* (28 August 1787), no. 168, 971. *Provinzialnachrichten* (29 August 1787), no. 69, 262: Bericht aus Prag, vom 21 August: "Die Prinzeßin Therese von Toskana, wird gegen die Hälfte des Monats Oktober in Prag erwartet."

39. *Courier du Bas-Rhin* (1 September 1787), no. 70, 581: EXTRAIT *d'une lettre de* Vienne, *du 18 Août:* "On avoit assuré qu'on ne donneroit aucune fête à l'occasion du passage de l'archiduchesse *Marie-Thérèse* par *Vienne*, par la raison qu'on croioit que l'empereur partiroit incessamment pour *Bonn*: On sait aujourdui que le départ du souverain pour cette derniere ville aiant été remis à une époque indéterminée, les ordres ont été donnés pour les préparatifs de plusieurs fêtes qu'on célébrera en honneur de l'auguste épouse." By now, delegates from the Austrian Low Countries had been invited to Vienna.

40. *Leipziger Zeitungen* (4 September 1787), no. 173, 997: Dresden: 2 September: "um die Mitte des Monats Octobers zu Außig eintreffen, daselbst von dem Churfürstl. Commissario übernommen."

41. *Laibacher Zeitung* (30 August 1787), no. 35: Wien: "Während dem 14tägigen Aufenthalt der Prinzeßin von Toskana sollen hier große Festins gegeben werden . . . zu Prag wird sie nur einige Tage bleiben, und man zweifelt, ob der Prinz selbst dahin kommen werde."

42. *Prager Oberpostamtszeitung* (1 September 1787), no. 70: Prague den 30. August: "Der k. k. Kammerfourier Hr. le Noble von Edlersberg ist . . . auch gestern Mittags hier angelangt. . . . Derselbe wird alsdann auch hier in Prag verschiedene Anstalten zu den abzuhaltenden Festins veranlassen, und es soll sowohl Freyball als Freytheater gegeben werden." This and the following citations from the *Prager Oberpostamtszeitung* are taken from the discussion in Weidinger, "Il dissoluto punito," section VI: Hochszeitpläne—Reisepläne—Festpläne.

80   CABALS AND SATIRES

"this month."[43] A few days later, the industrious Hofkammerfourier again passed through Prague, this time with a view to inspecting the accommodation in Deutschbrod (Havlíčkův Brod).[44] Thus far, it seemed likely that festive events would go ahead as planned.

But in late August an even more serious political crisis began to intrude on planning for the reception of Maria Theresia: the Ottoman declaration of war against Russia, to which Joseph was bound by treaty to respond with full-scale military assistance. In preparation for this, reinforcements were immediately sent to the front line and adequate protection put in place for the northern Bohemian frontier.[45] In the changed circumstances, news broke that the emperor was having second thoughts about the festivities planned for Prague and that a courier had been dispatched to Bohemia to cancel everything.[46] The nature of the abandoned events was still not spelled out; one source referred merely to "réjouissances."[47] Some commentators started to assume that Maria Theresia would adopt a low profile throughout her progress, even during her stay in Vienna.[48] News that the Prague celebrations had been called off must have been puzzling to those concerned with their planning, since only a few days earlier the Hofkammerfourier had confirmed some (limited) festivities. The result was confusion as to whether the new directive was intended to countermand

43. *Prager Oberpostamtszeitung* (1 September 1787), no. 70: Prague den 30. August: "die Bondinische italienische Operntruppe hier schon eingetroffen, und wird diesen Monats ihre beliebten Opern anfangen."

44. *Prager Oberpostamtszeitung* (8 September 1787), no. 72: Prague den 6. September: "Der k. k. Kammerfourier Hr. le Noble von Edlersberg, ist von Prag wieder nach Wien über Deutschbrod, wo für die ankommenden allerhöchsten Herrschaften gleichfalls Quartiere bereitet werden, abgereiset."

45. *Gazette de Berne* (19 September 1787), no. 75: De Vienne, le 6 Septemb.: "L'artillerie qui étoit en route pour les Pays-bas, a reçu ordre de revenir. On croit qu'on en sera passer la plus grande partie en Boheme."

46. *Augspurgische Ordinari Postzeitung* (14 September 1787), no. 221: Wien, den 8. September: "Gestern wurden durch eine nach Prag abgefertigte Estaffette alle öffentlichen Freudenfeste abgesagt, welche bey der Durchreise der Prinzessinn von Toskana nach Dresden bereits angestellet waren und in Erfüllung gesetzt werden sollten."

47. *Gazette de Berne* (19 September 1787), no. 75: De Vienne, le 6 Septemb.: "on a envoyé une estafette à Prague, pour contremander toutes les réjouissances qui devoient y avoir lieu à l'occasion du mariage."

48. *Bayreuther Zeitung* (17 September 1787), no. 111, Anhang, 799: Wien, Dienstags den 11. Sept.: "Es sind auch deswegen alle Hof-Feste bey der Durchreise der Prinzeßin Therese von Toscana, sowohl hier, als in Prag bereits abgesagt worden."

plans recently put in place, and the first notice of the cancelation in the Prague press ended with an unanswered question mark.[49] The war had yet to be formally declared, but its accompanying fog was already creating havoc.

And within days there was yet another twist of fate. In the spring of 1787, Joseph had categorically ruled out a Prague wedding for Maria Theresia, as in the circumstances it seemed impossible for him to consider traveling to Bohemia, but with war imminent and the possibility of an opportunistic attack by Prussia, an emergency tour of fortresses in the region now seemed more essential than ever. Adding greatly to the potential for further confusion, Prague now understood that the emperor was coming after all.[50] Franz was already in the city, having been sent on his own tour of Bohemia as part of his military training. He took up residence in the Castle on 1 September.[51] Two weeks later, he was reported to be in good health, occupying his time with military exercises and seeing the sights.[52] His accounts for 1787 include a significant number of unidentified payments to theaters in Bohemia, but these are not dated, and press reports do not give any details.[53]

Joseph left Vienna early on 10 September. In marked contrast to the relaxed atmosphere of his sojourn in Prague during September 1786, this was to be a whistle-stop tour, its haste determined by the exigencies of war. In particular, he wished to see demonstrations of the siege munitions with which the forthcoming siege of Belgrade would be prosecuted.[54] Having witnessed the display, he professed himself satisfied with the efficacy of the mines, and one commentator looked forward to seeing the Austrian

---

49. *Prager Oberpostamtszeitung* (11 September 1787): "auch sind die Festins, welche hier gehalten werden sollten, zurückgerufen.—?"

50. The powerful influence on musical events of press reports of last-minute changes of mind (or the lack of such reports) is highlighted in Glatthorn, "Imperial Coronation."

51. *Preßburger Zeitung* (12 September 1787), no. 73: Böhmen. "Den 1 September nach 6 Uhr sind Se. K. H. der Erzherzog Franz, zu Prag angelangt, und haben die Wohnung im K. Schlosse genommen."

52. *Gazette de France* (5 October 1787), no. 80: De Vienne, le 18 Septembre 1787: "L'ARCHIDUC François de Toscane, pendant son séjour à Prague, a visité tout ce que cette ville offre de remarquable."

53. Dunlop, " 'Kaisersammlung,' " 54.

54. Arneth, *Joseph II. und Leopold*, 118: "Je pars dans ce moment, à quatre heures du matin, pour la Bohême. Je vais faire le tour des forteresses et voir l'expérience des mines que j'ai fait arranger."

eagle fluttering over Belgrade.[55] Joseph's visit to Bohemia was summed up in a characteristically pithy statement in the *Times* on 15 October: "Vienna, September 25: His Majesty . . . returned from Bohemia, where he made a short excursion to convince himself of that Kingdom being in a good state of defence." As a matter of fact, he seems to have been unimpressed with Prague's fortifications, and he ordered urgent action to improve them.[56] In the light of its recent history, the city was well used to responding to threats from Prussia in the north, but now there were also wild rumors of an imminent assault by hordes of Turks.[57] Although Prague was nearly as far distant from Ottoman territory as it was possible to be in the main land mass of the Austrian Monarchy, the reputed conduct of the Turkish forces during battle and in the aftermath of victory always induced great unease. The *Courier du Bas-Rhin*, once again offering a different perspective, claimed that Joseph had made use of his brief stop in Prague to countermand the celebrations in person—including, one must assume, any gala opera that had been planned.[58]

Mozart's career as an opera composer was to be influenced significantly by this unfolding series of crises. In the space of a few months, he won a coveted commission for a festive opera, failed to have the chosen work ready on time, but then saw his earlier opera drafted in as a late replacement, much to the benefit of its wider reputation. Discussions about the festive commissions— including one to celebrate the marriage of Franz and Elisabeth, the date of which had been hastily brought forward—began at the start of July 1787 after Joseph's return from the Crimea. Da Ponte's account implies that three

55. [Bonn] *Annalen* (16 October 1787), no. 42, 166–67: Kaiserl. Königl. und Russische Staten: "Aber freylich könte bis daran Oestreichs Adler in Belgrad wehen, wenn es anders wahr ist, daß mit einer Belagerung dieser wichtigen Festung der Operationsplan anheben solle." No one was in much doubt that this was an achievable war aim. Stuwer had his celebratory pyrotechnic display ready more than a year before the city fell. *Bayreuther Zeitung*, 4 Aug. 1788, no. 92, Anhang, p. 628: Wien, vom 29 Julii: "Dieser Künstler hat noch immer die Decoration von Belgrad fertig liegen, welche er abzubrennen gedenkt, wann es einmal erobert seyn wird."

56. *Bayreuther Zeitung* (1 October 1787), no. 117, Anhang, 848: Prag, vom 25. Septr: "Die durch verschiedene Belagerungen sehr beschädigten Stadtmauern um Prag."

57. *World* (5 October 1787), no. 227: "Advices from Prague say, that the utmost exertion is now using in repairing and augmenting the fortifications and works of that city, as an attack is expected by a large army of Turks, which is now collecting on the borders of Transylvania."

58. *Courier du Bas-Rhin* (3 October 1787), no. 79, 662: EXTRAIT *d'une lettre de* Vienne, *du* 19 *Septembre*: "L'empereur en passant par *Prague* a contremandé les fêtes qui devoient s'y donner lors du passage de l'archiduchesses de *Toscane*, épouse du prince *Clément Antoine* de *Saxe*."

projects were agreed around 1 August. He recalled that the trio of composers had come at the same time, each to discuss his own libretto, although it is unclear whether he intended this to be taken literally.[59] He was hard pressed, but as retold in his famous story of an all-night stint, he made significant progress on all three commissions. Several years later, cast as the defendant in the satire *Anti-da Ponte*, he was made to respond to the charge of incompetence by conceding that gaps and inconsistencies remained in his reworking of *Tarare* as *Axur*; these could be blamed on the haste with which he had been obliged to produce the text.[60] But at least he did not have to worry unduly about political symbolism. By the late 1780s, the plot of a gala opera was no longer expected to allude to the happy political circumstances of its first performance; it was sufficient that it achieve a popular success, with the title page simply recording the event: usually an arrival ("per l'arrivo") or a marriage ("per le nozze").[61] The Temple of Diana was a popular subject in fashion journals, and women's taste was perhaps a significant factor in the choice of *L'arbore di Diana* for Martín y Soler's commission.[62] Certainly the performances of the women singers dominated the early reception of the opera. The main Vienna review recorded a consensus that the acting of Morichelli and Laschi left nothing to be desired.[63] A dissenting and idiosyncratic voice lambasted the exposure of

---

59. Martín y Soler and Mozart were in Vienna, while Salieri had to make the journey back from Paris. Unless his return was coincidental, he received an urgent recall at the start of July. The approximate date of his arrival back can be established through a reference in a letter written by Gluck on 3 August to thank a correspondent in Paris for the receipt of a score that Salieri had just delivered to him. Rice, *Antonio Salieri*, 403.

60. De Alwis, *Anti-Da Ponte*, 60: "so kann ich hierauf nichts wichtigeres sagen, als daß man dieß alles auf Rechnung der Eile, mit welcher ich dieses Stück liefern mußte, schreiben müsse."

61. Link, *National Court Theatre*, 304, summarizes the findings of Sommer-Mathis, "*Tu felix Austria nube*": "The book traces how the wedding operas changed from stately court functions at the beginning of the century to public entertainments at the end. Under Maria Theresia, wedding operas treated such themes as the uniting of kingdoms, the upholding of laws, princely virtues, and the like through allegory and mythology. The operas were one-time performances before invited audiences made up of heads of state, their representatives and some of their personnel. For the two imperial marriages that took place during Joseph's reign, operas were still commissioned, but they were produced within the context of the court theatre's operations and were intended to become part of the repertoire."

62. The *Cabinet des Modes*, Dixième Cahier (1 April 1786), included a plate of the Temple of Diana.

63. *Provinzialnachrichten* (10 October 1787), no. 81, 45–46: Kaiserl. Königl. Hoftheater: "alle Kenner und Liebhaber der Bühne gestehen übereinstimmend, daß das Spiel der Mad. Morichelli und der Mad. Laschi nichts zu wünschen übrig gelassen habe."

84 CABALS AND SATIRES

flesh required of Laschi, who had to crossdress in the role of Cupid.[64] Da Ponte himself later drew attention to the fact that he had managed to incorporate an element of political allegory in the plot: allusions to Joseph II's recent closure of the monasteries and convents. He claimed that the emperor recognized and appreciated the gesture.

The most urgent of the three commissions was the one awarded to Martín y Soler to celebrate the arrival of Maria Theresia in Vienna. At the end of the first week of August, many newspapers carried an announcement, giving the title of the new work as: *L'albero di Diana*. Its festive status was acknowledged, even if the reported dedication was not in the form that would eventually appear on the title page.[65] An Italian source, which failed even to identify the occasion for the commission, noted that 20 September was the target date.[66] The pressure placed upon the composer as a result of so tight a schedule was generally acknowledged.[67] In time, the commission awarded to Salieri also received advance publicity; a nationalist expressed some disappointment that the libretto selected was not the work of an author from the "fatherland."[68] In marked contrast, there is no trace of any prior public announcement of Mozart's festive opera.

Any consideration of how all these events impinged on the genesis of *Don Giovanni* must first consider the position of the two impresarios Pasquale

64. *Lettre d'un habitant de Vienne à son ami à Prague, qui lui avait demandé ses réflexions sur l'opera intitule l'Arbore di Diana*, cited in Michtner, *Das alte Burgtheater*, 435–39: "D'abord L'Amour paraît un homme, avec un buste ou corps de femme, la gorge nue, et comme c'est une femme qui joue ce rôle, on lui voit une paire de tétons découverts jusqu'aux mamelles."

65. *Kurfürstlich gnädigst privilegirte Münchner Zeitung* (17 August 1787), no. 128, 514: Wien, vom 11. August: "eine ganz neue Opera, betittelt: l'albero di Diana, in Musik gesezt von dem berühmten Kapellmeister Hrn. Martin aus Spanien, aufgeführt werden. Unter die Vignette des Tittelblattes dieser Oper wird gesezt werden:—Ihrer Königl. Hoheit der Frau Erzherzogin Maria Theresia von Toskana, bei ihrer Reise über Wien nach Dresden gewidmet." Artaria, with his usual impeccable timing in offering images of musicians for sale, had just advertised a pair of engraved portraits of Martín y Soler and Morichelli. Rice, "Twin Portraits."

66. *Gazzetta universale* (21 August 1787), no. 67, 532: Vienna, 9 Agosto: "Il Maestro di Cappella Sig. Martini deve per tale oggetto terminar la musica del nuovo Dramma l'*Albero di Diana*, che per il suddetto giorno 20. deve esser pronto per andare in scena."

67. *Gazzetta bolognesi* (21 August 1787), no. 34: VIENNA 8. Agosto: "Il Maestro Martini ha l'ordine di affrettarsi a terminare di porre in musica l'Opera intitolata l'*Albero di Diana*, per poter questa andare in Scena nel dì 20. dello stesso mese."

68. *Bayreuther Zeitung* (14 December 1787), no. 149, Anhang, 1099: Schreiben aus Wien, vom 8. Dec. "Beaumarchais hat nicht ohne Neid vaterländischen Schriftsteller, die Ehre, daß seine Oper Tarrare, in Musik gesetzt vom K. K. Capellmeister Saliere [sic], bey der Vermählung des Erzherzogs Franz aufgeführt wird."

Bondini and Domenico Guardasoni. Wherever they were currently based, both would have seen the developing speculation about a dynastic Habsburg wedding in Prague as it swept across Europe. An obvious question was whether they should take the initiative in offering something. If the established schedule was adhered to, Bondini's theater troupe would be in Prague for the summer season, leaving in early September for a brief visit to Leipzig before returning to Dresden. Guardasoni's Italian opera company on the other hand might have been expecting to perform in Leipzig during the summer before returning to its home base in Prague.[69]

It may be no coincidence that on 3 July, around the time that the wedding was announced, Bondini submitted an enquiry to the authorities in Prague as to the status of the ban on the Figaro play. In view of the popularity of this marriage drama in Saxony, he was perhaps hoping that Joseph would relent and allow a special performance to celebrate his new alliance with Dresden. The response was long delayed and demonstrated a curious lack of awareness about the local situation. It reaffirmed the ban on *Der tolle Tag* but granted formal permission for the performance of *Le nozze di Figaro*, more than a little redundantly, as Bondini had not asked about this, and the opera had already been playing to full houses in Prague for a year.

The explanation may be a recent change in the highest office of the local administration: that of Oberstburggraf, the emperor's representative in Bohemia. Since 1782, the holder of the post had been Franz Anton Graf von Nostitz-Rieneck, the music-loving aristocrat. In the summer of 1787, however, he asked to be relieved of his post owing to ill health, a request that was granted by Joseph II.[70] Some sources hinted darkly that certain "oversights" in the performance of his duties had led to his demise.[71] The *Courier du Bas-Rhin* offered a more specific explanation, alluding to his intemperate response to

---

69. For some reason, a newspaper in Graz saw fit to run a story on the transition between the two companies, even though this was part of an established cycle. The focus was on what the Prague theatergoing public had lost following the departure of Bondini rather than what it had gained through the arrival of Guardasoni. *Gräzer Zeitung* (15 September 1787), no. 74: Wien.

70. *Kurfürstlich gnädigst privilegirte Münchner Zeitung* (23 August 1787), no. 131, 525: Wien, vom 18 August (aus der Wienerzeitung): "Graf v. Nostiz und Rhinek . . . wegen mislicher Gesundheits Umstände . . . um die Entlassung gebeten hat."

71. *Journal politique de Bruxelles* (September 1787), 100: De Vienne, le 30 Août. "Le Comte de *Nostitz*, Grand Burgrave de Bohême, est aussi demis de sa charge, pour s'être justifié, dit-on, en termes peu mesurés, de quelques négligences dans l'exercice de ses fonctions."

criticism that he had failed to live up to Joseph II's high standards of public visibility.[72] In the background and perhaps at issue now was inevitably the language question. German was used in the governance of Bohemia, but on some formal occasions Czech was preferred for symbolic purposes.[73] At the end of 1786, Nostitz used Czech when opening the council, an act significant enough to be reported in Paris.[74] Whatever the reason for the resignation or dismissal, his replacement, Ludwig Graf von Cavriani, did not arrive in Prague until 18 September, and perhaps only then could a response to Bondini's request be set in motion.[75]

Although there were press stories about the "beautiful" festivities being planned for Prague, an opera is not once mentioned.[76] This raises a rather perplexing question: *Don Giovanni* was certainly intended as a gala work, as its libretto in the draft form printed in Vienna was permitted to bear the prestigious title-page announcement "Per l'arrivo di sua altezza reale," but that fact was not publicized. An idea worth exploring, admittedly in the absence of direct evidence, is that the decision to schedule the opera in Prague represented a change of plan. An early version of the timetable for Maria Theresia's journey, widely circulated, was very different from the one finally chosen; it anticipated a full two weeks of festivities in Schönbrunn and Laxenburg, lasting from 20 September to 4 October.[77] Writing to Franz on 25 August, Elisabeth von Württemberg told him that she would be there by 20 September, ready to

72. *Courier du Bas-Rhin* (29 August 1787), no. 69, 574: EXTRAIT *d'une lettre de* Vienne, *du* 15 *Août*: "Le Comte de Nostitz vient d'être démis de la charge de grand-burgrave du roiaume de *Boheme*, pour avoir écrit, dit-on, au gouvernement une lettre dans des termes peu circonspects, pour se justifier du reproche qu'il en avoit reçu il y a quelque tems de ce qu'il négligeoit une partie de ses fonctions, particulierement celle qui tient si fort à coeur à S. M. I. de visiter régulierement les chefs lieux des roiaume."

73. Nedbal, *Prague's Estates Theater*, 3.

74. *Gazette de France* (5 December 1786), no. 97, 416: De Prague, le 8 Novembre 1786: "Le Comte de Nostitz, Président du Conseil du Gouvernement, ouvrit, le 16 du mois dernier, l'Assemblée des États, & fit en langue du pays les propositions du Souverain."

75. *Preßburger Zeitungen* (29 September 1787), no. 78: Böhmen. "Am 18. d. M. gieng zu Prag die feyerliche Einführung des neuen Oberstburggrafen und Präsidenten des Böhmischen Landesguberniums, in der Person des Hrn. Grafen v. Kavriani, vor sich."

76. *Gazette van Gend* (30 August 1787), no. 70: WEENEN den 18 Augusti: "en dat zy, naer alvooren de Festen te *Schönbrunn* en te *Laxemburg* bygewoont te hebben, nae *Prag* zal vergeleyd worden, in welxe Stad ook zeer schoone Festen voor haer worden bereyd gemaekt."

77. *Leipziger Zeitung* (21 August 1787), no. 166, 957: Wien, 15 August: "Sowohl zu Schönbrunn, als zu Laxenburg, werden Hoffeste bey der Anwesenheit der Prinzessin von Toskana von 20sten Sept. bis 4ten Oct. gegeben werden."

greet her future sister-in-law.[78] Commentators in the press predicted that there would be lavish entertainments; an opera was said to be in preparation at each location, although there is no evidence as to the identity of either planned work.[79] One possibility is that a new essay in the genre of self-reflexive opera was being considered: opera about opera, in the manner of the two one-act pieces commissioned by Joseph for Schönbrunn the previous year.[80] A recent libretto, exactly fitting the template for this kind of festive comedy, featured an opera company rehearsing and then performing a short version of the Don Juan story.

Giovanni Bertati's *Il capriccio drammatico* was given its premiere in Venice on 5 February 1787. "Act I" depicts an opera troupe preparing a Don Juan drama in an attempt to win an audience. "Act II," for which Gazzaniga wrote music, is the opera: DON GIOVANNI / OSIA / IL CONVITATO / DI PIETRA. Either "act" could be given by itself. The rehearsal contains elements that could easily have been played up in Vienna as a lighthearted commentary on the intertroupe contest, as members of this fictional Italian troupe express grave reservations about presenting *Don Giovanni* in Germany. Although he later tried to disguise the fact, Da Ponte, under severe time pressure, took the decision to make use of Bertati's lighthearted version of the Don Juan story as his starting point. In his *Memorie*, he claimed to have selected the Don Juan subject himself during the frenetic weeks when all three festive works were under discussion. In the earlier *Extract*, however, he had let slip that it was the Prague impresario Guardasoni who made the suggestion: "Why did Mozart refuse to set to music the *Don Giovanni* (of evil memory) by Bertati, and offered to him by one Guardasoni . . . ? Why did he insist upon having a

---

78. Weyda, "Briefe an Erzherzog Franz," 29: "Je serais aussi fort charmée de faire la connaissance de Mme sa soeur; on va à Laxenburg le 20 et elle y arrivera le 22; J'ai bien de la joie d'être aussi de ce séjour qui sera, à ce que je crois, de 10 jours."

79. *General Advertiser* (11 September 1787): FLANDERS MAIL. *Vienna, August* 25. "The august Spouse of Prince Clement of Saxony is to be at Luxembourgh on the 29th of September, where, and at Schonbrunn, orders are given to prepare two grand tables, operas, and two masked balls."

80. The hypothesis that Mozart was aware of some plan to stage his work in Vienna is consistent with his off-the-cuff remark in a letter dated 4 November. Writing to Gottfried von Jacquin, he expresses the hope that *Don Giovanni*, by now an obvious success in Prague, will perhaps be performed in Vienna after all ("vieleicht wird Sie doch in Wienn aufgeführt?") Mozart: Briefe und Aufzeichnungen, vol. 4, 58; Anderson, *Letters*, vol. 3, 1357. It is of course a lot to read into a single perhaps casually chosen word, but one primary meaning of "doch" is "nonetheless," hinting at the revival of a previously held expectation. The theory that the opera's genesis lay in Vienna was proposed by Weidinger, "Il dissoluto punito," 833–39.

book written by Da Ponte on the same subject . . . ?"[81] Given that librettos were
inexpensive and easily transportable items in free circulation, either explanation is credible.[82]

But the original schedule for Maria Theresia's extended period of relaxa-
tion at Laxenburg soon fell victim to the exigencies of war. Thanks to Joseph's
emergency tour of Bohemia, he was now expected to be away from Vienna
until 20 September, and it would be several days after that before he would
be in a position to travel south to accompany his niece back to Vienna, as was
his standard practice. Her stay in Laxenburg was thus shortened drastically
and many of the planned festivities called off. A fireworks display had been
commissioned, but it was canceled, and there was no further mention of an
opera at Schönbrunn.[83]

Coverage of the events in preparation for the much shorter stopover at
Laxenburg remained light on detail. Some notices referred to unspecified
"Spektakel," while others stated that on 27 and 28 September there would be
German and Italian entertainments, preserving the current national equilibrium in the theatrical world. Several sources still expected a small Italian opera
("una piccola Opera Italiana") to be given.[84] Others went further, implying that
it would be a new work, written for the occasion.[85] The *Provinzialnachrichten*
spoke of an "expressly composed" operetta.[86] After the event, one Italian source

81. Da Ponte, *Extract*, 17–18.

82. A generally accepted possibility is that the singer Antonio Baglioni, who participated in
the Venice production of *Il capriccio drammatico*, took a copy with him when he traveled to
Prague, following short seasons in Parma in the spring and Bologna in the summer. Rice,
Mozart on the Stage, 119–34. This is a plausible transmission route, but there were other
singers in the Venice cast who had direct and recent links with Vienna. Antonio Marchesi
sang with the opera buffa during the 1785–86 season, as did Paolo Mandini, who had been
employed alongside his better-known brother Stefano. Link, *National Court Theatre*, 220.

83. *Notizie del mondo* (26 September 1787), no. 77: DA VIENNA, 19. Settembre: "La Corte
passerà nel 24. dell'andante in Laxenbourg . . . nelle presente critiche circostanze sono stati
ritirati tutti gli ordini . . . fin quello relativo all'erezione d'una macchina di fuochi artifiziali
per la quale Sua Maestà aveva assegnati 10. mil. fiorini."

84. *Gazzetta universale* (1 September 1787), no. 70, 557: VIENNA 20 Agosto. "Nel dì 26. e
27. i soliti divertimenti della Campagna di Laxemburgo, e chiusa la giornata con una piccola
Opera Italiana in musica, e piccol ballo."

85. *Gazzetta bolognesi* (16 October 1787), no. 42: VIENNA 5 Ottobre 1787. "[Laxenburg] . . . li
27 . . . in esso giorno, non meno che in quello de' 28, vi fu tra gli altri divertimenti lo
Spettacolo al Teatro di Corte, in cui venne rappresentata un'Opera Italiana, composta
espressamente per una sì lieta circostanza."

86. *Provinzialnachrichten* (29 September 1787), no. 78, 402: "An eben dem Tage, und am
28. war auf dem Laxenburger Schloß-Theater Schauspiel, und wurde unter andern eine zu
dieser frohen Begebenheit eigends komponirte italienische Operette aufgeführt."

stated unequivocally that *L'albero di Diana* was given on 28 September.[87] That Martín y Soler's commission was intended for Laxenburg as the high point of the original schedule cannot be ruled out altogether, especially given that 20 September was his widely reported deadline. Yet this raises in acute form a dilemma often encountered when evaluating press coverage: the possibility that two separate pieces of information, each correct in itself, could have been combined in error. It is not hard to imagine an editor in Florence splicing details of the original announcement of his commission with a more recent report that an opera composed "especially" for the occasion had indeed been performed. Given the general emphasis on the small scale of the Laxenburg work, a complete rendition of *L'arbore di Diana* seems unlikely, although a private preview of part of it is certainly possible.[88]

   A change of plan with regard to a Don Juan work is of course entirely speculative, but it might provide an explanation for what in some ways is the most puzzling question of all: why a one-act source text came to be selected as the basis for a full-scale opera. In such a scenario, there could have been a two-stage genesis: brief consideration of the Don Juan theme in a self-reflexive opera-about-opera, as part of a small festive work; followed by a decision to expand the well-known story into a two-act work. The change of genre would represent a change of both function and venue, and the draft libretto the process of enlargement at approximately its halfway point. Whether or not this was what happened, the award of a festive commission to Prague was a decision of symbolic significance. Joseph had refused to participate in the traditional Bohemian coronation ceremony for a new Habsburg ruler, for which a festive work would normally have been required. While an opera to celebrate the arrival of a relatively minor figure would not have quite the same prestige, it is arguable that political considerations now came into play. Prague had been expecting (wrongly) to play a major role in the wedding but had suddenly found itself written out of the script. With the region's participation in a full-scale war now inevitable, perhaps this was the moment to acknowledge that Bohemian national pride had again been roughly handled. If so, it would cast a very different light on the long-held theory that the omission of the whole of the act 1 finale in the draft libretto was a ruse to mislead the censors, who

---

87. *Notizie del mondo* (10 October 1787), no. 81, 647: DA VIENNA, 29. Settembre: "Jeri, giorno 28 . . . e nella sera un' Opera Buffa Italiana, intitolata l'*Albero di Diana*, spettacolo ch'ebbe per tutti i riguardi un esito corrispondente alle circostanze, ed all'espettazione."

88. Link, *Arias for Vincenzo Calvesi*, xxvii, citing Fuchs, "Nuevas fuentes," 263, and Sommer-Mathis, "*Tu felix Austria nube*," vol. 4, 232.

might have objected to the words "Viva la libertà."[89] On the contrary, this toast might have been inserted quite deliberately, to enable the loyal operagoing public in the city to witness a rousing patriotic gesture.[90]

The only obviously contemporary allusions in *Don Giovanni* come in the banquet scene with the wind band.[91] A political explanation for the choice of airs played as *Taffelmusik* deserves careful consideration.[92] Although Da Ponte's libretto indicates that the meal should be accompanied by a *Harmonie*, it was the composer's idea that the tunes played should be identified immediately by Leporello. In choosing three, Mozart may have been influenced directly by Bertati, who has three stage directions relating to the wind band. The selected airs come from *Una cosa rara*, *Fra i due litiganti*, and *Le nozze di Figaro*. Given the dramatic context, the introduction of instantly recognizable melodies, the choice of *Una cosa rara* to begin the Don's evening entertainment has always seemed puzzling, since in September 1787, Martín y Soler's hit opera, even if it had been given its Bohemian premiere, could hardly yet have become widely familiar in Prague. This suggests that the choice was made for the benefit of the imperial visitors rather than the local populace.

The schedule of operas during the period of the festivities in Vienna made a special feature of *Una cosa rara* and *Fra i due litiganti* in a German transla-tion.[93] The intention was surely to enable the two competing troupes each to present one of its most popular works.[94] The two operas were given (in

89. For a judicious evaluation of the various theories advanced during the nineteenth and twentieth centuries, see Weidinger, "'Dux Drafts.'"

90. The existence of a prior Vienna proposal for a Don Juan work, contributing to the even-tual composition of *Don Giovanni*, would in no way invalidate the possibility that Mozart was expecting to return to Prague in late 1787 or early 1788, to fulfil an invitation to com-pose a new opera following the triumph of *Figaro*, or that Guardasoni played some role in suggesting the topic.

91. Heartz, *Mozart's Operas*, 169, focused on the original texts of the cited works, but also cited Volek on possible Prague connections.

92. My reading of Don Giovanni's *Harmoniemusik* differs from that of Chong, "Last Supper," but we are in agreement that the selection of melodies was not a casual process.

93. The German version of *Fra i due litiganti* was titled *Im Trüben ist gut fischen*. *Wiener Zeitung* (19 September 1787), no. 75, 2274: "frey bearbeitet und auf die nämliche Musik des Hrn. Joseph Sarti übersetzt von Hrn. Johann André."

94. The practice of scheduling popular works on Friday opera nights continued. On 31 August, *Una cosa rara* and *Zémire und Azor* competed for an audience. The previous eve-ning, Stuwer took a balanced approach in his fireworks display. His main theme was a rep-resentation of *Zémire und Azor*, but the sixteen-part *Harmonie* employed to accompany it entertained the public as they assembled with a selection from *Una cosa rara*. Woodfield, "Fireworks and Wind Bands."

that order) on the traditional Habsburg occasion for "state" theater attendance: immediately following a return after a period of absence. Franz had been away for several months, Joseph for a much shorter period, but both traveled back to Vienna for the celebrations. The calendar for the ensuing three weeks is given in Table 2.1.[95] Plays were presented on the nights for which there is no entry.

After Maria Theresia's arrival in Vienna, the Singspiel troupe found itself in a difficult position with respect to festive entertainment, as the Kärntnertortheater was required for state balls. A slot for German opera was not available until the final night of her stay, but at least that allowed the festive period to come to an end on 8 and 9 October with the two works that had marked the return of Joseph and Franz three weeks earlier. If that was the plan, it was rapidly overtaken by events. The Habsburg party conspicuously failed to put in an appearance at the Kärntnertortheater, preferring instead to support the theater troupe.[96] The reason for this snub—it would probably have been so regarded, since opera was conventionally the genre chosen on the night before a formal departure—is easy to understand: a decision on which of the two troupes should be shut down had been pending and had finally been taken. On 6 October, Zinzendorf thought that it was the Italians who were under threat, but the decision went instead against German opera.[97] According to one source, the unpalatable announcement was made on 9 October, the very day the imperial party in normal circumstances might have been expected to attend the Singspiel as their farewell performance.[98] Such an appearance was now out of the question; even handed patronage of the Italian and German genres would be seen as a hollow gesture. An exchange of gifts

---

95. *Gazzetta universale* (16 October 1787), no. 83, 660: VIENNA 4. Ottobre: "dell'Augusta Sposa, che nelle precedenti sere ha goduto ancora dell'Opera Buffa italiana." *Kurfürstlich gnädigst privilegirte Münchner Zeitung* (15 October 1787), no. 161, 645: Wien, vom 6. Oktob. (aus Privatnachrichten): "Den 4ten . . . Abends um 7 Uhr in das Theater in der Leopoldstadt dem Spiel la Cosa rara beizuwohnen, welches mit vieler Zufriedenheit aufgeführt wurde."

96. *Provinzialnachrichten* (13 October 1787), no. 82, 50: "Abends wurde das Schauspiel besucht." Dunlop, '"Kaisersammlung,'" 55, records Franz's purchase of a comedy libretto on 9 October.

97. Link, *National Court Theatre*, 302: 6 October: "L'Empereur veut renvoyer l'opera Italien a cause de la guerre des Turks, et cet opera [lui?] coute 12. a 20,000 florins par an."

98. *Carlsruher Zeitung* (22 October 1787), no. 127, 604: Wien, vom 10 Oct.: "Bey den itzigen sehr Kriegrischen Zeitläuften ist die hiesige deutsche Oper im Hoftheater abgedankt worden, worüber gestern der Befehl kam."

Table 2.1 Operas performed during the festivities for Maria Theresia

	Venue	Opera	Comments
Sep 20			Franz arrives back in Vienna after a long absence, accompanied by Joseph II, returning from his short military tour of Bohemia.
Sep 21	B	*Una cosa rara*	No imperial attendance is recorded, but an appearance at the opera house was routine on the occasion of a Habsburg return to Vienna.
Sep 23	K	*Fra i due litiganti* (in the German translation *Im Trüben ist gut fischen*)	No imperial attendance is recorded, but Joseph's practice was to be seen to support both operatic genres even-handedly, especially during a festive period.
Sep 24			Franz and Joseph leave Vienna to travel to meet Maria Theresia and escort her to Laxenburg.
Sep 29			The imperial party, together with Maria Theresia, arrives back in Vienna.
Oct 1	B	*L'arbore di Diana*	The main festive commission is given.
Oct 3	B	*L'inganno amoroso*	A ball is scheduled for 9:00 p.m. until midnight, but Maria Theresia chooses to go to Guglielmi's opera.
Oct 4	L	*La cosa rara*	After a visit to Schönbrunn, the imperial party returns to Vienna, where some of them attend a performance of the Singspiel version of *Una cosa rara* at Leopoldstadt.
Oct 5	B	*Le due contesse*	Paisiello's opera is attended by some members of the imperial party.
Oct 8	B	*Una cosa rara*	The opera is attended by Joseph II and possibly by other Habsburgs.
Oct 9	K	*Fra i due litiganti* (in the German translation *Im Trüben ist gut fischen*)	This work is scheduled by the Singspiel troupe as its festive offering, but the Habsburgs do not attend.

B = Burgtheater; K= Kärntnertortheater; L =Leopoldstadttheater.

symbolized the Italian triumph. Martín y Soler presented Maria Theresia with a score of her opera and was generously rewarded with a ring worth 100 zecchini.[99]

In his briefing document for Joseph II, Rosenberg, notwithstanding his own predilection for Italian opera, had been even-handed, acknowledging that both genres of opera were likely to continue to need imperial subsidy. He identified large and potentially escalating costs: expensive recruitment trips; large salaries; pension contributions; and periodic upgrades to the structure and fabric of the theaters, including the Hetztheater used for animal baiting shows. The clinching argument in favor of the Italian genre, though, was the strength of its recent box office.[100] It was an unarguable point in view of the poor performance of the Singspiel troupe during the second year of the contest. When it mattered, the financial outlook carried more weight than any counter-argument that might have been advanced in favor of German opera at a moment of national crisis.

Once the celebrations in Vienna were over, press attention turned to the Bohemian sector of Maria Theresia's itinerary. The focus was on Aussig, the location of the handover, with Prague featuring merely as one of the stops on the route.[101] In Paris, there was sufficient interest in the niece of Marie-Antoinette to stimulate two short notices, predicting and then announcing the arrival of the bride.[102] A letter written by Karolina Waldstein in Prague on 5 October provides some additional details.[103] She passes on gossip about the appearance and deportment of Maria Theresia in a rather frank fashion, describing her

---

99. *Notizie del mondo* (24 October 1787), no. 85, 684: DA VIENNA, 10. Ottobre: "al Maestro di Cappella Martini, che le presentò lo spartito dell'Opera intitolata l'*Arbore di Diana*, un annello del prezzo di 100. Zucchini."

100. Hassmann, *Quellen und Regesten*, 130–31: "sehr zahlreich besucht, mithin ist auf die stärkste Einnahme von daher zu rechnen."

101. *Paderbörnisches Intelligenzblatt* (20 October 1787), no. 42: Wien, vom 3. Oct. "Den 10ten dieses geht die Toscanische Prinzessin von hier über Gnayin, Iglau [Jihlava], Colin [Kolin], Prag, Loboschitz, und Außig nach Dresden. Zu Aussig wird sie von der sächsischen Hofsuite übernommen."

102. *Gazette de France* (30 October 1787), no. 87: De Prague, le 1er Octobre 1787: "On apprend de Vienne que l'Archiduchesse Marie-Térèse de Toscane arrivera ici, le 13, avec sa suite; elle y séjournera le 14, & en repartira le lendemain pour continuer son voyage par Zehst [Zehista] à Dresde." *Gazette de France* (6 November 1787), no. 89: De Prague, le 15 October 1787: "L'ARCHIDUCHESSE Marie Térèse de Toscane, accompagnée de son frère l'Archiduc François, est arrivée ici, avant-hier, dans l'après-midi."

103. Volek and Bittner, *Mozartiana*, 34. The letter was discovered by Eva Mikanová in the Waldstein archives.

as plain and her dress as lacking in taste.[104] She was expecting the visitor to spend one day in the city, passing through as a private citizen without seeing anyone.[105] The idea that the whole journey should be undertaken incognito had been rejected back in July, but reports that her stay in the Bohemian capital would be without ceremony persisted. On the political front, Waldstein expresses no enthusiasm for the war now in prospect.[106] She refers to Mozart's new opera, of which much was expected.[107]

When Mozart chose the melodies for Don Giovanni's entertainment, he probably knew which operas were to close the festivities in Vienna and very likely too the reason for their selection. In constructing his little aural test for Franz, he could be confident that his pointed references to theater politics in the city—the latest (and as it turned out final) round in the intertroupe contest—would be understood. He began with a melody from *Una cosa rara*, the work representing the Italian troupe and first performed on Franz's fiancée's own name day. With Franz's marriage now only weeks away and his sister's having already taken place by proxy in Florence, the chorus of rejoicing from the act 1 finale ("O quanto un sì bel giubilo"), celebrating Queen Isabella's permission for two weddings to go ahead, was apposite. Leporello hails the choice: "Bravo, Cosa rara!" The second musical reference also came from an opera with a double wedding. Representing the German troupe, it came with a sharp edge, alluding not just to the ensemble with no future, but to the very piece scheduled on the day that its demise was announced. In these circumstances, its cited text—like a sacrificial lamb to the slaughter—took on an unambiguous political connotation. Leporello's response, the salutation—"and long live *Litiganti*"—spoke up for the German genre and by extension the troupe performing it. His asides on the two opera melodies do not appear in Da Ponte's libretto, and it is possible that their insertion in the autograph

---

104. Volek and Bittner, *Mozartiana*, 34: "L'archiduchesse doit etre fort Laide mais bien bonne Extrememem fagoté p[ou]r tout dire a l'Italienne, et parfaitement bien Elevé et belle Taille. Elle . . . est fort timide." The public awkwardness of the princess is echoed in Joseph's withering comments on the way Leopold had brought up his children. Beales, *Against the World 1780–1790*, 564: "The physical side seems to me as neglected as the moral. They don't know what to do with their arms and legs any more than they know how to make use in society of the pedantic knowledge that has been stuffed into their heads."

105. Volek and Bittner, *Mozartiana*, 34: "L'archiduchesse doit passer i jour a Prague sans voir personne. Elle voyage fort comodement."

106. Volek and Bittner, *Mozartiana*, 34: "puisque l'on chante la vielle chanson *la guerre la guerre contre les Turcs* pour contenter l'embitieuse Catherina."

107. Volek and Bittner, *Mozartiana*, 34: "le 15 doit etre Lopera qu'a composée Mosarthe, de la quelle on se fait [crossed out] promois beaucoup."

came late on, although the ink colors do not offer any decisive indications either way.[108] If Mozart incorporated the comment on Sarti's opera only after news confirming the closure of the Singspiel had reached Prague, which cannot have been much before 11 October, then it came with sharp irony.

Again from an opera with a double wedding, the third melody—the self-citation of "Non più andrai"—was equally double-edged: a none too subtle reminder to Franz (see fig. 2.1) of its composer's justifiable pride over his own Prague success, but also an unambiguous reference to the resounding conclusion of Figaro's aria ("Cherubino, alla vittoria, alla gloria militar"). In the circumstances, this could hardly have been seen as anything other than a public salute to the young Habsburg whose own military bearing was soon to be on display.

When *Figaro* was chosen "by desire" as a last-minute replacement for the commissioned festive work, this element was further politicized. At the conclusion of act 1, following the military march at the end of "Non più andrai," the signal for the departure of the imperial guests, a sonnet, ordered by several Bohemian patriots, was handed out.[109]

Gestures of this kind had a recent history. During his visit to Prague in September 1786, the emperor had gone out of his way to make it clear that his policy of establishing German as the administrative language of the Austrian Monarchy was not to be at the expense of Czech in other contexts, historical, cultural, and theatrical. His attempts to demonstrate respect for the language and (distant) history of Bohemia during a university visit—he read a passage from Jan Žižka's famed battle orders—were reported in many newspapers and not by accident.[110] Theater was also an arena in which he could make a clear statement about language. Dramatic works in Czech were incorporated

---

108. When the 1788 Vienna libretto was prepared, Leporello's lines were not added in, even though some attempt was made to correct other mistakes and omissions.

109. A curious feature of the report of this patriotic gesture of farewell is the apparent absence of the Oberstlandhofmeister Count Wieschnick and the new Oberstburggraf and his wife. Wieschnick had recently been in Prague for the ceremonial investiture of the new Burggraf. *Preßburger Zeitungen* (29 September 1787), no. 78: Böhmen. The reception of important Habsburg visitors was of course part of the job. Nostitz put on a "Konzert" for Albert, Duke of Teschen, when he called at Prague in March 1786. *Prager interessante Nachrichten* (11 March 1786) no. 11, 88.

110. *Bayreuther Zeitung* (10 October 1786), no. 122, 854: Prag, vom 30. October: "und einige der ältesten Handschriften, z.B. das alte Ewangeliarium der böhmischen Herzoge, die Liturgie der böhmischen Brüder, die in böhmischer Sprache geschriebener Kriegsordnung des Cizka, aus welcher Se. Majestät selbst eine Stelle vorlasen, und dabey über die böhmische Sprache einige Anmerkungen machten."

FIGURE 2.1 Franz II, Holy Roman Emperor (1768–1835); Portrait miniature (c. 1790), unknown artist.
Courtesy of Bildarchiv, Vienna

in the schedule of Nostitz's National Theater in 1785, a significant development attracting widespread comment.[111] The following year, a performance of
Václav Thám's *Břetislav a Jitka* was reported in Salzburg.[112] Toward the end of
his visit to Prague in the early autumn of 1786, Joseph made a great show of
attending a Czech-language production of Schikaneder's *Die Lyranten* at the
rival Vaterländische Theater, which presented German and Czech drama as
well as Singspiel. A widely distributed account in the press painted a striking

111. *Mannheimer Zeitung* (29 January 1785), no. 13, 50: Prag, den 20. Winterm.: "Auf dem
Gräflich Nostitzischen Altstädter Theater sahen wir heut zum erstenmal, was Prag vielleicht
noch nicht gesehen hat. Es war ein Lustspiel in der Nazionalsprache." Nedbal, *Prague's
Estates Theater*, 3–4.

112. *Oberdeutsche Staatszeitung* (25 January 1786), no. 18, 69: "Zu Prag wurde vor einigen
Tagen ein schönes Original-Schauspiel in Böhmischer Sprache, unter dem Titel: Brzetislib
und Judith aufgeführt."

picture. Accompanied by his leading generals, he made manifest his enjoyment of the performance, after which odes in Czech were distributed.[113] This political act was a direct precursor to the distribution of a sonnet—language unknown, but probably also Czech—as Franz and Maria Theresia left the Nostitz Theater on 14 October. It would probably have attracted more comment had it not been for the fact that it was a major news week elsewhere in Bohemia, following a terrible conflagration in Leipa that destroyed parts of the city.[114]

The early start on 15 October was necessary because of the distance Franz and Maria Theresia had to travel. Some concern had previously been expressed about the quality of the routes northward, and road repairs had been ordered.[115] They were about to pass through a sensitive border region with strong (and negative) resonance for both Austria and Saxony, retracing the route followed by invading Prussian armies. Some locations, such as Colin (Kolín), where Frederick the Great suffered a major defeat at the hands of the Austrians, had more positive associations. The initial destination was the historic town of Leitmeritz (Litoměřice), but very close by, a few miles to the west along the Elbe, was the smaller Lobositz (Lovosice), site of the opening battle of the Seven Years War, which had been followed by the early surrender of the Saxon forces and the ignominious retreat of the Austrian army.[116] The symbolic presence of a leading Habsburg close to the site of a major defeat for the Monarchy did not pass without comment on the unfortunate result of the battle.[117]

---

113. *Laibacher Zeitung* (5 October 1786), no. 40: Prag den 22. Sept. "Den nämlichen Tag beglükten Se. Majestät die Gesellschaft des vaterländischen Theaters auf der Neustadt mit allerhöchst Dero Gegenwart, und wohnten nebst den Feldmarschallen Laudon, Lacy, und dem Feldzeugmeister Kolloredo dem ganzen Stüke: Die Lyranten, welches in böhmischer Sprache gegeben wurde. . . . Am Ende des Stükes wurden böhmische Oden unter die Zuschauer ausgeworfen."

114. An exception was the geographically proximate Pressburg. *Preßburger Zeitung* (24 October 1787), no. 85.

115. *Prager Oberpostamtszeitung* (15 September 1787), no. 74: Prag den 13 Septemb. "Da die Reise der Prinzeßinn Therese kön. Hohheit über Außig nach Dresden geht, so werden dem Vernehmen nach die gefärlichen Wege bey Lobositz, Außig, u.s.w. repariret."

116. Many sources report Lobositz rather than Leitmeritz as the next destination of the party. *Preßburger Zeitung* (27 October 1787), no. 86.

117. *Gazzetta universale* (3 November 1787), no. 88, 701. VIENNA 22. Ottobre: "S. A. R. l'Arciduca Francesco fece ritorno giovedì scorso in ottimo stato di salute da Laboschitz. In questo Borgo piccolo sì, ma noto per la famosa battaglia ivi disgraziatamente perduta nella guerra de' 7. anni dalla nostra Armata condotta dal Conte Generale di Neuberg contro i Prussiani, il R. Arciduca Francesco aveva preso congedo dall'Arciduchessa Maria Teresa."

Details of the ceremony at Aussig, during which the person of Maria Theresia was formally handed over, were given in several newspapers.[118] She arrived at 10:00 on the morning of 16 October and was taken to the magnificently furnished room prepared for her by the Hofkammerfourier. Seated under a canopy with the Tuscan party to her left and the Saxon party to her right, she listened to an address given by Graf von Thurn, and later replied to another from Graf von Einsiedl. The following morning, she attended Mass before completing her odyssey, finally meeting Anton in the Elector's castle near Dresden.[119] Joseph had little to say about his niece's reception in Prague, briefly informing Leopold on 18 October that all had gone well.[120] But he was greatly annoyed by a late change to the schedule for the handover. The original plan had been that she should cover the short distance from Lobositz to Aussig and then after the ceremony proceed immediately northward to Pillnitz. At the insistence of the Saxon Court, however, this timetable had been changed to allow a full day's stop at Aussig. Writing in a cold fury and focusing on the dowry, Joseph commented acidly that the extra time was probably required not only to count the money but to weigh it.[121]

Maria Theresia's arrival at Pillnitz on the banks of the Elbe was a visually stunning piece of state theater.[122] The castle was illuminated by 24,000 lights colored, according to some reports, red and green. She was welcomed by Anton, who then retired to Dresden to await her arrival the following morning. There was no diminution in the music; a long description in a local periodical gave a flavor of its intensity.[123] The entertainment included Janissary

---

118. *Paderbörnisches Intelligenzblatt* (10 November 1787), no. 45.

119. *Preßburger Zeitung* (3 November 1787), no. 88.

120. Arneth, *Joseph II. und Leopold*, 132: "Mes nouvelles de Prague de votre fils sont très-bonnes; tout le monde se portait bien." On 22 October, the emperor commended the way Franz had undertaken his role during his sister's journey: "et je puis vous annoncer l'heureux retour de votre fils, qui s'est très-bien acquitté de sa commission de la remise de votre fille" (134).

121. Arneth, *Joseph II. und Leopold*, 132: Ce 18 Octobre 1787: "tout cela pour avoir le temps non seulement de compter, mais même je crois de peser les ducats que vous leur payez de la dot. Les chicanes faites à ce sujet sont incroyables et révoltantes."

122. *Budissinische Wöchentliche Nachrichten* (20 October 1787), no. 42, 166: Dresden, den 11 Oct.: "Heute Nachmittag wird die hohe Braut des Prinzen Anton von Sachsen, Maria Theresia, im Kurfürstl. Lustschlosse Pillnitz eintreffen . . . das Kurfürstl. Schloß am Bord der Elbe wird diesen Abend mit 24000 Lampen erleuchtet werden."

123. *Magazin der Sächsischen Geschichte* (1787), 632–38: "In allen Dörfern Sachßens, wodurch ihre Reise ging, ward sie mit Feyerlichkeiten empfangen . . . ließen sich Trompeten und Pauken vom Schloßthurme hören . . . Musicchören . . . zwey Hautboistenchöre . . . mit Capellconcert . . . ein feyerlich Te Deum von Haßen gesungen . . . Familientafel mit Music . . . ein feyerl. Te Deum . . . Kantate auf dem kl. Theater."

bands, which remained very popular despite the imminence of war with the Ottoman Empire.[124] The sound was not thought in the least inappropriate for a Habsburg daughter.[125]

DURING MOZART'S VISIT to Prague, fallout from the closure of the Singspiel troupe dominated theatrical news from Vienna. The initial response was to attribute its demise to the war-like times ("kriegerische Zeitläufte").[126] There was a consensus that Joseph's decision would be followed by other theatrical economies.[127] Even the acting troupe was not immune from speculation; one commentator suggested that payoffs were imminent, now that attention was focused on a different kind of theater: the theater of war.[128] With the benefit of hindsight, others pointed out that the Singspiel had been in trouble for some time. Pezzl observed that even though most inhabitants of Vienna did not understand Italian, the German troupe had not been as well supported as the opera buffa. The exceptional applause for Dittersdorf's farce *Der Doktor* had been just that: exceptional.[129] Based on the figures given by Link, the Singspiel's nightly average box office taking in the year of Dittersdorf's triumph seems to have been around 320 gulden, but in the 1787–88 season, it dropped sharply to around 170 gulden a night. The average for plays and Italian operas during the same period was down only slightly.[130]

---

124. On the Janissary bands, see Head, *Orientalism*, 57–64.

125. *Langensalzisches Wochenblat*, 27 October 1787, No. 44; aus Sachsen, vom 19. Oct.: "Der Prinz führte seine Braut unter der Jantscharenmusik."

126. *Leipziger Zeitungen* (16 October 1787), no. 203, 1193: Wien: 10 October: "Am nämlichen Tage wurde, der kriegerischen Zeitläufte wegen, die hiesige deutsche Oper abgedankt." The impact of the Austro-Turkish War on musicians and opera-giving in Vienna has been extensively discussed, especially with reference to Mozart's declining fortunes during the later 1780s. Recent studies that take account specifically of the slide toward war in 1787 include Link, "Mozart's Appointment to the Viennese Court," 172–73; and Rice, *Antonio Salieri*, 416–18.

127. *Vaterlandschronik* (November 1787), no. 38, 297: "Kürzlich, schafte er zur Aergerniß der Wiener die welsche Oper und—das deutsche Singspiel ab." *Augspurgische Ordinari Postzeitung* (18 October 1787), no. 250: Wien, den 13. Oct.: "So eben verbreitet sich das Gericht, daß Sr. Majestät das ganze Personale des deutschen Singspiels heute verabschiedet haben. Das nämliche Schicksal soll, heißt es, das wälsche Theater, und den Staab der gallizischen Garde treffen."

128. *Laibacher Zeitung* (15 November 1787), no. 46: Wien: "Deutsche Oper und deutsches Orchester—beyde haben ihren Abschied erhalten. Auch mit dem Deutschen Schauspiele fängts an zu hapern. . . . Man sagt, daß unser Kaiser, der nun die Impressa des Kriegstheaters auf seine Schultern zu laden hat, die Schaubühne der friedlichen Thalie mit allen ihren helfernden und habernden Huldinnen in Verpachtung geben werde."

129. Pezzl, *Skizze*, vol. 3, 425–26.

130. Link, *National Court Theatre*, 493 and 496.

A more trenchant explanation from a nationalist perspective was offered by Franz Kratter. He posed the question "what is to be expected in the Fatherland when audiences scuffle to get into a poor academy to hear a pair of arias negligently sung by the arrogant foreigner Storace, who possesses an equally large talent for impertinence as for art, when Mozart, that excellent artist, receives insufficient income from a good academy even to defray his expenses."[131] In a similar vein, he attributed the success of the opera buffa to the fact that Italian salaries were on average more than four and a half times those offered to German performers.[132] This rhetorical device—Italians receive more ducats than do Germans gulden—exaggerated the difference. In the 1786–87 season, for example, the average male Italian singer received nearly three times the amount paid to his German counterpart. The perception that the competing troupes had been unequally resourced, thereby skewing the contest, persisted well into 1788, but it was not just a question of money; if the Singspiel had been given appropriate encouragement, it would now be in a position of strength.

The closure was clearly a temporary defeat for the genre of Singspiel, although in the medium term its demise at the National Theater galvanized commercial providers.[133] An immediate consequence was the transfer of Dittersdorf's hit success. *Doktor und Apotheker* received its first performance at the Leopoldstadttheater on 15 April 1788, a few weeks after the closure of the Singspiel troupe.[134] The policy of acquiring arrangements of the most popular *opere buffe* at the National Theater had not been matched by equivalent

131. Kratter, *Philosophische und statistische Beobachtungen*, vol. 1, 48–49 (changes in the enlarged 1789 edition): "Aber, Talent des Künstlers, was erwartest du in deinem Vaterlande, wo man sich darum rauft, die hochmüthige Ausländerin Storaze, die für Kunst und Impertinenz ein gleich grosses Talent besaß, in einer schlechten Akademie ein paar Arien nachlässig singen zu hören, und seinem Mozart, diesem vortreflichen Künstler, für eine gute Akademie nicht einmal so viel bezahlt, um die Auslagen dafür bestreiten zu können. *M. Storaze machte in dieser Akademie eine Einnahme mehr als 4000 Gulden (von 4000 Fl.)." On Kratter, see Pfeiffer, "Freemason, Mozart's Contemporary, and Theatre Director."

132. Kratter, *Philosophische und statistische Beobachtungen*, vol. 1, 48–49: "Die welschen Operisten haben mehr Dukaten zu ihrem Gehalte, als die teutschen Sänger Gulden haben . . . Hätte die teutsche Oper [das Singspiel] seit ihrem Daseyn des beifalls, des Schutzes, der Ermunterung genossen, womit die welsche Oper von allen Seiten bis zur Raserei bestürmt wird, wer hätte an ihrer itzigen Vortreflichkeit zweifeln?" The first edition is dated 17 September 1787. Deutsch, *Mozart: A Documentary Biography*, 309.

133. Branscombe, "Music in the Viennese Popular Theatre," 107: "the shrewd director Marinelli [perceived] that the closure of the *Nationalsingspiel* at the Kärntnerthortheater in 1787 left a sizable section of the populace in need of undemanding Singspiels of the type exemplified by Dittersdorf, Martín y Soler, Schenk, and the best of Müller's own work."

134. Angermüller, *Wenzel Müller*, 52.

plunder of its German successes, but with the closure of the troupe, there was no longer any obstacle to this. With the future of Italian opera now so uncertain, the aesthetic debate took on a sharper edge, albeit still focusing on *Una cosa rara,* which was continuing to attract audiences to Leopoldstadt in droves.[135] Pamphleteers became very active. The author of *Nachricht für Vernünftige* dissects the supposed shortcomings of the German version of the opera, seeing no more striking proof of the depraved taste of the Viennese than its excessive run in Leopoldstadt.[136] Critics of German opera as a genre often aimed their fire at the perceived inadequacy of its performers: actors without the necessary vocal skills; singers with a weak or inexpressive speaking voice, unable to portray character. The writer wondered whether Marinelli's troupe had what it took to delight the ear or move the heart.[137] His comparative evaluations of singers pulled no punches, and the two leading women are both found wanting. The voice of "Mademoiselle Storaci Leopoldiana" is defective, while "Die deutsche Lasky" (who knows something of music) is little better.[138]

A response appeared in *Antwort auf die unverschämte Kritik,* which in essence defends Singspiel as entertainment rather than art. The anonymous author of the original piece, accused of depicting the theatergoing audience as lacking in discernment, is confronted with the unanswerable argument of popular taste.[139] The Viennese, admittedly, treasure the jokes of a Kasperl more than the serious performances of a Franz Brockmann, yet each has his place in the scheme of things; Brockmann stirs the soul, while Kasperl shakes

---

135. Angermüller, *Wenzel Müller,* 168: 21 May [1788]: "Una cosa rara wird zum 50. Mal gespielt."

136. *Nachricht für Vernünftige,* 7: "Kein auffallender Beweis eines ganz verdorbenen Geschmackes im Fache der schönen Künste können die Wiener geben, als durch ein übermäßig Zulauf zur Cosa Rara in der Leopoldstadt."

137. *Nachricht für Vernünftige,* 8: "Eben so, wer den Endzweck der Tonkunst erreichen will, der muß sie nicht allein gut verstehen, sondern auch alle nöthige Erfo[r]derniße dazu haben, ohne welche er weder das Ohr kützeln, noch das Herz angenehm rühren kann. Haben das Marinellis Leute? Wir wollen sehen."

138. *Nachricht für Vernünftige,* 9: "Mademoiselle Storaci Leopoldiana thut freylich was sie kann, allein sie hat so mangelhafte Sprachorganen daß sie im Reden dem Ohre schon weh thut, zu geschweigen erst im Singen. Die deutsche Lasky scheint etwas Musick zu wißen, aber vom Wahren derselben hat man Ihr nie was gesagt, wie sie sich sonst nie mit so einer mistönigen Stimme dem Theater in der Absicht gewidmet haben würde."

139. *Antwort auf die unverschämte Kritik,* 4: "Der Anfang dieser Brochüre sind Impertinenzen gegen das Wiener Publikum, das hier als ein Volk ohne Geschmak, und ohne Beurtheilungskraft erscheint."

the diaphragm.[140] The small pen-portraits of the performers are rejected as wholly laughable caricatures; there is nothing remotely amusing in the satirical description of the leading woman as "die Leopoldstädter Storazi." Why should any singer in a suburban theater be ridiculed simply because she cannot match the great Storace?[141] Like all her colleagues, she does her best, actually quite enough to entertain the public. The patronizing commentary on "Laski" is similarly laid bare, and the rebuttal works its way through the cast list. It was a classic confrontation between high art (subsidized opera buffa at the National Theater) and popular art (commercial Singspiel in the suburbs).

---

140. *Antwort auf die unverschämte Kritik*, 7: "Und hat nicht jeder sein eigen Verdienst, ein Brokmann rührt die Seele, ein Kasperl erschüttert das Zwerchsell."

141. *Antwort auf die unverschämte Kritik*, 9–10: "Mademoiselle Sartori wird spottweise die Leopoldstädter Storazi genennet, ob ich gleich nicht umhin kann, lächerlich zu finden, daß man einer Sängerinn auf einem Vorstadttheater, wenn sie nicht wie eine Storaza singt, spotten will."

3

Operatic Satire

DITTERSDORF'S *FIGARO*

AFTER TWO EXTENSIONS to his sabbatical, Dittersdorf left Vienna at the
height of the intertroupe contest in which he had become embroiled. As
was the agreement, he returned to his posts as Oberamtmann in Freiwaldau
(Jeseník) and Landrechtsbeisitzer in Johannisberg (Jánský Vrch), located in
the region of Austrian Silesia to the northeast of Moravia. Little is known for
certain of his musical activities in 1787, but to judge by the works he had ready
by 1788, the theatrical ferment in Vienna had not been far from his mind.
A primary goal was to capitalize on his triumph at the National Theater, as
nothing would contribute more to his employability in a major court position.
A visitor to Vienna in the spring of 1787 reported gossip that Dittersdorf had
a commission to provide new operas for next winter.[1] Such a contract would
have made commercial sense for the Singspiel troupe, which was featuring
his works, for the time being almost to the exclusion of everything else, as it
continued to compete against the Italians. The same visitor also noted that although Dittersdorf's operas, along with Josef Martin Ruprecht's *Das wütende
Heer* (premiere 1 June 1787), had more "artifice" ("Arbeit") than *Una cosa rara*,
they were still pleasing audiences.[2]

---

1. *Musik*, July 1789, 51: "und wie man sagte, hat der Herr von Dittersdorf einen Auftrag zu
Verfertigung mehrerer Opern auf den künftigen Winter bekommen."

2. *Musik*, July 1789, 51: "Sonst habe ich auch die drey Operetten von Dittersdorf: *Der Doctor
und der Apotheker*, die *Liebe im Narrenhause*, und *Betrug auf Aberglauben*; sodann auch
eine von einem gewissen Herrn Ruprecht, *das wütende Heer* betitelt, mit Vergnügen im
Kärnt[n]erthortheater gehört, und es ist wahrlich ein bischen mehr Arbeit in diesen Stücken,
als in jener *Cosa rara*. Sie haben aber doch auch gefallen."

On Dittersdorf's list of priorities was the preparation of a German version of *Democritto corretto*, as its success as a Singspiel would go some way to counteract its failure in Vienna as an opera buffa. Also "political" was his decision to work on a German version of the second Figaro play, which was certain to be viewed as a new round in his ongoing rivalry with Mozart. But any hopes he may have entertained for a return to the National Theater came to nothing when the closure of the Singspiel was announced. A new plan was needed. In an undated draft petition, probably written in the early autumn of 1788, he requested permission for three months' leave of absence to visit Berlin and Brünn and identified three works that were available for a short season in Moravia. In addition to a new German version of his failed Italian opera and *Figaro*, he had in his portfolio *Hieronimus Knicker*, which had already proved its popularity in Jauernig (Jarnovík). It could be described as comic but not low comic, exercising the diaphragm (through laughter) at least every fourth minute.[3] It was even starting to supplant *Der Apotheker*, a claim likely to attract the attention of the recipient of this petition, Baron von Kaschnitz, who was also administrator of the Brünn theater.[4]

Dittersdorf's desire to compete with Mozart is manifest not just in *Die Hochzeit des Figaro* but also in his composition of a set of string quartets, a new genre for him and one in which his efforts—he made certain of this himself—would be compared with his rival's latest oeuvre. If his own account is accurate, he worked on them over a period of fourteen months, beginning soon after his departure from Vienna.[5] It is possible that even before he left the city, he took action to prepare the ground for their reception. A new attack on Mozart's compositional prolixity appeared at the start of 1787 in the *Magazin der Musik*, a periodical that, like the political press, relied for some of its news on unsigned letters. It carried a report from Vienna as the third

---

3. Unverricht, *Carl von Dittersdorf: Briefe*, 93: "den Rest meines Urlaubs zu *Brünn* zu bringen kann, wo selbst ich nebst den *Democrit*, und *Figaro*, noch eine neue *operette. Hieronymus Kniker* gennant P: [crossed out] mit bringen, und dem 1: Brünner *publico* auftischen kann. Diese letztere deutsch [crossed out] *Opera* ist bey uns bereits aufgeführt, und ist so gut ausgefallen daß sie den Apotheker ganz verdrängt hat. . . . Da wir hier vor das Armeninstitut spielen, so haben 2 *Productionen* dieser *Opera*. . . . Sie ist durchaus komisch aber nicht niedrig komisch und während des ganzen Stükes hat das Zwerchfell kein Intervall auch nur von 4 Minuten, und diese soll dem Brünner Theater *pour la bonne bouche* dienen."

4. In 1787, *Der Apotheker* was given in the Brünn theater (which did not stage a large number of opera performances) on 3 and 10 July, 28 August, and 9 October. *Theaterspiegel*, 23, 24, and 26.

5. Unverricht, *Carl von Dittersdorf: Briefe*, 85: "und nach einen Zeitraum von 13 bis 14 Monaten brachte ich 6 zu Stande."

item in a miscellaneous selection.[6] The anonymous correspondent offered a very pointed summation of the views of the cabal associated with the Singspiel troupe. Mozart is praised unequivocally as a keyboard virtuoso, but this accolade is merely the preamble to a reiteration of the main line of attack, aimed this time at the set of quartets dedicated to Haydn.[7] These are beautiful and artful works, but the pity is that Mozart has aimed too high in his quest for originality, leaving little room for feeling or the heart. In sum, they are too highly seasoned: "whose palate can endure this for long, if the analogy with a cookbook may be forgiven?"[8] This wounding criticism, with its culinary analogy, certainly reads like Dittersdorf.

The set of quartets was ready by the summer of 1788, and a few weeks after the loss of his position in Freiwaldau, Dittersdorf contacted the publisher Artaria in Vienna to offer them for publication.[9] In a letter dated 18 August, he adopted what Rice has identified as one of his favorite techniques: "putting praise for his music in the mouth of an unnamed friend." In this instance, he added with some chutzpah that he could not comment himself, as self-praise sounds bad.[10] It is left to an unnamed connoisseur to express admiration for Pleyel's quartets and those of Haydn and then assert that both sets have now been surpassed by Dittersdorf's opus, a verdict with which the author can only concur![11] The sales pitch ends with comments on Mozart's recent set, the tone taking on a sharper edge.[12] Speaking now in his own name, Dittersdorf is convinced that his works will do better than those of his rival "which indeed I and still greater [!] theorists consider to deserve the highest praise, but which because of their overwhelming and unrelenting artfulness are not to everyone's taste." Dittersdorf writes that he is sure that his set will prove more profitable than Mozart's on account of its

---

6. *Magazin der Musik* (1787), 1273.

7. *Magazin der Musik* (1787), 1273: "Er ist der fertigste, beste Clavierspieler, den ich je gehört habe."

8. *Magazin der Musik* (1787), 1273: "nur Schade, daß er sich in seinem künstlichen und wirklich schönen Satz, um ein neuer Schöpfer zu werden, zu hoch versteiget, wobey freilich Empfindung und Herz wenig gewinnen, seine neuen Quartetten für 2 Violin, Viole und Baß, die er Haydn dedicirt hat, sind doch wohl zu stark gewürzt—und welcher Gaum kann das lange aushalten. Verzeihen Sie dieses Gleichniß aus dem Kochbuche."

9. Unverricht, *Carl von Dittersdorf: Briefe*, 82.

10. Rice, "New light on Dittersdorf's Ovid Symphonies," 458.

11. Eisen, *New Mozart Documents*, 54.

12. This critique—unqualified praise for Haydn and Pleyel followed by qualified praise for Mozart—strongly resembles the trajectory of the unattributed comments about quartets in the *Magazin der Musik* (1787), 1273.

"lucrum cessans."[13] This pointed remark alludes to the legal concept of ceased profits, allowing an appellant to sue for damages if an agreed service is suspended. Dittersdorf was hardly hinting that Artaria might wish to reclaim from Mozart actual losses incurred in the publication of his quartets in the event that there had been any; rather, he was using his powers of verbal artifice to add weight to the point that his chamber style had a more reliable appeal.

Dittersdorf probably began work on a libretto for his *Figaro* shortly after returning to Johannisberg in the spring of 1787. The text, "freely" adapted from the French original—extensively reworked would be closer to the mark—was a major undertaking in itself. The title page of the only extant exemplar is as follows: "Die / Hochzeit des Figaro / Ein / komisches Singspiel / In zwey Aufzügen. / Aus dem Französischen frei bearbeitet. / Brünn / Gedruckt bei Johann Sylv. Siedler, / 1789."[14] The author is not identified, but the nature of the satirical content points to Dittersdorf himself. While the aria texts are disappointingly generic in character, the spoken dialogue displays a talent for vivid farce. As to the score, now lost, the verso of the title page of the libretto simply states: "Die Musik ist vom Herrn Dittersdorf."[15]

Without question, Dittersdorf approached Beaumarchais through *Le nozze di Figaro*. He had personally witnessed the cabals surrounding the premiere of Mozart's opera and would have been well aware of the reasons for its mixed reception. For this reason, his Singspiel can be read as an early commentary on Da Ponte's drama. The following analysis will take into account three general issues: (1) the degree to which the text develops or changes the characters; (2) the manner in which it seeks to forestall possible objections from the censor;[16]

---

13. Unverricht, *Carl von Dittersdorf: Briefe*, 85: "und bin sicher, daß Sie bey meinen wegen den *lucrum cessans* der *Mozart*ischen: welche zwar bey mir, so wie bey noch grössern *Theoretiqu*ern alle Hochachtung verdienen, aber wegen der allzugrossen darinne beständig herrschenden Kunst nicht Jedermanns Kauf seyn: erhollen werden."

14. It is in the Schatz Collection in the Library of Congress and can be accessed online.

15. Lothar Riedinger, "Karl von Dittersdorf als Opernkomponist," 212–349, criticized the libretto severely, ranking it far below Da Ponte's effort. Either in person or through a contact in America, he had examined it, if cursorily. Bartolo's interest in Susanna is noted, but the description (239) of Basilio as a theatrical villain who is unmasked at the end of the opera does not suggest a close reading.

16. Italian opera texts did not have to be submitted to the office of the censor Hägelin. See Nedbal, "Sex, Politics and Censorship." After listing the personnel currently employed in the German theater and opera troupes, the author of *Wiens gegenwärtiger Zustand*, 366, summarized the managerial roles in the two theaters as follows: "Beide Hoftheater stehen unmittelbar unter dem Oberhofcämmerer izt Franz Xaver von Orsin und Rosenberg. Das Secretariat, und Oeconomat besorgt Johann Thorwart, und Theatralcensor ist der k. k. Regierungsrath Franz Carl Hägelin." Only then is there a section devoted to the "Italienische Hofoperisten." A Singspiel version of *Figaro* could not have avoided the censor in Vienna, and the outcome of the submission was perhaps difficult to predict.

and (3) moments when it seems to invite (or overtly avoid) comparison with the earlier work. But the main focus, throughout, will be on detail intended to satirize his opponents in the opera buffa ensemble. Viennese operagoers were to be entertained by references not just to the characters in *Le nozze di Figaro* but to the singers who had played them and, in the case of Cherubin, to Mozart himself. Dittersdorf wrote on the assumption that Joseph II would be in the audience, as he incorporated quite a few skits that lampoon opposition to Joseph's enlightened and rational policies.

As the plot of Dittersdorf's *Die Hochzeit des Figaro* is largely unknown, I begin with two summaries. Table 3.1 lists the cast of characters, indicating aspects of fictional personality aimed at facilitating satire of the original performers of these roles in the opera buffa troupe.

The perception that the Italian singers, led by Storace, had conspired to ensure the failure of *Democritto corretto* was reported by Perinet at the time, and several years later, the satirist responsible for *Anti-da Ponte* thought that Dittersdorf was still bitter about it.

Table 3.2 gives a plot synopsis, identifying passages where I read satirical intent toward (1) opponents of Josephinian political policies, and (2) Mozart. In casting the composer as Cherubino, his own character, Dittersdorf deployed the satirist's full armory, from uncomfortable verisimilitude, through exaggeration, to outright implausibility—Mozart as fifteenth-century warlord. The main argument in favor of regarding *Die Hochzeit des Figaro* as a satire is the sheer number of more or less plausible instances of caricature, where Dittersdorf departs radically from Beaumarchais and Da Ponte for no obvious reason. That said, the boundary between personal commentary and comic character development is not always easy to discern, and in the case of the former it is often difficult to read its tone. Some of the humor comes across as biting, but how much this stemmed from animus toward the subjects in real life is hard to say.

Act 1 begins, as in Da Ponte's libretto, with Figaro and Susanna in their designated bedchamber, but it is not long before there is an allusion to current circumstances in the Vienna theatrical world. Figaro's first aria (act 1, scene 2) includes a reference to the Singspiel ensemble's performance of *Im Trüben ist gut fischen*, the version of Sarti's *Fra i due litiganti* that was prepared as the ensemble's festive offering for the visit of Maria Theresia. Dittersdorf uses the exclamation "Ey, ey!" as a way of drawing attention to a satirical reference that might otherwise be missed. After the opening couplet, in which he swears that he will thwart the Count's desires for this particular dish (Susanna), he sings:

Ey, ey! du willst im Trüben fischen!
Wie fein war es nicht angestellt!

Table 3.1 Satirical roles in *Die Hochzeit des Figaro*

Role	Original performer	Satirical persona
Graf Almaviva	Stefano Mandini	The plot is adapted so that the Count is more often in the company of Marzellina than in Beaumarchais. In the original production of *Le nozze di Figaro*, these two roles were played by a married couple, Maria and Stefano Mandini.
Gräfin	Luisa Laschi	A statuesque, rather remote figure, with an eye-catching hairstyle, prone to striking poses, she nonetheless develops an exaggeratedly familiar relationship with her servant.
Susanna	Anna Storace	Exceptionally brusque in speech, she berates the Count and is often very sharp with Figaro. Her saccharine relationship with the Countess pokes fun at the sharp dealings between two *prime donne*.
Figaro	Franceso Benucci	The primo buffo's much-vaunted prowess at delivering a punchline seems to be caricatured. His reported affair with Storace may underlie some of the exchanges between Figaro and Susanna.
Cherubin	Dorotea Bussani	The persona of Cherubin, allocated to Mozart, allowed Dittersdorf to launch an entertaining satirical portrait of his rival
Marzellina	Maria Mandini	In order to develop onstage humor at the expense of the real-life Mandini couple, Marzellina sometimes substitutes for the Countess.
Bartolo	Francesco Bussani	A dyed-in-the-wool misogynist, a pompous lawyer with designs on Susanna, he is easily manipulated by Marzellina.
Basilio	Michael Kelly	A lampoon of a music master, he speaks a blend of broken (low) German and operatic Italian, while he dreams of food and riches.
Lieschen		Spoken role
Thomas [Don Curzio]		Spoken role [Role omitted]

Table 3.2 A synopsis of *Die Hochzeit des Figaro*

Scene	Synopsis	Political satire	Cherubin/Mozart
Act 1, scene 1	Figaro and Susanna measure up their bed chamber. Figaro learns about the Count's designs on his fiancée.		
Act 1, scene 2	Alone, Figaro expresses his fury at the behavior of the Count and Basilio, parodying Basilio as a castrato in an opera seria aria.	The aria text comes from Metastasio's *Il trionfo di Clelia*, performed in a setting by Hasse on the occasion of the birth of Joseph II's heir.	
Act 1, scene 3	Bartolo and Marzellina agree a plan to force Figaro to honor his promise. If it works, Bartolo hopes to claim Susanna as his wife.		
Act 1, scene 4	As agreed, Marzellina approaches Susanna to advise her that the more she rebuffs the Count, the more he will persist.		
Act 1, scene 5	Cherubin has been discovered in Lieschen's room, facing dismissal as a result. He snatches one of the Countess's ribbons from Susanna and tells her about the "Abschiedlied" he has composed.	Cherubin's threat to commit suicide "à la Werther" may allude to a decision by Joseph II in 1786 to lift the ban on Goethe's *Die Leiden des jungen Werthers*.	Cherubin/Mozart is a butterfly in love, flitting from one woman to the next.

(continued)

Table 3.2 Continued

Scene	Synopsis	Political satire	Cherubin/Mozart
Act 1, scene 6	The Count enters, and Cherubin hides. He informs Susanna of his posting to London and requests an evening meeting in the Summer House.		
Act 1, scene 7	Basilio's approach prompts the Count to hide. He speculates on the intended recipient of Cherubin's romance. The Count emerges and repeats his order that the page should be dismissed, in the process uncovering him.		Cherubin/Mozart is a beardless rent boy!
Act 1, scene 8	Figaro asks the Count to receive a chorus of village girls. He listens to them twice and offers them breakfast.		
Act 1, scene 9	Cherubin, Susanna, and Figaro join forces to plead for a stay of execution, so that Cherubin can attend the evening festivities. The Count refuses.		Cherubin/Mozart is obsessed with attending the evening dance.

Act 1, scene 10	Figaro and Susanna tease Cherubin over his posting to the army.	Cherubin/Mozart can no longer expect to have his hair dressed and his body anointed with perfume. He will have to put up with a diet of "stinking tripe" rather than capons.
Act 1, scene 11	The Countess enacts a parody of self-absorption. Susanna is worried about broaching the subject of the Count's infatuation, but her mistress receives the news calmly.	
Act 1, scene 12	An upbeat Figaro enters, still dwelling on Cherubin's fate. He outlines a plan to disguise the page in a dress and send him to the rendezvous.	Cherubin/Mozart will soon grow up physically. Military fare and exercise will toughen him up.
Act 1, scene 13	The Countess wonders whether women's clothing will suit the page. Susanna reassures her that a dress will fit him perfectly.	Cherubin/Mozart can carry off crossdressing to the manner born.

(*continued*)

Table 3.2 Continued

Scene	Synopsis	Political satire	Cherubin/Mozart
Act 1, scene 14	Alone, the Countess hopes that her fate is about to change for the better.		
Act 1, scene 15	Susanna returns with Cherubin. His song of farewell is a setting (in German) of Metastasio's "Ecco quel fier istante."	The text of Cherubin's canzonetta is Madame Herz's aria "Da schlägt die Abschiedsstunde" from *Der Schauspieldirektor*, commissioned by Joseph II.	Cherubin/Mozart can compose with much expression, but he is apt to go on too long.
	Cherubin starts to perform it but is rudely interrupted by the Countess.		Cherubin/Mozart has conspicuous frizzled hair.
	The crossdressing begins, and particular attention is paid to Cherubin's hair.		
Act 1, scene 16	The Count enters and interrogates Susanna and his wife. He orders the Countess to come with him to retrieve the key to the closet.		Cherubin/Mozart is of acrobatic disposition, well used to leaping around.
	Susanna helps Cherubin to escape, through the window.		
Act 1, scene 17	Figaro reports to Susanna that a tailor has arrived to make final alterations to her wedding dress.	Joseph valued the contributions the industrious lower and middle classes made to the state.	

Act 1, scene 18	Thomas the gardener enters with news of the damage done to his flower beds. The Count becomes suspicious, and Figaro, Susanna and the Countess start to dissemble.	In a striking inversion of social order, Figaro objects strenuously to being described as a rascal and threatens to quit the Count's service.
Act 1, scene 19	Basilio enters to report that he has recruited forty musicians from Seville to play for the minuets.	Joseph attended Dittersdorf's concert in the Augarten at which forty musicians played.
Act 1, scene 20	Marzellina offers the Count her good wishes in extravagant fashion.	
Act 2, scene 1	Cherubin needs to borrow a dress to disguise himself at the dance. Lieschen replies that her father possesses an old tome detailing a method of making oneself invisible.	Joseph was contemptuous of cabalistic texts.
Act 2, scene 2	Thomas is preparing a picnic for the evening's festivities. He asks Lieschen if the garlands are ready.	

(continued)

Table 3.2 Continued

Scene	Synopsis	Political satire	Cherubin/Mozart
Act 2, scene 3	Marzellina emerges from the feast, proclaiming that she is a sworn enemy of formal dinners.	Joseph was impatient with the flummery of events like guild feasts.	
Act 2, scene 4	Marzellina inveighs against Bartolo's pedantry and misogyny.		
Act 2, scene 5	Marzellina and Bartolo review the progress of their scheme. He reports that when he showed Figaro's letter to Susanna, the document became electrified, and she vanished in a puff of smoke.	Joseph displayed interest in the electrical experiments of Jan Ingenhous, his physician.	
Act 2, scene 6	Bartolo is outraged by Marzellina's comment "better luck next time." Why should he take this implied insult from a feeble-minded woman?		
Act 2, scene 7	Susanna ponders the content of the document she has just been shown. Could Figaro really be unfaithful? The Count enters and is given a ferocious tongue-lashing.	Norms of class behavior are inverted.	

Act 2, scene 8	Marzellina and Bartolo produce the letter. The Count decides in favor of Marzellina. Bartolo requests the right to woo Susanna.	
Act 2, scene 9	Marzellina recognizes Figaro as her son. Bartolo discovers that he is Figaro's father. The newly reunited parents think their son is too good for a mere servant, forcing Susanna to reveal that she, too, is of good birth.	Susanna's decision to live as a member of the productive classes rather than starve as an aristocrat would have met with Joseph's approval.
Act 2, scene 10	A quartet unites the new family.	Figaro's distinguishing mark is a malformed left ear that he has been keeping well hidden. A jibe at Mozart may be intended, even though Figaro is not "his" character.
Act 2, scene 11	Susanna informs the Countess about Figaro's parentage. The plan to crossdress Cherubin must go ahead. The fateful letter to the Count is written.	The text may be a sendup of the middle section of "Riconosci in questo amplesso."

(continued)

Table 3.2 Continued

Scene	Synopsis	Political satire	Cherubin/Mozart
Act 2, scene 12	The Count enters and invites his wife to join him in the park for the festivities. She declines, preferring to stay and converse with Susanna.		
Act 2, scene 13	Thomas, Lieschen, and Cherubin, dressed as a girl, are in the park. Basilio enters to inspect the lighting. He asks Thomas whether the girls have rehearsed his chorus.		
Act 2, scene 14	The Count enters with Marzellina, and the girls sing their chorus. He takes out Susanna's letter to read it and is pricked by the pin, which he throws away. Then, understanding its significance, he retrieves it with the help of Bartolo.		

Figaro is impressed with the Page's fluency as a brazen liar. Cherubin feigns sincere repentance, but he is nevertheless to be locked up in the Countess's antechamber until after the dance has ended.

Cherubin/Mozart is an accomplished liar.

Thomas asks Lieschen who the unfamiliar girl is, and Cherubin's identity is duly revealed to him. The Count at first fails to see through the disguise, whereupon Thomas asks him if he no longer recognizes the apricot thief.

Cherubin/Mozart is identified as an apricot thief, conceivably because the composer was involved in a real-life incident akin to the fictional one portrayed by Eduard Mörike.

Cherubin explains himself. He had been on his way to Seville as instructed, but his horse bolted back.

Cherubin/Mozart appears to be too slight to control a horse.

Cherubin threatens Figaro with violence if he fails to assist his escape.

Cherubin/Mozart single-mindedly pursues his obsession with attending the dance.

A reference to the Albanian warlord Skanderbeg, who confronted the Ottoman Empire in the fifteenth century, alludes to Joseph's forthcoming military campaign.

(continued)

Table 3.2 Continued

Scene	Synopsis	Political satire	Cherubin/Mozart
Act 2, scene 15	The Count recruits Lieschen to deliver his reply to Susanna. She is to say that at 10:00 p.m. the moon will come out, but Lieschen objects that it is a new moon.		
Act 2, scene 16	Marzellina and Bartolo discuss what the Count's letter might have contained and the significance of the pin.		
Act 2, scene 17	Marzellina and Bartolo encounter Lieschen and trick her into revealing her errand. She believes her message about the moon to be a lie. Albertus Magnus knows better than the "little milk soup face" that invisibility is possible.		Cherubin/Mozart has a pale, pock-marked countenance.
Act 2, scene 18	Figaro wonders whether he is worthy of the good fortune fate has delivered to him.		

Act 2, scene 19	Basilio enters and Figaro spins him an extraordinary yarn. He is not merely of good birth but is the son of the king of Persia. His bride-to-be is the daughter of the emperor of China. He is pleased to be able to offer Basilio the post of "Directeur des Spectacles."	A sendup of the follies of rank, this was calculated to appeal to Joseph, with the added spice of references to his own status. There is a short skit on bowing, scraping, and other servile practices recently outlawed.
Act 2, scene 20	Susanna goads Figaro by refusing to reveal details of what is going on.	
Act 2, scene 21	Marzellina, Bartolo, and Figaro enter with lanterns to observe. The Countess comes in, concealed from head to toe, her hair dressed as Susanna's.	
Act 2, scene 22	The three watch as the Count is duly deceived. When his wife is revealed, he apologizes and promises to reform. There is a perfunctory reconciliation between Figaro and Susanna.	
	A young woman approaches. It is Cherubin wearing his third dress. Basilio fails to recognize him and offers to act as an escort.	Cherubin/Mozart achieves his objective: to attend the dance.
	Figaro reveals his identity, and everyone leaves for the dance.	

Typically for satire, it is not altogether clear whether Dittersdorf wished to imply that *Im Trüben ist gut fischen* had gone well or not. The second line ("how nicely was it not done") could be a sarcastic reference to the politics surrounding this work—notably that it had been snubbed by the Habsburgs on the day that the closure of the Singspiel was announced.[17]

Figaro's remarks on the Count are merely a preamble to a harsh assault on Basilio, the role sung by Michael Kelly. A close associate of Storace, he is the first of the performers to come under sustained attack. There is an early indication (act 1, scene 1) that the singing master is to be the object of Figaro's contempt, when Figaro describes him as a Kerl (fellow) "with the voice of a he-goat" ("mit der Stimme wie ein Ziegenbok"). Should Basilio fall into his clutches when he has his barber's razor handy, he will be "tickled" so that he can sing the "highest discant" ("akutesten Diskannt"). The lampoon is developed in the lead-up to Figaro's aria. So far as he is concerned, the music master should return to Naples and "squeak" in the opera there, along with other "capons." (The castrated cockerel was often used as an image for castrati, many of whom were gangly individuals.) Kelly had studied in Naples, and in his autobiography comes across as a prolific name-dropper of castrati he knew—no doubt with his London readership in mind. Numbered among his acquaintances were Marchesi, Millico, Aprile, Pacchierotti, and Guarducci.

In the second stanza of the aria, Kelly himself is identified by inference:

> Und du Basil, du dummer Jackel!
> Es schadet nicht, du bist schon alt.

The seemingly gratuitous reference to the music master's age ("schon alt") points directly to the Irishman, who recalled in his autobiography how in Vienna he was universally known by the nickname "Old Gafferio."[18] He described a convivial evening in the company of Paisiello and Casti during which he was asked to do an impression of an aged miser.[19] Casti was so taken with his impersonation that he turned to Paisiello and remarked: "this is the very fellow to act the character of Gafferio in our opera; this boy shall be our old man!" The name stuck: "in short, wherever I went I was nicknamed 'Old Gafferio.'" Figaro's aria ends by conjuring up the improbable image of Kelly

17. The use of "Ey" as a marker for a sarcastic comment is seen in *Der Apotheker* (act 2, scene 25) when Claudia, laughing bitterly, retorts: "Ey das wäre ja vortrefflich."

18. Kelly, *Reminiscences*, vol. 1, 237–40.

19. Brown, "Beaumarchais, Paisiello and the Genesis of *Così fan tutte*," 312.

as a hero in an opera seria. The text, "De folgori di Giove," is from Metastasio's *Il trionfo di Clelia* (act 3, scene 8), which was performed in Vienna on 27 April 1762 to celebrate the birth of the first child of the (then) Archduke Joseph and Isabella of Parma.

For the would-be satirist of the original production of *Le nozze di Figaro*, there was mileage in its casting of two married couples and a further pair, Benucci and Storace, who were in a relationship if gossip is to be believed. Under the spotlight first are Stefano Mandini (the Count) and Maria Mandini (Marzellina). In the play, these characters do not interact much, but Dittersdorf makes minor adjustments to the plot throughout to allow for husband and wife humor. From the start, he characterizes Marzellina as a feisty woman, even spikier than the advocate of women's resistance portrayed in Beaumarchais.[20] In *Le nozze di Figaro*, a series of frosty exchanges between Marzellina and Susanna (act 1, scene 4) ends with Susanna playing her trump card: age ("l'età!").[21] In Dittersdorf's version, Marzellina herself introduces this touchy subject. She begins (after a stage sigh) by regretting that the Countess should be saddled with a husband who is so "abominably ugly" ("abscheulichen garstigen"). Maria is describing Stefano! Susanna objects that she finds the Count "attractive and finely shaped" ("schön und wohlgestalt"). Marzellina, glancing around nervously, clarifies: she is speaking of his character, not his appearance. She asserts that she knows him very well, as they were brought up together and are much of the same age ("so ziemlich in gleichem Alter—"), a claim that causes Susanna inward merriment. After Marzellina has taken a falsely affectionate farewell, she can conceal her amusement no longer: "Ha, ha, ha! Mit dem Grafen in gleichem Alter! Ha, ha, ha!" The relative ages of Maria and Stefano Mandini (thirty-six at the time of the premiere of *Le nozze di Figaro*) are not known, but the satire appears to be directed against them, as there is no reason why Marzellina's age in relation to the Count's should be of any interest.

At the start of the lighthearted episode in which Cherubin takes the Countess's ribbon from Susanna (act 1, scene 5), Dittersdorf's careful reading of Da Ponte's libretto is evident as he develops the vision of the page as an amorous butterfly. His Cherubin includes many elements that appear to parody Mozart's physiognomy and character.[22] For the moment, Susanna is

---

20. Allanbrook, "Pro Marcellina," 71–72.

21. Storace and Mandini had played opposite one another in Cimarosa's popular *L'italiana in Londra* as Madama Brillante and Livia. Da Ponte wittily evokes this when the two singers first meet onstage in *Figaro*: "Via, resti servita, Madama brillante."

22. Dittersdorf retained the Italian forms of personal names for the sung parts, with the exception of Cherubin: symbolically, the German Mozart among his Italian singers.

amused by the breathless haste with which the "amorous, small, fickle, variegated butterfly" ("verliebten, kleinen, flatterhaften, bunten Schmetterling") appears to bestow his affections first on the gardener's daughter, then on the Countess, and finally, even as she speaks, on herself. Dittersdorf's literary credentials are also on display, as Cherubin's declaration of love is "à la Werther," accompanied by a threat to blow his brains out. The reference is to Goethe's portrayal of a young man's unrequited love in *Die Leiden des jungen Werthers*, alluding to (and implicitly commending) the fact that in 1786 Joseph had overridden his own censor by removing this widely read novel from the list of banned books.[23]

An important satirical strand in Dittersdorf's libretto concerns Cherubin's canzonetta, the origin of which he is careful to establish. The page has spent the morning in the garden translating and versifying an Italian song of farewell: "ein Abschiedlied an die Gräfin." Susanna mocks the young poet, who has all the qualities necessary for a lover: "*Sus.* Ey, ey! Seht doch! der kleine Satan hat alle Requisiten zu einem Liebhaber, er ist auch schon Poet." This may be a mocking reference to Mozart's interventionist approach to the texts he chose for his operas, or conceivably to his recent public appearance as the author of a set of riddles.

Upon his entrance, Basilio is depicted as an ignoramus, a truly absurd caricature. He knows about Cherubin's canzonetta because he spied on the page in the "Sommer-aus" while taking his morning constitutional:[24]

BAS. (tritt ein) *Bon Giorno, cara Susannetta!*

SUS. Herr Basilio! Ich habe heute keine Zeit Lektion zu nehmen. Sie können wieder in Gottes Namen gehen.

BAS. *Tanto meglio* wenn Sie eute Keine *Lezione* nehm. Ik kann also einer albe Stunde mit Sie red. Ik ab *per via di Sua Excellenza* viel, viel guter Sak zu spreck.

SUS. (Ernsthaft) Wenn Sie nicht bald gehn, so—

BAS. Deren Sie mik ein klein Vizel!—*Sua Exzellenza* aben mir sak, ik soll ihnen wieder sak, daß *sua Excellenza* iß abseulik verlipp in die söne Susannetta.

---

23. Blanning, *Joseph II*, 162.

24. This resolves an issue in *Le nozze di Figaro* that has recently provoked discussion. Several critics have suggested that there is a musical reference in the terzetto "Cosa sento" to "Non so più," implying that Basilio must have overheard Cherubino singing it. How else could he have become familiar with the melody? Leeson, "Mozart's *Le nozze di Figaro*: A Hidden Dramatic Detail," 301–4; Woodfield, "Reflections on Mozart's 'Non so più cosa son, cosa faccio,'" 133–39; Rumph, "Unveiling Cherubino," 129–38.

[Susanna has no time for her lesson. Basilio is happy to hear this as he can now gossip. He has much to report concerning the Count, especially that he is in love with Susanna.]

Basilio's peculiar language, probably a caricature of Kelly's limitations, is a hybrid of operatic Italian (not deriving from Da Ponte) and a form of Low German, building upon the well-established use of such dialects by "fool" figures, but also indicating, through the frequency of dropped consonants, difficulty in pronunciation to the point of suggesting a speech impediment. (In the libretto, the two "languages" are typographically distinct. I have distinguished the Italian passages by using italics.) His command of spoken Italian also seems to be at issue. When he communicates with the Count (act 1, scene 7), he switches rapidly between the correct *"Eccellenza"* and the faulty *"Excellenza," "Ezcellenza"* and *"Exzellenza,"* possibly with the intention of evoking the double consonant sound (cs) of English/Irish pronunciation. The repeated use of this salutation in a single scene (nine times) indicates that the actor is supposed to be adopting a comic accent to produce laughs. Even though he reverts to the correct consonants on the final tenth occurrence of the word, its termination is now wrong, the punchline of the joke: *"Eccellenze!"*[25]

The music master struggles with articulation, alluding to Kelly's well-known parody of the old man with the tremulous voice and perhaps also his portrayal of Don Curzio as a stutterer.[26] Figaro's earlier reference to his having the voice of a he-goat ("Ziegenbok") implies this. While happy to poke fun at Kelly, Dittersdorf nevertheless deprives him of his role as the judge; the stutterer is not to be allowed to reprise his success with this manner of vocal delivery "in character." Susanna wants to send him packing, but the music master slyly introduces the subject of her preferences:

---

25. Another example of the comic blending of two languages may be seen in the character of the effete Frenchman Monsieur Girò in Anfossi's *Le fortunate gelosie*, played by Albertarelli, for whom Mozart wrote the substitute aria "Un baccio di mano" (K.541). He moves freely between French and Italian, even in the middle of a word: "Ah pourquoà, barbar amour / San mon coeur ici, ho da star."

26. Although Kelly does not refer to Anfossi's opera *Il trionfo delle donne*, which received its premiere on 15 May 1786, shortly after the first few performances of *Figaro*, it is possible that he was cast in the tenor role of Tiziano. His insistence that a stuttering rendition of the judge would work—it was part of the court scene in act 3 of *La folle journée*—may have been reinforced by rehearsing, or hearing someone else rehearse, the stuttering aria: "Ma, Signor, per carità: / Fatto male alcun non ho. / Son un che pa—pa—pa—pa—/ Pa—pascendo i Bovi io vò. / Che volete? di—di—dito. / Ma—ma—ma—ma voi sentite, / Ch'io tre—tremo di spavento; / E le bu—budelle io sento / Farmi in corpo blò—blò—blò."

sus. Kommen Sie mir schon wieder mit dem einfältigen Gewäsche? Packen Sie sich fort, oder ich rufe Figaro zu Hülfe, und der wird sie tüchtig ausklopfen.

bas. *Ma cospetto di Bacco!* Ik weiß nik, warum Sie ab mehr *inclinazione* vor die *Paggio* als *per sua Eccellenza?* Die *Paggio* iß sik ein—ein *bardasso, chi—chi—chi non ha nemenno la barba.*

[Susanna has no time to listen to Basilio's silly twaddle. If he refuses to leave, she will call Figaro, who will beat him up. Basilio wonders why she prefers Cherubin to the Count, as he is a rent boy who has yet to acquire a beard.]

Set upon developing a running gag, in which aspects of Cherubin's appearance and personality are seen to match those of Mozart, Dittersdorf begins with a startling insult; the epithet *"bardasso"* signifies a young male prostitute, beardless, a choice of word that begs for the censor's pen. A possible allusion to the composer's prominent nose comes when Basilio, reporting to Susanna what he has heard Cherubin say, makes use of a German proverb to the effect that he who tells the truth can expect a blow to the pate ("Kopf") or gob ("Maul"), but with "nose" substituted: *"Bas. Ah furbetta! ti ho colto!* Glt [Gilt]; wenn man geig der War-it, schmeiß man mit die Fidelbok auf der Nase!"[27]

The music master pointedly avoids using Cherubin's name, referring to him as "Die *Paggio*," a mixed-language label, also hinting at an unclear gender: Die (German feminine) *Paggio* (Italian masculine). The music master harps on about him, repeating this term eight times for comic effect. It is conceivable that Mozart's well-known objection to being categorized as a servant was Dittersdorf's target here, but for a Viennese audience, the emphasis on the term "page" might also have evoked the Rautenstrauch controversy, during which the name Cherubin appears to have become an issue. It is systematically avoided in *Der närrische Tag* and is not used in the lengthy review in the *Wienerblättchen.*[28] Susanna, like the other characters, has no qualms about referring to the boy by name and always gives the correct gender ("Der Page"). Aside from the personal satire, Dittersdorf's libretto repeatedly emphasizes that Cherubin is a young lad who has yet to reach the age of puberty and

---

27. This proverb appeared as the title page motto of the pamphlet *Kratter, B**n & Socii,* published the day after the premiere of *Figaro,* unfortunately in the year 1786 ("Leider anno 1786"), in which an unidentified Masonic brother comments on the controversy raging between Ignaz von Born and Franz Kratter: "Wer die Wahrheit geigt, dem schlägt man den Bogen um's Maul."

28. Woodfield, "Trouble with Cherubino . . . ," 178.

indeed is not particularly close to attaining sexual maturity. The playing down of his latent sexuality finds an echo in Joseph's unhealthy interest in "raging [male] adolescent passions," manifest in memoranda on the evils of masturbation in the armed forces and decrees confining ordinands to the seminary during vacations for fear of what lusty trainees for the priesthood might get up to in the world outside.[29]

Experienced teacher of Italian opera that he is, Basilio is immediately able to identify Metastasio as the author of the farewell song he has overheard, as he informs Susanna, once he can get the words out:

BAS. Deren Sie *questa mattina* bin geweß, spasier in der grosse Garten, und in der Sommer-aus ab ik incontrir die *Paggio.* Ik ab mik versdek, um su sau, was mak sik die *Paggio* da? Die *Paggio* nahm sik eine kleine Pappier aus die Sak, und fieng sie an zu *resitir* eine—eine—*canzonetta per congediarsi*—wie eist man auf Teutsch?—eine—eine—aha! eine Absiedlied, und der Lied war eine Uebersessung aus die celebre Metastasio—Sak Sie mir, *ma in confidenza*, ik werd nik weiter sak; Iß sik die *canzonetta* für die Susannetta, oder für die Frau Gräf?[30]

[While walking in the garden that morning, Basilio noticed Cherubin in the summerhouse and observed him taking out a small piece of paper from his sack. He then began to recite a song of farewell, a setting of a poem by Metastasio. Was it, Basilio wonders, for Susanna or the Countess?]

Well may Basilio recognize this canzonetta; Kelly himself had set one such text by Metastasio, an accomplishment in which he was known to take great pride. In his autobiography, he records that his "Grazie agl'inganni tuoi" was a favorite whenever he sang it and that it had "the good fortune to please Mozart," even if his advice to Kelly was to stick to his career as a performer.[31]

Basilio warns Susanna that the page is a little demon in love, liable to be transported by his emotions. When he sees the Countess at table, his eyes betray his feelings all too clearly. The ensuing trio takes "Cosa sento" as its starting point, but Susanna demonstrates the strength of her control. She knows exactly how to get rid of this pair of "apes"; she will pretend to pass out

---

29. Blanning, *Joseph II*, 62–63.

30. This might have been taken as an allusion to the difficulty Mozart apparently had in allocating arias for his two *prime donne*, Storace and Laschi.

31. Kelly claimed that Mozart composed a set of piano variations on his canzonetta, but these have not survived.

by descending into delirium, claim to feel off-color ("gelb und grün"), reel, and then collapse ostentatiously into the arms of Basilio.

After Cherubin is revealed, Dittersdorf introduces a subplot that will serve as the crux of the entire drama: the portrayal of the page as an insatiable dancer.[32] Accepting his punishment, Cherubin asks to be allowed to remain for one day in order to attend the festivities. The Count refuses, offering him a position as an ensign in his regiment, to qualify for which he must leave within two hours. In turn, both Susanna and Figaro come forward to support the page's request for a stay of execution, but the Count responds that it is precisely this deprivation—missing the dance—that is to be the main punishment for his offenses.

The leave-taking (act 1, scene 10) focuses on Cherubin's immaturity. Susanna observes that once he has joined his regiment, he will have to express himself a full octave lower ("um eine ganze Oktave herabstimmen"). According to information given to Vincent Novello, Mozart's voice was a tenor, "rather soft in speaking and delicate in singing." The page refuses to kiss Figaro, whose full beard might ruin his delicate complexion ("*Cher.* Ne, ne, ne, ne! nichts küssen. *Fig.* Warum denn nicht dummer Junge? *Cher.* Ne, ne, ne, ne! Sie haben einen starken Bart, und der könnte mir den Teint verderben.") Just to make absolutely sure that the point is taken, Figaro observes that in two years Cherubin will be piping a very different tune. At the moment, he really is only a child.

The great aria "Non più andrai" was the best-known piece in Mozart's opera. Dittersdorf could hardly avoid having a solo here, because he would be seen to duck a challenge. His solution was creative: a strophic aria with spoken dialogue in between each verse, a technique common in Singspiel. Satire of the name "Cherubino" again seems to be indicated. Whereas Basilio cannot bring himself to utter the actual name, Figaro uses it climactically as the third line of each quatrain, each time with an exclamation mark. Dittersdorf perhaps intended one of the German performers to caricature Benucci's stentorian tones and his famed skill at delivering a punchline.

The first line of Figaro's aria "Ja das Blatt hat sich gewendet" may be an allusion to the play *Das Blatt hat sich gewendet* by Friedrich Ludwig Schröder (after Richard Cumberland's *The Brothers*), some long-forgotten issue sparking

---

32. In a letter to his father dated 23 January 1783, requesting him to send a Harlequin costume, Mozart mocked his own appetite for dancing: "Last week I gave a ball in my own rooms . . . we began at six o'clock in the evening and kept on until seven. What! Only an hour? Of course not. I meant until seven o'clock next morning." Anderson, *Letters*, 837–38.

the reference.[33] After hearing the work, Zinzendorf commented on the implausibility of the metamorphosis—a subject of interest to Dittersdorf—of the henpecked husband into alpha male.[34] In the first stanza of the aria, the page is taunted about the joys he will miss. In particular, he will have to cease pining for girls. Moreover, an ostentatious appearance will no longer be possible, for who, now, will cut his hair or spread perfume over his body? The reference to hair again summons up the composer, described by Kelly as having "a profusion of fine, fair hair of which he was rather vain." Susanna objects that this is embarrassing the lad, but Figaro continues, making play with military imagery: "im Sommer exerzieren, avancieren, retriren." Instead of his customary chicken and capons, Cherubin will be served "foul stinking tripe," and his health will suffer. As Susanna opines that this is downright nasty, Figaro attempts to be more encouraging: once the page's cheeks are red with the evidence of wounds, what then of his beauty? But all will be well. A final stanza points out that in military life there will be girls aplenty, although "Präkaution"—an allusion to the *ossia* title of *Il barbiere* as well as the obvious—is advisable.

Following Da Ponte, Dittersdorf delays the first appearance of the Countess until her scene with Susanna. The manner in which she is portrayed is sufficiently exaggerated to suggest that parody of Laschi may have been in his mind, although so little is known about the personality of this important singer that it is difficult to identify what character flaws might have caused amusement. There are some hints in *L'ape musicale* (act 2, scene 2). Her husband, Domenico Mombelli, upon being reassured that his role will be "bellissima," retorts that it cannot be more beautiful than his "princess," a jewel in any language, a veritable pearl of the sea, and immensely rich.[35] The satirical persona is that of a glamorous woman who parades her looks at every opportunity, or at least is popularly thought to do so. On her first appearance, Dittersdorf describes her as "magnificently dressed," in marked contrast to Beaumarchais, who indicates in his preface that the Countess should be attired for private comfort rather than public display.[36] Nothing is known of the costumes used in

---

33. It was performed in opposition to *Die Entführung aus dem Serail* on the night of 19 November 1786 and then again on 9 January 1787. Link, *National Court Theatre*, 94 and 96.

34. Link, *National Court Theatre*, 283.

35. "Oh non sarà più bella / Della mia Principessa: / E un giojello, un bijou, / Una perla marina, anzi un Perù."

36. Earlier, Susanna comments (act 1, scene 4) that her mistress looks like an angel: "O heute sieht sie wieder wie ein Engel aus." Her appearance was often the first thing that was said about Laschi. Zinzendorf went to her benefit performance, noting that she was in a borrowed costume. Link, *National Court Theatre*, 330: "Benefice de la Laschi, elle avoit un bel habit du Pce Auersperg, satin rose, tablier a fleurs."

Le nozze di Figaro or whether Laschi had issues with her attire, but two weeks later, at the premiere of Anfossi's *Il trionfo delle donne*, Zinzendorf recorded that she had appeared dressed as a woman rather than an Amazon, with no helmet ("sans casque"). Somewhat cryptically, he observed that this seemed to cause her no embarrassment, a remark possibly implying that her choice of headdress could in certain circumstances cause problems.[37]

The Countess enters, engrossed in a book, and proceeds to enact a caricature of extreme tranquility. She sits down "with a calm serenity" ("mit einer ruhigen Heiterkeit"). A sign that parody may be in the air is that the stage directions begin to occupy more space than the dialogue. Susanna thinks that now may be the time to broach the awkward topic of her husband, but her mistress seems to be "in her greatest contentment" ("in ihrer größten Zufriedenheit"). With the Countess very likely striking a comic pose, Susanna continues: "her forehead is as serene as the morning sun" ("Ihre Stirn ist so heiter, wie die Morgensonne"); should she really ruin this air of well-being? The Countess momentarily relaxes her pose, letting her hand slip carelessly from her knee—she is still alive! Susanna seizes her chance. With a hesitation uncharacteristic of Storace and comical for that reason, she wonders whether she may be permitted to interrupt her mistress for a moment. Sending up Rousseau's feminine ideal, an inexhaustible "sweetness of temperament," the Countess starts to probe, her tone becoming ever more saccharine: "(sanft) [sweetly] . . . (noch sanfter) [still more sweetly]."[38] Finally, Susanna comes out with her problem: "Your husband is in love with me." The Countess receives the news with equanimity, merely observing that if she conducts herself with propriety, the rushing whirlwind of the Count's passion—the violence of the image is in striking contrast to the general tone of the conversation—will soon blow itself out.

Interrupting this mood of tranquility, Figaro marches in, and the plot is hatched. Hearing that Cherubin has been sent to join the army, the Countess objects that he is too small and too weak, but Figaro reassures her that military fare and exercise will stretch the young lad's limbs ("Komißbrod und exerziren strekt die Glieder auseinander"). In the next scene (act 1, scene 13) the two women avidly discuss his disguise. Crossdressing, a prominent theme both in the original play and in *Le nozze di Figaro*, was developed further by Dittersdorf. The Countess wonders whether a dress will suit Cherubin, but Susanna has

---

37. Link, *National Court Theatre*, 272: "La Laschi dans tout son brillant, sans casque en habit de femme, ne parut point embarrassée."

38. Hunter, "Rousseau, the Countess, and the Female Domain," 2.

no doubts. She is eager to see the page thus attired. When asked to take part in the intrigue clad as a woman, Cherubin takes little persuading.

At this point, the identity of the page's song of farewell is revealed to be Metastasio's canzonetta "Ecco quel fier istante" (La partenza). This "Abschiedlied" was the ur-text for an extended complex of poems in which leave-taking raises the fear that the beloved will in time not remember even the name of the departing one. The point of the satire is that Mozart, as Cherubin, opts for a German version, the well-known strophic poem "Da schlägt die Abschiedsstunde," by Johann Joachim Eschenburg. Although this had been set by other composers—Johann Adam Hiller and Friedrich Gottlob Fleischer under this title and Christian Gottlob Neefe and C. P. E. Bach as "Die Trennung" (The parting)—the Viennese context would have been obvious: the aria for Aloysia Lange in which Madame Herz displays her vocal talents at the start of *Der Schauspieldirektor*. In Dittersdorf's *Figaro*, the composer Mozart is thus cast unequivocally as his own Cherubin.

Dittersdorf may not have arrived in Vienna in time to see one of the performances of the festive skits in the Kärntnertortheater, but the double bill would still have been a major talking point. When he later came to construct his satire, it was natural to focus on *Der Schauspieldirektor*, but its Italian counterpart was also available to cross-reference. Salieri had left Vienna well before the premiere of *Der Apotheker,* and he played no known part in the failure of *Democritto corretto*. He was not satirized in *Die Hochzeit des Figaro*, but a comic episode involving him in *Prima la musica* may have given Dittersdorf a good idea. Casti good-humoredly subjected a performance of Salieri's music to an interruption. Eleanor has only just begun to sing "La prima cavatina di Salieri" when she is brusquely cut off by the poet, who thinks "more expression" ("maggior espressione") is needed. Interruption was a stock theatrical device, and it was perfectly suited to what Dittersdorf had in mind for Mozart.

The first four lines of Cherubin's song are taken directly from the Eschenburg poem, with the gender of the lover amended. Although sung by a woman, Cherubin is a male character, and he thus takes his leave from Daphne rather than Stephanie's Damon:

Stanza 1:
Da schlägt die Abschiedsstunde
Um grausam uns zu trennen.
Wie werd ich leben können.
O Daphne ohne dich?
Ein Fremdling aller Freuden
Leb ich um nur zu leiden

Und du?—vielleicht auf ewig
Vergißt nun Daphne mich.

[As the hour of departure strikes, cruelly to separate us, how will I be
able to live without you, Daphne? A stranger to all joys, I will live only
for sorrow. And you? Perhaps now Daphne will forget me for ever.]

Stanza 2:

. . .

Und du?—vielleicht auf ewig
Vergißt nun Daphne mich.

Stanza 3:
Ach—

As Cherubin is about to start a third stanza, the Countess intervenes
brusquely: "that's quite enough! really!—delivered with much expression!"
("*Gräfin.* Schon genug! wahrhaftig! mit vielem Ausdruck vorgetragen!")[39] It
is tempting to read this as direct satire of Mozart's compositional style, as
her hasty termination of Cherubin midflow could be taken as a witty dram-
atization of the critical stance currently gaining traction: that the composer's
music, expressive or not, was thought simply to go on too long.[40]

In the erotic dressing scene (act 1, scene 15), the page's inability to sit still,
charmingly captured in Susanna's aria "Venite iginocchiatevi," is played up.
Mozart's sister-in-law Sophie Haibel later recollected that he found it hard
not to fidget.[41] Dittersdorf's satirical target here, however, appears to be his
rival's hair. It is already clear that the page has something of a hair fixation,
having mentioned it while fantasizing (act 1, scene 5) about Susanna's role
dressing and undressing the Countess: "Sie friesiren ihr schönes Haar." In
Le nozze di Figaro, the question of how the page's hair should be presented is
quickly resolved by locating a bonnet to disguise it. Dittersdorf dwells on the
arrangement of the hair, which Susanna combs: ("Nimmt einen Kamm, und

---

39. The satirical response in *Der Schauspieldirektor* at the end of the aria is "Göttlich!" (heavenly!) "Unvergleichlich!" (incomparable!). In *Le nozze di Figaro*, the Countess exclaims, perhaps with irony: "Bravo! che bella voce!, io non sapea / che cantaste si bene."

40. In generic terms, the passage could also be read as taking a pot-shot at the verbosity of
sentimentality, especially apparent at moments of leave-taking. Faced with the pain of sep-
aration, the sentimental lover was liable to expatiate at length on his or her misery. A good
example is Mozart's own "Das Lied der Trennung" (23 May 1787) with its eighteen stanzas
of lachrymose F minor.

41. Deutsch, *Mozart: A Documentary Biography*, 537.

richtet die Haare des Cherubins"). When Thomas (the gardener) enters to complain about the damage done to his flowers (act 1, scene 18), he identifies the page's hairstyle, asserting that never in his life has he seen wind (blamed for this unfortunate occurrence) with hands, feet, and "gekraußte [curled or frizzled] Haar."

In *Le nozze di Figaro*, Da Ponte retained a certain amount of the risqué symbolism of the ribbon, but there are indications in the musical sources that much of this material was cut at an early stage. Dittersdorf's setting appears to confirm that this had been an issue. He removes all references to blood and the improved healing that the Countess's ribbon might afford. Indeed, Susanna has only just informed her mistress that the ribbon tied around Cherubin's arm is hers when the Count knocks on the door, diverting attention. The imagery of blood, which Joseph would surely have regarded as "anstössig" (scandalous) in this context, may have been identified as a lapse of judgment in an otherwise morally acceptable adaptation of the play, one that required immediate attention once the postpremiere revisions got under way.[42]

When Susanna is left alone with Cherubin, with both of them frantically seeking an exit for him, Dittersdorf evokes another aspect of Mozart's personality, famously described years later by Karoline Pichler. She recalled that after improvising variations upon "Non più andrai" while she played the bass line, the composer seemed to become bored: "he suddenly tired of it, jumped up, and, in the mad mood which so often came over him, he began to leap over tables and chairs, miaow like a cat, and turn somersaults like an unruly boy."[43] This striking description has generated much medical and psychological commentary. As Cherubin prepares to leap from the window, Dittersdorf sets up a reference to his rival, aligning him with the page's acrobatic prowess. Cherubin is not concerned by the drop ("Es ist nicht höher als ein Stockwerk [single story]"), but Susanna is worried that he will break his neck. Once Cherubin has made the leap unscathed, Susanna comments: "Ey der Luftspringer!" (the tumbler). Both markers of a satirical reference ("Ey" and "!") are present. This is Mozart as Harlequin, his favorite *commedia dell arte* character.

In view of Dittersdorf's espousal of the extended finale in *Der Apotheker*, his decision to avoid direct comparison with the climax of act 2 of *Le nozze di Figaro* appears significant, yet it may amount to nothing more than a consequence of the fact that the gardener, Thomas, is a speaking role. Only after

42. Woodfield, "Trouble with Cherubino," 186–88.

43. Deutsch, *Mozart: A Documentary Biography*, 557.

his withdrawal can the sung finale commence. Figaro, asked to explain how he could have been responsible for the damage to the flowers, resorts to fiction; he had seen Susanna walking in the garden and simply wished to join her. The Count is made to look like a fool. Implausible though his factotum's suddenly acquired limp is, he immediately accepts it as proof of the jump. But the gardener persists, asking why Figaro has changed clothes, revealing that Cherubin had been dressed in blue and white.[44]

The passages in which the suspicious aristocrat begins to probe the identity of the mysterious escapee, using as evidence the note picked up by the gardener, are among the most remarkable in the whole opera. Why Joseph allowed (as opera buffa) but forbad (as German drama) the play's attack on aristocratic privilege has been much debated. In Beaumarchais, Figaro seethes in private over the injustice of his situation and plots revenge, but in the lead-up to Dittersdorf's act 1 finale, he subjects his master to a prolonged and public humiliation. Frustrated by Figaro's prevarication over the note, the Count injudiciously orders the "villain" ("Schurke") to speak and immediately has cause to regret his intemperate choice of word. The response to this linguistic infringement, boldly and instantly delivered, is that the servant is no longer willing to serve under such an "honorary title." One out, both out! He and Susanna will experience no difficulty in earning their crust elsewhere: "Ich und Susanna werden schon anderwärts Brod finden." The shocked Count mutters to himself, apparently without irony, that he is being shown the door by his own servant. Although he adopts a more emollient tone, Figaro continues to assert his dominance. When asked why he is in possession of Cherubin's commission, he retorts: "examine it carefully and you will see why?" The Count does so but in vain and asks if he is being taken for an idiot. In response, Figaro reassures him that he is, offering a word of patronizing advice for his whole class: "great men are often blind, or at least do not want to see well" ("große Herren manchesmal blind sind, oder wenigstens nicht gut sehen wollen").

Eventually, he has to be told: the commission is not valid, as it has yet to be sealed. Cherubin has left for Seville, and the document is to be forwarded to him after accreditation. Why, wonders the Count, did he not get it sealed himself? It transpires that the page, following his "sacred" command to the letter, departed after his two hours were up, a minute after the stroke of the clock. For a moment, the Count softens toward his perpetual irritant: "Es ist doch ein braver Junge." He himself will pay for the document to be sent, but Figaro is

---

44. The colors probably derive from Beaumarchais, who described Chérubin's "riche vêtement" as "celui d'un page de cour espagnol—blanc et brodé d'argent—le léger manteau bleu sur l'épaule, et un chapeau chargé de plumes."

not yet finished. How do matters now stand as regards the use of the epithet "villain"? An abject apology is necessary to give satisfaction: "Ich bekenne hier vor allen, daß ich unrecht habe, und dieses öffentliche Bekenntniß soll euch allen zur Genugthuung dienen." This little scene enacted one of Joseph's most cherished if unattainable dreams, "to humble . . . the grandees."[45] Dittersdorf evidently thought it amusing, as he stages another such verbal exchange in act 2, scene 9. After showing Figaro the document containing his promise to Marzellina, the Count insists that he honor his word: "in short, I order it" ("Kurz: ich befehle es"). The servant's response—no trappings of serfdom are to remain in Joseph's realm—is truculent: "I will also be brief. I hereby renounce my position. Now there is nothing you can order me to do." ("und auch Kurz: ich kündige meinen Dienst auf; und nun haben sie mir nichts zu befehlen").

Basilio has been asked to provide music for the evening's entertainment. He reassures the Count (act 1, scene 19) that the minuets will be perfect: "*Eccellenza!* Sie ab mir befehlen / Daß ik soll die Musik bestellen Um su spiel *questa sera i Minuetti* / *E vi giuro che sono perfetti.*" With this reference, Dittersdorf appears to include himself in the satire, by alluding to the occasion of the Augarten performance of his Ovid Symphonies. Rice comments: "Dittersdorf took special care to give his minuets an important role in the program of each symphony. None of them can be dismissed as merely decorative."[46] Their high quality is thus assured! Basilio continues by describing the musicians he has hired: "*quaranta persone* / *Con violini, con corni e un Trombone.*" In his memoirs, Dittersdorf recalled that he hired a band of this size (without the trombone) for his Augarten evening.

Act 2 begins with a scene for Cherubin and Lieschen during which Dittersdorf sets up another skit for the amusement of Joseph II. As the curtain is being raised to reveal the park next to the castle, trumpets and drums are heard, repeatedly sounding an intrada. These offstage fanfares punctuate the ensuing conversation, prompting her to ask why there are so many. Cherubin explains that every time the Count's health is drunk, the instruments sound. By his calculation, they have at least another half hour before the guests will be able to take their leave. The punchline of the joke comes when Marzellina enters with the gardener (act 2, scene 3), thanking the heavens that she has finally been able to escape from this ordeal. Her next remark is aimed at the emperor: "Ich bin eine abgesagte Feindinn von allen Traktazionen!" Joseph II

---

45. Blanning, *Joseph II*, 101.

46. Rice, "New Light on Dittersdorf's Ovid Symphonies," 463–64.

had recently acted to restrict the power of the craft guilds, and he disliked over-
blown ceremonial events such as their formal feasts ("Traktazionen"), which
are being parodied here.[47]

Once the trumpet flourishes cease, Cherubin tries to persuade Lieschen
to lend him one of her dresses so that he will be able to participate in the
dancing. In *Le nozze di Figaro*, it is Barbarina who offers Cherubino the use of
one of her outfits. Cherubin is desperate to attend the "festival of the peasant
girls" ("Feste der Bauernmädchen")—that this might be a wedding celebration
is not clear—but he would need to make himself invisible first, an obvious im-
possibility. Lieschen begs to differ. Her father has an old book by . . . Alexander
Magnus . . . no Albertus Magnus . . . which describes dark arts of all kinds,
including a method of making oneself invisible, the type of cabalistic fantasy
scorned by Joseph.[48]

Dittersdorf's introduction of the dubious concept of a cloak of invisibility
may have been intended as satire of Cimarosa's popular *L'italiana in Londra*,
which features a bloodstone (heliotrope) said to confer invisibility on its pos-
sessor. When he saw the opera at Laxenburg on 9 June 1786, Zinzendorf
enjoyed the music but derided this aspect of its plot.[49] At least Benucci was
able to extract comedy from the actions of his character.[50] Dittersdorf's interest in *L'italiana in Londra* may have stemmed from a clash at one of the
Friday night operatic confrontations. The premiere of his opera *Betrug durch
Aberglauben* was unopposed on Tuesday 3 October 1786, but on Friday, the first
subsequent operatic head-to-head, his Singspiel had to compete with *L'italiana
in Londra*.[51]

Cherubin is scornful of invisibility, but he has a simple solution: Lieschen
must lend him a dress. She remains dubious, worried that if he is recognized
she will be punished, but he responds that women's clothing suits him very

47. *Handbuch aller unter der Regierung des Kaisers Joseph II*, 573: "Die Traktazionen, oder
sogennanten Jausen und Meistermahlzeiten bei der Ertheilung des Mei[ster]rechts, sollen
in natura abgestellt sein."

48. Several eighteenth-century magical texts associated themselves with the name of
Albertus Magnus, for example: *Secrets merveilleux de la magie naturelle et cabalistique du petit
Albert*, Lyon, 1782.

49. Link, *National Court Theatre*, 275: "Le sujet est si ridicule, cette Eliotropia, ces pierres,
dont Benucci remplit les poches de son habit."

50. Link, *National Court Theatre*, 280: "Elle s'amusa du jeu de Benucci quand il jette toutes
ces pierres."

51. The following Friday, the Cimarosa opera again clashed with a Dittersdorf work, this time
Der Apotheker und der Doktor.

well ("die Weiberkleider stehn mir gar gut"). This has already been established during the dressing scene, but it was perhaps important for Dittersdorf that "Mozart" himself makes the admission. In order to get his way, Cherubin has to resort to singing an aria in which he declares his eternal love.[52] Despite her reservations, Lieschen finally gives in.

In Dittersdorf's reworking of the play, the role of Bartolo is expanded. While the preposterous lawyer could be taken as a stock figure of fun, there may well be personal caricature embedded in the portrayal. Francesco Bussani was a controversial individual of whom Da Ponte remarked tartly that he knew a little of every profession other than that of gentleman. He had a minor managerial role looking after the costumes, and on occasion, as for the performances of *Der Schauspieldirektor*, he acted as stage director. There are no particular grounds for supposing him to have been a legalistic individual, even though it was he who alerted Rosenberg to the fact that Mozart had included a fandango in act 3 of *Le nozze di Figaro*. But if the severity of the caricature is anything to go by—Bartolo is depicted as an ineffectual misogynist—Bussani, too, had to take some of the blame for the failure of *Democritto corretto*.

Marzellina's attitude toward her coconspirator is that of a competent woman toward an idiot child; there is no doubt which of them is calling the shots. In a soliloquy, she recalls the condescension with which Bartolo had agreed to her scheme: "cooked up in the brains of a female head" ("In dem Gehirne eines weiblichen Kopfes gebaken!"). She expresses her contempt for him forcefully. Notwithstanding his learned manner, she can run rings round him ten times a day. It is laughable when a man takes pride in thumbing his nose at his wife, while failing to notice that she has already returned the favor a couple of dozen times. Glimpses of the balance of power in the Bussani marriage may be intended here.

Upon his entrance (act 2, scene 5), Bartolo receives the full Dittersdorf treatment. He is the wordy pedant par excellence, peppering his interminable pronouncements with Latin phrases. Marzellina has a lot of trouble keeping him to the point. Her attempt to curtail his long-windedness is met with an outburst of legal gobbledegook: "*Bart.* Das verstehn sie nicht. Ein species facti [a specific circumstance], ein Bericht [a report], ein Gutachten [expert evidence], ein referat [an address] & caetera, & caetera." In order to state the case clearly and precisely, he must include every "circumstantiam" no matter how trivial, and even the smallest interruption is ill-advised, as he then has

---

52. The location here of a solo for the page mirrors Da Ponte's libretto, in which the text of an arietta for Cherubino was mistakenly retained. A continuity direction in the autograph of *Le nozze di Figaro* indicates that it was cut only at the last moment.

to start again from the beginning. He swears by a legal codifier: "O göttlicher Justinian!"[53] Marzellina eventually reigns in the lawyer by alluding to his hopes of winning the soon-to-be-available Susanna for himself, an element in their original scheme (act 1, scene 3).

All this is merely the preamble to an inventive monologue in which Dittersdorf satirizes scientific experimentation. Bartolo describes Susanna's reaction to the document containing Figaro's promise. As she starts to read it, "elektrische Feuer" passes into her body with obvious physical effects. Once she is thoroughly stupefied ("durch und durch elektrisirt"), Bartolo seizes his chance, stating his case with elaborate rhetorical flourishes, but when this produces no reaction, a legal principle comes into effect: "qui tacet, consentire videtur" (silence implies consent). In order to demonstrate his good faith, Bartolo requests permission for a small kiss, but when his nose is still two inches from the brim of her bonnet, he receives a powerful shock. Upon regaining his senses, it seems to him that he is enveloped in a cloud, which turns out to be the powder from his wig. Alas, Susanna has disappeared in this puff of smoke, leaving behind the paper torn in half—another clear proof of the power of electricity. Marzellina, laughing, has a simpler explanation for all this: Susanna has simply boxed his ears, but Bartolo should not give up hope—he might perhaps have better luck when she is not electrified.

Experimental science was a popular topic for comedy in Viennese opera, and in this instance a well-known figure provided Dittersdorf with a model. Jan Ingenhousz, whose major contribution as a scientist was the discovery of photosynthesis, was summoned to Austria in order to inoculate the Habsburg children against smallpox. He was also well-known for his electrical experiments, on which subject he corresponded with Benjamin Franklin. Shortly after his return to England in 1779, he submitted a paper to the Royal Society of London titled "Improvements in Electricity" in which he claimed: "It is well known that writing and brown packing paper, when warmed, may acquire a considerable electrical power by being rubbed with hares' skin, or a piece of wood, or ivory, nay even (as I have found by experience) with a metallic body."[54] From 1781, he was back in Vienna, where he was in great demand as a presenter of experiments. As he informed Franklin, Joseph II was as interested as anyone: "a little while ago the Emperour came in my house to see

---

53. This passing reference was perhaps for the benefit of Franz, whose program of education included the study of this system of law. Beales, *Against the World 1780–1790*, 359.

54. *Philosophical Transactions of the Royal Society of London*, 14, 1776–1780: "Improvements in Electricity. By John Ingenhouz, F.R.S. Body Physician to their Imperial Majesties," 598.

some experiments relative to my discoveries. He Stayed in my room above three hours, and went away very satisfied."[55] Ingenhousz informed Franklin on 8 December 1781 that he had demonstrated "fire of beautiful brilliancy" to the emperor last winter and to Grand Duke Paul "this day."[56] Early in 1783, he informed his colleague, presciently: "I prepare a very powerfull Electrical machine. . . . And will make some decisive Experiments."[57] One experiment was decisive indeed, though hardly as anticipated. He recounted the effects to Franklin:

> The jar, by which I was Struck, contained about 32 pints, it was nearly full charged when I received the explosion from the Conductor supported by that jar. The flash enter'd the corner of my hat. . . . I neither saw, heared, nor feld the explosion. . . . I lost all my senses, memory, understanding and even sound judgment. My first Sensation was a peine on the forehead. . . . [he went home to record the experience]. . . . I . . . dipt the pen in the ink, but when I applied it to the paper, I found I had entirely forgotten the art of writing and reading. . . . [After a good night's sleep] . . . my mental faculties were at that time not only returned, but I feld the most lively joye in finding, as I thought at the time, my judgement infinitely more acute.[58]

Given the social prominence of Ingenhousz in Vienna—he was entertained by Rosenberg on 2 August 1784 with the scientist Alessandro Volta from Pavia and the librettist Casti—this startling incident is sure to have been the talk of Vienna society.[59] The skit in which the maid is electrified into complete silence may also have been intended to ridicule Storace's loss of voice during her brother's opera *Gli sposi malcontenti* and her subsequent absence from the stage.

In a monologue, Bartolo expresses some of the anger of the original character in Beaumarchais. He splutters over Marzellina's "perhaps," as it casts doubt on his ability to achieve his goal, even with an unelectrified Susanna: "Vielleicht mehr Glück haben?—vielleicht?—Doktor Bartholo, und

55. Jan Ingenhousz to Benjamin Franklin, Vienna, 23 May 1781, Franklinpapers.org.

56. Ingenhousz to Franklin, Vienna, 8 December 1781.

57. Ingenhousz to Franklin, Vienna, 28 January 1783.

58. Ingenhousz to Franklin, Vienna, 15 August 1783.

59. Link, *National Court Theatre*, 231.

vielleicht?" He will strike the word "perhaps" from his lexicon, replacing it with "gewiß" (certain), "zuverläßig" (dependable), "ohne Wiederrede" (without contradiction), and other similar terms of certitude. He rambles on: who will be able to resist the eloquence of a Bartolo? Who? A wench? ("ein Frauenzimmer?"); a weak creature? ("ein schwaches Geschöpfe?"). Francesco Bussani's attitude toward women is once again under the spotlight.

As events unfold, social inversion becomes the norm. In rejecting the Count's advances, Susanna shows how little respect she has for rank. There is no question of even token deference—in *Le nozze di Figaro* she at least addresses the Count as "Signor" or "Sua Eccellenza." She begins: "You mon- ster" ("Du Scheusal"). The Count asks her if she is mad. Does she know with whom she speaks? With whom I speak?, with whom I speak?, she snaps back. He is, she informs him, the lowest scoundrel in heaven or earth: "You, a gentleman, a Count? Ha!" On account of his black deeds, he is rather to be numbered in the class of lewd sailors who man the "rudder." Storace was fa- mously very direct in speech, her "peculiar characteristic bluntness" as Kelly put it.[60] Taken aback by the sheer ferocity of this verbal onslaught, the Count is reduced to dropping his family name into the conversation to remind her who he is—to no avail.

When Bartolo and Marzellina present the Count with the written evidence of Figaro's promise (act 2, scene 8), he at first thinks that it is waste paper, but the lawyer tells him that the tear is simply the effect of a violent electrical discharge. The Count reads the damning text out loud, reserving the right to judge, at which point Bartolo offers his services: if he cannot do it by the book ("secundum libellum"), he himself will hear the appeal. The Count hastily retorts that it will not come to this.

Impressive ancestries all round now come to light, starting with Figaro, whose own past history emerges when the Count tells him that he came from an orphanage in Madrid, a revelation that immediately awakens Marzellina's interest. The servant's distinguishing mark is not to be found on his right arm; instead, he is asked to present his left ear for public inspection: "Erlauben sie mir (zu Fig.) ihr linkes Ohr zu besehen." Marzellina immediately recognizes the signs of an accident that her young child, not yet six months old, had suffered from the broken glass of a coach: "und das zerbrochene Wagenglaß zerschnitte ihm das linke Ohr." Figaro has been taking good care to keep this

---

60. Kelly, *Reminiscences*, vol. 1, 244. The Irishman was much struck by the manner in which she had requested the emperor to fetch a glass of water for her. Link, *Arias for Nancy Storace*, xvi, cites another example of her plain speaking, taken sometimes as outright rudeness.

unfortunate defect hidden. The humor seems to be at Mozart's expense, his problem being a congenitally malformed lobe.

Dittersdorf goes to considerable lengths to fill in the backstory of Figaro's parentage. Further satire of the cast of *Le nozze di Figaro* appears to be embedded in a series of monologues. Marzellina is first to explain. In the original production, she was played by the Frenchwoman Maria Mandini. Dittersdorf selected for her birth-name, Isabella von Montarez, possibly referencing Mont Ares to the north of the Pyrenees.[61] Her story, if satirical, implies the cavalier treatment of a child. When her son was one year old, she had to leave for Paris in a rush in order to visit a rich aunt in her final hours, and so she placed him in the temporary care of an institution. Expecting a three-month stay, she ended up remaining for four years, staking her claim to the money, forgetting to forward the second year's fee to the orphanage, a regrettable lapse, as the Count's father had since offered her boy a place in his household. In the meantime, a fire had destroyed all the placement records and legal documentation, rendering him untraceable. After a near-fatal illness, her quest seemingly at an end, she had returned to Seville and changed her name. When pressed, she reveals the name of her deceased husband, Captain von Villanuova, who turns out to be Bartolo. He in turn embarks upon a lengthy tale of a battle wound, a premature obituary, and a voluntary name change. His research had uncovered Marzellina in Paris, but he had been unable to trace her further. Domenico Mombelli, born in Villanova Monferrato in Piedmont, may be implicated in the satire, but the allusion, if any, is obscure.

The discovery of Figaro's respectable parentage places an obstacle in the way of his forthcoming nuptials: the all-important matter of class. Marzellina would not dream of his marrying a mere chambermaid. This new impasse forces Susanna to reveal a secret that she has been hoping to take to the grave. She, too, is of good birth, her name, Susanna Malabini, being a punning reference to her failed marriage: "Mal-abbini" (*abbinare*, to go with) hints at a bad match. After the death of her parents, she had taken the decision to disown her aristocratic origins and find employment: "better to live comfortably in the middle class than starve as an aristocrat" ("ich lieber im Bürgerstand gemächlich leben; als im Adelstand erhungern wollte"). Marzellina wonders how she can bring herself to so degrade her status, but Susanna responds that the name Malabini would in any case have died out; the line cannot continue through a daughter. She reiterates her aphorism in favor of the industrious, a sentiment guaranteed to meet with warm imperial approval and therefore

---

61. Marzellina takes her leave of Susanna (act 1, scene 4) in French: "adieu!"

worth direct repetition. Now that Susanna's good breeding has been established, Marzellina and Bartolo abruptly change their tune; they have no further objection to their son marrying her.

All these discoveries are drawn together in a quartet that appears to be a
sendup of a passage in Mozart's sestetto "Riconosci in questo amplesso," according to Kelly the composer's favorite piece in the opera. The witty verbal
patter in the central section ("sua madre? tua madre? suo padre? tuo padre?")
sustains the whole of Dittersdorf's ensemble:

Fig.	O liebster Papa!
	O liebster Mama!
Sus.	O liebster Papa!
	O liebster Mama!
Bart.	Bin auch dein Papa.
Marz.	Auch deine Mama.
	Ist auch dein Papa
Bart.	Ist deine Mama

Mozart's parody of a sentimental recognition scene—the exclamations "sua /
tua madre?" and "suo / tuo padre?" occur a total of thirty-four times—turns
what could have been "a moment of intense emotion" into "a piece of farce."[62]
Whether Dittersdorf further exaggerated this lampoon of sentimentality or
referenced Mozart's music remains uncertain in the absence of his score.[63]

The Countess's aria is combined with the letter-writing episode (act 2,
scene 9). No historical source identifies friction between Laschi and Storace,
the evenly matched *prime donne*, but some of the revisions to the musical text
in the autograph and early copies of *Le nozze di Figaro* imply that Mozart may
have found this particular operatic triangle—the composer and his two leading
ladies—difficult to manage.[64] Such as it is, the evidence lies in an inversion of

---

62. Castelvecchi, *Sentimental Opera*, 194–99.

63. In *Die Liebe im Narrenhause*, there may be a fleeting allusion to the opening gesture of the
overture to *Le nozze di Figaro*. The thematic content of this fragment is sufficiently generic to
suggest a fortuitous resemblance, yet it comes at an undeniably ear-catching moment in the
asylum scene (the start of the septet). Dittersdorf was a calculating individual, and it cannot
therefore be ruled out that he was hoping to raise a laugh at his rival's expense when strains
of *Figaro* herald an attempt to feign madness of an altogether darker kind than that on show
during the "crazy" day.

64. Zinzendorf noted in his diary on 18 November that Laschi was complaining about her
role in the new opera by Storace, her rival's brother (*Gli equivoci*), but gives no further details.
Link, *National Court Theatre*, 283.

their relative vocal tessituras in ensembles, made part way through the composition of the opera, and in a late change of mind over the award of the prestigious genre title of rondò—a widely recognized accolade for the prima donna. The systematic scratching out of this word in the orchestral parts betokens an issue of perceived significance.[65] Following Beaumarchais, Da Ponte does no more than hint at the growing warmth between the Countess and her maid following a very brief and quickly resolved spat. Dittersdorf raises the emotional temperature considerably. On the face of it, the two women become affectionate in a matter of minutes. The exaggerated emotions caricature feminine sentimentality in opera; they may also depict an amusingly implausible friendship between the rival *prime donne* of the Italian troupe.

Susanna begins by addressing the Countess with the utmost formality as though addressing an equal at a high-society soirée; she has news of importance to impart that the Countess should not hear from the lips of another: "Ganz sicher würden es mir euer Exzellenz ungnädig nehmen, wenn sie eine Sache die mich angeht, und von so grossen Wichtigkeit ist, eher aus einem andern Mund als aus den meinigen erführen." The Countess responds "with condescending benevolence" ("mit herablassender Gütigkeit"): "Ey [again a clear signal that a specific satirical reference is imminent] liebes Mädchen!" Is she about to break further bad news? ("bringst du mir schon wieder eine Hiobspost?") The reference is to Dittersdorf's oratorio *Hiob*, performed in Vienna during Lent 1786. The Countess is delighted that she has her maid's confidence and urges her to pour out her "Jeremiasklagen" on her breast. Susanna, kissing the Countess's hand, has no bad tidings to impart; rather, joy is flowing through her innermost soul. Figaro, she reports, is of noble extraction but will marry her nonetheless. The Countess interjects a "tender warning" ("zärtlichen Warnung"); surely she cannot imagine that this is a piece of good fortune or that a joyful future beckons? (Storace's disastrous first marriage is perhaps the subtext here.) Susanna responds that she, too, comes from an old and respected family, which is news to her mistress. As evidence, she has her baptismal certificate, which the Countess reads and exclaims "in [a state of] the utmost ecstasy" ("in der äußersten Extasie") how charmed she is. Susanna falls before the Countess, who promptly raises her "dearest Malabini" up, unable to countenance such a servile gesture. As a commoner by birth herself, she sets little store by her title; moreover, their friendship should be sealed with a physical embrace: "come into my arms, give me your sweet friendship, and be assured of mine for ever."

---

65. After a detailed evaluation of the evidence, Edge, "Mozart's Viennese Copyists," 1578–83, concluded that Storace's "vanity" may have been driving some of these changes.

A favorite piece after the revival of *Figaro* in 1789 was the letter duet "Che soave zeffiretto," but it perhaps had yet to achieve this status, since Dittersdorf made no attempt to emulate it. The note, signed "Ihre Susanna Malabini," indicates that she will meet him in the garden at exactly 10:00 p.m. In a short scene with the Count (act 2, scene 22), Susanna covertly passes the letter to him. He asks his wife to join him in the festivities but is rebuffed. She would much prefer to stay indoors and converse with her maid.

The scene in which Cherubin is revealed (act 2, scene 14) begins with the village girls singing their chorus. As the Countess has declined an invitation to accompany her husband, her place is taken by Marzellina; the Mandini couple is once more on display. On cue, the Count pricks his finger on the pin attached to Susanna's note and throws it away, whereupon Marzellina and Bartolo observe closely as he reads his secret missive. Seeing how alarmed he suddenly becomes at the loss of the pin, Bartolo retrieves it. As he tells Marzellina, he is in no doubt that it is "from a beauty" (cue laughter), but he wonders which one it could possibly be? Maria Mandini appears to have several rivals for Stefano's affections. The girls start to repeat a strophe of their chorus, but the Count puts an abrupt stop to this, observing that "much singing ruins the chest" ("vieles Singen verdirbt die Brust"). The collective response from the girls and Cherubin is "Ne!" In recompense for their efforts, the Count invites them all to the ball. Will they come? "Ja!" Will their parents raise any objections? "Ne!" Will it be acceptable if the Count invites the village lads? "Ja!" It is becoming clear that the ball will be the climax of the opera.

Thomas's curiosity is piqued by a girl he does not recognize. He quizzes his daughter, forcing her to reveal Cherubin's identity. Another gratuitous epithet for the page makes its appearance: "Der lose Pursche, der so genäschig ist"—the dissolute lad who loves his delicacies.[66] Annoyed by this fastidiousness, Thomas decides to betray him to the Count. Lieschen is sent to fetch a military cap, and while she is away, Basilio claims credit for arranging the "*illuminazione*," as a reward for which he is presented with a watch.[67] When Lieschen returns with the cap, it is placed on Cherubin's head, but the Count again demonstrates that he is a dullard, commenting on how well the young girl looks in military headgear. In a second attempt to enlighten him, Cherubin is frogmarched into his presence. The moment

---

66. A glimpse of Mozart as a fine diner and connoisseur of delicacies is given by Leopold Mozart in a letter of 21 February 1785, which reports a meal at which meats (on a Friday and with a priest present) were followed by oysters and delicious glacé fruits.

67. Kelly, *Reminiscences*, vol. 1, 246, recalled that he "wore two watches (as was the custom of the country)."

of revelation is dramatic. Thomas asks the assembled company: "do you no longer recognize the apricot thief?" ("kennen sie den Aprikosendieb nicht mehr?") The instant response from all present is "Cherubin?" This takes up a comment made in passing by the gardener (act 1, scene 18), when asked to identify the figure who has just leapt from the window; it was, he stated, the page who the previous year had devoured "the large apricots" ("die großen Aprikosen"). With the imperial gardens open to the public—one of Joseph's most popular policies—it is easy to imagine that a youth might have been caught in the act of consuming some fruit. Yet Dittersdorf attributes the misdemeanor twice to Cherubin, with the possible innuendo that Mozart himself had been accused of fruit theft, that he had been pardoned, and that it was common knowledge. No such incident is recorded, yet it bears an uncanny resemblance to the central episode of Eduard Mörike's novella *Mozart auf der Reise nach Prag* (1856), in which the absentminded composer, passing through Moravia on his way to Prague, is caught by a gardener after picking an orange.

The revelation of Cherubin duly shocks the Count. Dittersdorf embroiders the fiction that the page has already complied with the order to leave for Seville. Figaro has to think quickly. He sticks to his story and prompts Cherubin's answers as the inquisition begins: he was on the road to . . . that's right . . . Seville, when his steed . . . yes indeed . . . went out of control. Having set him off, Figaro is astounded by the page's fluency as a brazen liar ("Der kleine Belzebub kann lügen"); not much more than a cannon-shot from Seville, his horse was alarmed by a bullock and galloped all the way back to the castle. Cherubin (Mozart) appears to be too slight to retain control of his horse.[68] He delivers his story with composure, feigning innocence. The Count is taken in by this explanation—he, too, has observed that the black charger is shy—but he points out that Cherubin has nonetheless committed two offenses: his failure to notify him of his return; and his lack of shame as a soldier in donning a dress. Cherubin, simulating repentance, pleads that if the Count will let him off just this once, he will be a reformed character for life. Figaro is again amazed at how the little "wheedler" is able to handle the Count: "Uiber die kleine Schmeichelkatze! wie er ihn herum zu drehen weiß." In deciding upon a punishment, the Count shows leniency but opts for something that will be painful enough: instead of attending the dance ("statt zu Tanzen"), Cherubin must be held in a locked room.

---

68. Little is known of Mozart as a horse-owner, other than that he sold his old nag ("Kleper") for 14 ducats in the autumn of 1791. Spaethling, *Mozart's Letters*, 439.

Dittersdorf reinforces his characterization of the page as a compulsive dancer, willing to take any action necessary (including physical violence) to get to go to the ball. Cherubin pretends to accept his punishment meekly, all desire to dance having left him anyway; rather than give the Count a moment's offense, he would give up dancing for life. But to himself he mutters darkly: nevertheless I *will* dance ("Und ich werde doch tanzen"). His public contrition again has an effect, as the Count observes that the lad has a good heart but is a little frivolous. (Mozart may be annoying but he has the gift of conciliating men of power.) Thomas is commanded to take Cherubin to the room attendant with orders that a bed be placed in the Countess's antechamber, the room locked, and the page confined in it. With its ready supply of dresses, to say nothing of an unbarred window, this proves an unfortunate choice for his captivity. In order to make certain that he will be able to escape from custody in time, though, Cherubin threatens Figaro that should he fail to arrange it, he will, upon his return as an officer, cut a wing from his body ("so haue ich ihnen einen Flügel vom Leib"). The image of the butterfly is turned back upon its author, who hastily agrees to see what he can do after muttering to himself: "just look at the little 'Skanderbeck.'" This casts the slight figure of the page as the celebrated fifteenth-century Albanian hero Skanderbeg, by repute a fearsome warlord who resisted the Ottomans, as Joseph II was soon to find himself doing. Cherubin is led away, accompanied by all the girls, and for the moment, the plotters appear to be checkmated.

The problematic sequence in act 4 of *Le nozze di Figaro* leading up to Figaro's aria is recast completely. In a comic scene (act 2, scene 15), the Count recruits Lieschen to return the pin to Susanna with the cryptic message that at 10:00 o'clock the moon will come out. Lieschen casually wonders what would happen if someone were to offer her a coin, perhaps a "Reale" or a "Filippo," to divulge her secret? The Count has no option but to fork out a gold "Dublone" to ensure her silence. In the next scene (act 2, scene 16), Marzellina and Bartolo reflect on the role Susanna is playing in the plot.[69] The lawyer's idiotic suggestion that the note might be a written reprimand from a jealous Countess is slapped down. Why, in that case, would he be kissing it so ardently? But neither of them can believe that it is from Susanna. For Marzellina, it would be unthinkable; for Bartolo, it is simply a question of good breeding: "Sie ist ja von guter Extraktion." Nonetheless, they decide to investigate further, and

---

69. The room is furnished with two tables on each of which are two lights. Writing materials have been placed on one—it is not clear why this is mentioned, as the dictation scene has already taken place.

when Lieschen enters (act 2, scene 17), she is questioned about her mission as postgirl for the Count. It is not difficult to elicit information.

The earlier satire on Albertus Magnus is revisited, allowing Dittersdorf to let rip with a particularly choice epithet for his rival. The Count's cryptic message, which Lieschen is instructed to repeat to Susanna, is: "the moon comes out around ten tonight." This puzzles her because she knows that it will be a new moon. How can the moon hide itself, she wonders? She has been told by Cherubin that physical invisibility is not possible, but it is now clear to her that Albertus Magnus knows much better than the "little-milk-soup-face" ("das Milchsuppengesichtchen"). We are to understand that Cherubin (Mozart) has not merely a pallid countenance but also, depending on the ingredients of this doubtless tasty but not necessarily visually attractive recipe, one somewhat pock-marked.[70] With his pale visage, Dittersdorf's page is the antithesis of Da Ponte's Cherubino, who has a roseate hue: "quel vermiglio donnesco color." The introduction of the moon as an example of invisibility satirizes Paisiello's *Il mondo della luna*. This opera had been in contention for imperial favor with Dittersdorf's *Der Apotheker* at a critical juncture of the intertroupe contest. When he returned from his long absence from Vienna in late October 1786, Joseph II was faced with a significant decision: on 20 October he had the choice of attending either this work by the much admired Paisiello, new to Vienna, or Dittersdorf's hit success. Not one to fudge the issue by putting in an appearance at both for part of the evening, Joseph decided to grace the Italian opera with his presence, and although two days later at a performance of Dittersdorf's Singspiel, he offered its composer and cast a great show of support, the order of precedence was clear. Despite this, *Il mondo della luna* was a flop, disappearing almost immediately from the schedules, but that did not protect it from Dittersdorf's satirical imagination. It ends with a starlit sky featuring a brilliant full moon that—the implication hardly needed to be spelt out—would vanish without trace as quickly as the opera itself.

Following the departure of Lieschen on her errand, Marzellina and Bartolo discuss the information obtained from her in a manner suggestive of a further satirical attack on Francesco Bussani. Bartolo again expresses contempt for the intellectual abilities of women; either they know nothing of the art of making deductions, or they do not want to understand it. Unable to convince his wife, he exhibits exasperation at the way women come to each other's support. In *Le nozze di Figaro*, Bartolo is not present to hear this statement of

---

70. It is clear that Mozart's face suffered some permanent scarring from his childhood smallpox, although the degree of disfigurement is uncertain.

female solidarity, whereas in Dittersdorf's reworking, he appears to consider himself a victim of it.

Figaro, now that he has been revealed as the young Herr von Villanuova, has no cause to inveigh against privilege; fortune is capricious, and the stupid are often the ones favored. The lead-in to his aria ("Figaro, Figaro! bist du dieses Glückes wohl werth?"), makes a clear rhetorical nod in the direction of the great soliloquy in Beaumarchais: "O femme! femme! femme! créature faible et décevante"; "Suzon, Suzon, Suzon, que tu me donnes de tourmens!" The end of the aria conjures up the image of Benucci, star dancer in the musical cast of *Le nozze di Figaro*: "Tralla, lara, lara. (Hüpft bei dem letzten Vers herum)." The instruction "he hops around" perhaps implies a sendup.

In his lighthearted mood, Figaro launches into an extraordinary flight of fantasy, which combines an extended satire of the greedy and gullible music teacher with a further attack on the follies of rank. Basilio enters and wonders why the servant seems so upbeat. News has spread that he is a gentleman but not yet the still more sensational tidings that he is in fact a royal prince, first-born of the king of Persia. Nor is it yet common knowledge that Susanna Malabini is actually the only daughter of the emperor of China. This Basilio can well believe on account of her appearance: "perche Susannetta ha propria una facia chinese." Figaro is thus in a position to reward the music teacher by offering him the post of "Directeur des Spectacles." He will require plenty of money to maintain his position, and he is informed that diamonds are the currency in Figaro's realm. Will he be content with two hundred bags-full? The response is: "soncontentissimo!" By his own admission, the original Basilio, Kelly, enjoyed flashing his diamond rings around.[71]

Basilio performs a catalogue aria (in Italian), "Son Conte, e son Marchese," the end of which enumerates the culinary and sexual delights to come:

Prosciuti, caponi
Caffe, maccaroni
E torte e pasticci
Legume salcicci
Salami con aglio
Ed uno Seraglio

---

71. Kelly, *Reminiscences*, vol. 1, 246: "At this period of my life, I was rather vain, and very fond of fine clothes; indeed, my greatest expense was the decoration of my precious person. I wore every evening full dress embroidered coats, either gold, silver, or silk . . . and a diamond ring on each of my little fingers; thus decked out, I had not of course the least appearance of a Paddy."

Con cente ragazze
Di persiche razze
Che gioia, che festa
La la la ra la!
Mi gira la testa
Non so dove sta.

[Hams and capons, coffee and macaroni, cakes and pastries, legumes, sausages, and salami with garlic, and a seraglio with a hundred girls of Persian extraction. What joy, what a feast. La, la, la, ra, la. My head is spinning. I don't know where it is.]

Food was standard fare for a catalogue aria and particularly appropriate for Kelly, who relished and often recorded his meals.

The scene ends with another vignette for the diversion of Joseph II. Dittersdorf had been in Vienna on 30 December 1786 when the emperor issued an edict forbidding all forms of bowing, hand-kissing, and curtsying, perhaps under the influence of the English Calvinist prison reformer John Howard, whom he met shortly before the announcement.[72] Such practices are thoroughly ridiculed. Once the gullible Basilio has learnt of Figaro's regal status, bowing and scraping will be the order of the day ("mit vielen Bücklingen"). Having awarded his new impresario a huge salary, Figaro (Benucci) with appropriate royal gravitas ("mit königlicher Gravität") instructs him to fall to his feet and kiss the dust from his shoes.[73] Basilio readily obliges and kisses Figaro's toes: "(fällt Figaro zu Füssen, und küsset seine Zähen.)"

With the unexpected introduction of a royal Persian ancestry for Figaro, the astute Dittersdorf was dropping in a gentle reminder of his oratorio *Ester*, enjoyed by Joseph in 1773 and heard again by him on 22 December 1785. The Persian kingdom is represented as an idyllic place where the winds are calm ("tranquilli i venti") and the sky serene ("serena il Ciel").[74] The contemporary subtext to the story of Esther, more pertinent in 1785 than it would have been

---

72. Beales, *Against the World 1780–1790*, 437.

73. An anecdote doing the rounds exploited Benucci's effectiveness in imperial roles and related an encounter between "fellow" emperors. *Musikalische Korrespondenz der teutschen Filarmonischen Gesellschaft* (29 December 1790), no. 26, col. 208: "Zu Mailand besuchte der Kaiser Joseph II. vor einigen Jahren den vornehmsten Operisten, welcher Tags zuvor eine Kaiserrolle vortrefflich gespielt hatte. Der Monarch traf ihn in völligem Negligee an; worüber der Sänger in große Verlegenheit gerieth. Aber der Kaiser befreite ihn bald davon, indem er sagt: 'Das thut nichts: wir Kaiserleute machen keine Ceremonien unter einander.'"

74. *Ester, ossia la liberatrice del popolo giudaico nella Persia*, Vienna, 1785, 32.

in 1773, is that it depicts a kingdom in which a ruler is taking action to improve the lot of his Jewish subjects.

The fantasy that Susanna is the daughter of the Chinese emperor seems to allude to *Prima la musica* rather than Metastasio's "Chinese" libretto. At one point, Tonina, the opera buffa star, disputes that she is mad, notwithstanding her appearance, strangely clothed ("stranamente vestita"), with staring eyes ("gli occhi stralunati"), a fixed gaze ("la guardatura fissa"), and a yellow face ("il viso giallo"). The explanation is that she is the bride arriving from China: "La bella Tonina / Che vien dalla China." Working from the libretto a year or more after the event, Dittersdorf perhaps assumed (as others have since) that Storace rather than Coltellini was cast as Tonina, in view of her acknowledged status as prima buffa of the troupe.

A distinctive feature of Dittersdorf's plotting in *Die Hochzeit des Figaro* is his insertion of several scenes for Figaro and Susanna. On one level, this marked a return to Beaumarchais, who included a sprightly conversation between them (act 2, scene 1) as they reflect on their changed circumstances. But in focusing on this relationship, Dittersdorf may have been intending to have some fun at the expense of Benucci and Storace, whose affair was reported to have ended in February 1787.[75] The tone is set in their first duet, in which Susanna describes Figaro as her "Goldjunge" (blue-eyed boy). A longer scene following Figaro's encounter with Basilio (act 2, scene 20) sees further strife. Figaro has committed a most grave crime; has he not denied that women have understanding? In turn, he wants to know why she called him a "Dummkopf." (In effect, this expands greatly on Susanna's comment in the first scene of *Le nozze di Figaro*: "Perchè io son la Susanna e tu sei pazzo.") Figaro is to be doubly chastised: his curiosity will not be assuaged; and he is about to be seriously provoked. Further teasing ensues before he arrives at the satirical heart of the matter, insisting that he has told Susanna countless times that he does *not* love her for her beautiful face ("schönen Gesicht") or her charming figure ("reizenden Gestalt") but only for her warm heart, honest character, and sublime intellect. At this point, character development of the maid probably tips over into satire of Storace's appearance, by no means universally appreciated.[76] Dittersdorf had landed an early blow on this

---

75. Link, *National Court Theatre*, 288: "16 Fevrier: Le soir a *l'opera Trofonio*. Benucci etant enroué [hoarse] il fut mal rendu. La Storace lui est infidele et s'en va avec Lord Barnard." The way this is put almost suggests a shouting match!

76. Pezzl, *Skizze von Wien*, vol.3, 425: "aber ihre Figur ist nicht vortheilhaft: ein kleines dikes Geschöpf, ohne irgend einem weiblichen körperlichen Reiz, ein paar grosse wenig sprechende Augen ausgenommen."

subject when Marzellina in her scene with the maid (act 1, scene 4), cruelly implies that rather than remaining faithful to his lovely wife, the Count is set on pursuing young women who are "very ugly" ("viel häßlicher"). The quarrel ends with Figaro leaving "for ever."

In the scene before the finale (act 2, scene 21), the Countess is observed making her way to the rendezvous. A note in the text requires her to dress from head to toe like Susanna so that the audience cannot spot the deception. As this seems slightly superfluous, it could represent a coded comment on the production of *Le nozze di Figaro*. The act 2 finale begins by listing the participants in the usual manner, but there is no mention of Basilio or Cherubin. When the Count arrives at his assignation, he makes a declaration of love to the woman he hopes will become his amour, accusing his wife of being too cold. Upon being unmasked, her cutting response seems to confirm this: "are you embarrassed, Count? that's what happens when you err" ("Nichtwahr, Herr Graf, sie sind verwirrt? So geht es, wenn man sich verirrt"). This is very far indeed from the transcendent reconciliation that the ending of *Figaro* came to represent.[77] Still more perfunctory is the renewal of relations between Susanna and Figaro: "*Sus.* Und du, junges Herrchen! Was sagst du dazu? *Fig.* Das Ende vom Liede schenkt mir wieder Ruh."

But all this is merely the prelude to Dittersdorf's denouement. Unheralded in the initial stage directions, two other characters enter. Everyone hides in the arbor to see who is coming. Cherubin saunters in, got up as a woman, the Count's plan to detain him in his wife's antechamber having backfired. In a reprise of his earlier escape, Cherubin has made off in a disguise that he hopes will enable him to gain admittance to the ball after all ("durch die ich noch heute den Ball werde sehn"). Luckily for him, the coffers containing women's clothing had been unlocked. The galant Basilio then wanders in to take the air, it being such a beautiful night. He spies a woman and, observing that "she" is unaccompanied, offers to escort her, noting that she is a "*bella ragazza*" (displaying his Irish charm), but the unknown young lady first wants to know who he is. The diamond-obsessed Basilio proudly responds: "Ik bin eine Conte, bin ein Cavalier, Ab *molti Diamanti*, so viel Sie begehr." Cherubin takes Basilio by the hands and dances, and for a moment *Le nozze di Basilio*— Kelly was unmarried—appears to be on the cards. But Figaro intervenes to perform the final revelation with the aid of a lantern, commenting: let us see

---

77. Will, "Ambivalence of Mozart's Countess," 31–54, questions the validity of the traditional interpretation.

who the vulture Basilio is to wed. Insouciant to the last, Cherubin simply takes off his costume (one form of crossdressing—the character's—is replaced by another, the performer's) and addresses the music master warmly in his own language: "*O caro Basilio.*" As he observes, the young lady has vanished and her place has been taken by "the young rascal" ("die kleine Spitzbub"). The page thus rounds off the long-running gag at his expense by acknowledging its truth, "Mozart" assenting to Dittersdorf's depiction of his character. A distant intrada announces the dance. The drama ends with a concluding jibe surely directed at Mozart. Everyone remarks: "Wir wollen nun tanzen, so viel jeder kann"—we are now going to dance, insofar as each can—a singularly loaded comment with which to end an opera. The page is perhaps not so good on the dance floor as he thinks he is. In portraying his rival as a fanatical dancer, Dittersdorf went beyond the irrepressibility of the page in Beaumarchais; his Cherubin is an obsessive.

DITTERSDORF'S SATIRE OFFERED a sustained assault on the preposterous follies of title and lineage, clearly calculated to win approval from Joseph II, who would also have relished seeing his celebrated virtuosi being got at. There is no clear sign that Mozart's imperial appointment, widely reported in the press at the end of 1787, was in his mind, with disappointment driving the sarcasm, but the degree to which he ransacked his lexicon of invective for epithets to throw at his rival (via the page) is impressive.

It is not possible to establish with any certainty when *Die Hochzeit des Figaro* was first performed. Dittersdorf ran his own small opera troupe in Silesia in which *Hieronymus Knicker* was tried out. It is conceivable that *Figaro* was also staged there during the summer of 1788, but Dittersdorf had his eye on a more prestigious venue. When it became apparent that the work could not be staged at the National Theater in Vienna owing to the closure of the Singspiel troupe, he made alternative arrangements, offering it as the first work in a short season in Brünn. A review in the *Brünner Zeitung* was favorable, praising the beauty of the music without mentioning the performers. The opera had provided the public with a good spectacle.[78] In its brief summary of the most successful operas of the Brünn season, the *Theater-Kalendar*

---

78. *Brünner Zeitung* (6 January 1789), no. 2, 16: "Verflossenen Donnerstag den 1 Januar ward in dem königlich städtischen Nationaltheater hier in Brünn eine neue deutsche Oper zu 2 Akten: die Hochzeit des Figaro, vom Herrn von Dittersdorf in Musik gesetzt, und nach dem Französischen frei bearbeitet, unter seiner Anführung mit allgemeinem Beifall aufgeführt. Die Schönheit der Musik wird von allen Kennern gerühmt und ist ganz des Künstlers würdig, der er sich so sehr angelegen seyn läßt, zur Unterstützung der Bühne und zum Vergnügen des Publikums zu arbeiten."

named *Hochzeit des Figaro*, along with *Der Apotheker* and *Una cosa rara*. All three operas had been given often, always pleasing the audience.[79] Apart from this brief period of interest in Moravia, Dittersdorf's *Figaro* disappeared from view so completely that it is missing in lists of stage works appended to early biographical accounts of its composer.[80]

---

79. *Theater-Kalendar auf das Jahr 1790*, 108: Brünn: "Opern, die oft gegeben, und immer mit Vergnügen gesehen werden: Doktor und Apotheker, Hochzeit des Figaro vom Herrn von Dittersdorf; und Una cosa rara."

80. Arnold, *Gallerie der berühmten Tonkünstler*, vol. 1, 146.

4

In Time of War

THE VIENNA *DON GIOVANNI*

THE NEXT PHASE of the struggle between Italian and German opera was played out against the backdrop of the Austro-Turkish War. The opera buffa troupe came under increasing threat of closure and then was served with notice of dismissal, only to be reprieved at the last moment, following a significant military victory. The year began with a splendid occasion. Despite the retrenchment in theatrical budgets necessitated by the looming war, Joseph decided that no expense should be spared in providing sets and costumes for the festive work *Axur*, commissioned to celebrate what was anticipated to be the most important dynastic event of his reign: the marriage between Franz and Elisabeth von Württemberg.[1] When he heard *Axur* in the theater, he was delighted and offered Salieri a public vote of thanks.[2] In a posthumous summary of his musical tastes, this work was identified as his favorite opera, a verdict with which few at the time would have disagreed.[3] Da Ponte also received some acclaim; one report described him and the composer as the "favorites" of Vienna.[4] With only a few weeks left before its closure, the Singspiel troupe

---

1. *Leipziger Zeitungen* (17 December 1787), no. 247, 1430: "17 neue Decorationen und 114 neue Kleidungsstücke im besten Costume."

2. *Kurfürstlich gnädigst privilegirte Münchner Zeitung* (1 February 1788), no, 19, 74: Wien, vom 26. Jäner (aus Privatnachrichten.): "Salieri! wir sind es, die ihnen für die Unterhaltung, die sie uns durch ihre schöne Komposizion verschaft haben, danken wollen." Mozart's participation in the festive celebrations is not recorded, although he may have contributed to a masonic musical academy on 12 January. *Auszug aller Europäischen Zeitungen* (31 January 1788), no. 27, 422. Black, "Masonic musical academy in Vienna," in Edge and Black, *Mozart*.

3. *Musikalische Korrespondenz* (1790), no. 4, col.30: 28 July 1790: "Salieri's Axur Rè d'Ormus' war Seine Lieblingsoper."

4. *Carlsruher Zeitung* (23 January 1788), no. 10, 47: Wien, vom 12 Jan.: "Axur Re d'Ormus von da Ponte und Salieri, die itzigen Lieblinge des musikalischen Publikums in Wien!"

presented *Richard Löwenherz*, a German translation of Grétry's opera, as its festive offering.[5]

In the weeks that followed the end of the opera season, Vienna witnessed a flowering of oratorio performances. An intensification of an existing tradition rather than a new one, this stemmed from the particular circumstances in the city: the conclusion of the intertroupe contest and the fast approaching war. Table 4.1 lists oratorio nights, a significantly larger number than recorded the previous year. Performances sponsored by the Tonkünstler-Societät were usually given unopposed at the National Theater, while oratorios in private residences were scheduled on play nights—during Lent, the theater company continued to perform on Sundays, Mondays, Tuesdays, and Thursdays—in order not to split the audience for music or the available performing forces. Large-scale musical productions of this kind required at least one full-scale rehearsal, unadvertised but often open to at least selected members of the public.[6] A few "concerts" for which no program details are known are included, as during Lent these sometimes featured selections from an oratorio.

By tradition, the Tonkünstler-Societät presented two pairs of fundraising events, one in Advent, the other just before the start of Holy Week.[7] These were magnificent occasions, and an invitation to perform between the acts was highly prized by instrumentalists.[8] As it was the society's practice to recruit the best singers, whether Italian or German, individuals from the Singspiel troupe tended to be experienced vocalists rather than actor-singers. At the end of the first year of the intertroupe contest, with the focus firmly on the rival Italian and German factions, the Tonkünstler-Societät's performances (30 March and 1 April 1787) were politically well balanced: an unidentified cantata by Georg Christoph Wagenseil, a Viennese composer of the previous generation, and an Italian import, Giuseppe Gazzaniga's *I profeti ad Calvario*.[9]

---

5. *Königlich privilegirte Stettinische Zeitung* (28 January 1788), no. 8: Wien, vom 9. Januarius. As yet, there is no comprehensive study of how mutual repertoire recommendations influenced the program choices of the Habsburg brothers in Vienna, Florence, Monza, and Bonn. Ferdinand's 1787 autumn season (following his weeks in Vienna during the autumn of 1786) was unmistakably Viennese: *Una cosa rara*; *Il barbiere di Siviglia*; and *Le nozze di Figaro*. The fourth work, *Riccardo cor di leone*, marked the start of what was hoped would become a significant initiative: the translation of popular *opéras comiques* into Italian. Castelvecchi, *Sentimental Opera*, 161.

6. According to the *Musikalischer Almanach für Deutschland* (1789), 121, two full rehearsals contributed to the success of C. P. E. Bach's *Die Auferstehung*.

7. Pohl, *Denkschrift aus Anlass des hundertjährigen Bestehens der Tonkünstler-Societät*.

8. Maria Theresia Paradis performed a concerto before taking her leave of Vienna for a concert tour. *Auszug aller europäischen Zeitungen* (January 1788), no. 7, 102.

9. Morrow, *Concert Life*, 268.

Table 4.1 Oratorio performances in Vienna (December 1787 to March 1788)

Date	Composer	Title	Location	Sponsor	Conductor	Comments
22 Dec	Kozeluch	*Moise in Egitto*	Burgtheater	Tonkünstler-Societät	Kozeluch	
23 Dec	Kozeluch	*Moise in Egitto*	Burgtheater	Tonkünstler-Societät	Kozeluch	
8 Feb	Pasticcio	*Il convito di Baldassare*	Burgtheater	Morichelli benefit		
9 Feb	Pasticcio	*Il convito di Baldassare*	Burgtheater	Morichelli benefit		
13 Feb	Pasticcio	*Il convito di Baldassare*	Burgtheater	Morichelli benefit		
14 Feb		Concert (unidentified program)		Prince Galitzin		Play night at the National Theater
16 Feb	Pasticcio	*Il convito di Baldassare*	Burgtheater	Calvesi benefit		
25 Feb?	C. P. E. Bach	*Die Auferstehung und Himmelfahrt Christi*		Count Johann Eszterházy	Mozart	Play night at the National Theater Full rehearsal?
26 Feb	C. P. E. Bach	*Die Auferstehung und Himmelfahrt Christi*			Mozart	Play night at the National Theater
4 Mar	C. P. E. Bach	*Die Auferstehung und Himmelfahrt Christi*		[Gesellschaft der Associierten Cavaliere]	Mozart	Play night at the National Theater
6 Mar		Concert (unidentified program)		Prince Galitzin		Play night at the National Theater
7 Mar	C. P. E. Bach	*Die Auferstehung und Himmelfahrt Christi*	Burgtheater		Mozart	Play night at the National Theater

Date	Composer	Work	Venue	Organizer	Composer	Notes
9 Mar?	Handel	*Judas Maccabeus*		Count Johann Eszterházy	Mozart	Play night at the National Theater / Full rehearsal?
10 Mar?	Handel	*Judas Maccabeus*		Count Johann Eszterházy	Mozart	Play night at the National Theater
11 Mar?	Handel	*Judas Maccabeus*		Count Johann Eszterházy	Mozart	Play night at the National Theater
13 Mar		Concert (unidentified program)		Prince Galitzin		Play night at the National Theater
14 Mar?	Mombelli	*La morte e la deposizione della croce di Gesu Cristo*	Burgtheater	Tonkünstler-Societät	Salieri	Full rehearsal?
15 Mar	Mombelli	*La morte e la deposizione della croce di Gesu Cristo*	Burgtheater	Tonkünstler-Societät	Salieri	
16 Mar	Mombelli	*La morte e la deposizione della croce di Gesu Cristo*	Burgtheater	Tonkünstler-Societät	Salieri	
29 Mar		Concert (unidentified program)		Count Johann Eszterházy		Play night at the National Theater
30 Mar	Sacchini	*Jefte*		Venetian ambassador		Play night at the National Theater

Following the end of the opera season on 5 February 1788, there was a significant innovation. In place of individual academies, by convention awarded
to leading singers about to depart, three Italians, Morichelli, Stefano Mandini,
and Vincenzo Calvesi, chose to present an oratorio, the pasticcio *Il convito di
Baldassare*, as a collective benefit. Morichelli received the proceeds of three
performances (8, 9, and 13 February) and Calvesi one (16 February). Mandini
performed on all these nights, but for his own benefit on 15 February he arranged a traditional concert to which the other two singers contributed. With
Joseph's departure for the battlefield only days away (29 February), the choice
of an oratorio may have been made with him in mind. Following an overture
by Gluck, an acknowledgment of his recent passing, the pasticcio begins with a
chorus by Ferdinando Bertoni, saluting the heroic and (so far) invincible ruler:

> Viva, e regna, o Rege invitto,
> Grand' Eroe, speme d'Egitto,
> Raro esempio di valor.

> [Live and reign, undefeated King, great hero, hope of Egypt, rare
> example of valor.]

This sent a bracing message of support to the emperor from his Italian singers,
relieved for the moment to have been spared the axe.

A few days after *Il convito* had ended its short run, a series of German
oratorios was sponsored by Johann Eszterházy: the well-known performances
of C. P. E. Bach's *Die Auferstehung* and two evenings devoted to *Judas Maccabeus*,
the evidence for which has only recently come to light.[10] The date of the Handel
performances is not known. One possibility, recorded speculatively in Table
4.1, is 10 and 11 March, with a full rehearsal the previous day. Another is during
Holy Week itself, perhaps 18 and 19 March. With this Lenten series, the society
that later was called the Gesellschaft der Associierten Cavaliere emerged decisively into the historical record after an unknown number of formative years
in the shadows. The singers who participated in the Bach oratorio were all
from the Singspiel troupe: Adamberger, Lange, and Ignaz Saal, with Mozart
conducting. The newspaper report of *Judas Maccabeus* does not state explicitly
that he also directed these performances, although the implication that he did
is a strong one. In the context of the imminent war, this particular Handel oratorio was an apt choice; there is hardly a more militaristic text in the canon,

---

10. Black, "Mozart Conducts C. P. E. Bach's *Die Auferstehung* and Handel's *Judas Maccabeus*,"
in Edge and Black, *Mozart*.

and its selection could easily have been taken as a musical salutation to the emperor on behalf of the German troupe as he left to command his army, a counterpart to the opening chorus of *Il convito*.[11]

Notwithstanding the strained atmosphere as the intertroupe rivalry came to an end, it would probably be wrong to read this episode as divisive: the incursion of competing national identities, sharpened by the opera contest, into the hitherto neutral world of the charitable oratorio. More likely, it was an expression of national unity in the face of war. If nothing else, Eszterházy's German oratorio series provided end-of-season engagements for leading members of the Singspiel troupe to match those available to the Italians. But a new (if temporary) sense of common purpose is unmistakable, symbolized above all by the emperor's attitude toward the musicians affected by his decision to end German opera. In the way of the world, lowly orchestral players had to fend for themselves, but no leading singer was cast adrift.[12] Indeed, as shown in Table 4.2, even middle-ranking performers were given consideration.

Lippert was the only important singer to leave Vienna.[13] Adamberger retained his operatic salary (to add to the 800 gulden he continued to receive as an employee of the Hofkapelle). Arnold and the Saal couple were also transferred with no loss of pay. Lesser singers may have lost some ground. Ruprecht had been paid 700 gulden as an opera singer but was offered a position in the Hofkapelle at 400 gulden.[14] A similar pattern is seen with the women. Lange and Teyber transferred with no reduction in salary. Hümlin was dismissed but received a full year's pay in compensation. Rothe, however, had to make do with a benefit that, while it attracted a good audience, brought in less than her salary.[15]

---

11. A fragment of an intended arrangement of the chorus "See the conqu'ring hero comes" in the hand of Franz Jacob Freystädler appears on a sheet of sketches for K.558. Woodfield, "Mozart's Jupiter," 33.

12. Some instrumentalists found work in the commercial sector. Buch, "House Composers," 15, notes that the Theater auf der Wieden recruited musicians from the discontinued Singspiel in the National Theater.

13. His move to the Prussian capital significantly facilitated the transfer of Viennese Singspiels there. In his letter of recommendation, Stephanie praised him as a good comedian, possessed of no bad voice. Brachvogel, *Geschichte*, vol. 2, 101. Following his early application for a salary increase, he was acknowledged to be an excellent comedian, but questions were asked about his skill in "bravura" singing. The interesting comment is made that the music director will already have cured him of "his Vienna faults" ("Seine Wienen Unarten"). Brachvogel, *Geschichte*, vol. 2, 132.

14. Link, "Mozart's Appointment," 164.

15. Link, *National Court Theatre*, 298–99 and 119.

Table 4.2 The remuneration of singers dismissed
from the Singspiel

Singer	Singspiel salary (gulden)	New position	Salary/payoff (gulden)
Men			
Adamberger	1,333.20	Opera buffa	1,333.20
Saal (and wife)	1,200	Opera buffa	1,200
Arnold	1,200	German theater company	1,200
Lippert	1,200	New appointment in Berlin	
Women			
Langin [Lange]	1,706.40	Opera buffa	1,706.40
Arnoldin [Teyber]	1,000 [1,400 from September]	Opera buffa	1,400
Hümlin [Katharina Himlin]	1,000	A year's salary in compensation	1,000
Rothin [Klara Rothe]	800	Receipts from the German theater company performance on 13 January 1788 by order of the emperor	535.5

To a significant extent, these transfers represented the reunification of the operatic world by the man who had split it asunder in the cause of his contest between national genres. At this critical juncture, Joseph II showed himself a fair-minded employer by the standards of his time. Although bitterness over the fate of the troupe was expressed by supporters of its genre, a degree of generosity was shown to its personnel.[16] The severance costs for the singers were in part recouped by savings on posts that no longer needed to be filled elsewhere. It is arguable that lower-ranking singers in the opera buffa whose contracts were not renewed at the start of the 1788 season—Trentanove, Giovanna Nani and Rosalinda Molinelli—lost out as a result of the retrenchment, having to make way for performers being redeployed from the German troupe. In general, Joseph

---

16. Many years later, Müller acknowledged that Lange, Teyber [Arnold], Adamberger, Saal, and Arnold had all been retained for service in the surviving companies. Müller, *Abschied*, 277.

now seemed to be going out of his way to maintain public parity of esteem, as when he selected one singer from each troupe, Adamberger and Cavalieri, to perform at a meal in honor of Elizabeth; each received 100 ducats.[17]

Mozart's new court appointment, the result of several factors, not least the death of Gluck, may also be seen in the context of this reconfiguration of imperial musical structures, one aim of which was to preserve the national balance.[18] It would be going too far to claim that he owed his long-awaited post to the declaration of war or that he was appointed primarily as a German, but it is striking that almost his first act as an "imperial" musician was to produce two small pieces with war-related titles. The first was the contredanse *Die Bataille* (K.535). A more overtly political composition was his setting of Johann Wilhelm Gleim's "Ich möchte wohl der Kaiser sein" (K.539) for the actor Friedrich Baumann to perform at the Leopoldstadttheater.[19] He entered it in his catalogue on 5 March 1788 under the heading "Ein teutsches Kriegslied." Both pieces were published, by which time the dance had already acquired a more descriptive title, alluding to one of the main objectives in the forthcoming campaign: *Die Belagerung Belgrads.*[20] The manner in which these pieces head an advertisement in the *Wiener Zeitung* is eye-catching:

Neues Kriegslied
Eines deutsches Soldaten, des Herrn Kapellmeister Mozart in
wirkl. Diensten Sr. Majestät des Kaisers
Ich möchte wohl der Kaiser Seyn, mit allen Stimmen, 1 fl.
Detto im Klavierauszug, 12 kr.
Die Belagerung Belgrads, mit allen Stimmen, 1 fl.
Detta im Klavier auszug, 12 kr.[21]

---

17. *Stralsundische Zeitung* (29 January 1788), no. 13: Wien, den 14 Januar. Link, *Arias for Vincenzo Calvesi*, xxvii, cites a court document dated 8 January 1788 mandating the payment of double the usual 50 ducat fee on account of the special occasion.

18. Press opinion inclined to the view that he had been offered a position in Franz's household. *Prager Oberpostamtszeitung* (29 December 1787): "Der berühmte Kompositeur Mozard ist mit jährlichem 600 Gehalt zum Hofmusikus bey Sr. Königl. Hoheit dem Erzherzog Franz ernannt worden." See also *Strasburgische privilegirte Zeitung* (9 January 1788), no. 4, 28: Wien, vom 31. Dec., and *Gräzer Zeitung* (1 January 1788), no. 1. Brauneis, "Mozarts Anstellung," 559–72.

19. Angermüller, *Wenzel Müller*, 168: 7 March [1788]: "Akademie von Friedrich Baumann d. J."

20. *Wiener Zeitung* (19 March 1788). A copy of the keyboard version is in the Gesellschaft der Musikfreunde in Wien: Sig. XV 46889. Plath, "A Sketch-Leaf," 115–25, demonstrates the care with which Mozart approached the composition of even a simple contredanse.

21. Deutsch, *Mozart: Die Dokumente*, 274.

To a casual reader, the impression might have been given that Joseph's newly appointed "Kapellmeister" was laying the foundations for a catalogue of war music.[22] Certainly he relished his new title. As Wolff observes, his apparent insistence upon using it stands in contrast to other composers with imperial appointments such as Gluck, Salieri, and Umlauf.[23]

By the time he left Vienna, Joseph II was resigned to the likelihood of a long struggle. Two attempts to seize Belgrade by stealth had been foiled by the weather, the result being that the enemy was fully forewarned as to Austrian intentions.[24] He faced a strategic problem typical for a landlocked empire. With potential threats from two directions, he had no option but to divide his army; a force would have to be stationed along the northern border with Saxony and Silesia and further to the east in order to discourage renewed Prussian territorial ambitions, while the troops distributed along the lengthy southern frontier—the so-called cordon facing the Ottoman Empire—were thinly spread and not easy to reinforce at speed.[25] Joseph set up his headquarters about halfway along this frontier at Semlin (Zemun) opposite Belgrade.

His journey southward took him through Trieste, where his appearance at Sarti's *Giulio Sabino* was greeted with heightened displays of patriotic fervor, including shouts of "evviva."[26] In Giovannini's libretto, the Roman emperor is faced with a rebellious northern Gallic province, its theme of resistance to imperial oppression being "impossible to miss."[27] As the Austrian Caesar headed off to war, with open revolt growing in his northern possessions, the plot suddenly acquired contemporary resonance. Tito, a young man in love rather than a bloody tyrant, eventually chooses reconciliation, and the rebels

22. Mozart is also reported to have appeared on the subscription list of Anton Stein's *Österreichische und türkische Kriegslieder*. Deutsch, *Mozart: A Documentary Biography*, 309, gave his name in this entry as "Hr. Mozart, Tonkünstler in Diensten Sr. k. k. apost. Majestät." A collection of war songs, by turn bellicose and lachrymose, it had an educative purpose as well, incorporating many definitions of Turkish and Islamic terms: Moslem, Imam, Koran, Allah, Bosphorus, etc. In one song (p. 72) the ubiquitous imagery of opera makes an appearance: "Horch! horch! Kaum schließt den frohen / Schmaus, / Das trunkene Desert, / So schallt im höll'schen Opernhaus, / Ein wohlbesetzt Konzert."

23. Wolff, *Mozart at the Gateway*, 78.

24. Mayer, "Price for Austria's Security," 267.

25. The threat from the north remained a real one throughout the period. In 1790, Prussia reached an agreement with the Ottomans (never implemented) committing it to an invasion of the Austrian Monarchy the following spring. Mayer, "Price for Austria's Security: Part II," 475.

26. *Gazzetta Toscana* (15 March 1788), no. 22, 175: TRIESTE. 5 Marzo.

27. Ketterer, *Ancient Rome in Early Opera*, 159–66.

agree to set aside the ancient hatred of the empire—"Deposto l'odio antico / Dell'Impero"—and swear allegiance to Rome.

When he left for the front line, the emperor was not accompanied by his wind band, as some of its members also played in the opera orchestra, but the imperial *Harmonie* marked his imminent departure with a performance of *L'arbore di Diana* on 22 February. The poster noted that there would be appropriate military bombast: "at the beginning, in the intermission and at the end, there will be choruses of trumpets and drums."[28] In wartime, wind bands were required for active military purposes as well as ceremonial functions. With respect to this particular enemy, the Ottomans, there was the obvious question as to how its own (very popular) martial music should be deployed. Vienna's undiminished enthusiasm for Janissary bands was considered in *Das alte und neue Wien*, which compared the soundscapes of the old and new city: in old Vienna, the lanes had resounded with stately church music and serenades, whereas a characteristic sound of the new Vienna was tasteless Turkish music. A footnote drew attention to a potential irony if Austrian warriors were now to make use of these very tones to inspire their forces in battle.[29] In the campaign itself, military music was available to both sides for the usual purposes of psychological warfare. Joseph Nikolaus de Vins, fighting with the Austrian forces in Croatia in 1788, was able to muster an impressive fifty or more oboists to reply in kind to a night of Turkish "lärmendes Musik und Tanz."[30]

Franz, now of an age to serve in the army, left Vienna a few days after his uncle. During the weeks he had been able to spend with his new wife, the couple's demeanor on the dance floor won approval.[31] His departure marked the end (at least for the time being) of personal Habsburg patronage of theater and opera in Vienna, since Elisabeth, playing the role of dutiful wife, took

---

28. Morrow, *Concert Life*, 271.

29. *Das alte und neue Wien*, Vienna, 1788, vol. 3, 18: "Das alte Wien: Wiens Gässen—ertönend von pompöser Kirchenmusik oder Serenaden"; 19: "Das neue Wien: Wiens Gässen—ertönend vom Kettengeklirre der Züchtlinge oder geschmakloser türkischer Musik. [footnote] Diese Musik reimt sich in der That mit unsrer übrigen militärischen Originalität nicht wohl zusammen und es wurde den Stolz der Türken nicht wenig kitzeln, wenn sie erführen, daß deutsche Krieger durch türkische Musik zur Schlacht begeistert werden."

30. *Wienerblättchen* (1 September 1788), 13: "Baron De Vins beobachtete selbst dieses türkische Freudenfest, und ließ noch den nemlichen Tag Nachmittag von mehr als 50 Hautboisten in unserm Lager ebenfalls eine lärmende Musik veranstallten."

31. *Courier du Bas-Rhin* (9 February 1788), no. 12, 89: EXTRAIT *d'une lettre particuliere de Vienne, du 26 Janvier.* "L. A. R. danserent dans 4 contre-danses, on admira l'habillement riche & noble de Mde. l'archiduchesse, qui, à un maintien majestueux, sait réunir toutes les graces de son sexe."

the decision not to continue attending. As she informed her husband on 28 March, four days after the start of the new season, she had not set foot in the theater since his departure, nor was it likely that she would do so soon, as it was too painful to enter the box that they had so happily occupied in recent years.[32] Her withdrawal was a news story.[33]

The prolonged absence of Joseph, Franz, and Elisabeth did little for the prospects of the National Theater, and the new season began with a crisis precipitated by the late arrival of Celeste Coltellini. Her appearance in Vienna, six weeks after the start of her contract, was recorded by Elisabeth von Württemberg on 16 April, but the reasons for the unusual delay are not clear.[34] Coltellini arrived with her sister Anna, who was engaged on a rolling monthly contract at the rate of 150 gulden.[35] The two made their debut in Paisiello's *La modista raggiratrice*, set in a fashion emporium, with Celeste taking the role of Perlina, the milliner. She may well have come to Vienna in possession of a score, as she and her sister had taken part in the premiere in Naples in 1787. Despite its topical setting, the opera failed to win over the Vienna audience; Zinzendorf was bored, and Joseph professed himself unsurprised by its lack of success.[36] A local newspaper commented that while Coltellini had no rival as an actress, Storace and Morichelli were the better singers.[37]

---

32. Weyda, "Briefe an Erzherzog Franz," 47: 28 mars: "Pour le théâtre je n'ai pas mis le pied et je doute qu'il me voie de longtemps, car cela m'affligerait trop encore de me trouver dans la même loge, où j'ai eu le bonheur d'être si souvent avec vous."

33. *Budissinische wöchentliche Nachrichten* (28 June 1788), no. 26, 102: Wien, vom 11 Juni: "Die Erzherzogin Elisabeth lebt seit der Abwesenheit Ihres Durchl. Gemahls ganz in der Stille, giebt keine Musik, und besucht kein Schauspiel."

34. Weyda, "Briefe an Erzherzog Franz," 67: 16 avril: "La Coltellini est enfin arrivée après s'être fait attendre assez longtemps."

35. Link, *National Court Theatre*, 315.

36. Link, *National Court Theatre*, 302: "Le mauvais succes de l'Opera ne m'etonne pas, ce n'est que le nouveauté qui a du prix à Vienne."

37. *Wiener Früh- und Abend-Blatt* (29 April 1788). Link, "Anna Morichelli," 5, citing Michtner, *Das alte Burgtheater*, 252–53: "Mlle Coltellini ist dieser Tage angelangt. . . . An Aktion wird sie von keiner Sängerin übertroffen, aber an Gesang sind Mme Morichelli und Storace ihre Meisterinnen." Coltellini certainly knew how to play to the gallery, the subject of an anecdote dating from her first engagement in Vienna. *Laibacher Zeitung* (29 December 1785), no. 52: Wien, den 28. Nov.: "Als neulich unsere beliebte Sängerin Tottellini [*sic*] in dem Stük ihrem Liebhaber eine Ohrfeige zu geben hatte, so war das Publikum so wohl mit ihrer Austheilung zufrieden, daß sie sowohl Gesang als Aktus wiederholen muste. So sehr auch der Sänger mit den lächerlichsten Stellungen dagegen protestirte, so muste der appetitus spurius der Zuschauer befriediget werden."

The indifferent reception accorded to *Don Giovanni* in Vienna looms large in the story of Mozart's declining fortunes, but its limited success reflected the deteriorating political context. Put simply, from the moment the production went into rehearsal through to the final performance, the opera had to make its way in a year of crisis for the Austrian Monarchy. The circumstances in which it was scheduled in Vienna remain obscure. An odd story in the *Prager Oberpostamtszeitung*, reprinted on 29 November 1787, suggested that Mozart was being urged by friends to see if he could get his new opera staged in his home city, seeming to imply that this had yet to be agreed.[38] The report went on to claim that Martín y Soler was working on a counterpart ("Gegenstück") to *Figaro*, a rather unlikely scenario, given that he had already left Vienna. On the face of it, this intriguing but very garbled piece of gossip seems to refer to *L'arbore di Diana*, even though its widely reported premiere had been two months earlier. But as the opera said to be in preparation is described as a competitive work, aimed in some unspecified manner at diminishing Mozart's reputation, one wonders whether rumors of Dittersdorf's riposte to *Figaro*, by then very likely well under way, was the ultimate source of the story. Mozart's unnamed supporters were arguing that he could fend off this challenge with *Don Giovanni*, as it was sure to receive high praise as a "non plus ultra" of composition. This cliché had recently been used against the composer in a newspaper report that claimed that even the Italians regarded Dittersdorf's *Der Apotheker* as worthy of this accolade.[39]

The casting of *Don Giovanni* took place in the immediate aftermath of the closure of the Singspiel and was influenced by the legacy of the intertroupe contest. One immediate problem was Laschi, who in view of her pregnancy was offered the generally less demanding role of Zerlina, despite her status in the troupe.[40] After their delayed arrival, the Coltellini sisters were cast in a work they already knew. The roles of Donna Elvira and Donna Anna were

38. *Auszug aller Europäischen Zeitungen* (29 November 1787), 816–17: "Der große Tonkünstler Mozart ist nun wieder in Wien angekommen; seine Freunde dringen in ihn, die letzte Oper: das steinerne Gastmahl auch da zu geben, weil er dadurch das *non plus ultra* hoffen kann, welches ihm der Verfasser der *cosa rara* schon wirklich zu vereiteln sucht, da es heißt, daß er ein Gegenstück des Figaro in der Arbeit habe, und es in Prag aufführen lassen werde." Black, "Mozart in Competition with Martín y Soler," in Edge and Black, *Mozart*.

39. *Erlanger Real Zeitung* (28 July 1786), no. 58, 499. This paper was read by Leopold Mozart and was reported by Johann Pezzl to be one of the most widely available titles in Vienna, but the degree to which comments in the foreign press filtered back to Mozart himself is not easy to establish.

40. Edge, "Mozart's Viennese Copyists," 1747.

therefore allocated to the two women singers who had personified the operatic
divide, ever since their contest in the Schönbrunn Orangerie. Now, in a very
real sense, Cavalieri and Aloysia Lange represented the reunification, even if
there was the awkward question of their salaries to consider, notably whether
the comparability principle would apply.[41] During her career, Cavalieri made
consistent use of this highly effective mechanism for driving up her remuneration. In 1782, she entered the Singspiel troupe on 1,200 gulden, a salary
she retained when she transferred to the opera buffa. At the start of the new
season in 1784, she was still on this rate, but after four months she won an increase to 1,400 gulden, when Laschi joined at a much higher salary. Her next
raise followed her contest with Lange at Schönbrunn, when the two women
attempted to outdo one another (in character and in person) in the trio "Ich
bin die erste Sängerin" in *Der Schauspieldirektor*. After this, she could hardly be
asked to start the new season on less than her rival's 1,706.40 gulden, which
she was duly awarded. Her final increase to 2,133.30 came on 7 April 1787.
When Lange transferred to the opera buffa troupe at the start of the 1788–89
season, it was on her established Singspiel salary of 1,706.40 gulden, which
was now significantly less than Cavalieri's. The disparity may have become a
matter of contention. After a pleasant day with the Mozarts, Joachim Daniel
Preisler recorded some anti-Italian animus he picked up in their company.
Of Lange's pay he wrote: "She receives scarcely half the salary given to the
Italians [a fair point, as Mombelli and Coltellini were on 4,500 gulden] and
yet she . . . can sing the longest and most difficult parts incomparably better
than the songstresses who are here pampered by the *Viennese* nobility."[42]
(In this context, Cavalieri, a German by birth, counted as an "Italian," as de-
fined by her employment and salary.) The question of remuneration was not
the only awkward issue; the perception of reputation was vital in the longer
term, as a singer with the status of prima donna could command consistently
higher fees. Although better paid, Cavalieri was cast as Elvira. If her role were
to be seen to match that of Donna Anna, she would need a significant en-
hancement, which Mozart duly provided in the form of "Mi tradì." Switching
the roles was probably precluded by the distinctive personalities of the two

---

41. As always, there were minor singers in the company. The *Wiener Zeitung* (4 June 1788),
no. 45, 1373, recorded the debut of Mlle Francesca Benuccini, niece of the famous singer, in
Le gelosie fortunate.

42. Deutsch, *Mozart: A Documentary Biography*, 324. Lange's transfer to the opera buffa
coincided with Mozart's completion of an Italian scena for her titled "Ah se in ciel, benigne
stelle" (K.538). It is conceivable that this aria, a score of which exists from around 1778,
served some kind of function as an audition piece, a demonstration that she could cope with
Italian bravura writing.

singers, Lange's warmth being well suited to Donna Anna, Cavalieri's brilliance to Donna Elvira.[43]

Negative reactions to the premiere of *Don Giovanni* focused on the writing for the singers. Zinzendorf heard that Madame Lippe considered the work not well suited to the voice ("peu propre au chant").[44] Elisabeth von Württemberg mentioned to Franz gossip that the opera had not enjoyed a particularly successful premiere, but she was not specific as to the reasons.[45] In his autobiography, Joseph Lange also recollected a cool reception. Referring to the death of Mozart, he stated that the opera, which now (in 1808) was usually full, did not please at first and had been temporarily discontinued after the third performance.[46] The work was not actually abandoned altogether; "zurücklegen" signifies "to put back." The sequence of performances has a gap of two weeks after the first six nights on 7, 9, 12, 16, 23, and 30 May, but whether this constituted the supposed withdrawal is a moot point. Many years later, Da Ponte conceded that the opera had failed to please, even after being changed in some unspecified manner.[47]

Up until the start of August, *Don Giovanni* received twelve performances. This is not indicative of an obvious failure, and it is necessary to consider why a sense of underachievement clung to the work. A significant factor was that May 1788 proved to be a problematic period for the National Theater as a whole, owing to the number of outdoor events in the Prater. The first display of Johann Georg Stuwer's new season of firework extravaganzas was set to clash with the fourth performance of Mozart's opera on 16 May. He advertised *Der Reiz des Frühling* for 15 May, nominating the next day as his

---

43. Gidwitz, "Ich bin die erste Sängerin," 573. In *Wiens gegenwärtiger Zustand*, 366, the kinds of roles allocated to the two singers are distinguished thus: "Cavallieri, Demoiselle Catharine. Sie spielt Liebhaberinnen, und Mädchenrollen. Lang, geborne Weber. Sie spielt Liebhaberinnen und naive Mädchen." In *Friedrich Ludwig Schröder. Beitrag*, 369, Lange received a warmer evaluation than her rival: "Demoiselle Cavalieri besaß Stimme und Kunst, aber keine vortheilhafte Persönlichkeit. Madam Lange, die sich auch durch ihr Gestalt empfahl, bezauberte durch die vollendete Kunst und Lieblichkeit ihres Gesangs."

44. The emperor's celebrated opinion was that *Don Giovanni* was "bien trop difficile pour le chant." Link, *National Court Theatre*, 315. If his reaction was based on a private performance arranged for him before his departure, some of the singers for whom he adjudged the writing too difficult would have left the company before the opera was staged in public.

45. Weyda, "Briefe an Erzherzog Franz," 91: 15 mai: "On a donné ces jours passés un nouvel opéra de la composition de Mozart, mais on m'a dit qu'il n'avait pas eu beaucoup de succès."

46. Lange, *Biographie*, 171: "Sein Meisterstück, Don Juan, welches nun fortgesezt das Haus zum Erdrücken füllet—gefiel Anfangs nicht, und wurde nach der dritten Vorstellung zurück gelegt."

47. Woodfield, *Vienna Don Giovanni*, 110–14.

reserve date. That the weather, not living up to the display's title, forced a further postponement, leaving *Don Giovanni* unopposed on 16 May, is likely to have limited rather than mitigated entirely the damage done to the box office. Next came Carl Enslen's aerostatic display *Die Calydonsiche Jagd*, which began at 5:30 p.m., overlapping with the start time at the National Theater. As its scheduling could not be announced until Stuwer had settled on his date, there was further uncertainty. When it took place on 19 May, over 6,000 people went to see it, and the effect on the box office takings for *La modista raggiratrice* in the Burgtheater is likely to have been significant.[48] The wave of populist entertainments in the Prater reached a peak following the arrival of news of the first small military success of the campaign. On 24 April, Joseph himself witnessed and rewarded the bravery of Prince Charles Antoine Ligne during the assault on the fort at Schabacz (Šabac) to the west of Belgrade on the river Sava, close to the border with Ottoman territory. The *Wiener Zeitung* announced this victory in an "extra" extra supplement—late-breaking news in modern parlance.[49] Stuwer was very quick off the mark, staging a spectacular (and doubtless preprepared) representation of the capture of Schabacz, which pulled in a huge crowd on 27 May.[50] *Don Giovanni* (on 30 May) can hardly have been helped by the publication of 29 May as the fallback date. In his next display, advertised for 24 or 26 June, Stuwer went for another popular theme: *Una cosa rara*.[51] Mozart's opera was again scheduled in close proximity. If *Don Giovanni* was generating a disappointing box office during the spring of 1788, the Prater displays were at least in part to blame.[52] Summing up this period, the *Bayreuther Zeitung* painted a striking picture of a half-empty theater echoing to the sound of the prompter.[53]

---

48. *Provinzialnachrichten* (31 May 1788), no. 44.

49. *Wiener Zeitung* (30 April 1788), no. 35, besondere Beylage.

50. *Auszug aller europäischen Zeitungen* (12 June 1788), no. 141, 998: Wien, den 28sten May.: "Gestern gab Stuwer sein erstes Feuerwerk. Es stellte die Einnahme von Schbacz vor."

51. Link, *National Court Theatre*, 300. Perinet, *20 und 4 Annehmlichkeiten*, 51: Neunzehnte Annehmlichkeit: Das Feuerwerk: "Herr Stuwer, der erst kürzlich die Eroberung von Schabacz vorstellte, gab eben an diesem Tage *Una cosa rara*."

52. There are no figures for opera receipts in 1788, but analysis of box office income in the spring of 1789 shows the adverse effect on theater attendance of the firework displays; extremely low receipts were recorded at the National Theater on 22 May 1789 (46 gulden) and 25 May 1789 (56 gulden).

53. *Bayreuther Zeitung* (7 June 1788), no. 68, 448: Wien, vom 31 May: "Das National-Theater spielt öfters nur für leere Logen und Bänke und man kann fast jedes Stück doppelt hören, einmal vom Soufleur, und dann auch vom Acteur."

By the early summer, the military campaign had taken a significant turn for the worse, and there was no significant victory to celebrate.[54] The Ottoman army, proving better organized than had been anticipated, took offensive action. There was great alarm when, following a breach of the cordon in the Banat, a border region in central south Hungary, major incursions into the territory of the Monarchy were reported, with villages and towns being systematically sacked.[55] With dormant atavistic fears reignited, Vienna itself seemed under threat.[56]

At the start of the campaign, Franz had been stationed with the emperor, albeit undertaking some independent visits. In late June, he went to Trieste, where his program of engagements was dominated by military inspections. Showing his inexperience, he neglected to put in an appearance at any of the musical or theatrical events arranged for him. The ladies of the city were unimpressed, and their displeasure at his failure to attend a musical academy became an unusual news story.[57] Culture could not be ignored in this cavalier fashion, even in time of war. When Franz traveled to Lemberg in Galicia in the summer, he did not repeat the mistake, attending the theater twice on 20 and 22 August.[58] In uncertain times, the high visibility of such appearances provided reassurance to the populace at large.

In the light of the major setback in the Banat, the emperor's own performance as a commander came increasingly into question. Commentators were not slow

---

54. Perinet, *20 und 4 Annehmlichkeiten*, 19: Siebente Annehmlichkeit, hinted at this, toying with the linguistic ambiguity of a "rare" thing in the title of *Una cosa rara*: it can signify both "very scarce" and "highly prized": "Alles in Wien ist aus Mode zur Cosa rara geworden. . . . A la cosa rara sind die guten Komödien und die vortreflichen Schauspieler, die unverschuldeten Opern, ein wichtiges Extrablatt, und der Sieg im Türkenkrieg."

55. *London Chronicle* (6–9 September 1788): Vienna, August 18: "Those who boasted of the excellent plan of this campaign, the chief end of which was to protect Austrian territory from the depradations of the enemy, are thunderstruck at hearing that the enemy had entered the Bannat."

56. Head, *Orientalism*, 33, accepts the view that the Russian-Turkish War (1768–74) marked a turning point after which Turkey was no longer taken to be a serious threat. In 1771, Joseph II opined that the Russians "are a thousand times more dangerous neighbours than the Turks can ever be." Contempt for Ottoman military prowess was particularly evident early in 1788. Mayer, "Price for Austria's Security," 269. The unexpected success of the offensive "irruptions" into the Banat and Transylvania thus seemed a genuine cause for concern.

57. *Bayreuther Zeitung* (5 July 1788), no. 80, 536: Venedig, vom 24 Juny: "des andern Tages war Concert im Cassino, wo seit kurzem eine neue Musikalische-Academie errichtet ist, aber alles umsonst, Se.Königl. Hoheit erschienen nirgends, und die vornehmen Triester Damen waren sehr übel auf ihn zu sprechen."

58. *Provinzialnachrichten* (3 September 1788), 71; Dunlop, "'Kaisersammlung,'" 55, records payments on both occasions.

to attribute poor morale to the defensive posture that was being maintained. It was accepted that he had fallen ill, but there were those who questioned the severity of his condition, and speculation was growing that he might soon return to Vienna.[59] In reality, there were cogent reasons for postponing offensive action: poor intelligence about the dispositions of the enemy, lack of action by his Russian allies, the rapid spread of disease, even the enervating summer weather.

The news from Vienna was also worrying. Discontent over the rising price of bread led to a small riot on 31 July, precipitated by the belief that bakers were using the war as an excuse to sell short measure and even to manipulate the price of a loaf by withholding supplies.[60] Order was restored by troops, but not before there had been significant damage to property.[61] Elisabeth informed Franz that there had been casualties: the son of a baker had been so badly beaten that it was uncertain whether he would recover; a child had been crushed by the crowd.[62] When punishments were handed out, the authorities acknowledged the justice of the complaints by pillorying some of the bakers. Instructions were issued that emergency stocks of food should be assembled, and even the Kärntnertortheater was pressed into service.[63]

Reverses on the battlefield and discontent in Vienna brought it home to Joseph that the war was not likely to be short and would be expensive to fund. Stringent economies in his expenditure, planned but not yet fully implemented, could no longer be delayed. The summer crisis of 1788 therefore sealed the fate of state subventions for opera buffa. It is worth quoting Blanning on the severity of the financial crisis:

As early as June 1788 Joseph was writing home calling for major reinforcements: twenty-seven battalions of infantry and three regiments

---

59. *The World* (29 August 1788): "The EMPEROR had quitted the camp sick. At Vienna they say, had it been any other man, they should have called it being *sick of the war*."

60. *General Evening Post* (19 August 1788): "An insurrection happened lately at Vienna, on account of the scarcity of bread, and even that scarcity short of weight, and held back from sale in order to enhance the price. The town guard was repulsed by the mob, and the bakers ill-treated, but the regiments of Kaunitz and Lasey restored the public peace."

61. *Whitehall Evening Post* (21 August 1788): "A violent commotion followed; and the populace destroyed 23 houses, distributed extensive hoards of provisions found in them; and would have gone to more immoderate excesses, if not prevented by some batalions of cavalry, that were called in on the occasion."

62. Weyda, "Briefe an Erzherzog Franz," 126: 2 août: "Le fils d'un boulanger a été tellement battu qu'on ne sait pas s'il en reviendra; un enfant a été écrasé par la foule."

63. *Preßburger Zeitung* (27 August 1788), no. 69: "das Theater am Kärnthnerthore zu einem Fruchtmagazine herstellen will."

of cavalry, together with the appropriate number of artillery, draft an-
imals and equipment. All this was clearly going to be very expensive,
he pointed out, especially as he had incurred already a great deal of
extraordinary expenditure due to the raising of free corps, the care of
50,000 refugees, the construction of dams, bridges and fortification
and the purchase of ships for coastal operations. He instructed his min-
isters to put their heads together and devise a scheme for raising the
money—and they were not to adopt the soft option of relying solely
on more loans, because "every patriot who wishes to enjoy protection,
honour and advantage in the state must in these circumstances reach
into his pocket."[64]

As early as 31 March 1788, Zinzendorf knew of Joseph's concerns, expressed in
a response to an enquiry from Storace about a new engagement: "The Emperor
does not want Storace and is even determined to dismiss the Italian opera company."[65] Negotiations with singers continued, however, on the assumption that
a new season would be funded, albeit with clear limits on expenditure. Joseph
wrote to Rosenberg on 3 May: "I am sending you back Storace's letter. You must
not offer her a farthing more than the 1,100 ducats that she has been offered, nor
allow her anything for the journey, nor any benefit other than that which is customary in Lent."[66] By the early summer, however, rumors that the opera buffa
would be closed became steadily more persistent. On 14 June, Elisabeth von
Württemberg was alarmed by gossip that most of the leading stars were to leave,
as this would result in a catastrophe for the opera.[67] The *Bayreuther Zeitung*, well

---

64. Blanning, *Joseph II*, 178.

65. Link, *National Court Theatre*, 314: "L'Emp. ne veut pas de la Storace, et est même
determiné a renvoyer l'opera Italien."

66. Link, *National Court* Theatre, 313: "Je vous renvoye ici la lettre de la Storace, il ne faut pas
lui donner un liard de plus que les 1100 Ducats qu'on lui a offerts, ni lui accorder quelque
chose pour le voyage ni autre benefice que celui qui est d'usage en carême." The singer was
negotiating her future, even as her 1788 London season was reaching its climax: Storace
to Prince Hoare, 29 February 1788: "I have no time to scold for I am hurried to death with
rehearsals every morning and performance every night. Stephen is composing an opera
which is to come out next week, and my benefit is also Thursday, so that with one thing or
other I have no time to Breathe, besides I have Oratorios, and Ancient Concert to attend and
with all these I have not been very well, but [unclear] when Lent is once over I shall be a little
at ease." Beinecke Library, Yale University, Osborn Files "F" 5228. Some English sources
thought the negotiation for her return to Vienna was already concluded: *The World* (22
March 1788): "The STORACE is re-engaged at the conclusion of this season, in the Opera,
and the Imperial Concert, at Vienna."

67. Weyda, "Briefe an Erzherzog Franz," 106: 14 juin: "On dit que Mombelli et sa femme
ainsi que la Coltellini doivent s'en aller à Pâques: ce sera une furieuse chute pour l'Opéra."

informed as always, preempted the actual decision to give notice to the singers by more than a month.[68] Another German commentator could scarcely conceal his pleasure that the opera buffa was struggling, its victory short-lived; regular income was barely enough to cover half the exorbitant salaries of the singers, to say nothing of other high costs. He hoped that the stringent economic climate would help to curb this extravagance.[69] To make matters worse, a furious dispute had broken out between Coltellini and Joseph, who regarded her very late arrival as a breach of contract. He decided that her engagement should be reduced from three years to one.[70] In response, she flounced out at the end of July.[71]

A decision to close the opera buffa was starting to seem inevitable. On 16 July, Joseph II wrote in a memorandum to Rosenberg that if the opera was not paying for itself, the time had come to close it altogether: "Si l'opera ne peut se payer de lui même je suis resolu de le renvoyer tout à fait." The bad news was that it was very far from breaking even. Its theoretical liabilities— loans not yet repaid—now stood at 80,000 gulden. Link has elucidated this figure. It consisted of 24,000 gulden of the original start-up grant and 12,000, 10,000, and 12,000 awarded during the intertroupe contest.[72] This implies that a puzzlingly large sum of 22,000 gulden was added to the accumulating debt during the first part of the 1788–89 season. No box office figures are available, yet while there were surely losses during the spring, a significant upturn during the final months is possible, driven by factors such as the arrival of Ferrarese del Bene, the return of Joseph and Franz, a decisive Russian victory, and the reprieve of Italian opera.

---

68. *Bayreuther Zeitung* (3 July 1788), no. 79, 527: Wien, vom 29. Junii: "Die Italiänische Opera scheint bald einzugehen, da die vorzüglichen Subjecta ihre Entlassung erhalten haben."

69. *Auszug aller europäischen Zeitungen* (19 July 1788), no. 173, 262–63: "Die welsche Oper kömmt hier, zum Triumph der deutschen Muse, beynahe täglich in größern Verfall. Die gewöhnlichen Einnahmen reichen nicht zur Helfte zu, die übermässigen Besoldungen der Operisten nebst dem andern ungeheueren Aufwande bestreiten zu können. Man hoft mit Grunde die strengste Oekonomie unserer Zeiten werde auch auf sie einen Einfluß haben."

70. *Auszug aller europäischen Zeitungen* (19 July 1788), no. 173, 262–63: "Mlle Coltellini gefällt nicht, und läßt sich im Grunde besser sehen, als hören. Sie war hier auf drey Jahre mit einem Gehalte von 1000 Dukaten engagirt; da sie aber den großen Erwartungen nicht entsprochen hat, und 6 Wochen später, als sie sollte, gekommen ist, so hat man mit ihr den Kontrakt aufgehoben. Mit Ende des Faschings verläßt sie Wien wieder." See also *Bayreuther Zeitung* (24 June 1788), no. 75, 497.

71. Payer von Thurn, *Joseph II. als Theaterdirektor*, 74–81. Da Ponte recollected, though not with his usual certainty, that Coltellini, fearing that she had fallen foul of Salieri, had written a sharp letter to the emperor prompting his order to dismiss the entire company. Her abrupt departure is probably the reason for the repetition of *Le gelosie fortunate* on 31 July, replacing *Don Giovanni*, in which she was not cast. Link, *National Court Theatre*, 128.

72. Link, *National Court Theatre*, 302.

On 29 July, Joseph gave his ruling: "I believe that the time has come to renounce completely the opera for next year."[73] The news was made public on Sunday 3 August, a night upon which there was no opera. (During the vacation of the acting troupe between 1 July and 15 August, opera was given on every second night.) Joseph confirmed his decision on 18 August, sending further instructions to Rosenberg: "Notices will be sent immediately to all members of the opera, both those in Vienna and abroad."[74] The dismissals were announced in Italy.[75] In London, the disbanding of the troupe was reported as part of a general drive to economize.[76] Some commentators discerned a personal dimension to the decision, sensing that the emperor was starting to display increasing annoyance at the caprices of his star singers, who were never at peace with one another and who always seemed discontented even with large salaries. Mombelli and his wife (Laschi) were singled out for criticism, and there was a claim that they had been sacked.[77] The first premiere after the announcement of the closure was Cimarosa's *Il fanatico burlato*, scheduled probably for Celeste Coltellini, as she had sung in it during Lent 1787 in Naples, but she left before the first performance on 10 August.[78]

The general picture was of out-of-touch opera stars provoking an exasperated commander-in-chief. In Salzburg it was noted that the Italian singers had embarked upon their swansong.[79] There was increasing speculation that the German theater troupe would be offered to a commercial

---

73. Payer von Thurn, *Joseph II. als Theaterdirektor*, 81: "Je crois que c'est le moment de renoncer entierement à l'Opera pour l'année prochaine."

74. Payer von Thurn, *Joseph II. als Theaterdirektor*, 83: "Les Denonciations seront donc faites incessament à toutes les membres de l'opera tant à Vienne qu'en pais etranger."

75. *Gazzetta universale* (2 September 1788), no. 71, 566: VIENNA, 22 Agosto: "Fu notificata jermattina la Sovrana risoluzione ai Cantanti della nostra Opera Buffa Italiana, che terminato il pross. Carnevale, restano congedati."

76. *London Chronicle* (4 September 1788): Vienna, 15 August: "His Majesty, in order to save as much money as possible for the necessary expenses of the war, has made some considerable alterations in his household, and particularly in the Royal Hunt, by which alone 30,000 florins per annum will be saved. The Italian opera, which cost annually 40.000 florins, is also paid off. Many other alterations are talked of."

77. *Gazzetta bolognesi* (19 August 1788), no. 41, 349: VIENNA 11. Agosto: "e questi Cantanti non sono mai in pace tra essi, nè mai pagati abbastanza, come essi pretendono. Per questo motivo S. M. ha fatto licenziare il Sig. *Mombelli*, e sua Moglie *Laschi*; i quali non si credevano forse pagati a sufficienza con 1000. Zecchini per ciascheduno, Quartiere ec."

78. *Calendrier musical universal*, vol. 10 (1789), 171.

79. *Oberdeutsche Staatszeitung* (26 August 1788), no. 168, 684: Wien, den 20sten August: "Indessen fingen unsre italiänischen Operisten ihren Schwanengesang."

impresario.[80] The *Bayreuther Zeitung* claimed that the Italian company had been dismissed and that a similar fate was now thought likely for the entire National Theater.[81] The conclusion to be drawn from this depressing news was the usual one: the loss of the opera meant that prospects for peace were poor, and it was a near certainty that a second campaign in 1789 would be necessary.[82] The care with which musical runes were read during the war years as evidence of military fortune is remarkable. With rumors from Croatia flying about, patriotic opinion inferred from the "ausserordentlich Hofmusik," heard in the Hofkapelle on 12 September in Joseph's continuing absence, that news of a successful action had reached Vienna and that a Te Deum had been sung.[83] It is interesting that Zinzendorf, back in Vienna after an absence of seven weeks, noted in his diary that day: "on dit que l'Emp. veut la paix."[84]

A few days after the bread riot had demonstrated that the crisis facing the emperor had a Vienna dimension, Mozart composed the most overtly political song of his career, "Beim Auszug in das Feld." As Beales has argued, the significance of the small number of patriotic texts set by Mozart has been underestimated: "There is no need here, as in the case of the operas, to make a leap of faith and infer from a generalised expression of feeling or from a contrived situation, ostensibly located in some remote age and country, first the librettist's and then, by extension, Mozart's attitudes to current issues. Here the composer conspicuously associated himself with a highly specific and elaborate piece of war propaganda."[85] Mozart entered this war-song in his catalogue on 11 August, and it was subsequently published in a periodical titled *Wochenblatt für Kinder*. Among the notes to this text is the observation that the

---

80. *Oberdeutsche Staatszeitung* (26 August 1788), no. 168, 684: Wien, den 20sten August: "und das Nationaltheater sammt dem fürchtlichen Ausschuße geht aus der Kaisers Händen an Pächter über."

81. *Bayreuther Zeitung* (18 August 1788), no. 98, Anhang, 678: Ein anderes Wien vom obigen Dato. [12 August]: "Die Welsche oper ist auch abgedankt, und man sagt sich im Vertrauen, daß dem Nationaltheater ein gleiches bevorstünde."

82. *Kurfürstlich gnädigst privilegirte Münchner Zeitung* (19 August 1788), no. 130, 531: Wien, vom 13ten August (Aus Privatnachrichten): "Auch hat der Monarch befohlen, daß das ganze kostspielige Personale der wälschen Oper nach Endigung des heurigen Theatraljahrs verabschiedet werden soll . . . welches auch um so nöthiger ist, als noch gar kein Friedensanschein, sondern vielmehr alle Vermuthung vorhanden ist, daß es noch zu einer zweiten Kampagne mit den Türken kommen werde."

83. *Bayreuther Zeitung* (18 September 1788), no. 112, 786.

84. Link, *National Court Theatre*, 318.

85. Beales, "Court, Government, and Society," 17.

bread riot would not have happened if Joseph II had still been in Vienna.[86] In essence, the song is a justification for the war, as it praises the emperor's honorable adherence to his treaty obligations. In the final four verses, Joseph addresses his men directly, reassuring them that he values the sacrifices they are making. As the rousing conclusion puts it, "the brave troops are fighting for the right and for mankind; God will reward the heroes whose blood is shed; future generations will bless them; and their heroism will not have been in vain."[87] Whether prompted by others or offered as a gesture on his own behalf, Mozart composed a song that recognized in timely fashion the urgent need to address propaganda failings—neither the commander-in-chief nor his armies were thought to be acquitting themselves particularly well.

In a response to the stalled military campaign, Joseph tempted Laudon (fig. 4.1) out of retirement. A flattering letter of invitation was widely reported, and when the ageing hero signed up to head the troops in Croatia, there was general elation, if some uncertainty as to what the terms of his engagement were.[88] Concerns were being voiced as to how Laudon's anticipated successes would play with Joseph's for the moment rather tarnished reputation as a war leader.

It was the age-old question of distributing credit between monarch and star general. As it happened, the Vienna stage provided the perfect proxy for this debate, one that was seized upon by both sides in the intensifying propaganda for and against Joseph. At a critical juncture in *Axur*, a youthful oracle is consulted as to who should be appointed leader: Axur (the king) or Atar (the soldier). Several German sources reported that some members of the audience at a performance in early August hijacked this solemn moment, breaking out into chants of "Laudon, Laudon."[89] In the months leading up

---

86. For a discussion of the accompanying annotations, see Head, *Orientalism*, 38–39.

87. Beales, "Court, Government, and Society," 16.

88. *World* (25 August 1788): "Marshall LAUDOHN's appointment fills *Vienna* with acclamation. He received a very flattering letter from the EMPEROR: and in the conduct of the war, it is said, the *Marshal* is to act solely from his own discretion, subject to no superior orders whatever. There are those, however, who doubt much of the last article, from an opinion, that fear may be entertained, lest the martial talents of LAUDOHN might be manifested in achievements that would discredit and reproach the character of others."

89. *Bayreuther Zeitung* (21 August 1788), no. 100, 690: Wien, vom 15. August: "Als ein Beweiß des großen Zutrauens, welches man allgemein in diesen versuchten Krieger setzt, verdient angeführt zu werden, daß, als neulich die wälsche Oper: Axur, König von Ormus, aufgeführt wurde, in welcher das Orakel gefragt wird, ob Axur oder Artor General werden soll, die ganze Versammlung in die Worte ausbracht: Laudon, Laudon." It was also printed, with minor variants, in the *Brünner Zeitung* (12 August 1788), no. 65, 523. The report is dated: "Oesterreich, vom 8 August."

FIGURE 4.1 Field Marshal Gideon von Laudon; portrait (c. 1780), unknown artist. Courtesy of Heeresgeschichtliches Museum, Vienna.

to this unusual occurrence, the hero was assumed to be standing aloof from the war, generating speculation as to when he would finally join the Austrian forces. In Germany, at least, the story was presented as a simple demonstration of the public confidence he inspired. On 6 September 1788, the *London Chronicle* took a similar line in the following news item:

FOREIGN INTELLIGENCE *Vienna, Aug. 23.*
      Besides the flattering letters which the Emperor wrote to induce old General Laudohn to take command of the army in Croatia, that veteran has received another great public compliment: the other evening during the performance of the Opera d'Axur King of Ormuz, in the scene where the oracle is consulted, which of the two Generals Axur or

Artar, should be sent against the enemy, the audience with one voice, cried out Laudohn, Laudohn!

Another London source, the *Morning Post and Daily Advertiser*, adopted a very different stance. Claiming to have the inside story, it ran an article on the conduct of the war highly antagonistic to Joseph:

TURKS AND AUSTRIANS *Extract of a Letter from Vienna, Aug. 22*. . . .

The Emperor having proved to demonstration his utter incapacity to direct the operations of war, and conscious of his inability, and perceiving himself to have been for some time past not only the sport and ridicule of the best experienced of his general officers, but the jest even of the soldiery, his Majesty absented himself as much as possible from the army, under the pretence of visiting the military hospitals, employing at the same time his emissaries here to sound old Laudon, whether he would like to have the command. The veteran fought shy, and always evaded giving a direct answer, or even an opinion on the conduct of his Sovereign; but when the news arrived of the irruption of the Turks into the Bannat and Transilvania; that 13,000 of the enemy had invaded the former and defeated most completely his best disciplined troops, and that General Fabris had been compelled to retreat in the latter province, the question was more direct put to the Field Marshal, who refused to answer, until the application was made to him officially and in form; in consequence of which the Emperor immediately wrote to him in his own hand a long letter, supplicating him in the most earnest manner, to take upon him the command of the army in the following terms: "*I do not order you, my dear Marshal, but ENTREAT of you to come immediately, and take upon you the command of the army, for the salvation of my Empire, and the love of me.*" And in order to flatter the vanity of the old man, and engage him to a compliance, a number of people were judiciously distributed the same evening at the Opera of Axur King of Ormuz, which was commanded as if for the purpose; and when the oracle was consulted, which General should be employed, Axur or Attar, against the enemy, the name of Laudon resounded from all parts of the theatre. Thus you see how degraded and how fallen this MAXIMUS *in minimis* is, even in the opinion of his Austrian subjects, whom [sic] I assure you, execrate him as cordially as their fellow-sufferers in the Netherlands, and would express their abhorrence and contempt of him in stronger terms than they ever did in Brabant, if they were not over-awed by a military force.

This reading of the incident comes close to attributing it directly to Joseph, who is reduced to ordering the formation of a claque at his own opera in a desperate attempt to flatter the old man and obtain his services. To be fair, the London editor felt it necessary to outline the circumstances in which he had received this hardly impartial diatribe. Expressing his thanks for the article, he noted that there had been little time to check it: "Such was the very important intelligence with which we were favoured last night just as the paper was going to press. . . . We cannot omit acknowledging our gratitude . . . with the above very circumstantial account."

An unprovoked outbreak of war-related chanting in the Burgtheater seems improbable, yet hardly more so than the idea that Joseph staged the incident himself. If the demonstration did actually happen, bearing in mind that it exhibits some of the hallmarks of an anecdote, a supporter of the emperor could easily have arranged it. As to its date, *Axur* was performed on 4 and 8 August, but Zinzendorf, who would surely have said something, was away during that period. The Brünn report from Vienna is dated 8 August, and its use of the word "neulich" (recently) points firmly to 4 August. This is plausible on other grounds, as it was the first chance the opera audience had to express their disappointment over the decision to close the opera buffa, announced the previous day. They perhaps gave vent to their feelings by seeking to demean the emperor's reputation as a military commander. Spontaneous or contrived, real or imaginary, this unusual instance of audience intervention made for eye-catching copy; Joseph's favorite opera had been commandeered to give voice to the Vienna public's views on the military situation in a fashion far from respectful of his leadership.

The difficulties facing *Don Giovanni* steadily mounted. Joseph Lange recalled that his wife's contract had been terminated on 3 August, the date on which the closure was announced, but he described her dismissal as a personal setback, someone having apparently told Joseph that she had lost her voice.[90] He neglected to mention the salient fact that she was pregnant. Preisler wrote on 20 August: "Between 10 and 11 [a.m.] the actor *Lange* came to fetch us, to see his collection of pictures by himself and to hear his wife sing.—A melancholy ecstasy was to be read at once in her eyes. She was great with child and could not perform in that condition. Too bad for us! for she was, although a

---

90. Lange, *Biographie*, 151: "Allein es erfolgte noch ein weit härterer Schlag. Am 3. August folgenden Jahres wurde meiner Frau der Contract aufgekündet. Man hatte dem Kaiser vorgegeben: sie hätte die Stimme verloren."

German, the *prima donna* of the *Italian opera*."[91] Preisler also implied that her dismissal (seemingly yet to be confirmed) was in some manner a separate decision from the disbandment of the troupe as a whole: "The *Italian Opera* was given notice today and will only continue to play until *Lent*. I am now eager to hear the *Emperor's* decision whether this delightful *Madame Lange* is to be got rid of with the others."[92]

If Lange had to withdraw on the grounds of her pregnancy after appearing in *Don Giovanni* on 2 August, then someone else must have sung Donna Anna when performances resumed briefly on 24 October.[93] Her dismissal was accompanied by the award of a 900 gulden supplement to her husband's salary, although what was intended as a generous gesture resulted in marital dissension. Joseph Lange had been on 1,400 gulden as an actor, she on 1,704.40 as a member of the Singspiel troupe; now he was awarded a supplement of half of his wife's salary. The Court Theater accounts for the next two years have not survived, but in the 1791–92 season, he was on 2,300 gulden (1,400 + 900), a very large remuneration for an actor.[94] This solution, though part of a general policy of looking after the interests of established singers and actors when a troupe folded, involved some reputational damage. Joseph Lange, who by the time of writing had long since divorced her, recalled her irritability and suggested that her melancholy had undermined her health. Rather than continue in Vienna under these circumstances, she embarked upon a lengthy tour. She is recorded in Mainz, where she hoped to sing in *Zémire und Azor* on 28 March as "eine durchreisende Sängerin."[95]

---

91. With the benefit of hindsight, Joseph Lange recollected that he had not been expecting his wife to shine in her new troupe: Lange, *Biographie*, 151: "es war voraus zu Sehen, daß sie hier nie in dasselbe helle Licht, wie in der deutschen Oper, gestellt werden würde."

92. Deutsch, *Mozart: A Documentary Biography*, 324. The delay in giving notice to singers who had recently transferred from the Singspiel troupe, Arnold and his wife, Saal, and Lange, might suggest that the option of retaining a core of German performers had yet to be ruled out. They would be on hand to provide music for theatrical productions if required, and in the event that the less expensive genre of Singspiel was substituted for Italian opera, as was briefly considered at the end of the year, they would be immediately available.

93. At some point, Donna Anna's rondò may have been temporarily removed from the opera. The original violin 1 part for the Vienna *Don Giovanni* was annotated with the name of the performer at the head of each aria, but no singer is identified for "Non mi dir."

94. Link, *National Court Theatre*, 433.

95. *Dramaturgische Blätter* (24 December 1789), vol. 2, pt. 3, no. 13, 193. By the summer she was in Berlin, where she sang in a performance of *Die Entführung aus dem Serail*.

The pregnancies of Lange and Laschi also affected the visual spectacle. Especially in the wake of *Una cosa rara*, costume remained a vital aspect of any production, as demonstrated by Laschi, who turned her benefit performance of *L'ape musicale* into something of a fashion parade.[96] As Link has pointed out, there is a clear correlation between the staging of a work "en robe de chambre" and the indisposition of singers.[97] If a performer fell ill but the advertised performance went ahead, it was sometimes given without full dress. The whole cast, not just the replacement performer, apparently dressed down, possibly for reasons of aesthetic consistency. On 16 June, Zinzendorf saw *Don Giovanni* given this way, the ostensible reason being that Therese Teyber had had to take over the role of Zerlina from the heavily pregnant Laschi.[98] After the death of her newborn child, Laschi was set to make her return in *Axur*. She had not regained her full health, however, and in her absence on 24 October, *Don Giovanni* again had to be performed "en robe de chambre."[99] On 28 January 1789, *Una cosa rara*, indubitably the costume opera of the age, had to proceed without the full magnificence of its Spanish dresses.[100]

Difficulties with women members of the cast hindered the performance run of *Don Giovanni*, but the new male singers, both accorded a poor reception, were not unproblematic either. Morella and Albertarelli, the latter in particular failing to impress, were the subject of scathing comments by Preisler following a visit to the opera house on 20 August 1788.[101] It did not help that Albertarelli's indisposition resulted in a four-day postponement of the much-anticipated debut of Ferrarese del Bene in *L'arbore di Diana*. When it took

96. Link, *National Court Theatre*, 330: "6 Mars [1789]: A l'opera. Benefice de la Laschi, elle avoit un bel habit du Pce Auersperg, satin rose, tabliera fleurs, Albertorelli un joli habit de satin. La ferraresi proprement mise."

97. Link, *National Court Theatre*, 253: "3 October 1785: Chez moi puis a l'opera des litiganti, qui fut tres fort en robe de chamber, Benucci ne jouant pas."

98. Link, *National Court Theatre*, 317: "16 Juin: Dela a l'opera *Don Giovanni*. Il fut en robe de chambre, la Taeuberin fesant le rôle de la Monbelli." "Die Arnoldin," as she was also known, entered the troupe as a lesser singer, but her salary had been rising; originally 800 gulden a year, it now stood at 1,400. She brought youthfulness to the cast: *Friedrich Ludwig Schröder. Beitrag*, 369: "Die der Demoiselle Teyber war jügendlich Frisch."

99. Link, *National Court Theatre*, 321.

100. Link, *National Court Theatre*, 327: "28 Janvier: La ferraresi et la Monbelli enrouées, par consequens le spectacle en robe de chambre."

101. Deutsch, *Mozart: a Documentary Biography*, 323–33. The *Wiener Zeitung* (26 April 1788), no. 34, 1021, restricted itself to a bare factual announcement; the absence of any positive comment indirectly indicated poor or indifferently received debuts: "Noch sind zwey neue Sänger seit Ostern bey der hiesigen Oper zum Vorschein gekommen: Herr Franccesco Morella als Conte Almaviva beym Barbiier von Sevilla; und Herr Francesco Alberttarelli als Biscroma in dem tragisch-komischen Singspiele: Axur Re d'Ormus."

place, Zinzendorf noted that his "awkwardness" had damaged his duet with the new star.[102] Outside Vienna, it was reported that a new tenor singer was being sought. According to a notice in Mannheim, Luigi Simonetti had recently traveled to Vienna to take up an engagement with the Italian opera company, though there is no indication of this in the theater records.[103]

All in all, a very difficult situation confronted the Italian opera troupe in the summer of 1788, as it struggled with the late arrival and then the unexpectedly early departure of the prima donna, two unfortunate male recruitments, and two pregnancies, to say nothing of external factors such as the continuing absence of Joseph, Franz, and Elisabeth and the military situation. Most debilitating of all was the persistent threat of disbandment, a subject of speculation after only three months of the theatrical year.

It seemed to some observers in the autumn of 1788 that the Leopoldstadttheater was starting to benefit from the deteriorating prospects for opera at the National Theater, cementing the advantage it had gained from its coup with *Der seltene Fall*. An obvious next step had been to commission Eberl to produce a German version of *L'arbore di Diana*. Its first performance on 17 July 1788 prompted a renewed exchange of pamphlets. As before, a leaflet in support of the Leopoldstadttheater met with a harsh rebuttal. The author of *Etwas für Alle*, who eulogized the new production, noted that the desire to stage it stemmed from the success of the German version of *Una cosa rara*.[104] The new translation, it was claimed, marked a decisive turning point for suburban opera, as audiences now comprised both the aristocracy and the middle classes: "At last the nobility decided to throw their weight behind him [Marinelli] and started to reserve boxes, whereupon the middle classes followed suit, and in short order all the boxes were taken."[105] So packed was the house that there was hardly room to draw

---

102. Link, *National Court Theatre*, 321: 13 October 1788: "Le joli Duo alla mal a cause de la maladresse d'Albertorelli." He had sung during the spring season at the Teatro di via della Pergola in 1786 as "secondo buffo," but apparently not in the autumn, when Ferrarese arrived in Florence to join the troupe. By the summer of 1787, he had achieved the rank of "primo buffo caricato" in Florence, albeit at a different theater. *Calendrier musical universal*, vol. 9 (1788), 133 and 136.

103. *Musikalische Real-Zeitung* (1788), no. 4, col. 29: Mannheim vom 10ten Julius: "Herr Simonetti . . . gieng am Ende des vorigen Monats hierdurch nach Wien, wo er zu der dasigen Italienischen Oper engagirt ist."

104. *Etwas für Alle*, 4: "Die glükliche Aufführung der seltnen Sache auf dem Leopoldstädter Theater, die bereits drey und fünfzigmal das Theater gefullt hatte, erwekte den gedanken, sich auch an den Baum der Diana zu wagen."

105. *Etwas für Alle*, 8: "Endlich entschloß sich der Adel, ihn aufzumuntern und fieng an, sich Logen zu bestellen, ihm folgte der Bürgerstand und im kurzen waren alle Logen besetzt." Link, "Vienna's Private Theatrical and Musical Life," 231.

breath.[106] A particular talking point was the interpretation of the role of Amor by the wife of Wenzel Müller, director of music at the Leopoldstadttheater since 1786, which Mombelli (Laschi) had eye-catchingly made her own in the Italian production. The author obviously felt it advisable to forestall criticism that Madame Müller was better suited to her role as Ghita in *Der seltene Fall*.[107] The all-important production values were thought to have reinforced the acting performances, a point also made a few days after Joseph had confirmed the closure of the opera buffa. The staging of *Der Baum der Diana* was perhaps treated as a newsworthy phenomenon in the *Provinzialnachrichten* for this very reason.[108]

Another favorable appraisal appeared in *Mein Urtheil*, a pamphlet by Herr J. K. known from the trenchant rebuttal of its views in the *Kritisches Theater-Journal*.[109] This periodical had already been severely critical of what it saw as Madame Müller's attempts to imitate Mombelli's (Laschi's) acknowledged grace.[110] It now attacked the pamphlet's assertion that Wenzel Müller had a particular talent for music. If, as claimed by J. K., musical experts are of this opinion, why does he not name one? The *Kritisches Theater-Journal* offered its own opinion that Müller's best opera is *Der lebendige Sack*, but only because it is replete with beautiful arias lifted from the three Dittersdorf Singspiels and *Una cosa rara*.[111] In the end, the two German translations of Martín y Soler

106. *Etwas für alle*, 8: "Der Tag erschien, und das Schauspielhaus war so voll, daß man, mit der gemeinen Art zu sprechen, keine Steknadel hinab zu werfen im Stande war, die nicht auf Menschen fiel."

107. *Etwas für alle*, 18: "Madame Müller, in Amors Rolle, gefällt nicht weniger, ob sie ihre Ghittha gleich mit mehr Natur spielt—aber, freylich ist Amor nicht ihre Natur."

108. *Provinzialnachrichten* (9 August 1788), no. 64, 192: Wien, den 9. August 1788: "Aber Herr Marinelli unterläßt auch nichts, um diesem Beyfall des Publikums werth zu seyn, den in jedem Betracht wirklich Dekorazion und Kunst der Schauspieler in vollkommnen Grade verdienen. So sind z. B. die Verkleidung des Alten, die Grotte, der Temple und Hain der Diana, so wie der Göttersaal mit allem möglichen Theaterprunke ausgeziert."

109. *Kritisches Theater-Journal*: Zwölftes Stük. Den 22 Jäner 1789: Wien 1789: " 'Mein Urtheil über die marinellische Schaubühne in der Leopoldstadt.' Eine Brochure."

110. *Kritisches Theater-Journal*: Viertes Stück, 27 November 1788, 95–96: Theater in der Leopoldstadt: "Seit der berühmten Cosa rara hat sich diese Aktrisse [Madame Müller] bemüht, die allgemein beliebte Madame Mombelli in ihrem Spiele zu kopiren. Wie schlecht ihr diese Kopirung glücke, kann man sich täglich überweisen; da Madame Müller gar keine Rolle mehr anders spielt, als: à la Mombelli. Die unnachahmliche Grazie der Madame Mombelli, äußert sich bei der Madame Müller durch Zückungen; das Köpfchen, die Hände, der Leib etc. sind in stäter Bewegung; und dazu wird immer gelächelt und gegrimmassiret."

111. *Kritisches Theater-Journal*: Zwölftes Stük. Den 22 Jäner 1789: Wien 1789: "Seine beste Oper ist, der Lebendige Sack, in der zum Erstaunen aller Musikverständigen, und der berühmtesten Kappellmeister die schönsten Arien aus den drei Ditersdorfischen Opern der Cosa rara u.s.w. glänzen."

were among the Leopoldstadttheater's greatest successes, and the management could afford to ignore accusations of "theft." Yet with so much money at stake, it is hardly any wonder that the phenomenon continued to polarize opinion sharply.

Although the decision to disband the opera buffa troupe at the end of the season was presented as an irrevocable fait accompli, Joseph was notorious for his abrupt changes of mind, and it was therefore premature to lose hope altogether. A new factor was the arrival midseason of Adriana Ferrarese del Bene. The low standing of Italian opera suggested that it would be politic for her to make her first appearance in *L'arbore di Diana*; not only would the opera buffa troupe be able to confront Leopoldstadt with the performance of a top Italian singer in the title role, there would also be a timely reminder that the work had originated as a Habsburg festive commission for the Italians. Her debut performance was well received, due allowance having been made for the indulgence of the Viennese public toward a singer on her first appearance.[112] After a single hearing, Elisabeth von Württemberg thought less favorably of her as a singer than Storace and rated her acting as "frightful," especially when compared to that of Morichelli.[113] The *Grundsätze zur Theaterkritik* tellingly identified her main limitation as a sameness of tone.[114] But over time she developed a following significant enough to result in a sustained upturn in audience figures.

As the end of the year approached, Joseph remained adamant: the Italian opera troupe would have to disband. Speculation that the less expensive Singspiel—during the two years of the contest it ran for less than half the cost of the opera buffa—might be revived in its place proved groundless.[115] It

---

112. *Oberdeutsche Staatszeitung* (21 October 1788), no. 216, 841: Wien, den 15ten Oktober: "Madame Ferrarese hat sich diesen Mondtag in L'Arbore di Diana das erste Mahl sehen, hören, und bewundern lassen. Man kennt zwar die Gutherzigkeit des wienerischen Publikums, mit der es sonst jeder neuen Schauspielerinn, oder Sängerinn huldiget . . . ob es besser sey die Augen zu verschließen, um bloß zu hören, oder die Ohren zu verstopfen, um nur zu sehen; wirklich wetteiferten Natur, und Kunst dem gesammten Publikum den lautesten Beyfall abzuzwingen."

113. Weyda, "Briefe an Erzherzog Franz," 177: 8 Novembre 1788: "Il y a à présent une nouvelle chanteuse ici qui s'appelle Ferrarese . . . mais j'avoue qu'elle ne me plaît à beaucoup près autant que la Storaci; son jeu est affreux d'autant plus que dans L'Albore di Diana elle fait le rôle de la Morichelli qui était pétrie de grâces comme vous savez." Zinzendorf disagreed, noting that she had sung "ravishingly." Rice, *Mozart on the Stage*, 210.

114. Link, "Anna Morichelli," 15: *Grundsätze zur Theaterkritik*: "der Morikelli aber ein ermüdendes Einerlei hat."

115. Link, *National Court Theatre*, 324, cites a comment of Zinzendorf: "il est question d'un opera allemand." The *Rapport von Wien* (13 December 1788), 421, speculated that the high cost of buying out the Italian singers was proving to be an obstacle to this alternative proposal.

was rumored that one "Wetzlar" might take over as an independent impresario.[116] A formal confirmation of the closure was released in early November, the timing being perhaps not unconnected to the fact that a special war tax was about to be imposed, backdated to 1 November.[117] Knowing the emperor's inherent unpredictability, though, Elisabeth von Württemberg suspected that a change of mind still could not be entirely discounted.[118] When Franz returned to Vienna on 16 November 1788 at the conclusion of that year's campaign, he lost no time in placing an order with Lausch for the two insertion arias, the latest changes to his sister's Vienna gala opera, along with another recently premiered work, Salieri's *Il talismano*.[119]

IF ALL OPERA was to be discontinued at the National Theater, seemingly now an inevitable consequence of the failure to bring the war to a conclusion, opportunities would open up for the commercial stage. In timely fashion, a relatively new theater under the management of the actor Johann Friedel rose rapidly to prominence. The German press, alert as always to the nuances of theatrical politics in Vienna, now had a new contest to report: that between the established Leopoldstadttheater and the emerging Theater auf der Wieden. During the second half of 1788, the impact of Friedel's troupe became increasingly apparent. In June, a notice was already implying that the offerings at the Burgtheater were so poor that the audience was now willing to make the slightly longer trip out to the Freihaus.[120] Some of the difficulties being experienced by Joseph's troupes were attributed to overzealous censorship, resulting

116. The man in question was probably Philipp Raimond Wetzlar. Zinzendorf wondered whether the public might be better served by this arrangement. Link, *National Court Theatre*, 318.

117. *Kurfürstlich gnädigst privilegirte Münchner Zeitung* (10 November 1788), no. 177, 726: Wien, vom 4. Novemb. (aus Privatbriefen): "Auch ist dieser Tagen von Seiten des Kaisers Majestät eine durchaus eigenhändig geschriebene Resoluzion von 2 Bogen, das Nazionaltheater und das Personale der wälschen Oper betreffend, eingelaufen."

118. Weyda, "Briefe an Erzherzog Franz," 177: 8 November 1788: "Tout le monde est au désespoir qu'il n'y aura plus d'Opéra après Pâques, mais on se flatte pourtant encore que Sa Majesté changera d'idée là-dessus."

119. The receipts are dated 21 November 1788. On 15 January he paid Lausch 13 gulden for the keyboard arrangement of Weigl's *Il pazzo per forza*, advertised at this price the previous day. Dunlop, " 'Kaisersammlung,' " 58; *Wiener Zeitung* (14 January 1789), no. 4, 94.

120. *Oberdeutsche Staatszeitung* (19 June 1788), no. 120, 487: Wien, den 14ten Junius: "Herr Friedel hat dem Nationaltheater bereits den Vorsprung abgewonnen. Man bezahlt lieber den Wagen, und fährt zu ihm in die Vorstadt, als daß man sich im Nationaltheater bey dem unausstehlichen Gewinsel und Maulaufreißen zu Tode ennuiirt."

in the loss of many of the best lines.[121] Conversely, Friedel's success seemed in part to stem from the fact that the censor's impositions for his productions came across as less stringent.[122] Friedel's strengthening profile was the prelude to an ambitious plan. A piece in the *Kritisches Theater-Journal* dated 5 February 1789 noted that he intended to form a Singspiel company that would begin after Easter and alternate with comedy.[123] This optimistic prospectus claimed that German opera was the favorite spectacle ("Lieblingsspektakel") of the Vienna public. In the event, the Theater auf der Wieden changed hands. Friedel died in March 1789, whereupon his partner, Eleanore Schikaneder, invited her estranged husband to take over the direction.[124] He thus had the good fortune to assume control of what was already well on the way to becoming a going concern.

The Leopoldstadttheater, too, was seeking to enhance its roster of performers and continued its successful policy of presenting translations of popular works from the repertoire of the National Theater. When the subject of Salieri's *Tarare* is raised in the satire *L'ape musicale*, Farinelli (Laschi) raises a laugh by commenting: "it will soon be given at Leopoldstadt!" ("La faranno tra poco a Leopoldstadt!").[125] An unnamed singer was reported to have been engaged for a salary of 2,000 gulden, only half the amount top performers had come to expect at the Burgtheater but at least an indication of some quality. It was predicted gloomily that lovers of opera in the city were going to have to make do with this.[126] Baron Karl Philipp von Reitzenstein, who arrived in

121. *Oberdeutsche Staatszeitung* (10 July 1788), no. 135, 549: Wien, den 5ten Julius: "daß die Theatercensur vorzüglich daran Schuld sey, weil sie die besten Stellen durchstreichet, und die guten Köpfe also abschreckt, für das Nationaltheater zu arbeiten."

122. *Oberdeutsche Staatszeitung* (22 August 1788), no. 166, 672: Wiener-Neuigkeiten: "Des Herrn Friedels Theater im Freyhause auf der Wieden macht noch immer sehr glückliche Fortschritte. . . . Auch setzt ihm die Zensur weniger Schwierigkeiten, als den Nationaltheater entgegen."

123. *Kritisches Theater-Journal*, Erstes Stück, 5 February 1789, 3: Theater auf der Wieden: "Es ist bekannt, daß sich Herr Friedel auch eine Gesellschaft deutscher Operisten verschrieben hat, die künftiger Ostern eintreffen, da er dann Komödie mit der Oper abwechseln lassen wird." The lack of a musical director was already causing some problems in maintaining good orchestral discipline. Buch, "House Composers," 16.

124. It has been pointed out that there is no solid documentary evidence for the traditional assumption that Eleanore was Friedel's sole heir. Lorenz, "Neue Forschungsergebnisse," 6.

125. Siniscalchi, *L'ape musicale*, 136.

126. *Bayreuther Zeitung* (2 October 1788), no. 118, 834: Schreiben aus Wien, vom 26 Sept.: "die Liebhaber des Gesangs sich mit der deutschen Opera des Leopoldstädter Theaters begnügen müssen, wozu eine Sängerin verschrieben worden, welche jährlich 2000 Gulden erhält."

Vienna at the start of 1789, considered that Singspiel in the suburban theaters would be excellent, if only the vocal parts were to be taken by performers who could equal the quality of the orchestral players. So far, though, the best singers in the suburbs could not match the smoothness of tone production displayed by Italians in the National Theatre.[127]

All things considered, the months during the second half of 1788, when the closure of the opera buffa seemed inevitable, had a notably invigorating effect on the commercial stage. The private sector was further assisted by the low standing of the theatrical troupe at the National Theater. Reitzenstein observed that Singspiel productions in the suburbs were attracting better audiences than plays in the Burgtheater.[128]

---

127. Reitzenstein, *Reise nach Wien*, 347: "sie würden vortreflich seyn, wenn die Singstimmen so gut besetzt wären als das Orchester. Allein die ersten bleiben weit hinter den Italienern zurück, die eine eigene Gabe bestitzen, das Gleitende der Melodie, das Hinüberschmelzen von einem Tone indem andern, ihrem Vortrage mitzutheilen."

128. Reitzenstein, *Reise nach Wien*, 347: "Mehr als dieses [German theater] werden die deutschen Operetten in den Vorstädten Leopoldstadt und Wieden besucht."

5

Italian Opera Reprieved

L'APE MUSICALE

THE MOOD AMONG aristocratic supporters of opera buffa at the start of 1789 was somber, but the prospects for their favored genre were about to be transformed. A courier arrived in Vienna on 2 January with news of the capture of Ochakiv by Prince Potemkin. The seizure of this strategically important city, located on the western bank of the river Dnieper where it controlled access into the Black Sea, was one of Catherine II's main war aims in the Crimea, and Joseph immediately ordered a sung Te Deum.[1] This piece was easily outshone by the spectacular work provided by Sarti for the St. Petersburg celebration, which incorporated cannon fire, a musical demonstration of Russia's military might that was not lost on commentators.[2] The success at Ochakiv resulted in a distinct if short-lived lightening of the public mood, as the belated entry of Russia into the war and her decisive victory indicated that the long-term outcome was no longer in doubt.

---

1. *Strasburgische privilegirte Zeitung* (19 January 1789), no. 8, 31: Wien, den 8. Jänner: "Den 4ten Jänner ist hier in Gegenwart des Kaysers wegen der Eroberung von Oczakow das Te Deum gesungen worden." Black, "Mozart and the Practices of Sacred Music," 146, discusses the circumstances in which Salieri composed a Te Deum around this time. According to Mosel, it was written to celebrate the return of Joseph to Vienna late in 1788. The autograph is headed "di Ant Salieri l'anno 1790" over an erasure. Black suggests that the piece could have been written in 1788 and then recast for one of the coronations in the period 1790–92. Although plausibly close in time to the Te Deum for the Ochakiv victory, Salieri's work cannot be linked directly to this occasion.

2. *Vaterlandschronik* (31 March 1789), no. 26, 207: "Das neue Tedeum des herrlichen Sarti, wo in die Worte: Herr Gott der Heerschaaren! Kanonen taktmäsig einstürzen. . . . Potemkins Kapelle besteht aus 200 Personen!! Welcher deutsche Fürst, nicht einmal unsern Kaiser und den König von Preussen ausgennommen, kann sich dieses rühmen?—So hebt sich Rußland in Allem; denn die Tage seiner Größe sind kommen."

In celebration of the good news, Joseph was regaled with a "musikalische Scherz." According to a report in the *Musikalische Real-Zeitung*, it was a surprise arranged by Franz (violin) with his fiancée, Elisabeth von Württemberg (bass), and a number of gentlemen- and ladies-in-waiting. The Countess von Chanclos, Joseph's head of female staff, played drums, signaling that the occasion was intended as comic relief.[3] The performance of a musical "Scherz" leads one to wonder whether Mozart's "musikalischer Spass" (K.522) was somehow acquired by Franz or Elisabeth after its completion in 1787, or whether knowledge of it inspired a similarly lighthearted trifle. But a piece with an unusual instrumentation might also have qualified as comedic in some sense, and there is some evidence to suggest that during their long courtship Franz and Elisabeth made music together on the "hölzernes Gelächter" (glockenspiel) and string bass.[4]

In the changed circumstances, it no longer seemed out of the question that Joseph would have a last-minute change of mind, and an additional reason for hope was that after his return to Vienna he was able to resume, if only on a very much more limited basis than before, his habits as an operagoer. During the recently concluded military campaign, he had not been without music, having had recourse to it, at least on rainy days.[5] It was reported that Nicholas Eszterházy sometimes loaned him his Kapellmeister and two oboists.[6] With his ill health a matter of acute concern, the pattern of his theatrical attendance was now taken as a barometer of his well-being. The early signs were not good. News that a crowd had waited (in vain) for him to mark his return to Vienna as usual at the opera buffa made headlines everywhere.[7] That this was his first

3. *Musikalische Real-Zeitung* (4 February 1789), no. 5, 39: Wien, am 7ten Jenner: "wegen der Eroberung Oczakows. . . . Es kamen nemlich der Erzherzog und seine Frau Gemalin, einger Kammerherren und Kammerfrauen mit musikalischen Instrumenten in die Zimmer des Kaisers, welche sie zum Ausdruk ihrer Freude ertönten liesen. Der Prinz spielte die Violin, die Prinzeßin strich den Baß. Die Gräfin von Chanclos schlug die Pauken und die andern von der Gesellschaft hatten gleichfalls ihre ausgetheilten Instrumenten; Dieser musikalische Scherz ergözte die höchsten Herrschaften ungemein."

4. Edge, "Joachim Perinet Refers to 'Mozarts Fortepiano,'" in Edge and Black, *Mozart.*, draws attention to a set of variations by Paul Wranitzky for two violins, cello, drum, cymbals, and "hölzernes Gelächter."

5. *Freiburger Zeitung* (16 July 1788), no. 57, 493: "An Regentägen in der wenigen Stunden ihrer Muße erheitert sich der Monarch mit Musik, an hellen Tägen mit Besuchen des Lagers." Other reports spoke of daily music, whatever the weather: *Stralsundische Zeitung* (17 July 1788), no. 85: Wien, den 2 Julii: "Der Kaiser unterhält sich täglich des Abends im Lager mit Musik."

6. *Auszug aller europäischen Zeitungen* (14 July 1788), no. 168: Semlin, vom 16 Juny: "Se. Maj. der Kayser unterhalten sich täglich des Abends mit Musik, wozu Höchstdieselben den Kapellmeister und 2 Hoboisten von Niklas Esterhazy berufen lassen und jedesmal reichlich beschenken."

7. *Gazzetta bolognesi* (16 December 1788), no. 75, 623: VIENNA 8. Dicembre. "Venerdì 5. del corr . . . Nella sera dello stesso giorno il Popolo si portò in folla al Teatro dell'Opera-buffa *Italiana* colla speranza di vedere l'amatissimo suo Sovrano, il quale però non v'intervene."

opportunity to see Salieri's *Il talismano* contributed to the sense that a crisis was imminent.[8] There was general relief when he appeared at a performance of Johann Heinrich Friedrich Müller's *Der Optimist.*[9] His much-publicized return to the theater seems at odds with a passage in a letter to his sister Marie Christine dated 16 December in which he confided that he had been too ill to go yet.[10] One explanation is that he did not count this brief appearance as a visit to the theater per se.[11] It is not out of the question that he attended the final performance of *Don Giovanni,* but it seems most unlikely.

In the New Year, two appearances at the Italian opera were enough to suggest that Joseph might be regaining a measure of health.[12] On 4 February, he went again.[13] Link's performance calendar for the early winter months of 1789 shows an unusually high level of inconsistency between sources. This was the result of a general desire to schedule works the ailing emperor was known to like (or had requested), in conjunction with the uncertainty, often resolved only at the last moment, over his fitness to attend.[14] On 13 February, three different operas are recorded.[15] In the circumstances, late changes of plan were inevitable.[16]

---

8. *Bayreuther Zeitung* (15 December 1788), no. 149, Anhang, 1073: Wien, vom 8. Dec.: "Abends ward der Talismann in der Ital. Oper gegeben; Se. Majest. fanden sich aber nicht daselbst ein."

9. *Gazzetta bolognesi* (23 December 1788), no. 77, 640. VIENNA 15. Dicembre. Zinzendorf noted that he had come in during an act and was applauded at the end of it: "L'Emp. aparut pendant un acte subitement, et fut applaudi apres la fin del'acte." Link, *National Court Theatre,* 324.

10. Wolf, *Leopold II. und Marie Christine,* 283: Wien, 16 December 1788: "Ich war noch nicht im Theater."

11. *Brünner Zeitung* (19 December 1788), no. 102, 821. Oesterreich, vom 16 December: "Der Monarch verweilte aber kaum eine halbe Stunde, und kehrte alsdann in die Hofburg zurück."

12. *Bayreuther Zeitung* (22 January 1789), no. 10, 71: Wien, vom 16 Januar: "Se. Majestät haben geruhet schon ein paarmal auszufahren, die Italienische Opern zu besuchen, und sehen Gott Lob! wieder ganz gesund aus."

13. *Gazzetta universale* (17 February 1789), no. 14, 108: VIENNA 5. Febbrajo: "Jeri poi si trasferì anche al Teatro, ove ascoltò l'Opera buffa."

14. Link, *National Court Theatre,* 11, notes that *Das Wienerblättchen* announced pieces on the day or one day in advance of the performance, thereby sometimes not reflecting last-minute changes.

15. The three were: *Axur; Il pazzo per forza;* and *Il pastor fido.* Link, *National Court Theatre,* 137. *Journal Historique et Litteraire* (1 March 1789), 370: VIENNE (le 14 Février): "L'empereur, qu'une nouvelle indisposition avoit obligé de garder le lit, se trouve encore une fois mieux. Il a paru avant-hier dans la salle de spectacle, & hier il a assisté à la représentation de l'opera d'Azur [sic] qui est généralement applaudi."

16. The *Journal des Luxus und der Moden,* reporting after the event, listed *Don Juan* (Mozart's opera) for 14 January, rather than *Una cosa rara.* Possibly another attempt had been made to schedule this work for Joseph, before it became evident that he was too ill to attend. Link, *National Court Theatre,* 134.

The campaign to secure a last-minute reprieve for the opera buffa troupe was led by Da Ponte, whose position at the National Theater was by now an influential one, as is shown by the steady growth in the dominance of his works during successive theatrical years. While there are a few evenings for which the evidence is ambiguous, the general trend exemplified in Table 5.1 is obvious.[17] He put together a specific proposal: if the emperor would allow him the use of a theater, he would act, in effect, as a commercial impresario with a consortium of backers.

In order to encourage a change of heart, it made good sense to pander to the emperor's tastes with special assiduity. There was thus a strong emphasis on the gala operas and indeed the play *Das Kleid aus Lyon*, resulting in something of a festive retrospective. A glimpse into Da Ponte's campaign to overturn the decision to abandon Italian opera is provided by a news report that a new work was in preparation. Based on a favorite Italian poet of Joseph, it was as yet only half ready, but all of Vienna was hoping that it would crown the closing months of the season.[18] Salieri's setting of Giovanni Battista Guarini's *Il pastor fido*, probably the work in question, received its premiere on 11 February, but with only three performances it was not a success; when it was restaged in the autumn, it was with many changes.[19] The failure was not forgotten. In the satirical pamphlet *Anti-da Ponte* published in 1791, Guarini, a witness for the prosecution in a mock trial, alleged that Da Ponte had "completely deformed" his beautiful poem *Il pastor fido*, to which the defendant had replied, rather insolently, that he had given his poetry "a new impetus, as it were, and, I dare say, a new luster."[20]

Table 5.1 **Performances of Da Ponte's works at the National Theater (1784–91)**

1784–85	1785–86	1786–87	1787–88	1788–89	1789–90	1790–91
6 (1)	6 (2)	38 (4)	42 (3)	76 (4)	83 (2)	99 (2)

(Figures in brackets refer to premieres)

17. Pillgrab, "Lorenzo Da Ponte's Work for the Stage," 59–60.

18. *Oberdeutsche Staatszeitung* (26 January 1789), no. 18, 139: Wien, den 21sten Jäner: "Die neue Oper, die sich unter der Feder des berühmten Abate d'Aponti befindet, und aus einem italiänischen Lieblingsdichter S. M. bearbeitet wird, ist bereits zur Hälfte fertig, und ganz Wien hoffet, daß ihre Vollendung und Aufführung den Theaterunterhaltungen in diesem Fasching die *Krone* aufsetzen werde."

19. Edge, "Mozart's Reception," 107. Two librettos are extant, one of which reduces the opera from four to three acts. Rice, *Antonio Salieri*, 429–30.

20. De Alwis, *Anti-Da Ponte*, 51 and 57.

Thanks to all these factors—the Ochakiv victory, the emperor's partial resumption of his habits as a theatergoer, and Da Ponte's careful deference to his tastes—the rescue plan was given the go-ahead, and the change of mind was announced on 21 January 1789.[21] The decision, of course, meant that hopes for peace must now be improving.[22] Interesting insights into the state of opera in Vienna at this critical juncture are provided by Reitzenstein. Writing around the time the reprieve was announced, he reported that opera had been in decline for several months. A number of outstanding singers had yet to be replaced, although there were hopes that this might happen. Nothing could be said for certain. Contributing to the instability was the frequency of change; every three months, an Italian came and went—a reference, seemingly, to the Coltellini debacle. Reitzenstein acknowledged that significant resources had to be deployed by the management to attract singers who might be reluctant to come, given the high salaries in their own countries. He was also very struck by the role of public opinion in the formation of the opera troupe, a revealing observation in the light of the overtly populist policy that Da Ponte was about to introduce.[23]

Details of the new arrangements began to trickle out. A group of fourteen unnamed aristocratic backers, led by Prince Alois Joseph Liechtenstein, were said to have agreed to underwrite the new initiative, which would stage eight operas during the course of the year.[24] The consortium presumably had to accept liability for any expenses not covered by subscriptions and nightly receipts. No other source confirms this arrangement, yet Liechtenstein's involvement is by no means unlikely. He is known to have hosted a series of *comédies de société* in 1784 at which operas were performed.[25] That these

21. Link, *National Court Theatre,* 327: "Chez le grand *chambelan*. Il m'annonça que l'opera reste aux frais de la Cour."

22. *Bayreuther Zeitung* (31 January 1789), no. 14, 101: Wien, vom 23. Januar: "Endlich haben Se. Majest. dem Wunsch des Adels und des gesammten Publikums nachgegeben, und die bereits abgedankte Italiänische Opera wiederum auf dem alten Fuß zu behalten geruhet, woraus man neuerdings große Hofnung zum Frieden schöpfen will."

23. Reitzenstein, *Reise nach Wien,* 342: "Ueberhaupt läßt sich über die Besetzung der Oper nichts Gewisses sagen. Jedes viertel Jahr gibt es Veränderungen, denn die Italiener laufen ab und zu. Uebrigens wendet die Direction viel Geld an gute Sänger und Sängerinnen. Das ist aber auch nöthig, wenn man sie ihrem Vaterlande entreißen will, wo sie außerordentlich gut bezahlt werden. Das Publicum hier trägt viel zur Bildung der Operisten bey; es ist sehr eigensinnig, so wohl was die Musik im Ganzen, als auch den Vortrag betrifft."

24. *Preßburger Zeitung* (7 February 1789), no. 11, 85: Wien, vom 4. Feb: "Die italienischen Opern allhier werden nun auf Kosten einer Gesellschaft von 14 Kavaliers, worunter der Fürst Louis Lichtenstein der erste ist, unterhalten; der Hof giebt das Theater gegen dem, daß sie die Garderobe ablösen müssen; es werden wöchentlich zweymal, und alle Jahr 8 Opern gegeben."

25. Link, "Vienna's Private Theatrical and Musical Life," 235; Link, *National Court Theatre,* 197.

were full-scale productions is evident from Mozart's letter of 20 March 1784 in which he complains of having to reschedule his concert, as Prince Liechtenstein has "not only abducted the cream of the nobility but the best musicians from the orchestra."[26] As a patron of music, he remains a rather shadowy figure, but in the summer of 1789 he promoted a concert series for an otherwise unknown society, the "Gesellschaft der Musikliebhaber." On one occasion sponsored by this group, battle music by Wenzel Müller was given in the garden of Liechtenstein's palace.[27] It is not known whether any society members were connected to the group backing the opera troupe.

Da Ponte said nothing about a formal group of aristocratic supporters in his memoirs, but he did outline his core scheme, which involved a retrenchment in expenditure and the setting-up of a fund of 100,000 gulden, made up from box subscriptions and London-style packages for single seats.[28] He optimistically anticipated that this would produce a clear profit of 25,000 gulden a year. He recalled that Rosenberg received news of the reprieve with delight but that the auditor Johann Thorwart, whose duties included management of the sets and the wardrobe, thought the plan would not work. At the time, Zinzendorf noted significant interest among foreign diplomats, a group with a clear professional interest in seeing a program of opera.[29]

The start of the 1789–90 season also saw significant changes to the organization of the German theater company. It was announced on 2 March that Franz Karl Brockmann would henceforth be in sole charge under Rosenberg, replacing the existing committee of five, the much-maligned "Ausschuß."[30] The *Bayreuther Zeitung*, often a useful source of information about management changes in Vienna, published an overview.[31] According to its assessment of the new arrangements, Brockmann was set to receive an additional 200

26. Spaethling, *Mozart's Letters*, 366.

27. Edge, review of Morrow, *Concert Life*, 151, 156, and 157.

28. Da Ponte, *Memoirs*, 181–83.

29. Link, *National Court Theatre*, 326, points out that in the absence of an official court in Vienna, foreign diplomats valued the chance to meet the emperor during his frequent visits to the theater: "15. Janvier: Chez le grand *Chambelan*. L'abbé *da Ponte* lui parla d'un projet de souscription pour garder ici l'opera Italien, ou tous les ministres etrangers veulent souscrire." Ferrarese was present at this meeting to bolster support for the new initiative.

30. *Bayreuther Zeitung* (10 March 1789), no. 30, 221: Schreiben aus Wien, vom 2 März: "Herr Brockmann . . . ist . . . Selbstherrscher Director geworden, steht unmittelbar unter dem Graf Rosenberg." A long report on German theater appeared in the *Grätzer Zeitung* (21 March 1789), no. 23. Link, *National Court Theatre*, 483.

31. *Bayreuther Zeitung* (28 March 1789), no. 38, 279. Schreiben aus Wien, vom 20 März.

gulden per annum, bringing his combined salary (with his wife's) to 3,000. A new appointment was that of Johann Friedrich Jünger, who was made poet at a salary of 600 gulden.[32] One of his plays had been selected as the festive work for Maria Theresia in Laxenburg, and there is thus a clear parallel with Mozart and Salieri. In all three cases, the provision of a gala work was followed by career advancement, when a position became available.

It is not known exactly when Da Ponte began work on *L'ape musicale,* but the plan to organize a collective benefit, a lighthearted satire with music from the most popular operas of the season, was conceived well before the reprieve of the opera buffa troupe was announced.[33] A commentary published in Salzburg acknowledged the commercial potential of the scheme but adopted a rather cynical tone.[34] It stated that two such operas were in preparation. This could have been a misunderstanding of the evolving nature of the pasticcio, but equally Da Ponte may have been intending that every leading member of the troupe should be offered a spot, this being a general end-of-contract occasion.[35] In the event, the welcome crisis precipitated by the reprieve forced a sudden change of plan. The pasticcio, probably conceived initially as part of the campaign to ensure a continuation of opera buffa, could now be presented to Joseph as a heartfelt expression of gratitude. A work in the tradition of the emperor's memorable publicity coup at Schönbrunn—opera about opera— was ideally suited to both purposes. Making use of a framework in which singers could first discuss and then perform their favorite arias from the recent past, it would be possible to salute Joseph's taste and to celebrate the very real popular success his program had enjoyed. The inclusion of Benucci's aria from Salieri's *La scuola de'gelosi,* which the new opera buffa ensemble had

---

32. Link, *National Court Theatre,* 434.

33. The title page reads: "L'APE MUSICALE / COMEDIA per MUSICA / IN DUE ATTI / DA RAPPRESENTARSI / LA QUADRAGESIMA DELL'ANNO / M.DCC LXXXIX. /NEL TEATRO DI CORTE / A / BENEFIZIO DI ALCUNI VIRTUOSI. / IN VIENNA / NELLA IMPER. STAMPERIA DEI SORDI, a MUTI." On the texts of these pasticcios, see Siniscalchi, *L'Ape Musicale.* Link, *National Court Theatre,* 18, suggests that he borrowed the idea of a collective benefit from Morichelli's oratorio performances in February 1788.

34. *Oberdeutsche Staatszeitung* (26 January 1789), no. 18, 139: Wien, den 21sten Jäner: "Künftige Fastenzeit bleibt die Nationalhofschaubühne verschlossen. Die Gesellschaft der wälschen Operisten ist daher auf den glücklichen Einfall gerathen, noch vor ihrer Auflösung die Gutmüthigkeit des Publikums tüchtig zu plündern. Sie stückeln aus allen zuvor gegebenen Opern Musik und Text zusammen, machen zwey neue Opern daraus, und unterhalten die Liebhaber während der Fasten auf eigene Rechnung damit. Daß es geld trägt, daran ist kein Zweifel."

35. After the benefit for Madame "Feraresa" on 7 March, the next performance was "mit neuen Veränderungen." *Journal des Luxus und der Moden* (June 1789), 243.

given on 2 April 1783 as its debut performance, enabled the satire to embrace the era as a whole.

The contents of *L'ape musicale* as it evolved can be established from three sources, as shown in Table 5.2. The libretto provides a list of source operas, including incipits of the original texts, and names the composers. It also gives a cast list, identifying the performer of each character. Two advertisements in the *Wiener Zeitung* publicized some of the replacement pieces, but while the first lines, genres, and voice types are identified, there is no indication of character, and in only a few instances is the performer named.[36] The number of solos allocated to each member of the cast reflected their status: Benucci, Ferrarese, Laschi, and Albertarelli received three each. (Benucci's farewell song is not listed but appears as a fourth solo.) Although Mombelli only had two arias, he also featured twice as a composer. Francesca Benucci, a lesser singer, had only a single solo. A note in the libretto advised the reader that should any piece fare less well than expected, it would be changed.[37] By this measure, Albertarelli was the least successful; all three of his offerings in the original libretto had to be replaced, although one may have been reinstated. The most eye-catching addition was Benucci's "Non più andrai." Mozart, who had yet to depart for Berlin, perhaps heard the great performer who had so electrified everyone at the original rehearsal of *Le nozze di Figaro*. Figaro's aria had since marked the conclusion of Franz's visit to the Nostitz Theater in October 1787, and its performance now welcomed back the minimally battle-hardened Habsburg heir. The response to this piece could even have been a contributory factor in the decision to schedule a new production of the opera.

From the start, the pasticcio celebrates the emperor's tastes, and it is thus not surprising that Salieri's music should feature so prominently. The poet Bonario, representing Da Ponte himself, decides to begin his work with the terzetto "Venite donne meco" from *La grotta di Trofonio*, an acknowledgment of the primacy of Joseph's favorite composer. An annotation in Salieri's hand on the autograph of this piece states: "it has always been regarded as one of the best pieces in the opera."[38] The first solo piece, from which the title *L'ape musicale* itself derives, is a cavatina from Joseph's prized opera *Axur*. Da Ponte

---

36. Link, *National Court Theatre*, 139. *Wiener Zeitung* (21 March 1789), no. 23, 687; (28 March 1789), no. 25, 763.

37. "Si avverte che sì cangeranno di sera in sera tutti quei pezzi che faranno minor effetto di quello che si spera."

38. Hunter, *Culture of Opera Buffa*, 270: "fu sempre riguardato come una dei pezzi particolari dell'opera." Its appearance in Hoffmeister's series of operatic arrangements for flute quintet confirms its appeal. Ridgewell, "A Newly Identified Viennese Mozart Edition," 122.

Table 5.2 The contents of *L'ape musicale* (1789)

No.	Libretto	*Wiener Zeitung* 21 March 1789	*Wiener Zeitung* 28 March 1789
Act 1			
[1]	Il Terz. del Trofonio *Venite Donne meco* Del Sig. Sal.	L'Introduz. *Sedete amici miei*	L'Introduz. *Sedete amici miei*
[2]	La Cavatina d'Axur *Com'Ape ingegnosa* Del Sig. Sal.	Cav. Basso *Com'ape ingegnosa*	Cav. Basso *Com'ape ingegnosa*
[3]	L'Aria della Cosa rara *Dolce mi parve undì* Del Sig. Mart.		
[4]	Il Terz. del Ricco d'un G. *Permettete Emilia bella* Del Sig. Sal.	Terz. *Permettete o Madamina*	Terz. *Permettete o Madamina*
[5]	L'Aria delle vendemmie *Quando saprai chi sono* Del Sig. Gazza.	Ar. B *Donne mie voi siete quelle*	Ar. B. *Donne mie voi siete quelle*

(continued)

Table 5.2 Continued

No.	Libretto	Wiener Zeitung 21 March 1789	Wiener Zeitung 28 March 1789
[6]	Il Terz. della Cosa rara *Dirò che perfida* Del Sig. Mart.	Q[uartetto] (Bonario participates briefly) *Chè una petegolla senza creanza*	Q[uartetto] *Chè una petegolla senza creanza*
[7]	Una Scena francese *Dell'Amor Artigiano* Del Sig. Gasm.	Recitativo. Cavatina Soprano *Que vos yeux sont touchants / Votre coeur aimable flore*	Recitativo. Cavatina Soprano *Que vos yeux sont touchants / Votre coeur aimable flore*
[8]	Una Cavatina francese *Amour nous parle* Del Sig. Anf.	[Cavatina] Soprano col Mandolino *Amour nous parle sans cesse*	[Cavatina] Soprano col Mandolino *Amour nous parle sans cesse*
[9]	Un'Aria franc. del Tarar. *Je sui ne* Del Sig. Sal.	Romance Tenor (Ahi povero Calpigi) *Je sui né natif de ferrare*	Romance Tenor (Ahi *Je sui né natif de* povero Calpigi) *ferrare*
[10]	Un'Aria delle Gel. fortun. *Lasciatemi stare* Del. Sig. Cim.	[Romance] B. (Non posso parlare lasciatemi star) *Un vate Signora*	[Romance] B. (Non posso parlare lasciatemi star) *Un vate Signora*
[11]	Un'Aria dell'Arb. di D. *Sereno raggio* Del Sig. Mart.	Cavatina Soprano *Da questi Liniamenti, intendo chiaramente*	Cavatina Soprano *Da questi Liniamenti, intendo chiaramente*
[12]	Un Duetto del D. Giov. *Là ci darem la mano* Del Sig. Moz.		Duet. S e T *Là ci darem la mano*
	Finale	Finale	Finale

Act 2

		Recitativo Rond. S.	Dunque per un infido / Il mio cor gli affetti miei	Recitativo Rond. S.	Dunque per un infido / Il mio cor gli affetti miei
[1]	L'Aria del Falegn. Trattar le cause Del Sig. Cim.	A[ria] T.	Voi che sapete che cosa è	A[ria] T.	Voi che sapete che cosa è amor
[2]	L'Aria delle Trame D. Le Donzellette Del Sig. Cim.	d S.	Le Donzellette che sono amanti	d S.	Le Donzellette che sono amanti
[3]	L'Aria Ti lascio al caro amante Di Giordan.				
[4]	Il Duetto dell'Ital. in Lond. Care piante Del Sig. Mon.	Duet. S. e T.	Care piante fortunate	Duet. S. e T.	Care piante fortunate
				Cavatina S. Die Alt.	Quantunque vecchierella
[5]	L'Aria della Scol. dei Gel. Adagio allor potrei Del Sig. Sal.	Trz.	Ah chi sa questo suo male	Trz.	Ah chi sa questo suo male

(continued)

Table 5.2 Continued

No.	Libretto	*Wiener Zeitung* 21 March 1789	*Wiener Zeitung* 28 March 1789
[6]	Il Quartet. della For. d. D. *Se colui non osservasse* Del Sig. Mar.	Aria Basso *Non più andrai farfallone amoroso*	Aria Basso *Non più andrai farfallone amoroso*
[7]	La Cavat. dei Viag. Fel. *Per una picca* Del Sig. Pic.		Cavatina Basso *Per una picca per un puntiglio*
[8]	La Scena dell'Ingl. Strav. *Non sai che farmi* Del Sig. Mom. *Paris son io* [not listed in table of contents]	Cavatina Soprano *Sento che in seno mi batte il core*	Cavatina Soprano *Sento che in seno mi batte il core* Recit. B. Die Beurlauberung des Hrn. Benucci *Paris son ivi che per destin fatale*

[9]	La Sce. dell'Arb. di Diana.	Ah se tu m'ami Del Sig. Tarch.		Recit. Rond. S.	Ah se tu m'ami / Ah sol bramo e mia speranza	Recit. Rond. S.	Ah se tu m'ami / Ah sol bramo e mia speranza
				Recit. Rondeau S.	Sposa! Consorte! / cari ogetti del mio core / Compatite e i casi miei, / Compiangete il mi dolor)	Recit. Rondeau S.	Sposa! Consorte! / cari ogetti del mio core / Compatite e i casi miei, / Compiangete il mi dolor)
	Finale		Finale Duetto S. e T. Die Beurlaubung des Herrn und Frau Mombelli von Wien "gesungen den 14. März d. J. in der letzten Vorstellung dieser Opera"	Qui dove lieu instanti (Die Stadt die mich belebte)		Finale Duetto S. e T. Die Beurlaubung des Herrn und Frau Mombelli von Wien "gesungen den 14. März d. J. in der letzten Vorstellung dieser Opera"	Qui dove lieu instanti (Die Stadt die mich belebte).

develops a metaphor: just as a bee sucks pollen in order to make honey, so a treasury of musical gems can be assembled.[39] A signal that Da Ponte saw his pasticcio as a chance to put right earlier difficulties with Salieri was his inclusion of a substantial piece from *Il ricco d'un giorno*, the terzetto "Permettete Emilia bella." In his memoirs he recollected that after the total failure of this opera, Salieri had declared that he would never again set one of his texts. The appearance of "Permettete" might have been taken as a conciliatory, even self-deprecating gesture: saluting the quality of the music, now that it bore a completely new text.[40]

Salieri's music dominates the opening scenes of *L'ape musicale*, but Martín y Soler's *Una cosa rara*, the most widely admired opera of the era, also makes an early appearance with the aria "Dolce mi parve un dì." Brunetto (Albertarelli) enters with a touch of humor, as he appears to be practicing the opening statement of an operatic canon from the same opera "Perchè mai nel sen perchè." (This piece is not identified in the list of contents.) Da Ponte, who evidently had a good deal of respect for the depth of the emperor's operatic knowledge, knew that not all his carefully planted references would be picked up by the imperial ear, but no one seemed in any doubt that Joseph enjoyed such challenges.

As the singers assemble and start to propose arias, a desire to sing in French is debated at surprising length. Ferrarese (Zuccherina) is the first to express her wish: "Ma voglio che tu faccia / Il mio *rolo* in francese." Bonario points out that he speaks French badly and writes it even less well. Several French operas are suggested as sources for arias, including Salieri's *Les Danaïdes*, but Ferrarese settles on one by "un celebre autor," Florian Gassmann, previously well known to the emperor as one of his chamber musicians. Although in French, "Que vos yeux sont touchants" comes from his most popular Italian opera, *L'amore artigiano*. Farinelli (Laschi) is enthusiastic, but she can ill afford to be seen to be less capable than her rival, and so it is incumbent upon her to sing in French as well—she chooses "Amour nous parle sans cesse," a cavatina by Anfossi with mandolin accompaniment. A certain amount of banter ensues between the two singers married in real life, as Mombelli (Don Capriccio) now joins those intending to sing in French. His wife (Laschi) immediately casts aspersions upon his pronunciation, but he refuses to back down, choosing the romance with guitar accompaniment for Calpigi, the male

39. Siniscalchi, *L'ape musicale*, 119; Brown, *W. A. Mozart: Così fan tutte*, 58.

40. In February 1789, Franz purchased a piano score of *Il ricco d'un giorno* from Sukowaty. Some connection with the benefit seems probable. Dunlop, " 'Kaisersammlung,' " 58.

slave character in *Tarare*. Husband and wife thus compete in singing to the accompaniment of a plucked instrument. The extended discussion of French music seems curious in a lighthearted satire on opera buffa, but it recognizes Salieri's achievements in French opera and Joseph's keen interest in them. It may also allude to an incident known only from Ignaz von Mosel's biography of the composer, which describes (in the manner of an anecdote) how Joseph's attempt to familiarize himself with Salieri's music in advance of the premiere of *Axur*, his Italian version of *Tarare*, was thwarted when performing materials for the two versions could not be made to match up.[41] Encountering him a while later, the emperor wondered why his beautiful French music had needed to be changed.

Much humor in *L'ape musicale* stems from the comical onstage depiction of real-life pairings. Ferrarese excoriates the efforts both of Martín y Soler ("bestia di maestro") and of her own lover, whose lines are enough to make cats weep ("e che versi / Da far piangere i gatti"). Given Da Ponte's relationship with Ferrarese, it must have been amusing when in a scene with her rival Laschi (act 1, scene 7), his character (Bonario) seems to enact the beginnings of an affair. After Farinelli has sung "Sereno raggio" from *L'arbore di Diana*, the two of them discuss a future engagement in Naples. A marriage between music and poetry is on the cards, but innuendo, in typical Da Ponte style, dominates: "*Far* . . . frattanto Compagni di viaggio / Per Napoli sarem . . . e poi . . . e poi . . . *Bon*. Sì, vita mia, come più piace a voi." They then perform "Là ci darem la mano," with Da Ponte parodying his own lyric.[42]

As the climax of act 2 approaches, the rivalry between the two *prime donne* comes into focus. In act 2, scene 4, both refuse to concede precedence: "[Ferrarese] Vo che la parte mia / Sia la prima dell'opera; "[Laschi] In tal caso / M'oppongo: perchè voglio / Che sia prima la maï." In order to keep the peace, Bonario promises equality. In effect, this was a rerun, for Joseph's benefit, of his Schönbrunn commissions, which depict rival sopranos quarreling over their status until parity is agreed. The last solo in the pasticcio is Ferrarese's rondò, for which there is a substantial satirical buildup. In the aftermath of the Ochakiv victory, the war was not off limits for humor. As the choice of music is considered, Bonario mistakenly refers to the well-known Italian opera composer as Angelo "Turchi." The instinctive response is: "Ohime!" Bonario does not like Turkish music: "La musica dei Turchi a

---

41. Mosel, *Ueber das Leben*, 130.

42. The Mozart parodies in *L'ape musicale* were discussed by Küster, "Lorenzo da Ponte's Viennese Librettos," 221–31.

me non piace." Everyone immediately interjects: "Ah, ah, ah," and it is left to
Zuccherina (Ferrarese) to explain reassuringly: "Angelo Tarchi, / E non angelo Turchi." The rondò is Tarchi's scena "Ah se tu m'ami / Ah sol bramo, o
mia speranza," one of two pieces by that composer inserted into L'arbore di
Diana for Ferrarese.[43] But the advertisement in the Wiener Zeitung suggests
that at some point she replaced this with another Tarchi piece, "Cari oggetti
del mia core," the aria heard by Zinzendorf when he attended her benefit on
7 March 1789: "le soir a l'opera . . . Ensuite La ferraresi chanta le rondeau de
Giulio Sabino. Compatite i casi miei, compiangete il mio dolor." It had been
performed in Vienna by Marchesi as an insertion aria in Sarti's Giulio Sabino,
the production personally ordered by Joseph II.[44] It was then chosen by Casti,
doubtless because of this, as one of the pieces to be parodied in Prima la
musica.[45] The reason for its inclusion at the climax of L'ape musicale is clear
enough: on behalf of the whole troupe, Ferrarese was saluting the emperor in
his role as impresario, acknowledging both his success with Marchesi and the
evening in the Schönbrunn Orangerie. Da Ponte does not say that Joseph II
was able to attend a performance, but he recalled that he at least paid for his
box, offering double the amount on the night of his own benefit.[46]

THE UNEXPECTED REPRIEVE of Italian opera prompted commentators to
take stock of the situation that now confronted the theatrical world in Vienna.
There was still much insecurity over the long-term prospects for both the

43. Armbruster, "Salieri, Mozart und die Wiener Fassung des Giulio Sabino," 153.

44. Link, National Court Theatre, 370.

45. Armbuster, "Salieri, Mozart und die Wiener Fassung des Giulio Sabino," 157.

46. L'ape musicale appears to have been a financial success, but the scheduling of Laschi's
benefit performance on 6 March 1789 raises a puzzling question. According to a hand-
written note on a copy of a libretto for Messiah, there was a performance of the oratorio at
the residence of Count Johann Eszterházy the same night. Deutsch, Mozart: A Documentary
Biography, 335. This is surprising, because direct clashes of this kind were almost always
avoided through the simple expedient of scheduling oratorios on play nights, as demonstrated
in Table 4.1. (The memorial Requiem for Gluck on 8 April 1788 was similarly on a play night.)
There was no point in splitting the audience for music or risking the unavailability of the
best performers. Zinzendorf attended a performance of Messiah on 7 April, and as large-
scale oratorio productions were often given on consecutive nights, a possible explanation
is that the unknown author of the annotation simply got the month wrong. Link, National
Court Theatre, 332: "Avant 7h au Concert chez Jean Eszterházy. Der Meßias, au musique de
haendel. J'y pris un peu d'ennui quoique la musique fut bien belle." A consequence of this
redating would be that the letter written by Gottfried van Swieten on 21 March 1789, in which
he comments favorably on Mozart's decision to replace an aria with recitative, would gain
credibility, as the chronological inconsistency implied by a 6 March performance of Messiah
would disappear.

troupes at the National Theater, and in consequence the debate as to the merits of the competing national genres was renewed with some venom. The focus remained the two hit operas by Martín y Soler. An anonymous pamphlet considered questions of morality and reformation of taste, deploring what was on offer at the Leopoldstadttheater. The author remarked that Eberl, one of its dramatists, was notorious for his bungling ("Verpfuschung") of *Una cosa rara* and implored him not to indulge in another such castration.[47] Franz Kratter, lamenting what he regarded as the indifference of the public toward German theater, laid the blame firmly on opera buffa. Admitting that its performers were talented, he regarded its music as barely mediocre and its plots inadequate.[48] This did not seem to matter, as an opera's triumph would be guaranteed if one of its tunes were to seize the public imagination and end up being sung in coffee shops and taverns and echoing in lanes and walkways. Yet his fears for the future of German theater in Vienna were unfounded. After a difficult period in 1788, the acting troupe, like the opera buffa, was about to experience a revival of its fortunes.[49]

---

47. *Bitte an Damen Wiens,* 15: "Eberl ward durch die Uebersetzung, oder Verpfuschung der cosa rara berühmt; aber ich möchte ihn im Namen der Kunst, des Dichters und des Kapellmeisters inständigst gebeten haben, derlei Geschöpfe nicht mehr so elendiglich zu kastriren."

48. Kratter, *Philosophische und statistische Beobachtungen,* vol. 1, 200: "Die vorzüglichste Ursache an dem Kaltsinne der Nation gegen das vaterländische Spiel war die welsche Oper. . . . Wahr ist es, die Gesellschaft hatte ihre musikalischen Talente. . . . Allein ihre Musik war oft kaum mittelmässig; die Poesie ihrer Stücke beinahe immer tief unter allem gesunden Menschen verstande."

49. This was led, ironically, by the success of Kratter's own work *Der Vicekanzler. Stralsundische Zeitung* (16 April 1789), no. 46: Wien, den 1 April: "Seit mehreren Jahren hat hier kein neues Stück so vieles Aufsehn gemacht, als das neue Schauspiel des Herrn Kratter, der Vicekanzler. Bey den beyden ersten Vorstellungen war die Einnahme, die Logen und abonnirten Plätze ungerechnet, 1200 Gulden."

6

Da Ponte as Impresario

THE REVIVAL OF *FIGARO*

IN ORDER TO construct a commercially viable season for the reprieved opera buffa, Da Ponte first had to locate additional singers, no easy task owing to the loss of the entire recruitment period. A news item published in Bologna identified individuals who were leaving and those who were expected to come.[1] It is interesting to have confirmation that Morella and Albertarelli had not been highly regarded, and the published list for the 1789–90 season in the *Indice de' teatrali spettacoli* shows that these two singers did indeed leave the troupe. The entry for Vienna is given in Table 6.1.[2]

The departure of Morella and Albertarelli excludes the possibility that one of them sang the role of the Count in the 1789 revival of *Figaro*.[3] The return of Vincenzo Calvesi, who in effect had to be rehired, was urgent enough to warrant the dispatch of an express courier.[4] Girolamo Cruciati seems also to have been recruited in haste. Having sung in the soirées presented by

---

1. *Gazzetta di Bologna* (31 January 1789), 72: VIENNA 22. Gennajo: "Martedì 20. del corrente S. M. l'*Imperadore* si degnò di far riconfermare al suo servizio la Compagnìa dell'Opera buffa *Italiana*. Partono però di quà il Tenore *Mombelli* con la *Laschi* sua moglie, il buffo *Benucci*, ed i due mal graditi *Bertarelli*, e *Morella*. Rimangono però la *Ferraresi*, la *Cavalieri*, la *Taiber*, il *Bussani* per Direttore delle Scene, e guardarobba ec., la sua moglie, ed il Signor *Nicoletto* dal *Sole*; e si attendono ora il Tenore *Calvesi*, il buffo *Morelli*, una prima donna, ed un Mezzo carattere."

2. *Indice de' teatrali spettacoli*, vol. 1, 853.

3. Edge, "Mozart's Viennese Copyists," 1668–75.

4. *Preßburger Zeitung* (7 February 1789), no. 11, 85: Wien, vom 4. Feb. Calvesi had been due to return to Vienna along with Stefano Mandini. Link, *Arias for Vincenzo Calvesi*, xxv. Whether a letter he wrote to Joseph, forwarded to Rosenberg on 11 June 1788, represented his acceptance of terms for the voiding of his contract is unclear. Payer von Thurn, *Joseph II. als Theaterdirektor*, 80.

Table 6.1 Singers listed in the Vienna entry in *Indice de' teatrali spettacoli*
(1789–90)

VIENNA
Dalla Quaresima 1789 a tutto il Carnivale 1790
Nel R. teatro Nazionale della R. I. Corte si rappresentarono varj Drammi giocosi in musica, oltre le Tragedie, e Commedie Tedesche dalli Comici della Real Corte, e Virtuosi Cantanti . . .

SIGNORI ATTORI

Adrianna Ferraresi	Francesco Benucci
Caterina Cavaliere	Valentino Adamberger
Luigi [*sic*] Villeneuve	Vincenzo Calvesi
Dorotea Bussani	Francesco Bussani
Francesca Benucci	Gio. Battista Brocchi
Luigia Colombati	Nicola del Sole
Mad. Saal	Girolamo Cruciati
	Giuseppe Calvesi
	Mons. Saal

I Signori Accademici Armonici in Florence on 8 and 15 March, he might have been expected to complete the series, but his name is omitted in reviews of the performances on 22 and 29 March, perhaps suggesting that he had already left for Vienna.[5] At some point, the idea of hiring the "leading" basso buffo Giovanni Morelli as a replacement for Benucci seems to have been mooted, perhaps with the intention of pleasing Joseph, who had been impressed by Morelli in Italy.[6] Such a recruitment would have seen a direct switch of *buffi* between London and Vienna, but if this was the idea, it proved unworkable, and Da Ponte turned instead to Giovanni Battista Brocchi, the singer who had created Figaro in the original St. Petersburg production of *Il barbiere di Siviglia* in 1782.[7] This could have been the result of a recommendation by Ferrarese,

---

5. *Gazzetta Toscana* (1789), nos. 11, 12, 13 & 14.

6. Payer von Thurn, *Joseph II. als Theaterdirektor*, 42: "J'y ai trouvé un Buffon qui chante la Basse appellé Morelli, qui a une excellente voix et plus forte encore que celle de Bennucci, ce talent se trouve reuni avec celui d'etre un très bon acteur." Joseph might have received an update on Morelli's virtues from his sister Marie-Antoinette in Versailles. In the summer of 1787, following the end of the season in London, a group of Italian singers traveled to France to present a series of operas. In its extended coverage of this bold initiative, the *Calendrier musical universal*, vol. 9 (1788), 114, noted that Morelli was possessed of "une voix de basse superbe."

7. Edge, "Mozart's Reception," 84 and 98.

whose up-to-date knowledge of the Italian opera scene would have enabled her to offer useful recruitment advice. After a contract in London, she returned to Italy in the autumn of 1786 to sing in Florence.[8] In Lent 1787, she took part with Brocchi in a concert in the Teatro di via della Pergola, and their duet was singled out for special acclaim.[9] Another singer with whom Ferrarese sang at the Pergola in the autumn of 1787, Giuseppe Calvesi, was also recruited for Vienna. He made his debut in a new run of Cimarosa's *Il falegname*. The strength of the Florentine connection during the emergency at the start of 1789 is clearly seen in the pattern of hiring. Another recruit known personally to Ferrarese was Luigia Colombati; both had taken part in a performance of *Il conte di Saldagna* in Milan in 1787.[10]

As the new season got under way in the spring of 1789, it quickly became clear that the hastily assembled troupe of singers was failing to impress. In part this was because the National Theater was facing stiff competition from the revitalized suburban stage. Improbable though it would have seemed a few months earlier, when the demise of opera at the National Theater appeared unstoppable, there were some evenings on which operagoers had their pick of three works. On 30 April 1789, *Der Wienerbothe* listed: "Im k.k. Nazionaltheater: Der Türke in Italien. In der Leopoldstadt: Talismano. Im Theater auf der Wieden: Die Entführung aus dem Serail."[11] In view of the degree of choice available, the opera buffa troupe needed their new singers to have successful debuts, but the first two on 28 April were to little effect.[12] A supplementary round of recruitment suddenly seemed an urgent necessity. Several years later, on the verge of dismissal from his post, Da Ponte wrote a memorandum outlining the case for retaining Ferrarese del Bene. He recalled the state in which the opera troupe found itself following the failure of a series of highly recommended singers: Coltellini, so famous in Naples; Brocchi, so highly praised by Paisiello; Colombati—the name passes without

---

8. *Calendrier musical universal*, vol. 9 (1788), 133.

9. *Gazzetta Toscana* (1787), no. 9, 35: FIRENZE 3. Marzo: "diverse Arie dette con gran maestria dalla rinomata Sig. Adriana Ferraresi, non meno, che dai bravi Professori. . . . Gio Batista Brocchi, il quale cantò con la Donna un duetto così grazioso, e scritto con una Musica talmente espressiva, e piacevole, che meritò una generale richiesta di replica dalla numerosa udienza." The concert series is mentioned in *Calendrier musical universal*, vol. 9 (1788), 154.

10. The performance was dedicated to Ferdinand and his wife in the customary manner: "Alla Scala la Primavera Dell'Anno 1787. Dedicato Alle LL. AA. RR. Il Serenissimo Arciduca Ferdinando . . . e la Serenissima Arciduchessa."

11. Edge, "Mozart's Viennese Orchestras," 87.

12. Link, *National Court Theatre*, 333: "Le Soir a l'opera . . . C'etoit *Il Turco in Italia*. Musique de Seidelmann. Mlle Colombati y debuta assez mal et le buffo Cruciati."

comment; and Cruciati, sent by a famous agent with so many plaudits.[13] This was the reason for the "haste with which we were obliged to hire Villeneuve and Benucci."[14]

Luigia Villeneuve was singing in Monza in the autumn of 1788, and it is possible that Joseph's brother Ferdinand agreed to release her to assist the Vienna troupe.[15] At her debut on 27 June, she was well received.[16] But the key hiring success was Benucci, who had been lured away to London by Sir John Gallini during the period when the opera buffa seemed on the verge of dissolution.[17] After six years of secure employment in Vienna, Benucci was worried about his prospects and asked for a letter of recommendation. The emperor wrote to Leopold: "Benucci . . . has requested me urgently to send you this small note. I should do him the justice to say that during his six years here he has conducted himself in an exemplary fashion."[18] The singer had to make decisions about his future, but by the time the reprieve was announced, he had already committed himself to a London engagement. The departure of its most highly regarded performer was a blow to the Italian opera ensemble, but Benucci's absence proved to be for a period shorter than expected, as his London contract was terminated following a fire at the King's Theatre. He made his return debut on 15 September in a performance of *Una cosa rara*, for which a bill stated that Herr Benucci would sing the role of Tita "again

13. Michtner, "Der Fall Abbé Da Ponte," 190–91: "lo stato in cui ci siam ritrovati alla venuta della Coltellini, tanto famosa in Napoli, di Brocchi dal Paisiello tanto lodato, della Colombati, dei Crociati mandatici con tanti elogi da un famoso sensale."

14. Michtner, "Der Fall Abbé Da Ponte," 190–91: "e la fretta con cui abbiamo dovuto procurarci la Villeneuve e il Benucci."

15. *Indice de' teatrali spettacoli*, vol. 1, 748. She had attained the status of prima donna by the time of her appearances in Venice during Carnival 1788. *Calendrier musical universal*, vol. 10 (1789), 189: "Femmes 1. Luiggia Villeneuve."

16. *Preßburger Zeitung* (1 July 1789), no. 52, 446: "Mademoiselle Louise Villneuve in der Rolle des Amors debutirte. Das Publikum bezeigte eine unaussprechliche Zufriedenheit über den Wohlstand, die Wahrheit, und den Nachdruck, mit dem sich die junge Sängerin produzirt hat; ihre Fähigkeit in der Schauspielkunst, und ihre Methode im Singen erhielt den ungetheilten Beyfall der zahlreichen Zuhörer."

17. *Morning Herald* (14 July 1788): "Sir J. GALLINI is going to Paris and Italy to muster troops for next season." It seems likely that he remained in Paris for most of the time, attempting to put together a dance troupe. The story was reported regularly in the *Courier de l'Europe* in the autumn of 1788: nos. 301, 318, 349, and 374.

18. Arneth, *Joseph II. und Leopold*, vol. 2, 214: "Benucci que vous connaissez, partant d'ici à la fin de ce carnaval, tout l'opéra buffa cessant, m'a instamment prié de vous envoyer ce petit mémoire. Je lui dois la justice qu'il s'est pendant six ans parfaitement bien conduit ici."

for the first time."[19] He had lost none of his rapport with the audience. Critics remained positive, and in 1790 he was highly rated in a review of performers.[20]

In addition to these recruitment successes, the troupe began to benefit from a marked improvement in the reputation of Dorotea Bussani. Although Da Ponte disliked her, her new standing was eventually reflected both in her salary level and in increasingly favorable notices.[21] In successive seasons, her husband, Francesco, had seen his pay creep up (2,424 to 2,445 to 2,451 to 2,520 gulden), possibly in recognition of the ancillary duties he took on. In his fourth year, his new wife was hired on a salary of 1,350 gulden, and in the two seasons following their marriage, the couple received a combined payment of 3,870 (2,520 + 1,350). The accounts are lost for the years when Da Ponte was impresario, but by the time the new regime came into force in 1791, Francesco's salary had gone down to 2,250, while Dorotea's had increased to 2,000.[22] Zinzendorf remained unconvinced, rating her far below Luisa Laschi (Mombelli).[23]

In these circumstances, it was inevitable that there would be speculation about the return of the one singer guaranteed to boost receipts: Storace. Like Benucci's, her season in London had come to a premature end on 17 June as a result of the fire. Although there is no concrete evidence that Da Ponte made any attempt to recruit her, an engagement was reported in early August in a usually reliable source.[24] A London newspaper was speculating about this alarming prospect even before the fire: "The STORACE, it may be feared, returns to Vienna—for the best buffa singing, Imperial JOSEPH knows when he is well, though *John Bull* may not."[25] Such was her reputation in Vienna

---

19. Edge, "Mozart's Reception," 98.

20. Link, *Arias for Francesco Benucci*, xvii, citing *Grundsätze zur Theaterkritik*: "bei der italienische Gesellschaft ist der einzige Benucci, sonst war es Mandini, der durch Spiel und Gesang, die Handlung zu erhaben weiß. Hätte er Fischers Stimme, dann wäre er ohne keines Gleichen."

21. *Preßburger Zeitung* (19 September 1789), no. 75, 690: "Madame Dorotea Bussani hat sich wie gewöhnlich in der Rolle der Gitta mit Sang und Spiel zur Zufriedenheit der sehr zahlreichen Zuhörer ausgezeichnet."

22. Francesco Bussani was perhaps fortunate to be kept on at all. Rice, *Antonio Salieri*, 503, notes Leopold's determination to remove from him any management role: "Bussani will from now on no longer have any say in the direction of the theatre, or in the distribution of roles."

23. Link, *National Court Theatre*, 376: 6 May: "Le soir au spectacle. *Il Talismano*. Le jeu de la Bussani n'approcha pas a cent piques de celui de la Mombelli."

24. *Bayreuther Zeitung* (13 August 1789), no. 97, 701: Wien, vom 7. August: "Madame Storace kommt auf den Winter aus London wieder nach Wien, um die Italiänische Oper in bessere Aufnahme zu bringen."

25. *World* (15 June 1789).

that the local press had been following her progress in London. It was disappointing to have to report that in a performance of Paisiello's *Il re Teodoro* she had not appeared to such good effect "as her zealous partisans had hoped."[26]

While the longer-term future of state-sponsored opera in Vienna still looked very uncertain, Frederick William II's operatic publicity machine in Berlin was working very smoothly. Reports praised the musical credentials of the new ruler, implying that he was attempting to outdo his rival in Vienna. Stories started to appear promoting his image as an active participant in opera. In a piece commending the accuracy of his ensemble, a writer claimed that "no cappella in the world," could match it, which most readers would have assumed meant Vienna![27] The *Schlesische privilegirte Zeitung*, published in Breslau, proved an effective organ of publicity. Breslau had been part of the Monarchy until 1742, but now that it was firmly under the control of Prussia, its coverage of opera in Berlin was fulsome. Early in 1789, there was a glowing report on the opera house itself, followed by an enthusiastic review of a production.[28] The attendance of the king was routinely noted, usually as part of the lead story. Even to a general reader, Berlin, unlike Vienna, would have come across as a city in which state-sponsored opera was thriving. It is probably no coincidence that during this uncertain period for musicians in the Austrian Monarchy, both Dittersdorf and Mozart traveled to Berlin in order to investigate what opportunities might be available.

In Dittersdorf's case, the visit was part of an ongoing campaign to boost his standing in Prussia. This had begun back in November 1786, shortly after the accession of Frederick William II, when he submitted a request for consideration, pointing to the enthusiastic public reception of his operas in Vienna.[29] Although the response was negative, he was not a man to give up easily, and after his return to Silesia, he continued to promote his Viennese Singspiels in Breslau, hoping to exploit its well-known function as a musical conduit to Berlin. By September 1788, *Der Apotheker* was an established favorite in the

---

26. *Auszug aller europäischen Zeitungen* (15 January 1788), no. 13, 208: "als es ihre eifrigen Partheygänger hoffen."

27. *Budissinische wöchentliche Nachrichten* (29 December 1787), no. 52, 208: Aus dem Brandenbergischen vom 18. Dec.: "Da der Monarch ein großer Freund der Musik ist, so hat Er sich gnädigst herabgelassen, bey den Opernproben Selbst mitzuspielen. . . . Die Accuratesse, mit welcher das Ganze dirigiret wird, kann keine Kapelle in der Welt übertreffen."

28. *Schlesische privilegirte Zeitung* (16 January 1789), no. 7, 57; (19 January 1789), no. 8, 67.

29. Unverricht, *Carl von Dittersdorf: Briefe*, 69: "In Ansehung meiner Fähigkeiten in der *Composition* für die Kammer *musique* hab ich vorlängst schon die Gnade gehabt *Eyer Mayestätt* meine Werke zu Füssen zu legen. Meine Fähigkeit in der *Composition* für das *Theater* ist aber *Eyer Mayestätt* nicht so bekannt wie ich es wünschte."

city.[30] In December, *Die Liebe im Narrenhause* was introduced, and although
a reviewer thought the plot offensive to suffering humanity, he conceded that
the music was excellent.[31]

With his instinctive feel for publicity, Dittersdorf would also have taken note
of the extensive coverage generated by his friend Haydn's gift of symphonies
to the Prussian king. A widely circulated extract from a letter of thanks signed
by Frederick William II himself ended with the pointed assurance that he
would always treasure the composer, something that, by implication, the emperor could hardly be said to be doing.[32] Having identified a new opportunity,
Dittersdorf sent a set of six new symphonies to Berlin, for which he received
a ring worth (he claimed) 1,500 gulden.[33] When he met the king in Breslau
in August 1788, he took the opportunity to indulge in some of his trademark
flattery. As he recalled it later, the conversation had echoes of his more famous exchanges with Joseph II, although the topic this time was spontaneity.
In response to the observation that if musical ideas did not come easily then
everything was lost, Frederick William replied that this seemed already to have
happened with "K." Dittersdorf countered that this individual might just be
"written out," but the king persisted, claiming that he found a certain *stérilité*
in his works, an observation that provoked an effusive response: what a fortunate prospect for music, now that the art can count on the understanding of
"another" ruler (the first being Frederick the Great).

A visit to Berlin, the culmination of this campaign, was assured, but in a
further demonstration of political acumen, Dittersdorf took great care over its
timing. He later recalled that Princess Wilhelmina, wife of the Stadholder of
the Dutch Republic, was scheduled to make a state visit to the city and that a
whole month was to be given over to the festivities. As he drily observed: "I
chose to go at that favorable moment."[34] He claimed to have made a profit of

---

30. *Neues Theater Journal für Deutschland*, vol. 1, 39: Breslau: September 1788: "Auch hier
hat dieses allgemein beliebte Singspiel außerordentlich gefallen, und ist bereits einige
dreyßigmal auf geführt."

31. *Neues Theater Journal für Deutschland*, vol. 1, 42: Breslau: December 1788: "Schade von der
herrlichen Musik! Das Sujet ist ganz abscheulich und beleidiget die leidende Menschheit."

32. *Budissinische wöchentliche Nachrichten* (2 June 1787), no. 22, 88: Wien, den 16 May: "daß
Allerhöchst dieselben von jeher die Werke des Herrn Kapellmeister Haydn zu schätzen
gewußt, und jederzeit schätzen werden."

33. Unverricht, *Carl von Dittersdorf: Briefe*, 86: "daß ich erst gestern von *Breslau*
zurükgekommen bin, wo selbst ich *Seiner Majes*tätt dem König von Preussen bey
Höchstderoselben Daseyn meine Aufwartung gemacht, und so glüklich ware, für 6 neue
Sinfonien einen Brillantenen Ring von 1500 fl: an Werth zu erhalten."

34. Dittersdorf, *Lebensbeschreibung*, 252.

2,675 gulden from his benefit performance of *Hiob* and could only account for the size of this sum by assuming that a significant number of overpaid tickets had been bought by aristocratic well-wishers.[35] Dittersdorf's success in Prussia is not directly relevant to events in Vienna, but it demonstrates the growing cultural pull of Berlin, as the Austro-Turkish War dragged on into its second year. His carefully choreographed appearance casts an unforgiving light on his rival's visit.[36] Mozart could not match his flair as a self-publicist, and in consequence the results for Mozart were meager.

When the new season got under way, Mozart's operatic fortunes in Vienna underwent a rapid revival. Whether he knew before leaving for northern Germany that *Le nozze di Figaro* was to be restaged remains an open question. In a discussion of a sketch of the new aria for Ferrarese ("Al desio"), Janet Page and Dexter Edge note that its paper type is unlike any other used by the composer and thus perhaps part of a batch purchased in Germany or Bohemia. If Mozart began work during his time away from Vienna, it would imply prior knowledge of the casting of Susanna, but the use of a leftover sheet after his return home cannot be ruled out.[37] Several factors contributed to the transformation in the reputation of *Figaro*, sealed by the second performance run in Vienna. The most significant, perhaps, was its acquisition of festive status at the gala evening in Prague on 14 October 1787. In recognition of this accolade, other Habsburg performances had followed quickly. The opera was presented to Ferdinand and his wife in Monza on 18 November:

LE NOZZE / DI FIGARO / COMMEDIA PER MUSICA / DA RAPPRESENTARSI / NEL TEATRO DI MONZA / L'Autunno dell' anno 1787. / DEDICATA / Alle LL. AA. RR. / IL SERENISSIMO ARCIDUCA / FERDINANDO / Principe Reale d'Ungheria, e Boemia, Arciduca d'Austria, / Duca di Borgogna e di Lorena ec. Cesareo Reale / Luogo Tenente, Governatore, e Capitano / Generale nella Lombardia Austriaca, / E LA / SERENISSIMA ARCIDUCHESSA / MARIA RICCIARDA / BEATRICE D'ESTE / PRINCIPESSA DI MODENA. /

---

35. More than any other composer of this period, Dittersdorf understood the value of high-profile oratorio evenings in generating publicity. *Hiob* was a tremendous success with performances in Vienna, Johannisberg, Brünn, Berlin, and Breslau.

36. A sign of Mozart's growing status in the world of news reporting is that his departure for Berlin was announced (with an incorrect date) in Stralsund. *Stralsundische Zeitung* (30 April 1789), no. 52: Wien, den 15 April: "Der berühmte Kapellmeister, Herr Mozart, hat vorgestern eine Reise nach Berlin angetreten."

37. Page and Edge, "A Newly Uncovered Autograph Sketch," 601–6.

IN MILANO / Appresso Gio. Batista Bianchi Regio Stampatore./ Colla
Permissione.

The Florence production for Leopold took place over two nights on 11 and 16
June 1788, making use of sources obtained from Prague. In Bonn, Maximilian
Franz had closed the stage for financial reasons, but in a revealing comment, one
month after the Prague gala night, Christian Gottlob Neefe reported that he had
come under pressure to make an arrangement.[38] In effect, *Figaro* gained belated
admittance into a small but prestigious canon of Habsburg festive works, joining
the major commissions *L'arbore di Diana* and *Axur* and other works, such as *Una
cosa rara* and *La grotta di Trofonio*, that were first performed on a name day.

The reputational value of this semipolitical status lay not only in the prestige of the premiere but in repeat performances on subsequent state occasions.
Some festive repetitions were necessary simply because the political dedicatees
had not been present on the night of the original performance. By failing to
travel south into Bohemia to meet and escort Maria Theresia back to Dresden,
Anton missed the gala performance of *Figaro*. The symbolism was put right in
the summer of 1788, when Domenico Guardasoni arranged a festive presen-
tation in Leipzig.[39] Given in a specially illuminated auditorium on the name
day of the Elector (3 August), the diplomatic ledger was thereby brought into
balance, although it is not known whether Anton himself was there.[40] If he
missed it again, another opportunity came when the Habsburg clan began to
gather in Vienna for the double wedding of two of Maria Carolina's daughters
on 19 September 1790, an event set to strengthen the Austrian alliance with
Naples. Anton and his wife arrived on 19 August and were seen by Zinzendorf
in the theater the same evening. Her two festive operas were scheduled for
the next available opera nights (20 and 22 August), with both works enjoying
a rise in box office receipts. A month later, during the coronation festivities
for Leopold II in Frankfurt, *Figaro* occupied a central and arguably prestigious
position in the schedule, with a performance on 10 October 1790, the day after

---

38. Leipzig, Universitätsbibliothek, Sondersammlungen, Sammlung Kestner, I C II
283: Neefe to Großmann, 13 November 1787: "Jetzt denk ich mich auf vieler Aufforderung an
Nozze di Figaro zu machen." Woodfield, "Christian Gottlob Neefe and the Early Reception
of *Le nozze di Figaro* and *Don Giovanni*," 4–6.

39. *Leipziger Zeitung*, 30 July 1788: "Diesen Sonntag wird zum ersten Male, bey ganz
erleuchtetem Hause, gegeben werden: Le nozze di Figaro, o sia: La folle giornata. Oder: Die
Hochzeit des Figaro. Ein großes, neues komisches Singspiel mit Chören, in vier Aufzügen.
Die vortreffliche Musik hat der berühmte Capellmeister, Herr Mozart, componiert."

40. In 1786, the Elector's name day had been marked by a performance of *Il burbero di buon
core*. Woodfield, *Performing Operas for Mozart*, 50.

the ceremony itself.[41] An intriguing possibility is that the Mainz troupe was also planning to present *Don Giovanni* as a festive performance, as Leopold and Franz had yet to see it. In his letter of 3 October, Mozart mentioned that his opera was to be given on Tuesday, which was the day after Leopold made his ceremonial entrance into Frankfurt. There was apparently a change of plan, as a result of which the opera may not have been given in the presence of a Habsburg audience until 1791, when on 2 September, shortly before the Prague coronation, Guardasoni staged a performance for a full imperial party "by highest desire."[42] In some sense, attendance by its dedicatees was necessary to fully validate a work's festive status.

The decision to revive *Figaro* in Vienna thus had a direct political aspect in that Joseph himself had yet to see the opera as a festive work, following its gala performance in Prague. After a brief respite at the start of 1789, his health had started to decline sharply.[43] In April his condition became so grave that he was given the final rites and the theaters were instructed to close.[44] But it became evident that this was premature when his doctors pronounced him out of immediate danger. Once this crisis was over, Joseph resumed his duties with typical devotion. According to one report, he still habitually worked until 6:00 p.m., after which he sometimes listened to the Kammermusik, albeit without joining in himself.[45] But another story claimed that he was still able to participate.[46] As his health fluctuated, there was much discussion as to

---

41. Glatthorn, "Imperial Coronation," 89–110.

42. *Preßburger Zeitung* (10 September 1791), no. 73, 739: Böhmen: Prag den 5. September: "Abends beehrten Ihro KK. KK. Majestäten mit Dero durchlauchtigsten Prinzen und Prinzessinnen KK. HH. das hiesige altstädter Nationaltheater mit Ihrer höchster Gegenwart, wo auf höchstes Verlangen die italiänische Oper: Il dissoluto punito, oder Il Don Jovanni gegeben wurde. Das Theater war stark mit Lustern beleuchtet, und die kais. Logen verziert."

43. Although he cut an isolated figure during his final months, he was not deserted by Elisabeth von Württemberg. In March she attempted to arrange some music for him, but he had to retire to bed as a result of a shivering fit. *Strasburgische privilegirte Zeitung* (6 April 1789), no. 41, 162: Wien, den 18. März: "Gegen Abend wollte die Erzherzogin dem Monarchen eine Musik bringen, diese unterblieb aber, weil derselbe auf einmal von einem solchen Schauer überfallen war, daß er sich vor der Zeit zu Bette begeben mußte."

44. *Bayreuther Zeitung* (24 April 1789), no. 49, Anhang, 357: Wien, vom 17. April.

45. *Der Wienerbothe* (2 May 1789), 30: "Diese Staatsbeschäftigungen währen fort bis 6 Uhr, nach welcher Zeit der Monarch bisweilen der Kammermusik beiwohnt, ohne doch wie sonst dabei mitzuspielen."

46. *Bayreuther Zeitung* (13 June 1789), no. 71, 520. Laxenburg, den 6. Junii.: "und kehren in den wenigen Erhohlungsaugenblicken zu Ihrem Lieblingsvergnügen, der Musik, zurück, ja akkompagniren auch zum öftern Selbst."

whether he should move to Laxenburg for the traditional summer recess, and
on 19 May it was agreed that he should relocate there. The condition of the
emperor was a matter with far-reaching political implications, a news story
across Europe. By mid-July, many newspapers had been fed the optimistic
message that he might soon be well enough to come back to the city.[47] But the
improvement was short-lived, and an operation for hemorrhoids on 18 August
once again rendered an immediate return out of the question.[48] Only at the
end of the month did flooding at Laxenburg force him to leave, but after just
four days in Vienna he was taken to Hetzendorf near Schönbrunn.[49] It is likely
that the plan was to schedule the first performance of a new run of *Figaro* to
coincide with his return to Vienna, so that he would have the opportunity to
attend, if fit enough on the night, but it proved hard to predict when this might
happen, and the window of opportunity was very brief.

Mozart had "Al desio" and other minor changes, such as the revision of
the Countess's aria "Dove sono" to suit Cavalieri, ready in time for a new production in July, but he, too, was affected by the delay.[50] At one point, he wrote
to his wife that he was planning to come and see her in Baden the following
morning, but that he would have to be back in Vienna on 19 August to attend
rehearsals.[51] Any hopes that Joseph might be well enough to see the opera,
though, came to nothing, as the state of his health precluded even the briefest
appearance in the theater. Elisabeth von Württemberg, who accompanied him
back to Vienna, also missed the revival of *Le nozze di Figaro*. Now that she was
visibly carrying the third in line to the Austrian Monarchy, it was necessary
for her to be seen in public, but the intense summer heat was making theater
attendance uncomfortable. On 3 September, she went to the Prater but did
not stay to see Stuwer's firework display. She felt obliged to put in an appearance at the next performance of *L'arbore di Diana*, although it is plain that she

---

47. *Staats- und gelehrte Zeitung* (24 July 1789), no. 117: Schreiben aus Wien, vom 15 Julii: "Man
hat nunmehr die angenehme Hoffnung Se. Majestät in kurzem wieder in der Hauptstadt
zu sehen."

48. *Courier du Bas-Rhin* (5 September 1789), no. 71, 653: "le séjour de Laxembourg sera
prolongé, dit on, jusqu'à l'arriere saison."

49. Link, *National Court Theatre*, 339.

50. As Gidwitz pointed out, the new version contained a bravura element lacking in 1786.
Gidwitz, " 'Ich bin die erste Sängerin,' " 572. Edge, "Mozart's Viennese Copyists," 1668–1742,
discusses the 1789 revisions in depth. Some of the changes to the tessitura of the Count's
role may date from the period of the new performance run, but uncertainty over who sang
the part hinders a clear conclusion.

51. *Mozart: Briefe und Aufzeichnungen*, vol. 3, 96; Anderson, *Letters*, vol. 3, 1388.

went solely to please the emperor. Even so, the heat drove her away after the first act.[52]

A review of the revived *Figaro* was published in the *Preßburger Zeitung*.[53] Its description of the work as "long-awaited"—a modern cliché but one less often encountered in eighteenth-century opera journalism—suggests more than a short postponement. As usual, the reviewer focused on the prima donna, commenting that Ferrarese's skill was especially evident in her new showpiece rondò "Al desio," but Brocchi was also commended now that he was cast in a role suited to his talents.

Two months before the revival of *Figaro*, audiences in Vienna had a chance to hear some of Dittersdorf's music for Cherubin. His opera *Hieronimus Knicker* had been well received in Brünn, where a reviewer had commended the "new and witty" music and acknowledged its composer's "great expertise in the refinement of German opera."[54] It transferred to Vienna, opening at the Leopoldstadttheater on 7 July. In one scene, a would-be opera star expresses admiration for the part of Cherubin, the cue for Dittersdorf to self-cite two arias from *Die Hochzeit des Figaro*. Perhaps by design, neither piece has an equivalent setting in Mozart's opera. The first is the aria Cherubin sings to Lieschen "Gutes Mädchen! Mein Begehren"; the second is a section from the act 2 finale, comprising the six lines sung by the page as he explains how he

---

52. Weyda, "Briefe an Erzherzog Franz," 196: 10 Sept: "La santé de l'Empereur va à merveille . . . Hier je fus pour la première fois un instant au théâtre, où on donnait 'l'arbre di Diane' et cela pour contenter l'Empereur et lui faire voir qu'il n'y a jamais de grimace dans mon fait, lorsque je ne fais pas telle ou telle chose; la chaleur y était insoutenable et je dus m'en aller tout de suite après le premier acte."

53. *Preßburger Zeitung* (2 September 1789), no. 70, 634: Wien, den 31ten August: "Samstag als den 29ten v. M. wurde in k. k. Nationalhoftheater das lang erwartete italiänische Singspiel die Hochzeit des Figaro, wozu die Poesie von Herrn Abbé de [*sic*] Ponte Dichter am k. k. Hoftheater, und die Musik von Hr. Kapellmeister Mozart aufgeführt. Das Publikum war damit sehr zufrieden, und legte seine Zufriedenheit mehr an Tag, als vor 3 Jahren, wie das Stück zum erstenmal erschien. Madame Ferrarese spielte als Prima Donna, und sang mit ihrer bekannten Geschicklichkeit, und Kunst, zeugte sich besonders in einem künstlich-harmonischen Rondeau, wo die Musik des Herrn Mozart mit dem Gesang der berühmten Sängerinn um die Wette stritten; gleiches Lob verdient der neu angekommene Bassist Herr Brocehi, dessen wahre Verdienste in der Schauspielkunst im ersten von ihm gespielten Stücke nicht gehörig glänzen konnte, weil die Rolle nicht für ihn beschaffen war, und überhaupt alle übrigen Mitglieder der Gesellschaft haben sich viele Ehre gemacht."

54. *Brünner Zeitung* (30 January 1789), no. 9, 71: Brünn, den 23 Januar: "Den 21 dieses gab der berühmte Herr von Dittersdorf die zweite neue komische Oper von seiner Komposition unter seiner eigenen Anführung: Hieronymus Knicker. Der Beifall, mit dem dieses Singspiel aufgenommen wurde, entspricht dem Werth dieser neuen und launigten Musik . . . um so mehr als der hiesige Adel und das Publikum sein Talent so wie seine große Kenntniß in Verfeinerung der deutschen Singspiele nicht verkennt, und bereits überzeugt ist, um wie viel durch seine obgleich kurze Gegenwart die hiesigen Singspiele sich schon verbessert haben."

came by his final dress. In the spoken text of *Hieronimus Knicker*, which was revised by Christian August Vulpius in 1791, crossdressing is presented as a particular attraction for the maid, who brags about being a prima donna.[55] Her favorite parts are trouser roles such as Cherubin: "Ach! Sie glauben kaum, wie gern ich Beinkleiderrollen spiele, und mit welchem Affekt und Effekt ich den Pagen gespiele habe." Both women agree that it is a sweet scene, and a second aria is performed. In the absence of a score of Dittersdorf's opera, it is not possible to demonstrate that the verbal citations made use of his own music, although the character of the second (tiny) piece is certainly consistent with it, having been a section for solo voice in a finale.

Few in Vienna would have been familiar with Dittersdorf's *Figaro*, unless the unattributed opera given by the Wilhelminische Gesellschaft in its 1789 summer season at Baden was his.[56] But *Hieronimus Knicker* proved very popular and spread quickly across Germany.[57] As it did so, the two texts from *Die Hochzeit des Figaro* remained embedded in it, even though the source opera had long since vanished. By the time of its Weimar premiere on 24 November 1791, just twelve days before Mozart's death, its references to Cherubin would have brought to mind *Le nozze di Figaro*, an ironic conclusion to Dittersdorf's attempt to compete with his rival's setting.

Once the revisions to *Figaro* were out of the way, Mozart began to take on some tasks of the kind traditionally associated with the duties of a "house" composer. One was the provision of substitute arias in which the newly arrived Villeneuve could demonstrate her talent. The first of these was "Alma grande e nobil core" (K.578) for Cimarosa's *I due baroni*, but the opera failed soon after its premiere on 6 September, receiving only two performances. A third was canceled as a result of the illness of Dorotea Bussani.[58] In September, Mozart composed two major arias for the revival of Martín y Soler's *Il burbero*—"Chi sà, chi sà qual sia" (K.582) and "Vado, ma dove" (K.583). He may also have been asked to provide new *accompagnato* introductions for some arias, compositional tasks too insignificant to merit entry in his catalogue of works. The best known of these is a short orchestral lead-in to his own "Vado, ma dove?" It is not attributed in any source, and the evidence for his authorship is

---

55. Hieronimus Knicker. / Eine / komische Operette in zwei Aufzügen. / Nach Dittersdorfs Musik / neubearbeitet. / Aufgeführt zum erstenmal den 24.November 1791 / auf dem Hoftheater zu Weimar. / Weimar, 1793. / in der Hoffmanischen Buchhandlung.

56. *Theater-Kalendar auf das Jahr 1790*, 118: "Una cosa rara. L'arbore di Diana. Barbier von Siviglia. Il Talismano. La Condatina [*sic*] in Corte. Die Hochzeit des Figaro."

57. Baumann, *North German Opera*, 244.

58. Link, *National Court Theatre*, 147.

inconclusive.[59] Another, a lead-in to Cimarosa's aria "Consola pur mia bella," included in the pasticcio version of Guglielmi's *La quacquera spirituosa*, is attributed to him in a single source.[60]

During the summer months of 1789, as the assault on Belgrade drew near, commentators began to forecast the end of the war.[61] As usual, the evidence came in the form not of military evaluation but of speculation about opera; Joseph, it was claimed, had instructed the theater management to hire a troupe of singers to perform *opere serie*, the most expensive version of the art form. This was of course wishful thinking, but it provided an accurate reflection of the state of hostilities; if a lavish state-funded program of opera was being planned, the conflict must now be close to an end.[62] When the fall of Belgrade was announced on 14 October, the atmosphere in Vienna was transformed and with it prospects for the opera season. There was widespread jubilation. Duty obliged Elisabeth von Württemberg to appear at the theater, and once again she found the heat oppressive.[63] Buoyed by the good military news and his enthusiastic reception, Joseph started to attend theater again. On 28 October he went to *Axur*.[64] Then on 9 November he was well enough to appear at the revival of *Il burbero*, where correspondents were struck by the enthusiasm with which he applauded his favorite, Benucci; one source gave his name as "Benutschn," an affectionate diminutive form.[65] This was probably

---

59. The discovery of this piece was announced by Edge in a lecture at Cardiff University on 8 March 1994, and it was subsequently discussed by Link, "A Newly Discovered Accompanied Recitative." Edge, "Mozart's Viennese Copyists," 1909. See also, Edge, "Attributing Mozart (i)," 197–237.

60. Edge, "Mozart's Viennese Copyists," 1961–73.

61. While they waited, keyboard players could keep up their spirits by reenacting Laudon's successful siege of Novi in 1778. Lausch advertised a series of titled dances, such as "der Bascha bedauert seinem Verlust," which depicted the inevitable victory. *Wiener Zeitung* (17 January 1789), no. 5, 121.

62. *Gazzetta bolognesi* (11 August 1789), no. 64, 512: Altra di VIENNA 3. Agosto: "Per ordine di S. M. l'*Imperadore* la *Direzione Teatrale* deve provvedere molti Cantanti bravi, anche per le Opere Serie, che si daranno nel venturo Anno: Ciò fa credere, che non sia distante la Pace."

63. Weyda, "Briefe an Erzherzog Franz," 232: 15 oct: "pour moi j'y fus aussi, mais il était impossible d'y rester, car la chaleur était si étouffante qu'on se serait trouvé mal."

64. *Gazzetta universale* (10 November 1789), 90, 716: VIENNA 29. Ottobre.

65. *Bayreuther Zeitung* (23 November 1789), no. 140, Anhang, 1043: Wien, vom 17. November: "In der Opera am 9ten waren Se. Majest. so wohl gemuthet, daß Höchstdieselbe den Operisten Benutschn wegen der sehr gut ausgeführten Rolle des gutherzigen Murrkopfs die Höchste Zufriedenheit durch Händklatschen zu erkennen gab." This account was clearly derived from the *Neuester Rapport von Wien 1789* (18 November 1789), 225, which optimistically claimed that Joseph still "almost always" attended opera, applauding any actors who played their characters well. Link, *National Court Theatre*, 345.

the last occasion on which the emperor heard Mozart's music—the substitute arias—in the theater. Elisabeth, who witnessed some of his dark periods of depression, reported that he was still deriving enjoyment from his favorite recreation. She joined him on 16 November at August Kotzebue's *Menschenhaß und Reue*, which she thought one of the best plays she had seen in a long time.[66] There was even speculation that Joseph was intending to see a performance of Paul Wrantisky's *Oberon* at the Theater auf der Wieden, following its premiere on 7 November 1789. Had the visit taken place, it might well have been seen as a gesture of some symbolic significance in support of German opera.[67]

Franz returned to Vienna at the end of November 1789 and immediately purchased an unnamed opera for 36 gulden. His accounts also include an intriguing payment dated 7 January 1790: "Vor Spaisen vor dem Don Govani."[68] His attendance at a private performance of the opera cannot be discounted, although, given the popularity of Goldoni's works at the *comédie italienne*, it seems as likely that he went to the play *Don Giovanni Tenorio*.[69] On 11 January, he invested in a copy of *Die Belagerung Belgrads* for violin and piano, perhaps with the idea of playing it with his wife on her new Walther fortepiano.[70] A conventional programmatic battlepiece, it ends with the salutations "Es lebe Joseph der IIte; Es lebe Laudon der Siege." The speed with which this bombastic celebration came out suggests that Mozart's pupil Franz Jacob Freystädtler had prepared it in advance for the expected victory.[71] Edge has drawn attention to an advertisement published in Munich in which, with or without permission, the work's composer included an endorsement from the most famous

---

66. Weyda, "Briefe an Erzherzog Franz," 256: 17 November: "Je me suis très-bien amusée hier au théâtre, la pièce était charmante, remplie de sentimens, c'est une des meilleures que j'aie vue depuis longtemps. . . . Sa Majesté était de fort bonne humeur et bien gracieuse."

67. The emperor would have witnessed the success of a Jewish singer from Berlin. *Bayreuther Zeitung* (27 November 1789), no. 142, Anhang, 1058: Wien, vom 21 Nov.: "Ein Jude, Hr. Herzfeld aus Berlin spielt die Hauptrolle, und gefällt ausserordentlich. Das ist doch wahre Toleranz!" The comment was topical. The Galician Patent, granting a measure of freedom to the large Jewish population in the region, came into force in October 1789. Beales, *Against the World 1780–1790*, 600–603.

68. Dunlop, "'Kaisersammlung,'" 52.

69. On 5 February 1790, Zinzendorf saw a performance of Goldoni's comedy *L'amor paterno*.

70. Rice, *Empress Marie Therese*, 18.

71. *Wiener Zeitung* (31 October 1789), no. 87, 2779–80. On a leaf of Mozart sketches dating probably from the late spring or summer of 1788, Freystädtler drafted a few bars of the start of an arrangement for four-part chorus and keyboard of the celebrated aria from *Judas Maccabaeus* "See the conqu'ring hero comes." Woodfield, "Mozart's 'Jupiter,'" 33. Possibly he was caught up in the jingoistic mood in Vienna during those months, when few observers imagined that the Turkish forces would put up much resistance.

"Mozard," who was reported to have been unstinting in his praise for this celebration of the victory of "der mächtigste Kaiser Joseph der 2te."[72] What Mozart
would have made of this can only be inferred, but it is telling that in his album
an inscription dated 31 October 1789, entered by his friend Dr Anton Schmith,
linked his name to that of Laudon:

PALLAS IN LOVDON IN MOZART REGNAT APOLLO
VIVET VTERQVE INGENS ARTE PER AEVA SVA

The message is straightforward: Mozart reigns supreme in his field, as does
Laudon in his. The roman numerals (in bold) add up to 1789.[73]

In this altogether more positive atmosphere, two new works were prepared for their premieres: Salieri's *La cifra* on 11 December and *Così fan tutte*
on 26 January. The discovery that Salieri started and then abandoned work
on a setting of *Così fan tutte* raises many unanswerable questions. Bruce Alan
Brown and John Rice considered it unlikely that he would have collaborated
with Da Ponte after February 1789, following a quarrel over the allocation of
benefits. If so, a brief period of work took place around the time Da Ponte
was compiling *L'ape musicale*, which on the whole seems respectful toward
Salieri's achievements.[74] The structural parallel between the two dramas is
certainly striking: both require a cast of six: an authority figure, his young
female assistant, and two pairs of men and women. In the published libretto
of the pasticcio, the characters are laid out in the hexagonal shape sometimes
used to demonstrate the symmetrical relationships in the opera.[75] Benucci is
placed at the top and his niece at the bottom, with two singers either side.
There are occasional similarities between the two texts. In *Così* (act 1, scene
2) Fiordiligi resorts to astrology, reading Dorabella's palm: "Dammi la mano;
io voglio astrologarti." In *L'ape musicale*, Bonario (Da Ponte) is asked to present his hand to Farinella (Laschi): "*Far.* Datemi un po la mani bravo poeta."
Having started the reading, she comments that he came into the world under

72. Edge, "Freystädtler Advertises His *Die Belagerung Belgrads* with an Endorsement from
Mozart," in Edge and Black, *Mozart*. In view of Freystädtler's "rather casual relationship with
the truth," Edge reasonably speculates that this endorsement was an invention.

73. Deutsch, *Mozart: A Documentary Biography*, 357. Loudon was the spelling current in the
eighteenth century; most modern writers prefer Laudon.

74. Brown and Rice, "Salieri's *Così fan tutte*," 36. If Salieri had started work as far back as late
1788 or early 1789, a factor in his cessation could have been the uncertain fate of the troupe
itself.

75. Steptoe, *Mozart-Da Ponte Operas*, 133.

a favorable planet: "Venisti al mondo sotto un buon pianete." There is at least
an echo of Despina's espousal of bogus Latin, when Don Capriccio (act 2,
scene 1) cannot stop spewing out random phrases: "Salve tu Domine / Gens
philharmonic / Tibi salute / Dicit per me."[76]

In my study of the autograph score of Così fan tutte, I considered textual
evidence that it had a two-stage genesis, either side of a short hiatus. Among
many signs of a break are the following: a change in paper types; differences
in ink colors; a rethink over the spelling of the name Guglielmo; a reordering
of the two bass parts in the score; and perhaps also a similar change affecting
the hierarchy of the two sisters.[77] Little remains upon which to base an appraisal of the text offered to Salieri. It is generally agreed that the title Così fan
tutte was Mozart's idea, implying that his colleague started work on the text
while it was still titled La scuola degli amanti. An intriguing explanation for the
change may be found in an inventory of books owned by Mozart, which included a copy of Baron Adolf Knigge's Dramaturgische Blätter. On 18 May 1789,
this journal carried a long review of Le nozze di Figaro. Knigge contributed a
piece on the text, which he and his daughter had been translating, while "W"
(probably Anselm Weber) reviewed the score. Toward the end of the musical
discussion, he lists pieces he rated highly. The penultimate item—the only
section listed, as opposed to a complete piece—is the setting of Basilio's mi-
sogynistic intervention in the first trio, "Ja so machens alle Schönen" ("Così
fan tutte le belle"), which receives a striking commendation: it is a veritable
"stroke of genius." Weber's warm appreciation of this "Geniezug" may be the
explanation for Mozart's choice of title and his ostentatious use of Basilio's
theme in the overture, a decision that placed the new work in conversation
with its predecessor, now a success on the Vienna stage.[78]

A sensitive issue was the choice of disguises for the men. When Ferrando
and Guglielmo return to begin their campaign of deception, there are no stage
instructions concerning their appearance, and details of their names and nationality emerge only at the end of the opera. The first clue as to their identity
comes when Despina cannot decide whether they look like Wallachians or
Turks. Located between Habsburg Transylvania to the north and the Ottoman

---

76. Siniscalchi, L'ape musicale, 226.

77. Woodfield, Mozart's Così fan tutte. A possibility I did not consider in relation to changes
in the casting of the male roles is that the leading buffo Brocchi could still have been in the
Vienna troupe when work on the opera started and that his departure occasioned a reallo-
cation of roles.

78. Deutsch, Mozart: Die Dokumente, 303: "Basil's eingeschobener Gesang im ersten Terzette
des ersten Acts: 'Ja so machens alle Schönen' ist ein wahrer Geniezug."

Empire to the south, Wallachia was caught up in the conflict. Long under Turkish sovereignty, it was seized by Prince Coburg on 22 September 1789. Zinzendorf heard the news as he was leaving a performance of *Una cosa rara* on 5 October, and Schikaneder was quick to celebrate the victory by reciting a couplet in honor of Coburg at the Theater auf der Wieden on 8 October.[79] In January 1790, Wallachia was highly topical, and Mozart himself was certainly aware of Coburg's victory, as he entitled one of twelve *teutsche* completed in December 1789 "einen Contre-danse, der Sieg *vom Helden Koburg.*" Yet Despina's initial assumptions prove incorrect, as the officers are eventually identified as Albanian noblemen, hailing from across the Adriatic.[80] In an early draft of the opera, Ferrando was to have introduced himself as a "Cavaliere dall Albania," presumably in the middle of act 1, but for some reason this passage was cut before the final version of the opera emerged. As a result, the citation of its music in the denouement, aimed at embarrassing Ferrando by recalling this moment, loses its effect. Close though it was to Italy, Albania had the power to conjure up an image of oriental savagery, as in the summer of 1788 when a notorious incident shocked Vienna. In the hope of fomenting internal dissent in the Ottoman Empire, Joseph II had approached the pasha of Scutari with an offer of 100,000 gulden to launch an attack. There was outrage when he pocketed the money and sent the heads of the two military emissaries to Istanbul as a pledge of loyalty.

Some Albanian territories, though, such as the coastal regions of southern Dalmatia, the Albania Veneta, owed their loyalty to Venice and were populated by a mix of orthodox and western Christians.[81] As further information about these mysterious strangers is revealed, everything points to their allegiance to Italy, if not the Christian religion. When he introduces himself and his friend in "Rivolgete a lui / me lo sgardo" (in a version of the plot subsequently abandoned), the disguised Guglielmo appears entirely au fait with European culture. As Heartz put it: "Figures from myth, for example, Narcissus and Cyclops, jostle historical figures such as Croesus and Mark Antony. Aesop, the ancient Greek writer of fables, shares honours with Boiardo's fifteenth-century *Orlando inammorato.* Da Ponte does not stop short of citing the name of a contemporary ballet dancer, Charles le Picq."[82] This amounts to a very

---

79. Link, *National Court Theatre,* 342.

80. In Locke's recent reading of *Così,* the "unconstrained" behavior of the two officers is taken to represent their otherness. Locke, *Music and the Exotic,* 320.

81. There was also a population of Christian Albanians in Naples, the location originally chosen for the opera. Locke, *Music and the Exotic,* 393; Mellace, "'Questi, nobili albanesi.'"

82. Heartz, "When Mozart Revises," 356

reassuring appraisal of the strangers' cultural background, with the text making no mention of their outlandish costumes and disguises. In the replacement aria, by contrast, Guglielmo takes great pride in their "mustacchi" as his clinching argument; these bushy growths may be regarded as triumphs of their manhood, their plumes of love. The failure to follow up the question of the men's appearance, so immediately eye-catching to Despina, suggests that some thought may have been given to downplaying the oriental aspect of the men's appearance only to reemphasize it in the wake of 14 October, when Turks once again seemed less threatening. Perhaps only at that point was the military chorus ("Bella vita militar") added as a patriotic gesture, a jingoistic response to the fact that the war had turned decisively in Austria's favor.

The most striking aspect of the plot of Così in the context of an ongoing war is that Don Alfonso sets out to demonstrate that women are unlikely to remain faithful when their lovers are called up to serve their country. The main hypothesis of my study of the opera was that a plot with lovers unswitched was given serious consideration as a way of addressing shortcomings in its dramatic credibility, yet a war-related element in the discussion should not be discounted. Sweethearts ought to be there for their military other halves when they return from the battlefield, even if their eyes have been wandering in the meantime!

No published review of the premiere of Così fan tutte has come to light, but for an assessment of how some of the singers were currently regarded, an appraisal of Salieri's La cifra, given its premiere on 11 December 1789, is a useful substitute.[83] The seria performers are praised for the quality of their singing, others for their acting ability. Ivo Cerman has recently drawn attention to an entry in the diary of Countess Maria Sidonia Chotek, a member of the audience at the premiere of Così fan tutte. Hers is a very negative evaluation.[84] Evidently aware of the prevailing consensus about the learned quality

---

83. Preßburger Zeitung (19 December 1789), no. 101, 949: Wien, den 17ten December: "Madame Ferraresi durch ihren unnachahmlichen vortrefflichen Gesang, Monsieur Benucci nach seiner bekannten Geschicklichkeit in der Schauspielkunst, Monsieur Calvesi im Gesange, und Madame Bussani, die abermahls Beweise ihrer Fähigkeiten im Spiele abgelegt hat." The report in the Gazzetta universale (2 January 1790), no. 1, 5, is more or less a translation, although it ends with strong approval of Bussani: "che in quest' Opera, come in molte altre si è mostrata degna di un applauso universale."

84. Black, "Report of the First Performance of Così fan tutte," contributed by Ivo Cerman; Edge and Black, Mozart.: "on a donné aujourd'hui un nouvel Opera dont la Musique de Mozart, est si savante qu'elle n'est pas du tout agréable, le sujet est pitoyable, les Acteurs ne savoit pas trop leur rôle, ainsi le public n'a pas été content." This is in striking contrast to Zinzendorf's short but upbeat appraisal. In the margin of her diary, Chotek noted the work's title as: "Tutte fan cosi ò sia la Scuola d'amore." This inversion of the title is also seen in a score copied by Wenzel Sukowaty. Nedbal, "Domenico Guardasoni's Prague Conducting Score," 6. Chotek's use of "d'amore" rather than "degli amanti" is interesting.

of Mozart's musical language, she found this aspect of the work disagreeable, and she expressed outright contempt for Da Ponte's "pitiful" plot, implying further that the singers had not yet mastered their parts.

The first performance of *Così fan tutte* came toward the end of Da Ponte's first year in the role of impresario. Box office receipts for the season as a whole tell the story of a considerable success. The nightly totals in gulden for each work performed that year are given in Table 6.2.[85]

The receipts from works composed by the triumvirate of Salieri, Martín y Soler, and Mozart together generated 75 percent of the total income. Their box office per night averaged around 235 gulden, as opposed to 105 for works by nonresident composers. In his memorandum of 1790, Da Ponte indicated the depth of the crisis he had faced that summer. The new recruitments had doubled his costs, while for half a year, the "Turchi," "Conti," "Baroni," "Falegname" and similar stopgap operas ("opere di ripiego") had set income back by 20,000 gulden.[86] This may have been an exaggeration, but the figures bear out a significantly lower level of takings for these works.[87] The press, too, was of the opinion that the Italian troupe was not making the most of its period without competition from the theater company.[88]

The damage being inflicted by competition in the suburbs can be seen in a snapshot from the May 1789 issues of *Der Wienerbothe*. When aligned with the box office receipts at the National Theater, the problem is clear. At its premiere on 28 April 1789, *Il turco in Italia* took 418 gulden. Its second performance on 30 April was in competition with *Die Entführung aus dem Serail* at the Theater auf der Wieden and *Der Talismann* at Leopoldstadt. Receipts plummeted to 114 gulden. The third performance on 2 May, again in competition with *Der Talismann*, generated only 71 gulden. Of course the trajectory of receipts for any work tended to decline anyway, but the strength of the competition was perhaps responsible for a disappointing fourth night for *I due supposti conti* on 26 May, when it coincided with *Der Talismann* and *König Theodor* at the Theater auf der Wieden. The box office takings for the work's first four nights were: 248; 258; 174; 107. Even the evergreen *Una cosa rara*, which took in 235

---

85. The figures are taken from Link, *National Court Theatre*, and Edge, "Mozart's Reception."

86. Michtner, "Der Fall Abbé Da Ponte," 191.

87. If the less popular works had taken something closer to the average for the popular works, that would only have boosted box office receipts by a sum of the order of 7,500 gulden.

88. *Bayreuther Zeitung* (2 July 1789), no. 79, 582: Wien, vom 26 Junii: "Unsere National-Schauspieler haben anjetzo Ferien auf 6 Wochen, dafür gurgeln uns die Sänger und Sängerinnen in einer Opera täglich etwas vor, was wir freylich schon weit besser gehört haben."

Table 6.2 The nightly box office takings (gulden) for *opere buffe* (April 1789 to February 1790)

Composer	Opera	Nightly receipts	Total	Average
Popular works				
Martin y Soler	L'arbore di Diana [rev]	410 481 273 163 176 228 177 145 144 125 267 155 174 119 234 267 308	3846	226
Martin y Soler	Una cosa rara	235 148 189 142 160 268 160 214 101 460 201 157 216 195 228 201 192 192	3659	203
Mozart	Le nozze di Figaro [rev]	376 245 212 176 222 235 182 209 220 216 158 204 181	2836	218
Salieri	La cifra	485 463 278 282 365 165 211 253	2502	312
Salieri	Axur	459 216 276 193 173 193 173 190 147 142 170 122	2453	204
Mozart	Così fan tutte	553 305 223 343 234	1658	331
Martin y Soler	Il burbero [rev]	255 129 228 102 142 98	954	159
Salieri	Il pastor fido [rev]	378 125 206	709	236
Less popular works				
Cimarosa	I due supposti conti	248 258 174 107 83 79 43 78 40 52 92 39 136 80 67 123	1719	106
Cimarosa	Il falegname	301 98 223 111 51 69 48 91 67 94 83 79 46 53 110 47	1571	98
Johann Nikolaus Franz Seydelmann	Il turco in Italia	418 114 71 75 52 47 46 72 87 33	1015	101
Sarti	Fra i due litiganti	257 116 75 89 96 40 76 42 44	835	92
Anfossi	Le gelosie fortunate	147 108 79 62	396	99
Cimarosa	I due baroni	169 91	260	130

gulden on 24 May, was reduced to 148 gulden four days later when competing with *König Theodor*.

It is a testament to Da Ponte's flair as an impresario that he quickly understood what was happening. During the month of May, the *Wienerbothe* advertised the following operatic performances in the suburban theaters: at the Leopoldstadttheater *Der Talismann* (2, 3, 11, and 26 May); *Una cosa rara* (9 May); and *Der Apotheker* (13 May); and in the Theater auf der Wieden *König Theodor* (26, 27, and 28 May). In effect, the National Theater was having to compete against commercial productions of its own most popular pieces. Da Ponte's policy was to emulate his rivals, welcoming (as an impresario) rather than seeking to undermine (as a poet anxious for new commissions) what was the emergence of a canon. Using the resources at his disposal, he matched debuts, role debuts, and (in the case of Benucci) role resumptions with revivals of popular works: Villeneuve in *L'arbore di Diana* on 27 June; Brocchi in *Una cosa rara* on 27 July; Ferrarese and Brocchi in *Le nozze di Figaro* on 29 August; Benucci in *Una cosa rara* on 15 September; and perhaps Ferrarese in *Axur* on 23 September. The combination of durable works with new star singers proved a most effective recipe, the magic formula indeed of the modern world: operas with a proven track record, decoupled from one set of performers and handed on to the next, allowing new stars to shine. There was one important difference in the 1780s: the text of a revived opera was not sacrosanct, and composers or their proxies were expected to provide adaptations as required. Mozart composed "Al desio" to suit the strengths of the new singer, yet at the same time he was fitting out his opera for a subtly different world. In 1786, he had done without a climactic rondò for his prima donna (perhaps a diplomatic decision, there being two of them), but since then, this distinctive type of aria had reached its fashionable apogee in Vienna, and a piece in this vein might have been expected, whoever the new Susanna was.[89]

The final illness of Joseph II led to the closure of the theaters, which remained shut throughout Lent. When Leopold arrived in Vienna, a clear priority was to negotiate a peace accord with Prussia to forestall its threatened entry into the conflict. At a conference on 26 April, Frederick William II's demands were discussed: either a return to the position that had existed before the war or a series of territorial exchanges.[90] If Austria were to retain her acquisitions in the south, Prussia would be looking for balancing gains. What was being proposed amounted to a reconfiguration of a slice of central-eastern

89. Rice, "A Bohemian Composer Meets a Mozart Singer."

90. Mayer, "Price of Austria's Security: II," 496.

Europe from top to bottom: Prussia would take territory from Poland in the north; Poland would reacquire Galicia from the Monarchy, which would receive Wallachia and Moldavia from the Ottomans, whose remaining European possessions would in turn be guaranteed.[91] Leopold's first foreign policy success, an accord with Prussia, was sealed at the Convention of Reichenbach on 27 July 1790.[92] An approximate return to the frontiers as they had existed *ante bellum* was now recognized as a prudent outcome, one characterized by Zinzendorf on 21 July as peace with little honor ("une paîx peu honorable").[93] Even after the Austrian Monarchy reached agreement with Frederick William II, the Russian offensive down the western coast of the Black Sea continued, culminating in a decisive engagement on 22 December 1790, when the fort of Izmail south of Odessa fell to its besiegers with the usual bloody slaughter of its inhabitants. This victory was celebrated by Stuwer in September 1791, the last in his series of battle representations that had begun with the Austrian capture of Schabacz.[94]

The reform of Italian opera was low on Leopold's list of priorities as he faced the maelstrom of political and military problems bequeathed to him, and the existing arrangements were allowed to continue for a further year. When the theaters reopened after Easter, the jubilation following the capture of Belgrade had passed, and the public mood was quieter. This was reflected in a significant drop in average receipts. Table 6.3 gives approximate monthly totals of takings for theater and opera combined, a crude measurement that takes no account of annual holidays, theater-free memorial days, or Christmas but is nonetheless indicative of broad trends.

The overall picture is strikingly episodic: very low box office in the summer of 1789 as the war dragged on; a significant peak in the winter season, the feel-good factor of Belgrade adding to the usual improvement in receipts; and then a distinctly lower level in 1790, after the resumption of performances in a period of political uncertainty, but picking up during Leopold's first extended residence in Vienna as emperor.

In view of the financially successful end to the 1789–90 season, a similar approach to planning the repertoire for the coming year made sense. Continuing to favor revivals, Da Ponte restaged Paisiello's *Il re Teodoro*, a decision perhaps

---

91. Blanning, *Joseph II*, 176–82.

92. Blanning, *Joseph II*, 201.

93. Link, *National Court Theatre*, 358.

94. *Vertraute Briefe*, vol. 2, 68: "So stellte er im Septe. d. J. 1791 die Eroberung der Türkischen Festung Ismael vor."

Table 6.3   Monthly box office takings (gulden) for the National Theater
(1789–90)

Jul	Aug	Sep	Oct	Nov	Dec	Jan	May	Jun	Jul	Aug
2,467	3,656	6,131	6,769	8,088	7,333	8,184	5,756	4,413	4,966	6,687

taken in the last days of Joseph's life in the hope of celebrating his role in the commission. The audience verdict was decisive: the box office at the first performance exceeded 600 gulden, a rare occurrence, and Zinzendorf praised Benucci unreservedly.[95] But neither of the works commissioned toward the end of the previous season sustained the audience's interest; performances of *La cifra* and (especially) *Così fan tutte* dwindled. Mozart's appearance as conductor on 12 June coincided with a very poor box office taking (76 gulden), no better than the sum taken for *Der Kobold* on 15 June (77 gulden), which suffered from a direct clash with Stuwer's second firework display. An additional hurdle for *Così* was that the emperor's death had interrupted the established pattern of dissemination through which operatic music was made available in arrangements for keyboard and string quartet. Nothing from the opera was advertised other than Artaria's edition of "Il core vi donno," a notable lacuna, implying that those engaged in the music business rated any *Così* arrangement, for the time being at least, a poor investment. The lack of interest in commercial spinoffs, once the mourning period for Joseph II was over, is a good indicator of that work's waning popularity.

Da Ponte's final season as an opera impresario was dominated by the prolonged visit of the king and queen of Naples, in Vienna to celebrate the double wedding of two daughters of Maria Carolina to Franz and his brother Ferdinand, Leopold's second son. A new festive opera was commissioned to celebrate the arrival of the Neapolitan party, *La caffetteria bizzarra*, which received its first performance on 15 September.[96] In the press it was portrayed as a total failure.[97] Although Joseph Weigl's score had its *longeurs* as well as its attractive moments, a wretched libretto was primarily responsible for

---

95. Link, *National Court Theatre*, 354: "Benucci anime tout."

96. The dedication in the libretto ran: "in occasione del felicissimo arrivo di sua maestà il re e la regina delle due Sicilie." Link, *National Court Theatre*, 157.

97. As the most recent work in Da Ponte's oeuvre, *La caffettiera bizzarra* also came under fire in the satire *Anti-da Ponte*, notably on account of its supposed pilfering of material from farces at the Leopoldstadttheater. De Alwis, *Anti-Da Ponte*, 49.

its fate, and its author's attempts to insist on the merits of his drama were
rejected with derision.[98] In his autobiography, Weigl admitted that the work
had deserved to fail but blamed his inexperience and the poor advice he had
received.[99] The perception that Da Ponte was producing indifferent work was
gaining ground and was soon to feature in the satire *Anti-da Ponte*.[100] Weigl's
failure demonstrated that "festive" status alone could not save a poor work
from deserved oblivion, but this debacle, abject though it was, did not represent the critical moment for the future of Italian opera: that occurred on 20
September 1790, when Leopold, who had not been in Vienna to hear the gala
opera written for the first marriage of his eldest son, Franz, finally attended
Axur, now selected to celebrate the double wedding.[101] He was of course
watched as he watched with close attention. General approval was one thing—
given the nature of the occasion the royal party was unlikely to leave before the
end—but interested observers wondered whether he would betray in his eyes
evidence that he was a discerning musician. As ill luck would have it, the composer himself was unable to direct the performance, owing to his departure
for Frankfurt, where the same opera was to be given in a German translation.
In his absence, the duty fell to the violinist Thomas Woborzill, who failed to
capture the requisite spirit. One commentator surmised that had Salieri been
present, *Axur* might well have made his fortune a second time.[102] That it had

---

98. *Musikalische Korrespondenz der teutschen Filarmonischen Gesellschaft* (10 November 1790),
no. 19, col.145: Wien vom 23sten Sept. 1790: "Der Operntext ist äußerst elend von unserm
Hofpoeten Abbate da Ponte, der es sogar vor der Produktion, für sein chef d'oeuvres ausgab,
und noch behauptet, er könne nichts dafür, wenn alle Menschen—wären und nichts verstehen, er sey überzeugt, daß das Werk gut sey: Eine allgemeine Vorrede zum schlechten
Poeten—!"

99. Angermüller, "Zwei Selbstbiographien"; cited in Rice, "Operatic Culture," 5.

100. De Alwis, *Anti-Da Ponte*, 32: "Obschon das Wiener Publikum ihm schon seit geraumer
Zeit sein Mißfallen über seine elende Poesie zu erkennen gegeben hat."

101. Both of the bridegrooms knew the work. On 3 September 1789, Elisabeth von
Württemberg informed her husband, Franz, that his brother Ferdinand had written to her to
express his thanks for the copy of *Axur* she had sent to him: "Votre frère Ferdinand m'a aussi
écrit, il me remercie pour l'opera 'Axur' que je lui ai envoyé." Weyda, "Briefe an Erzherzog
Franz," 189. A score had been purchased from Sukowaty on 6 August 1789. Rice, *Empress
Marie Therese*, 20.

102. *Musikalische Korrespondenz der teutschen Filarmonischen Gesellschaft* (10 November 1790),
no. 19, col.145: Wien vom 23sten Sept. 1790: "Schade, daß Salieri eben diesen Tag nach
Frankfurt abgereiset war, und die Orchesterdirektion dann von dem schläfrigen Woborzil
dependirte, wobei alle die Stellen, die mit Geist und Feuer vorgetragen werden müssen,
verlohren giengen. Sonst hätte Salieri mit seinem göttlichen Axur zum 2tenmal beim Hofe
gewiß sein Glük gemacht."

been Leopold's brother's favorite opera may not have helped its cause, but others concurred that the German version given in Frankfurt was better.[103]

In the changed political circumstances, *Figaro* continued to demonstrate its durability.[104] There was a slight spike in receipts when Benucci returned to the title role on 24 July 1790. The roster of singers reported to the *Indice de' teatrali spettacoli* for that season confirms that Brocchi was no longer a member of the troupe.[105] From the start of the season up until Benucci's reappearance, there were seven performances of *Figaro* for which the casting of the title role remains uncertain.[106] A pronounced dip in receipts during the spring may have been related to a less than inspiring performer in the title role. Around this time, Mozart told his wife that an unnamed scoundrel ("Hundsfott") was being pleasant to his face but running down *Figaro* in public. A date of 2 June 1790 has tentatively been assigned to this letter—simply headed Wednesday— because Mozart mentions in passing that he has been to see Benedikt Schack's *Der Fall ist noch weit seltener*, given its premiere on 10 May.[107] The poor receipts at the 19 May performance of *Figaro* were probably down to advertisements for Stuwer's firework display the previous night, a representation of the Siege of Belgrade that attracted large crowds.[108]

103. Glatthorn, "Imperial Coronation," 95, cites a report in the *Privilegirte Mainzer Zeitung* (25 September 1790), no. 137: "in keinen Oper ist wohl mehr gut geordnetes Theaterspiel, besseres Sujet, schönerer Text und angestandene hinreißende Musik."

104. In December 1790, in his only known comment on the revived *Figaro*, Da Ponte expressed the view that the work "does not displease" ("che pur non dispiace"), a remark not seeming to indicate a particularly high level of personal enthusiasm. Michtner, "Der Fall Abbé Da Ponte," 189.

105. *Indice de' teatrali spettacoli*, vol. 1, 928.

106. A *Theaterzettel* for 26 June 1790 announced that it had been necessary to perform *Figaro* as a replacement for *Una cosa rara* on the grounds of Benucci's illness. "This would seem to imply that Benucci was *not* in the cast of *Figaro* at that time." Edge, "Mozart's Reception," 104. A *Theaterzettel* for the next performance on 24 July notes Benucci's appearance in the title role, something usually done on a first occasion.

107. *Mozart: Briefe und Aufzeichnungen*, vol. 4, 110, and vol. 6, 395. According to his letter to Puchberg written on or before 12 June, Mozart was staying with Constanze in Baden to save money, coming in to Vienna only when necessary. He could have heard this work, a sequel to *Una cosa rara*, here as well, as a production was staged by the Wilhelminische Gesellschaft in the summer of 1790. *Theater-Kalender auf das Jahr 1791*, 255.

108. *Wiener Zeitung* (27 May 1789), no. 42, 1337: "Gestern gab Hr. Stuwer, im Prater, sein erstes diesjähriges Feuerwerk, dessen Hauptfront die Belagerung Belgrads vorstellete." The receipts for *Marie Stuart* on 18 May (60 gulden) and *Figaro* on 19 May (68 gulden) fell far below the prevailing average.

A further short run for *Figaro* began early in 1791, and the audience on 9 February included the Neapolitan royalty, fresh from an outdoor excursion to Schönbrunn.[109] Edge has proposed that "Un moto di gioa," once automatically assumed to have been composed in 1789 as a second new aria for Ferrarese, might in fact date from as late as the first months of 1791.[110] The letter in which Mozart refers to this "arietta" is undated, and the piece is not entered into his catalogue. As Da Ponte was arguing vehemently for the retention of Ferrarese at the end of 1790, he may have requested a new piece so that his mistress could demonstrate her aptitude in a simpler Neapolitan manner. Mozart doubted whether she could bring it off in the naïve fashion required, seeming to imply that he had followed instructions, notwithstanding his professional opinion that this style was unsuited to her.[111] But the presumed musical tastes of the new regime were certainly making their mark. Imported works such as Guglielmi's *La pastorella nobile* and Paisiello's *La molinara* were doing very well.[112]

DA PONTE'S APPOINTMENT came to an end in March, and the event was significant enough to warrant news coverage abroad.[113] He received a very harsh evaluation.[114] Using a Lutheran term of abuse for a priest overly interested in a good life ("Bauchpfaffe"), an anonymous writer characterized him as a thoroughly bad lot, whose dismissal had more to do with his lifestyle than his merits as a poet and dramatist. The satirist responsible for *Anti-da Ponte* attributed his dismissal to the machinations surrounding his attempt to retain Ferrarese, but her career at the National Theater was nearly over. Even now, she remained a draw, and reports of the 1791 benefit performances suggest

---

109. *Gazzetta universale* (22 February 1791), no. 18, 124: Vienna 10 Febbrajo: "Jeri in contemplazione delle LL. MM. Siciliane la Corte dette una superba corsa di Slitte fino a Schombrun . . . Nel ritorno . . . si trasferirono all'Opera in Musica le *Nozze di Figaro* al Teatro Italiano. " Edge, "Habsburg Court and Guests Attend *Le nozze di Figaro*," in Edge and Black, *Mozart*.

110. The orchestral parts were marked with a cue for a recitative ending—the words of which no longer exist. Edge, "Mozart's Viennese Copyists," 1687–99.

111. *Mozart: Briefe und Aufzeichnungen*, vol. 4, 97: " 'glaub' ich soll gefallen, wenn anders sie fähig ist es naiv vorzutragen, woran ich aber, sehr zweifle." Anderson, *Letters*, vol. 3, 1389.

112. Link, *National Court Theatre*, 490–91, citing Rice, "Emperor and Impresario."

113. *Laibacher Zeitung* (26 April 1791), no. 33: Wien den 20. April: "Der gewesene Hof Poet Abee la [*sic*] Ponte hat seine Charge quittiret, und ist bereits von hier abgereiset; statt desselben soll ein anderer von Florenz hieher kommen."

114. *Chronik* (1791), no. 71, 585: "Den Abt da Ponte, Verfasser der Cosa rara und des Baums der Diana verwies er mit noch 5 andern Bauchpfaffen aus Wien, weil sie abscheuliche Grundsäze unter dem Volke verbreiteten und ein asottisches Leben führten."

that she was making large sums of money.[115] Throughout her time in Vienna, she demonstrated the consistent pulling power of a true prima donna. Rarely during her first year did the box office takings fall to a two-figure sum in the five operas in which she sang major roles: *L'arbore di Diana: Il pastor fido; Le nozze di Figaro; La cifra*; and *Così fan tutte*. But a new-look troupe was in the process of being formed, and Leopold was determined to recruit opera seria singers from Italy. It was reported that some performers from the disbanded ensemble at Eszterháza had been offered a trial.[116] With the departure of Da Ponte and his mistress Ferrarese, the Josephinian era of opera came to an end.

---

115. *Laibacher Zeitung* (12 April 1791), no. 29: Wien den 6. April: "Die Madame Ferraresi hat in 3 malen bey Produzirung der neuen Opera der König David eine Einnahme von 3470 Gulden gehabt, die Unkösten mögen Ihr etwa auf 1000 Gulden zu stehen gekommen seyn."

116. *Preßburger Zeitung* (25 December 1790), no. 102, 1141: Wien: Aus Privatnachrichten, den 23 Dez.: "Der Fürst Anton Eszterhazy hat die in seinen verstorbenen Hrn. Vaters Gehalt gestandenen Operisten sammt den ganzen Orchester bis auf den Capellmeister Hayden, und einen der besten Violinisten mit einem vierteljährigen Gehalt der Dienste entlassen, von denen Operisten und Operistinen sind inzwischen 4 allhier bei dem National Theater zur Probe auf einige Zeit angestellt worden, die besten davon werden als dann auf längere Zeit engagirt werden."

Conclusion

THE NEW OPERATIC order with its programs of opera seria and ballet was scheduled to begin in the autumn of 1791. In the year and a half leading up to this, Leopold was at pains to demonstrate his support for German theatrical traditions. According to Lange, his first visit to see a production in Vienna as emperor was on 9 June 1790, when he attended the premiere of *Virginia*.[1] Suburban theater soon began to feature prominently in this campaign of reassurance. A large Habsburg party went to see *Merkur der neue Modezauberer* at Leopoldstadt.[2] In due course, Leopold visited a Kasperl performance, just as his brother had done, and it was made known that he intended to come regularly.[3] By mid-February, Leopold had also been several times to the Theater auf der Wieden.[4] On two occasions Habsburg parties went to see *Der Stein der Weisen*.[5]

---

1. Lange, *Biographie*, 166. Zinzendorf noted the presence of Maria Luisa. Link, *National Court Theatre*, 356. Lange stressed the emperor's even-handedness when it came to funding. *Biographie*, 171.

2. Angermüller, *Wenzel Müller*, 173: 21 November [December?] 1790: "Erzherzogin Christine, Erzherzog Franz mit Gemahlin, Erzherzog Ferdinand mit Gemahlin, Maria Luisa, Erzherzogin Marie Anna und die Erzherzöge Carl Ludwig, Alexander Leopold und Joseph Anton, besuchen."

3. *Bayreuther Zeitung* (10 February 1791), no. 18, 117: Wien, vom 4. Jan.: "Unser allgeliebter Kaiser zeigt sich öfter Seinem Volk, als vormals. Vor einigen Tagen beliebte es Demselben, das Leopoldstädter Theater zu besuchen, und den famosen Casperle zu belachen. Der Monarch gedenkt öfters dahin zu fahren, um sich zu zerstreuen."

4. *Bayreuther Zeitung* (1 March 1791), no. 26, 182: Wien, vom 21. Febr.: "Unser lieber guter Kaiser . . . besucht das deutsche Schauspiel fleißig, und hat schon zweymal das Theater des unermüdeten Schikaneder mit seinem Besuch beehrt, und freudigen Beyfall zu erkennen gegeben."

5. *Kurfürstlich gnädigst privilegirte Münchner Zeitung* (22 February 1791), no. 31, 161: Wien, vom 16 Febr. (Aus der Wienerhofzeitung): "Sonntags Abends besuchten II. KK. HH. des Wiedner Theater, wo die beliebte Oper, der Stein der Weisen, von Hrn. Schikaneder, gegeben wurde welche auch schon am 4ten d. M. Se. Majestät der Kaiser, sammt II. Siz. MM. und KK. HH gesehen, und mit Allerhöchstdero Beifall beehret hatten." Edge, "Habsburg Court and Guests Attend *Der Stein der Weisen*," in Edge and Black, *Mozart*.

The second of these visits may have been a consequence of a last-minute program change at the Burgtheater, where Ferrarese was too ill to appear in *La cifra*.[6] That there were spontaneous changes of plan demonstrates just how readily the Habsburgs were now frequenting the commercial theaters. On 12 November 1791, when the indisposition of a singer caused a cancelation, Franz headed off to the Leopoldstadttheater to see what was on offer.[7] Evidence of the frequency of his patronage of the suburban theaters during the early months of 1791 comes in his accounts: February 1791: 108 gulden at the Theater auf der Wieden; 54 gulden at the Theater auf der Landstraße; 108 gulden at the Theater auf der Wieden; March 1791: 54 gulden at a comedy (Kasperltheater); 54 gulden at a Kasperltheater; 54 gulden at Schikaneder's Theater (Theater auf der Wieden); May 1791: 54 gulden at Schikaneder's Theater (Theater auf der Wieden).[8] All in all, the three months at the start of 1791 witnessed the most intense period of imperial patronage of suburban theater yet seen.[9]

Once it became clear that the new emperor would be a regular visitor to the commercial stage, competition to catch his attention became correspondingly sharp. When someone acting on behalf of the Leopoldstadttheater planted rumors that its rival was in serious financial trouble, Schikaneder took the unusual step of placing a notice in three successive issues of the *Wiener Zeitung* (2, 5, and 9 February) denying gossip that he was in difficulty. Needless to say, the cost of this thrice-repeated rebuttal implies the existence of a campaign of denigration that had the potential to inflict some damage.

With Leopold II, Maria Luisa, Franz and his new wife, and other members of the Habsburg dynasty frequenting the suburban theaters, Schikaneder took

---

6. Link, *National Court Theatre*, 164.

7. *Bayreuther Zeitung* (25 November 1791), no. 140, Anhang, 1039: Wien, vom 19. Nov.: "Vergangene Woche hatten wir wohl einer Theaterzettel, aber keine Opera und keine Comödie, dann ein Sänger war krank, der andere aber nicht zu finden. . . . Der Erzherzog Franz setzte sich lächelnd in Wagen und beehrte noch an diesem Abend das Leopoldstädter Theater, wo zum Glück ein nettes Stück gegeben wurde."

8. Dunlop, "'Kaisersammlung,'" 54. The Josephstadttheater is less frequently mentioned at this period, although on 13 February the king of Naples went to a performance. *Kurfürstlich gnädigst privilegirte Münchner Zeitung* (28 February 1791), no. 34, 177: Wien, vom 20. Febr. (Aus Privatbriefen).

9. Leopold also patronized the Theater auf der Landstrasse, which had run into trouble early in 1791 when the police had intervened to close a comedy performed by a traveling French troupe; itinerant players of this nationality were easily cast as suspect purveyors of a dangerous ideology. *Bayreuther Zeitung* (13 January 1791), no. 6, 35: Wien, vom 6. Jan. After his return to Vienna in the summer, the emperor went to a performance there, apparently with the explicit aim of boosting the audience and saving the theater from probable closure. *Bayreuther Zeitung* (22 August 1791), no. 100, Anhang, 795: Wien, vom 16 August.

the decision to offer commissions to leading composers, in addition to those
he employed in-house.[10] Dittersdorf's *Der neue Gutsherr, oder Der Schiffspatron*
was given on 2 March 1791.[11] Mozart, whose connections with the Theater
auf der Wieden had been steadily strengthening during 1790 as a result of
commissions for individual pieces, was now offered the opportunity to com-
pose a new Singspiel. Having failed to attract Leopold's attention following
the death of Joseph II, first with a memorandum and then with his concert
in Frankfurt, he now had an excellent opportunity to demonstrate his talent
as a composer for the stage, with every prospect that his new sovereign would
in due course attend a performance. As Cairns commented: "The notion that
Mozart composed *The Magic Flute* only because of poverty and neglect by
the court—that he was driven to the expedient of slumming it at a suburban
theatre in a working-class district for want of anything more worthy of his
genius—dies hard. It was always an insufferably condescending idea, and a
snobbish one."[12]

A lengthy review of theatrical news was published in Bayreuth at the end
of April 1791, constituting a significant appraisal of the state of the Vienna
stage on the eve of *Die Zauberflöte*.[13] The Leopoldstadttheater was thought to
be doing well, as Hensler was attracting particular attention for his *Kasperl' der
glücklich Vogelkrämer*. Featuring a precursor of the birdman figure Papageno, it
received its premiere on 3 March 1791.[14] Franz and his new wife attended a performance on 31 March.[15] Other successes followed, notably *Kaspar der Fagottist*
on 8 June, but Schikaneder was also enjoying full houses.[16] A telling sign of
the strength of this competition is precisely that reviewers saw it as a competition, comparing accounts of their productions. As *Die Zauberflöte* came to the
stage, Leopoldstadt was featuring the actor Friedrich Baumann, whose turn as
a comic orangutan proved very popular. A teasing geographical choice faced
theatergoers in the center of Vienna: north to see the ape, or south to see the

---

10. Buch, "House Composers."

11. Link, "È la fede," 125.

12. Cairns, *Mozart and His Operas*, 200.

13. *Bayreuther Zeitung* (7 May 1791), no. 55, 486–87: Wien, vom 30 April.

14. Branscombe, *Die Zauberflöte*, 100.

15. Angermüller, *Wenzel Müller*, 174.

16. *Bayreuther Zeitung* (7 May 1791), no. 55, 487: Wien, vom 30 April: "Hr Schikaneder
geibt gute Stücke, hält brave Leute, und hat sein Hauß täglich voll. Er hat Achtung für das
Publicum, und das Publicum Zuneigung zu ihm, und auf diese Weise sind beyde Theile
zufrieden."

bird-catcher. Few enterprises were as effective in hastening an individual's bankruptcy as commercial theater, yet at times like this, with packed houses night after night, it must have looked like a good investment.[17]

Although his attention was now focused on the Theater auf der Wieden, Mozart may have made one final contribution to Italian opera. Aloysia Lange was back in Vienna, where she performed "No, no, che non sei capace" (K.419), a substitution aria written for her back in 1783. With a new *accompagnato* it was inserted into Paisiello's *Fedra*, the work selected for the Tonkünstler-Societät's annual performances on 16 and 17 April 1791.[18] There is nothing in its generic musical style to support a strong conclusion about authorship, but if Mozart wrote it, he was offering a small gesture, aimed at assisting his sister-in-law's reentry into the opera establishment in Vienna.[19] In any event, she was hired for Leopold's opera seria troupe. In a poignant coincidence, the *Bayreuther Zeitung* carried a notice informing its readers of Lange's new engagement on the very day of her brother-in-law's death.[20]

Mozart's high status as an opera composer, very evident in the early months of 1791 as he started work on a major new commission, was above all the result of the revival of *Le nozze di Figaro*. A measure of its popularity is that its music occupies a prominent position in the 1791 version of Da Ponte's collective benefit, now entitled *L'ape musicale rinnuovata*.[21] Before this satire could be staged, there was the inevitable controversy over women singers, there being three candidates for the two main roles. Ferrarese was allocated one, leaving Villeneuve and Bussani to contest the other.[22] After his dismissal,

---

17. A new suburban theater was announced a few days before Mozart's death. *Laibacher Zeitung* (9 December 1791), no. 98: Wien den 3. Christm.

18. Edge, "Mozart's Viennese Copyists," 1391–93.

19. Mozart and Lange both contributed to Joseph Bähr's concert on 4 March 1791. Mozart played a concerto (K.595), but it is not known which arias Lange sang. Deutsch, *Mozart: a Documentary Biography*, 386–87.

20. *Bayreuther Zeitung* (5 December 1791), no. 144, Anhang, 1065: Wien, vom 29. Nov.: "Madame Lange, unsere so gerne gehörte Sängerin ist wieder bey der Opera seria mit dem ganze vorigen Gehalt angestellt, und sie wird uns größeres Vergnügen gewähren, als die Cantatrice buffa welche bereits im achten Monat schwanger ist, und in eben der Zeit Wochenbette hält, wo man sie hatte wollen singen hören."

21. The title page reads: "L'APE MUSICALE / RINNUOVATA / COMEDIA per MUSICA / IN TRE ATTI / DA RAPPRESENTARSI / LA QUADRAGESIMA DELL'ANNO / M.DCC LXXXIXI. / LEL [sic] TEATRO DI CORTE / A / BENEFIZIO DI ALCUNI VIRTUOSI. / IN VIENNA / PRESSO GIUSEPPE NOB. DE KURZBEK, STAMPATORE DI S. M. I. R."

22. The former was still a member of the troupe, and if she had not done so already, she perhaps now took the role of Cherubino. Edge, "Mozart's Viennese Copyists," 1509.

Da Ponte penned a series of memoranda in which he identified his enemies and their attempts to undermine him. Francesco Bussani is named as his third major antagonist for a variety of reasons, among which was his belief that the poet had failed to acknowledge the merits of his wife.[23] But the second slot in *L'ape musicale rinnuovata* went to her, as Da Ponte had in the meantime fallen out with Villeneuve, who was accused of forgetting the courtesies he had shown her.[24]

The new edition of Da Ponte's satire marked the end of an era, as Leopold was about to sweep away his brother's operatic order. Franz attended *L'ape musicale rinnuovata* twice in March and April 1791, on both occasions offering a generous 225 gulden, no doubt in recognition that many were about to leave.[25] He had spent his formative years attending *opere buffe* given by the troupe recruited by his uncle, and it is quite possible that he felt some regret at the passing of the old order. Leopold's enthusiastic patronage of the commercial stage, representing, so far as anyone at the time knew, a major realignment of imperial aesthetic priorities, reawakened the intergenre satirical rivalry that had been quiescent for a few years in the absence of a Singspiel troupe at the National Theater. Given Dittersdorf's seminal contribution to the Josephinian regime, it seems very appropriate that he should feature in the final skirmishes.

After the discussion of the French pieces, retained from the 1789 edition of the benefit pasticcio, the banter turns to German music. Don Capriccio (Calvesi) expresses the wish to have "una scena tedesca," but Farinella (Bussani, a native German speaker) questions his pronunciation. She offers to sing in German if the poet can provide a scena that meets her requirements; it must be "buffissima," as she yearns for applause and encores. It is left to Zuccherina (Ferrarese) to recommend "Wenn man will" from Dittersdorf's *Der Apotheker*.[26] She is not disappointed with the performance, exclaiming: "Oh che cosetta amena."[27] But Don Capriccio (Calvesi) then proceeds to lampoon the work, commenting that its music may be graceful ("grazioso") but it is odd ("bizzarro"); it sets the blood coursing through the veins, tickles the ears,

---

23. Michtner, "Der Fall Abbé Da Ponte," 201: "Perchè ho detto sempre a tutti che sua moglie non poteva fare la prima donna in Vienna."

24. Michtner, "Der Fall Abbé Da Ponte," 201: "Costei dimenticò tutte le beneficenze e cortesie della mia amicizia perchè non l'ho fatta entrare nell' *Ape musicale [rinnuovata]*."

25. Dunlop, "'Kaisersammlung,'" 54.

26. The text was not given in the 1791 version but appears in full in the 1792 Trieste edition. Siniscalchi, *L'ape musicale*, 212.

27. Siniscalchi, *L'ape musicale*, 241.

Conclusion

provokes bystanders to dance, and above all keeps the cash rolling in ("E in fine è quello che fa. far. contanti"). Events in the summer of 1786, when the scale of *Der Apotheker*'s triumph had adversely affected receipts for opera buffa, had not been forgotten.

Da Ponte was an inventive satirist, and his attack on Dittersdorf continues with a skit on a celebrated aria in *Hieronymus Knicker*, in which one of the characters sings in mock Turkish. Composed late in 1787 or early 1788, this Singspiel coincided with the start of the Austro-Turkish War. Dittersdorf's inspiration was very likely Goldoni's libretto *La conversazione*, which derives much of its humor from language, including an aria in the dialect of the Bologna region. The linguistic climax is a Turkish word. Alone (act 3, scene 3), Lucrezia states her intention to go to the masked ball dressed "alla turca," mimicking "la lingua di Turchia." Accordingly, her aria begins with the Arabic greeting "Salaam" ("Sala melecch"). Dittersdorf, writing with war imminent if not actually under way, went for a sharper take-off of the sounds of the enemy language. Ferdinand enters (act 2, scene 8), accompanied by two Moors, and greets Knicker with a Turkish bow ("mit türkischer Verbeugungen"). His aria begins with the salutation but continues with nonsense: "Sala ma mi lecka / Ma ka kara becca / Ma li ma ti kala / Pa Hubabala!"[28] Mockery of Turkish is the intent, and it is doubtful whether any semantic content could have been discerned after the initial greeting. The music is off-the-peg *alla turca*: A minor in 2/4, with short, square-cut phrases and passages of reinforced tonic pedal. Where Mozart in K.331 is succinct, treating the two-bar phrase after the first double bar to a single sequential repetition, relative major to tonic, Dittersdorf runs his through several keys. Knicker of course cannot understand a word, but Ferdinand reassures him that he speaks his tongue too: "Seyn ohne Sorgen, hubabala auch so sprechen kann, wie Du." At the end of the scene, Ferdinand takes his leave in Turkish fashion with a bow ("mit einer türkischer Verbeugung"). Knicker is now confident enough to imitate him: to Ferdinand's "Salamilek!" he responds "Sala milek gleichfalls."

When he decided to include a satirical reference to the "Turkish" aria, Da Ponte could be fairly confident that the Vienna opera audience would make the connection with the piece in Dittersdorf's popular comedy. In the 1789 edition of *L'ape musicale*, the Turkish theme had been limited to a brief skit based on the similarity between Tarchi (the composer) and Turchi (the language). This was now replaced with a set-piece lampoon. At the end of the discussion about which languages to sing in (act 1, scene 5), there is a surprising

28. Thanks to my colleague Dr. Zeynep Bulut for helpful comments on this.

twist: Don Capriccio (Calvesi) proposes, hesitantly, to sing in Turkish: "Ed io . . . canterò . . . in turco." The poet questions this ("In Turco?"), but he has not misheard: "In Turco. Non è una bella Lingua, Halà Bàlà." Despite being warned that Turkish is incomprehensible, Don Capriccio is adamant: either he is allowed to sing in this language, or he will not be singing at all: "O canterò turchesco o non mi avrai / Nell'Opera che faì'. In the ensuing scene (act 1, scene 6), Bonario, representing the views of Da Ponte, refers to the "madman" who wants to sing in Turkish: "El matto che in turco / Pretendete cantare / Ha la La bha Lha."[29] In casting Calvesi as a singer intent on singing in Turkish, Da Ponte may have intended a further allusion. The current repertoire of the Italian troupe included Seydelmann's *Il turco in Italia*, which features a Turkish prince named Selim.[30] Fortuitously, this work had just acquired a contemporary resonance of its own, as a new sultan, Selim III, ascended to the throne on 7 April 1789, thereby assuming responsibility for the war. The full cast list is not known, but it is possible that Calvesi took the Turkish role.

Further satire is directed toward Bussani and her inadequate command of Italian. Ferrarese sarcastically thanks the poet, her other half, as "il signor correttore" upon his rectification of one of her mistakes ("propotipo" for "prototipo"). The conversation turns to the choice of an arietta, and there are three suggestions: "Serena raggio di bella calma" from *L'arbore di Diana*; Giordani's "Sento che in seno"; or one by a celebrated master, "Batti, batti, o bel Masetto / La tua poverina Zerlina." Don Capriccio (Calvesi) comments that the beauty of these pieces depends on the orchestra even more than the voice. Is it not possible to suggest something that is attractive (vocally) in its own right?[31] What the proposed pieces have in common is elaborate obbligato writing for a solo instrument—oboe, flute, and cello, respectively. The satirical issue is that of overrich orchestration, a complaint regularly leveled against Mozart. In Giordani's case, Don Capriccio's comment is apt; the orchestration of "Sento che in seno," introduced in the 1789 version of *L'ape musicale*, is remarkably rich.[32] With a prelude of thirty-two bars, a postlude of sixteen bars,

---

29. Siniscalchi, *L'ape musicale*, 216.

30. Wolff, *Singing Turk*, 285.

31. Siniscalchi, *L'ape musicale*, 239: Don Capriccio: "Ascolti Signorina / Quest'arie son bellissime, ma tutte / Piu assai che dal cantante / Dipendon dall'orchestra: / Or madama maestra, / Dica qualche arietta / Che sia bella in se stessa."

32. While it is not known who chose to insert this piece in the pasticcio, Cavalieri had previously sung an unnamed aria by this composer with a flute obbligato part in Tonkünstler-Societät programs on 20 December 1778 and 12 March 1779. On the latter occasion, it was advertised with Ludwig Gehring playing the flute. Morrow, *Concert Life*, 246 and 248.

and an interlude of fourteen bars, the instrumental content, amounting in total to almost half the piece, makes the satirical point perfectly, as does the colorful scoring. The opening sonority is striking; a solo flute has the melody, accompanied by pizzicato strings, while the viola, marked "sempre forte," arpeggiates remorselessly, if less elegantly, than the cello in "Batti, batti." A five-piece wind ensemble consisting of two clarinets in C, two horns in C, and a bassoon, further enriches the tutti texture and occasionally acts as a dialogue partner for the singer.

Shortly before the climax of act 2, the poet decides that he needs a rondò to crown his opera and asks for ideas. Ferrarese suggests the one from *L'arbore di Diana*, but that is dismissed brusquely by the poet as too old.[33] What about *Figaro*, she asks? Bonario replies that it is beautiful but that he would not know how to introduce it. These passing references to Mozart's music in the banter are followed by a more substantial set piece, featuring "Che soave zeffiretto" and the practice of improvising ornamentation.[34] The critical factor in establishing a good reputation as an opera composer was not the existence of past failures or modestly received works—even Paisiello had plenty of these—but success in providing the National Theater with a durable Italian work. The high profile of *Le nozze di Figaro* in Da Ponte's final satire attests its composer's growing status.

The final round in the satirical exchanges provoked by the termination of Da Ponte's contract went to the anonymous author of *Anti-da Ponte*. Describing himself as a "cosmopolitan," he dissects a letter to Leopold II written by Da Ponte to justify himself against what he terms "a malicious plot" ("ein boshaftes Komplott") instigated by his detractors.[35] The pamphlet appears to postdate the start of the new theatrical season, as it makes reference to the debut of Irene Tomeoni in *La bella pescatrice* on 26 April 1791.[36] In the mock trial that constitutes the second section of *Anti-da Ponte*, Von Diedersdorf (Dittersdorf), appearing as a witness for the prosecution, alludes to the debacle over his *Democritto corretto*, reopening the wider debate as to whether German composers could write competent and stylish Italian opera: "Von Dittersdorf said many bitter things to Da Ponte about his having once foisted such a miserable text upon him when he wanted to write an Italian opera for

---

33. The reference, nevertheless, is to a relatively recent piece, the substitute rondò by Tarchi. Gidwitz, "Mozart's Fiordiligi."

34. Woodfield, "Che soave zeffiretto," 126–27.

35. De Alwis, *Anti-Da Ponte*, 39.

36. De Alwis, *Anti-Da Ponte*, 69.

the Italian theatre. He brought up several incidents in which Italian singers strove to cause his works to fail, and he insisted that German composers, if supported, would easily bring just as much proficiency and just as much taste to bear in an opera as an Italian Kapellmeister."[37] In his response, Da Ponte is made to acknowledge the poor quality of his text: "If I foisted a bad text on Herr von Dittersdorf, he should not give me grief about it. Why did he accept it? The blame is his alone. Could he have reasonably imagined that Italian singers would want to contribute to elevating a German composer?"[38] The wider context of this exchange is the "rift between Italian and German opera" that had dominated theater politics in the later 1780s.[39]

MY STUDY OF the high politics and low cabals that impinged on the creation and reception of Mozart's Italian comedies has led me to question whether Salieri, widely cast as his nemesis, conspired against his junior colleague in any meaningful fashion at all. The primary evidence for the existence of a hostile relationship during the late Vienna phase of Mozart's career consists of two passing references in the tense weeks leading up to the premieres of *Le nozze di Figaro* and *Così fan tutte*; both could very easily have concerned matters of no lasting significance. Kelly, it is true, depicts Salieri as "a clever shrewd man" who conspired to have *La grotta di Trofonio* staged before two other works in preparation.[40] With an eye on his place in history, he asserted that he alone had been a "stickler" for Mozart, but his memory of these events is highly suspect. Salieri may well have been conspiratorially active early in 1785 on behalf of his latest opera against *L'incontro inaspettato* by Vincenzo Righini and one other unidentified work, but *Figaro*, as yet, was barely in the planning stages. A further hint of trouble came several years later in a letter—written shortly before

---

37. De Alwis, *Anti-Da Ponte*, 50–51: "Von Diedersdorf sagte dem *da Ponte* sehr viel bitteres darüber, daß dieser ihm ehemals, als er für das italienische Theater eine Oper schreiben wollte, einen so elenden Text untergeschoben habe. Er brachte mehreres auf die Bahn von den Bemühungen der welschen Sänger, seine Stücke fallen zu Machen, und er beharre darauf, daß deutsche Musik-Kompositeurs, wenn sie unterstützt würden, eben so viele Kenntniße, und eben so viel Geschmack bey Opern zu zeigen wüsten, als ein italienischer Kapellmeister nur immer thun könne."

38. De Alwis, *Anti-Da Ponte*, 56–57. "Wenn ich dem Hr. von Diedersdorf einen schlechten Text untergeschoben habe, so darf er sich deßwegen nicht über mich beschweren. Warum hat er ihn angenommen? Die Schuld ist bloß sein. Und hat er sich denn vernünftiger Weise einbilden können, daß welsche Sänger etwas dazu beytragen würden, einen deutschen Kompositeur empor zu heben?"

39. De Alwis, *Anti-Da Ponte*, 8.

40. Deutsch, *Mozart: A Documentary Biography*, 533.

the premiere of *Così fan tutte*—in which Mozart referred to Salieri's intrigues, albeit noting that these attempts to interfere had so far come to nothing. Yet if the memory of Constanze in old age can be trusted, this enmity, which she attributed to his jealousy over her husband's successful completion of this project, was of recent origin.

Against this evidence, such as it is, must be set the pride with which Mozart reported Salieri's glowing appreciation of *Die Zauberflöte*. The suspicion, at times almost paranoid in character, with which Mozart and, more particularly, his father had viewed Salieri as a figure of authority in the opera buffa troupe of the early to mid-1780s, has dissipated entirely. With nothing at stake and an obvious success to celebrate, the camaraderie between the two men is obvious:

> I fetched Salieri and Mad.me Cavalieri with a carriage and took them to my box—then I quickly drove back to pick up Mama and Carl, who were waiting for me at Hofer's. You can't believe how sweet they both were—and how much they enjoyed not only my music but the libretto and everything.—Both of them told me it was an *opera* ["operone"] fit to be played at the grandest festivity, before the greatest monarch—and they would certainly go and see it more often because they had never seen a more beautiful and more pleasant spectacle.—Salieri listened and watched with great attention, and from the overture all the way through to the final chorus there was not a single number that did not elicit from him a "bravo" or "bello." He and Cavalieri went on and on thanking me for doing them such a great favour. They had wanted to see the performance yesterday but would have had to get their seats by 4. o'clock—so, this way, they were able to see and hear it all without being rushed.[41]

Dated 14 October 1791, this is Mozart's last known letter, and there is hardly a warmer account of a fellow composer in his entire correspondence; no trace of animosity can be detected. A more balanced summation might be that the two men had a professional, perhaps even a collegial working relationship, ruffled every now and then by the conflicts of interest that inevitably arise in the running of an opera house.

But Dittersdorf's relationship with Mozart is another matter. My study suggests that this rivalry went deeper than is commonly supposed. In many ways, Peter Shaffer's image of a successful composer struggling to come to terms

---

41. Spaethling, *Mozart's Letters*, 442.

with a genius seems to fit Dittersdorf better. The clash between *Le nozze di Figaro* and *Der Apotheker* was not of either man's making, but Dittersdorf was certainly visible in the publicity campaign for his own work and thus for the Singspiel troupe, as was his duty. Whether he went further, engaging in the dark arts of theater politics by encouraging the dissemination of an exaggerated account of the mixed reception of *Figaro*, remains unproven, although the suspicion that he did so seems justified. In any event, he soon had to contend with a problem of his own. Faced with a difficulty in the scheduling of his new Italian opera, he lobbied the emperor hard, but the power of the Storace faction proved decisive, and he had to defer to them. The opera's miserable failure was attributed by Joachim Perinet to the activities of an Italian cabal, prejudiced against Germans on nationalistic grounds. Whether Dittersdorf agreed with this conspiracy theory or not, there is little doubt that this failure rankled.

After his return to Silesia, Dittersdorf may never have encountered Mozart again, but his choice of projects suggests a strong desire to continue competing with him. He started work on his first set of string quartets, offering them to Artaria with the insinuation that they would make a more profitable investment than Mozart's had been. Effective pitch though this was, it betrayed feelings of inferiority. It was hardly credible to claim that his rival lacked talent—this much he always acknowledged; better to argue that he had too much of it, that it was out of control, and that the resulting lack of moderation was commercially damaging.

Dittersdorf's extraordinary version of *Die Hochzeit des Figaro* also represents the competitive side of his nature: his desire to demonstrate that a musical setting of the Beaumarchais drama could achieve a level of popularity in Vienna not attained by *Le nozze di Figaro*. In fashioning Cherubin as a recognizable version of his rival, he presented a memorable satirical portrait of an immature dandy obsessed with dancing. It may be that when he conceived this idea, the possibility of an imperial appointment was at the back of his mind, as Heartz is surely right to suggest that Vienna remained the composer's career goal. Writing of an earlier chance to enter imperial service, which Dittersdorf claimed to have turned down, Heartz put it thus: "had he actually received an offer . . . not all his Silesian titles and emoluments would have kept him in the provinces."[42] But in a critical piece of ill luck, he was not on hand when Joseph executed an emergency rearrangement of his musical structures. Dittersdorf's operatic music nevertheless remained very popular in Vienna. Indeed, by the start of the new decade, something close to equilibrium had been established

---

in the theatrical fortunes of the two men, both making a successful transition to commercial theater, whose extraordinary flowering was the lasting musical legacy of the war.

Exactly two weeks after Mozart's death, Dittersdorf wrote a letter to Johann Friedrich Reichardt in Berlin, floating the possibility of a new commission.[43] At the end he remarked: "*Mozard* ist also Todt—und wieder ein grosser Mann weniger" ("So Mozart is dead; again, one fewer great man"). Its matter-of-fact tone is striking, as earlier in the letter he had alluded with rather more feeling to the death of "unser brave Landeshauptmann und Praesident." Altogether startling is the manner in which he wrote the name of Mozart. The letter is fluently penned with no more than the occasional very minor slip. "Mozard," however, was originally written as "Mazard," the wrong vowel being corrected ostentatiously. Something in Dittersdorf's brain or hand had conspired to prevent the unproblematic committal of his rival's name to paper.

---

43. Unverricht, *Carl von Dittersdorf: Briefe*, 102–3, pl. 6.

Bibliography

PRIMARY SOURCES

Periodicals

Allgemeine deutsche Bibliothek
Allgemeine musikalische Zeitung
Berlinische musikalische Zeitung
Cabinet des Modes
Calendrier musical universal
Chronik
Der neue deutsche Zuschauer
Der wienerische Zuschauer
Dramaturgische Monate
Gründsätze zur Theaterkritik
Journal der Moden
Journal des Luxus und der Moden
Kritisches Theater-Journal
Magasin des modes nouvelles, Françoises et Angloises
Magazin der Musik
Musik (previously Magazin der Musik)
Musikalische Korrespondenz der teutschen Filarmonischen Gesellschaft
Musikalische Real-Zeitung
Musikalischer Almanach
Musikalisches Wochenblatt
Neues Theater Journal für Deutschland
Pfeffer und Salz
Rapport von Wien
Theater-Kalendar
Vaterlandschronik
Wochenblatt für Kinder

PAMPHLETS

Anti-da Ponte: I. Das von dem Abbate da Ponte vor seiner Abreise von Wien aufgestellte Denkmal des tiefesten Respekts gegen den Monarchen, und der gränzenlosen Achtung und Dankbarkeit gegen die österreichische Nation, Vienna: Hraschanzky, 1791.

Antwort auf die unverschämte Kritik über die Leopoldstädter Cosa rara, Vienna, 1787.

Apologie der marinellischen Schaubühne in der Leopoldstadt gegen das "Etwas für Alle über die Aufführung des Baums der Diana," Vienna: M. L., 1788.

Bitte an Damen Wiens, Vienna: [self published], 1789.

Ein paar nachdrückliche Worte über die Aufführung des Trauerspiels: Die Verschwörung des Fiesko gennant, als es zum Zweytenmale mit einigen Abkürzungen den 8. December 1787 auf der Nationalhofschaubühne vorgestellt ward, Vienna, 1787.

Etwas für Alle über die Aufführung des Baums der Diana in dem Marinellischen Schauspielhause in der Leopoldstadt, Vienna, 1788.

Kaiser Joseph wird doch geliebt: Ein kleine Antwort auf die kürzlich erschiene Schrift: Warum wird Kaiser Joseph von Seinem Volke nicht geliebt, Vienna, 1787.

Kratter, B**n & Socii, Vienna, 1786.

Les Metamorphoses d'Ovide mises en Musique par Mr Charles Ditters Noble de Dittersdorf, Vienna: Kurzbek, 1786.

Meine Gedanken über die Broschüre: Warum wird Kaiser Joseph von Seinem Volke nicht geliebt, Vienna, 1787.

Nachricht für Vernünftige über die Vorstellung der COSA RARA in der Leopoldstadt, Vienna, 1787.

Szekelys Vertheidiger Strafbarer als Szekely, an Joseph, Prague, 1786.

Über das deutsche Singspiel den Apotheker des Hrn. v. Dittersdorf, Vienna, 1786.

Warum wird Kaiser Joseph von seinem Volke nicht geliebt?, Vienna: Wucherer, 1787.

Books

Anekdoten und Bemerkungen über Wien. In Briefen gesammelt, Vienna: Höring, 1787.

Arnold, Ignaz Ferdinand, *Galerie der berühmten Tonkünstler: Karl von Dittersdorf,* Erfurt: Müller, 1810.

Das alte und neue Wien, Vienna: Wucherer, 1788.

Dittersdorf, Ditters von, *Karl von Dittersdorf Lebensbeschreibung,* Leipzig: Breitkopf und Härtel, 1801.

Da Ponte, Lorenzo, *An Extract from the Life of Lorenzo da Ponte,* New York: Gray & Co, 1819.

Da Ponte, Lorenzo, *Le nozze di Figaro, Il Don Giovanni, e l'Assur re d'Ormus,* New York: Gray & Co, 1826.

Da Ponte, Lorenzo, *Memoirs of Lorenzo Da Ponte*, trans. Elizabeth Abbott, New York: Orion, 1929.

Friedrich Ludwig Schröder. Beitrag zur Kunde des Menschen und des Künstlers von F. L. W. Meyer, Hamburg: Campe, 1819.

Handbuch aller unter der Regierung des Kaisers Joseph des II für die k. k. Erbländer ergangenen Verordnungen und Gesetze in einer Sistematischen Verbindung enthält, vol. 3, Vienna: Moesle, 1785.

Kelly, Michael, *Reminiscences*, vol. 1, London: Colburn, 1826.

Kratter, Franz, *Philosophische und statistische Beobachtungen vorzüglich die österreichischen Staaten betrefend*, Frankfurt and Leipzig, 1787.

Lange, Joseph, *Biographie des Joseph Lange k.k. Hofschauspielers*, Vienna: Rehms, 1808.

Leben und Geschichte Kaiser Josephs der Zweiten, vol. 5, Amsterdam, 1791.

Mauntner, Helen, trans., *Life of Mozart (Leben des K.K. Kapellmeisters Wolfgang Gottlieb Mozart. 1798) by Franz Niemetschek*, with an introduction by A. Hyatt King, London: Hyman, 1956.

Mosel, Ignaz von, *Ueber das Leben und die Werke des Salieri*, Vienna: Wallishausser, 1827.

Müller, Johann Heinrich Friedrich, *Abschied von der k.k. Hof- und National-Schaubühne*, Vienna: Wallishausser, 1802.

Niemetschek, Franz Xaver, *Leben des K. K. Kapellmeisters Wolfgang Gottlieb Mozart*, Prague: Herrlischen Buchhandlung, 1798.

Niemetschek, Franz Xaver, *Lebensbeschreibung des K. K. Kapellmeisters Wolfgang Amadeus Mozart*, Prague: Herrlischen Buchhandlung, 1808.

Perinet, Joachim, *20 und 4 Annehmlichkeiten in Wien*, vol. 3, Vienna, 1788.

Perinet, Joachim, *30 Annehmlichkeiten in Wien*, vol. 2, Vienna, 1787.

Pezzl, Johann, *Skizze von Wien*, Vienna and Leipzig: Kraussischen Buchhandlung, 1787.

Philosophische Fragmente über die praktische Musik, Vienna: Taubstummeninstituts-buchdruck, 1787.

Rautenstrauch, Johann, *Das neue Wien. Eine Fabel von Rautenstrauch*, Vienna: Mößle, 1785.

Reitzenstein, Baron Karl Philipp von, *Reise nach Wien*, Hut: Grau, 1795.

Stein, Anton, *Österreichische und türkische Kriegslieder*, Vienna: Hraschanzky, 1788.

Theaterspiegel aller Trauer-Schau-Lust-Sing-und Nachspielen, Balleten und Neben-vorstellungen, Brünn: Traßler, 1788.

Urkunde über die vollzogene Krönung Seiner Majestät des Königs von Böhmen Leopold des Zweiten, Prague: Haase, 1818.

Vertraute Briefe zur Charakteristik von Wien, vol. 2, Görlitz: Hermsdorf und Anton, 1793.

Wiens gegenwärtiger Zustand unter Josephs Regierung, Vienna: Wucherer, 1787.

SECONDARY SOURCES

Allanbrook, Wye J., "Pro Marcellina; The Shape of 'Figaro,' Act IV," *Music & Letters*, vol. 63 (1982), 69–84.

Anderson, Emily, ed., *The Letters of Mozart and His Family*, 3rd ed., London: Macmillan, 1985.

Angermüller, Rudolph, *Wenzel Müller und "sein" Leopoldstadt Theater*, Vienna: Böhlau, 2009.

Angermüller, Rudolph, "Zwei Selbstbiographien von Joseph Weigl [1766–1846]," *Deutsches Jahrbuch der Musikwissenschaft*, vol. 16 (1971), 46–85.

Armbruster, Richard, "Salieri, Mozart und die Wiener Fassung des *Giulio Sabino* von Giuseppe Sarti," *Studien zur Musikwissenschaft*, vol. 44 (1995), 133–66.

Arneth, Alfred Ritter von, *Joseph II. und Leopold von Toscana. Ihr Briefwechsel von 1781 bis 1790*, vol. 2, *1786–1790*, Vienna: Braumüller, 1872.

Arthur, John, "New Light on Mozart's Late Letters," in *Haydn, Mozart, and Beethoven: Studies in the Music of the Classical Period*, ed. Sieghard Brandenburg, Oxford: Oxford University Press, 1998, 127–45.

Bauer, Wilhelm A., Otto E. Deutsch, and Joseph H. Eibl, eds., *Mozart: Briefe und Aufzeichnungen: Gesamtausgabe*, Kassel: Bärenreiter, 1962–75.

Bauman, Thomas, "The Music Reviews in the Allgemeine Deutsche Bibliothek," *Acta Musicologica*, vol. 49 (1997), 60–85.

Beales, Derek, *Against the World 1780–1790*, vol. 2 of *Joseph II*, Cambridge: Cambridge University Press, 2009.

Beales, Derek, "Court, Government and Society in Mozart's Vienna," in *Wolfgang Amadè Mozart: Essays on His Life and Music*, ed. Stanley Sadie, Oxford: Clarendon Press, 1996, 3–20.

Beales, Derek, *Enlightenment and Reform in Eighteenth-Century Europe*, London: I. B. Tauris, 2005.

Bebermeier, Carola, *Celeste Coltellini (1760–1828): Lebensbilder einer Sängerin und Malerin*, Vienna: Böhlau, 2015.

Beer, Adolph, and Joseph Ritter von Friedler, *Joseph II. und Graf Ludwig Cobenzl: Ihr Briefwechsel*, vol. 2, 1785–90, in *Fontes Rerum Austriacarum*, vol. 54 (1901).

Bellini, Alice, "Music and 'Music' in Eighteenth-Century Meta-operatic Scores," *Cambridge Opera Journal*, vol. 6 (2009), 183–207.

Black, David, "Mozart and the Practice of Sacred Music, 1781–91," Ph.D. diss., Harvard University, 2007.

Black, David, "Mozart's Association with the Tonkünstler-Societät," in *Mozart Studies 2*, ed. Simon Keefe, Cambridge: Cambridge University Press, 2015, 55–75.

Blanning, T. C. W., *Joseph II*, London: Longman, 1994.

Brachvogel, A. E., *Geschichte des königl. Theaters zu Berlin*, vol. 2, Berlin: Janke, 1878.

Branscombe, Peter, "Music in the Viennese Popular Theatre of the Eighteenth and Nineteenth Centuries," *Proceedings of the Royal Musical Association*, vol. 98 (1971), 101–12.

Branscombe, Peter, *W. A. Mozart: Die Zauberflöte*, Cambridge: Cambridge University Press, 1991.

Braunbehrens, Volkmar, *Mozart in Vienna*, New York: Grove Weidenfeld, 1990.

Brauneis, Walther, "Mozarts Anstellung am kaiserlichen Hof in Wien. Fakten und Fragen," in *Mozart Experiment Aufklärung*, ed. Herbert Lachmayer, exhibition catalogue, Ostfildern, Germany, 2006, 559–72.

Brown, Bruce Alan, "Beaumarchais, Paisiello and the Genesis of *Così*," in *Wolfgang Amadè Mozart: Essays on his Life and Music*, ed. Stanley Sadie, Oxford: Clarendon Press, 1996, 312–38.

Brown, Bruce Alan, "*Lo specchio francese*: Viennese Opera Buffa and the Legacy of French Theatre," in *The Culture of Opera Buffa in Mozart's Vienna*, ed. Mary Hunter, Princeton: Princeton University Press, 1999, 50–81.

Brown, Bruce Alan, *W. A. Mozart: Così fan tutte*, Cambridge: Cambridge University Press, 1995.

Brown, Bruce Alan, and John A. Rice, "Salieri's *Così fan tutte*," *Cambridge Opera Journal*, vol. 8 (1996), 17–43.

Buch, David J., ed., *Der Stein der Weisen*, Middleton: A-R Editions, 2007.

Buch, David J., "Die Zauberflöte, Masonic Opera, and Other Fairy Tales," *Acta Musicologica*, vol. 76 (2004), 193–219.

Buch, David J., "The House Composers of the Theater auf der Wieden," *Israel Studies in Musicology Online*, vol. 5, iss. 2: *Mozart in Context* (2006).

Buch, David J., *Magic Flutes, Enchanted Forests: The Supernatural in Eighteenth-Century Musical Theater*, Chicago: University of Chicago Press, 2008.

Buch, David J., "Mozart and the Theater auf der Wieden: New Attributions and Perspectives," *Cambridge Opera Journal*, vol. 9 (1995), 195–232.

Cairns, David, *Mozart and His Operas*, Berkeley: University of California Press, 2006.

Castelvecchi, Stefano, *Sentimental Opera: Questions of Genre in the Age of Bourgeois Drama*, Cambridge: Cambridge University Press, 2013.

Chong, Nicholas T., "Music for the Last Supper: The Dramatic Significance of Mozart's Musical Quotations in the *Tafelmusik* of *Don Giovanni*," *Current Musicology*, vol. 92 (2011), 7–52.

Clark, Caryl, "Reading and Listening: Viennese *Frauenzimmer* Journals and the Sociocultural Context of Mozartean Opera Buffa," *Musical Quarterly*, vol. 87 (2004), 140–75.

Corneilson, Paul, "Mozart in l'indice de'teatrali spettacoli," *Newsletter of the Mozart Society of America*, vol. 16, no. 1 (2012), 5–8.

De Alwis, Lisa, *Anti-Da Ponte*, n.p.: Mozart Society of America, 2015.

Deutsch, Otto Erich, *Das Freihaustheater auf der Wieden 1787–1801*, 2nd ed., Vienna: Jugend und Volk, 1937.

Deutsch, Otto Erich, *Mozart: Die Dokumente Seines Lebens*, Kassel: Bärenreiter, 1961.

Deutsch, Otto Erich, *Mozart: A Documentary Biography*, trans. Eric Blom, Peter Branscombe, and Jeremy Noble, London: Simon & Schuster, 1966.

Dunlop, Alison, "La Kaisersammlung: Franz II/I come musicista e collezionista," *Fonti Musicali Italiane*, vol. 19 (2014), 49–67, with English translation "The Kaisersammlung: Franz II/I as Musician and Collector."

Edge, Dexter, "Attributing Mozart (i): Three Accompanied Recitatives," *Cambridge Opera Journal*, vol. 13 (2001), 197–237.

Edge, Dexter, "Mozart's Fee for *Così fan tutte*," *Journal of the Royal Musical Association*, vol. 116 (1991), 211–35.

Edge, Dexter, "Mozart's Reception in Vienna, 1787–1791," in *Wolfgang Amadè Mozart: Essays on His Life and Music*, ed. Stanley Sadie, Oxford: Clarendon Press, 1996, 66–120.

Edge, Dexter, "Mozart's Viennese Copyists," Ph.D. diss., University of Southern California: Los Angeles, 2001.

Edge, Dexter, "Mozart's Viennese Orchestras," *Early Music*, vol. 20 (1992), 64–88.

Edge, Dexter, review of *Concert Life in Haydn's Vienna*, by Mary Sue Morrow, *Haydn Yearbook*, vol. 17 (1992), 108–66.

Edge, Dexter, and David Black, *Mozart: New Documents*, first published 12 June 2014, http://sites.google.com/site/mozartdocuments.

Eisen, Cliff, *New Mozart Documents: A Supplement to O. E. Deutsch's Documentary Biography*, Stanford: Stanford University Press, 1991.

Fuchs, Ingrid, "Nuevas fuentes para la recepción de las óperas de Martín y Soler en Viena, y en particolar, de *Una cosa rara*," in *Los siete mundos de Vicente Martín y Soler*, ed. Dorothea Link and Leonardo J. Waisman, Valencia: Institut Valencià de la Música, 2010, 255–64.

Gidwitz, Patricia Lewy, "'Ich bin die erste Sängerin': Vocal Profiles of Two Mozart Sopranos," *Early Music*, vol. 19 (1991), 565–79.

Gidwitz, Patricia Lewy, "Mozart's Fiordiligi: Adriana Ferrarese del Bene," *Cambridge Opera Journal*, vol. 8 (1996), 199–214.

Girdham, Jane, "A Note on Stephen Storace and Michael Kelly," *Music & Letters*, vol. 76 (1995), 64–67.

Glatthorn, Austin, "The Imperial Coronation of Leopold II and Mozart, Frankfurt am Main, 1790," *Eighteenth-Century Music*, vol. 14 (2017), 89–110.

Goehring, Edmund, *Three Modes of Perception in Mozart*, Cambridge: Cambridge University Press, 2004.

Greisenegger, Wolfgang, "Höfische Theaterfeste in Wien," in *Mozart und Salieri*, ed. Paolo Budroni, Vienna: Vienna University Press, 2008, 67–74.

Haberl, Dieter, "Beethoven's erste Reise," *Neues musikwissenschaftliche Jahrbuch*, vol. 14 (2006), 215–55.

Haberl, Dieter, *Das Regensburgische Diarium (Intelligenzblatt) als musikhistorisches Quelle: Erschießung und Kommentar der Jahrgänge 1760–1810*, Regensburger Studien 9, Regensburg: Stadtarchiv, 2012.

Hadamowsky, Franz, *Die Wiener Hoftheater (Staatstheater) 1776–1966: Verzeichnis der aufgeführten Stücke mit Bestandsnachweis und täglichem Spielplan*, vol. 1, 1776–1810, Vienna: Prachner, 1966.

Hassmann, Elisabeth, *Quellen und Regesten zur Schatzkammer, Gemäldegalerie und zu den drei Kabinetten aus dem Archivbestand des k. k. Oberstkämmereramtes 1777 bis 1787*, *Jahrbuch des Kunsthistorischen Museums Wien*, nos. 15–16, 2015.

Head, Matthew, *Orientalism, Masquerade and Mozart's Turkish Music*, Royal Musical Association Monographs, no. 9, London: Royal Musical Association, 2000.

Heartz, Daniel, *Haydn, Mozart and the Viennese School 1740–1780*, New York: Norton, 1995.

Heartz, Daniel, *Mozart, Haydn and Early Beethoven, 1781–1802*, New York: Norton, 2009.

Heartz, Daniel, "Susanna's Hat," *Early Music* vol. 19 (1991), 585–89.

Heartz, Daniel, "When Mozart Revises: The Case of Guglielmo in *Così fan tutte*," in *Wolfgang Amadè Mozart: Essays on his Life and Music*, ed. Stanley Sadie, Oxford: Clarendon Press, 1996, 355–61.

Hubmayer, Thomas, "Hieronymus Löschenkohl im Kontext der Kultur- und Sozialgeschichte des Josephinismus," M. Phil. diss., University of Vienna, 2012.

Hunter, Mary, *The Culture of Opera Buffa in Mozart's Vienna*, Princeton: Princeton University Press, 1999.

Hunter, Mary, "Rousseau, the Countess, and the Female Domain," in *Mozart Studies 2*, ed. Cliff Eisen, Oxford, 1997, 1–26.

Hunter, Mary, "'Se Vuol Ballare' Quoted: An Early Moment in the Reception History of Figaro," *Musical Times*, vol. 130 (August 1989), 464–67.

Joubert, Estelle, "Dittersdorf's Doktor und Apotheker," in *The Cambridge Companion to Eighteenth-Century Opera*, ed. Anthony R. DelDonna and Pierpaolo Polzonetti, Cambridge: Cambridge University Press, 2009, 190–201.

Keefe, Simon, *Mozart in Vienna: The Final Decade*, Cambridge: Cambridge University Press, 2017.

Ketterer, Robert C., *Ancient Rome in Early Opera*, Urbana: University of Illinois Press, 2004.

Knepler, Georg, *Wolfgang Amadé Mozart*, Cambridge: Cambridge University Press, 1994.

Küster, Konrad, "Lorenzo da Ponte's Viennese Librettos," in *Music in Eighteenth-Century Austria*, ed. David Wyn Jones, Cambridge: Cambridge University Press, 2006, 221–31.

Landon, H. C. Robbins, *Haydn at Eszterháza 1766–1790*, London: Thames and Hudson, 1995.

Landon, H. C. Robbins, *Mozart in Vienna*, New York: Schirmer, 1991.

Leeson, Daniel N., "Mozart's *Le nozze di Figaro*: A Hidden Dramatic Detail," *Eighteenth-Century Music*, vol. 1 (2004), 301–304.

Link, Dorothea, "Anna Morichelli, Vicente Martín y Soler's Champion Singer," English rev. (2010) of "La Cantante Anna Morichelli, Paladin de Vicente Martín y Soler," in *Los Siete Mundos de Vicente Martín y Soler*, ed. Dorothea Link and Leonardo J. Waisman, Valencia: Institut Valencià de la Música, 2010, 328–62.

Link, Dorothea, *Arias for Francesco Benucci: Mozart's First Figaro and Guglielmo*, Recent Researches in the Music of the Classical Era, Middleton: A-R Editions, 2004.

Link, Dorothea, *Arias for Nancy Storace: Mozart's First Susanna*, Recent Researches in the Music of the Classical Era, Middleton: A-R Editions, 2002.

Link, Dorothea, *Arias for Vincenzo Calvesi, Mozart's First Ferrando*, Recent Researches in the Music of the Classical Era, Middleton: A-R Editions, 2011.

Link, Dorothea, "Courtly Entertainments at Laxenburg under Joseph II and Leopold II," in *Antonio Salieri (1750–1825) e il teatro musicale a Vienna: Convenzioni, innovazioni, contaminazioni stilistiche*, ed. Rudolph Angermuller and Elena Biggi Parodi, Lucca: LIM, 2012, 341–44.

Link, Dorothea, "'È la fede degli amanti' and the Viennese Operatic Canon," *Mozart Studies*, ed. Simon Keefe, Cambridge: Cambridge University Press, 2006, 109–36.

Link, Dorothea, "The Fandango Scene in Mozart's *Le nozze di Figaro*," *Journal of the Royal Musical Association*, vol. 133 (2008), 69–92.

Link, Dorothea, "Mozart's Appointment to the Viennese Court," in *Words about Mozart: Essays in Honour of Stanley Sadie*, ed. Dorothea Link and Judith Nagley, Woodbridge: Boydell, 2005, 153–78.

Link, Dorothea, "Nancy Storace's *Annus Horribilis* 1785," *Newsletter of the Mozart Society of America*, vol. 18 (2014), 1–7.

Link, Dorothea, *The National Court Theatre in Mozart's Vienna: Sources and Documents 1783–1792*, Oxford: Clarendon Press, 1998.

Link, Dorothea, "A Newly Discovered Accompanied Recitative to Mozart's 'Vado Ma Dove?,' K.583," *Cambridge Opera Journal*, vol. 12 (2000), 29–50.

Link, Dorothea, "Vienna's Private Theatrical and Musical Life 1783–92, as Reported by Count Karl Zinzendorf," *Journal of the Royal Musical Association*, vol. 122 (1997), 218–19.

Locke, Ralph, *Music and the Exotic from the Renaissance to Mozart*, Cambridge: Cambridge University Press, 2015.

Lorenz, Michael, "Light on Vincenzo Calvesi's Origin," *Musicological Trifles and Biographical Paralipomena* (March 2013), http://michaelorenz.blogspot.co.uk/2013/03.

Lorenz, Michael, "Mozart in the Trattnerhof," *Musicological Trifles and Biographical Paralipomena* (September 2013), http://michaelorenz.blogspot.co.uk/2013/09.

Lorenz, Michael, "Neue Forschungsergebnisse zum Theater auf der Wieden und Emanuel Schikaneder," *Wiener Geschichtsblätter*, vol. 4 (2008), 15–36.

Lorenz, Michael, "Wolfgang von Mozart," *Musicological Trifles and Biographical Paralipomena* (June 2013), http://michaelorenz.blogspot.co.uk/2013/06.

Lütteken, Laurenz, "The Depoliticized Drama: Mozart's *Figaro* and the Depths of Enlightenment," in *The Oxford Handbook of Music Censorship*, ed. Patricia Hall, online.

Mayer, Matthew Z., "The Price for Austria's Security: Part I. Joseph II, the Russian Alliance, and the Ottoman War, 1787–1789," *International Historical Review*, vol. 26 (2004), 257–99.

Mayer, Matthew Z., "The Price for Austria's Security: Part II. Leopold II, the Prussian Threat, and the Peace of Sistova, 1790–1791," *International Historical Review*, vol. 26 (2004), 473–514.

Mellace, Raffaele, "'Questi, nobili albanesi': Neapolitan Couleur Locale in *Così fan tutte*," in *Mozart Studien*, ed. Manfred Hermann Schmid, vol. 24, Vienna: Hollitzer, 2016.

Michtner, Otto, *Das alte Burgtheater als Operbühne*, Vienna: Böhlau, 1970.

Michtner, Otto, "Der Fall Abbé Da Ponte," *Mitteilungen des Österreichischen Staats Archivs*, vol. 19 (1996), 170–209.

Morrow, Mary Sue, *Concert Life in Haydn's Vienna: Aspects of a Developing Musical and Social Institution*, Stuyvesant, NY: Pendragon, 1989.

Nedbal, Martin, "Domenico Guardasoni's Conducting Score for *Così fan tutte*," *Newsletter of the Mozart Society of America*, vol. 21 (2017), 5–10.

Nedbal, Martin, *Prague's Estates Theater, Mozart, and Bohemian Patriotism*, n.p.: Mozart Society of America, 2017.

Nedbal, Martin, "Sex, Politics, and Censorship in Mozart's Don Giovanni/Don Juan," in *The Oxford Handbook of Music Censorship*, ed. Patricia Hall, online.

Page, Janet K., and Dexter Edge, "A Newly Uncovered Autograph Sketch for Mozart's 'Al desio di chi t'adora' K577," *Musical Times*, vol. 132 (1991), 601–6.

Parker, Roger, *Remaking the Song: Operatic Visions and Revisions from Handel to Berio*, Berkeley: University of California Press, 2006.

Payer von Thurn, Rudolph, *Joseph II. als Theaterdirektor*, Vienna: Heidrich, 1920.

Pfeiffer, Gabriele, "Freemason, Mozart's Contemporary, and Theatre Director on the Edge: Franz Kratter (1758–1830) and *Der Friede am Pruth* ('The Treaty of Prut,' 1799). Cataloguing the Komplex Mauerbach, Vienna," *Thema*, vol. 1 (2012), 19–64.

Pillgrab, Daniela, "Lorenzo Da Ponte's Work for the Stage during His Time as a Librettist in Vienna," in *Maske und Kothurn, Internationale Beiträge zur Theater-, Film- und Medienwissenschaft*, vol. 52, no. 4, ed. Michael Hüttler, Vienna, 2006, 49–94.

Plath, Wolfgang, "A Sketch-Leaf for Mozart's Contredanse 'La Bataille,'" in *Haydn, Mozart, and Beethoven: Studies in the Music of the Classical Period*, ed. Sieghard Brandenburg, Oxford: Clarendon Press, 1998, 115–25.

Platoff, John, "A New History for Martín's *Una cosa rara*," *Journal of Musicology*, vol. 12 (1994), 85–115.

Platoff, John, "'Non Tardar Amato Bene' Completed. But Not by Mozart," *Musical Times*, vol. 132 (November 1991), 557–60.

Pohl, Carl Ferdinand, *Denkschrift aus Anlass des hundertjährigen Bestehens der Tonkünstler-Societät*, Vienna: Selbstverlag des "Haydn" Stadt, 1871.

Rice, John, *Antonio Salieri and Viennese Opera*, Chicago: University of Chicago Press, 1998.

Rice, John, "A Bohemian Composer Meets a Mozart Singer: Koželuh's Rondò for Adriana Ferrarese," in *Mozart in Prague: Essays on Performance, Patronage, Sources and Reception*, ed. Kathryn L. Libin, Prague: Mozart Society of America, 2016, 201–26.

Rice, John, "Emperor and Impresario: Leopold II and the Transformation of Viennese Musical Theater, 1790–1792," Ph.D. diss., University of California, Berkeley, 1987.

Rice, John, *Empress Marie Therese and Music at the Viennese Court*, Cambridge: Cambridge University Press, 2003.

Rice, John, "Grand Duke Pietro Leopoldo's Musical Patronage in Florence, 1765–1790, as Reflected in the Ricasoli Collection," https://sites.google.com, updated March-April 2014.

Rice, John, "Leopold II, Mozart, and the Return of a Golden Age," in *Opera and the Enlightenment*, ed. Thomas Bauman and Marita Petzoldt McClymonds, Cambridge: Cambridge University Press, 1995, 271–98.

Rice, John, "Mozart as Soprano," *Mozart Jahrbuch*, vol. 2006 (2008), 345–53.

Rice, John, *Mozart on the Stage*, Cambridge: Cambridge University Press, 2008.

Rice, John, "New Light on Dittersdorf's Ovid Symphonies," *Studi musicali*, vol. 29 (2000), 453–98.

Rice, John, "The Operas of Antonio Salieri as a Reflection of Viennese Opera 1770–1800," in *Music in Eighteenth-Century Austria*, ed. David Wyn Jones, Cambridge: Cambridge University Press, 2006, 210–20.

Rice, John, "The Operatic Culture at the Court of Leopold II and Its Connections to *La clemenza di Tito*," paper presented at Nordic Network for Early Opera, Stockholm, 24–27 August 2013.

Rice, John, "Twin Portraits: Morichelli and Martín y Soler in Vienna in 1787," *Newsletter of the Mozart Society of America*, vol. 21, no. 2 (2017), 11–12.

Ridgewell, Rupert, "Biographical Myth and the Publication of Mozart's Piano Quartets," *Journal of the Royal Musical Association*, vol. 135 (2010), 41–114.

Ridgewell, Rupert, "A Newly Identified Viennese Mozart Edition," in *Mozart Studies 2*, ed. Simon Keefe, Cambridge: Cambridge University Press, 2015, 106–39.

Riedinger, Lothar, "Karl von Dittersdorf als Opernkomponist," *Studien zur Musikwissenschaft*, vol. 2 (1914), 212–349.

Robinson, Michael, "Paisiello, Mozart and Casti," in *Internationaler Musikwissenschaftlicher Kongreß zum Mozartjahr 1991*, ed. Ingrid Fuchs, Tutzing: Schneider, 1993.

Rumph, Stephen, "Unveiling Cherubino," *Eighteenth-Century Music*, vol. 4 (2007), 129–38.

Salter, Lionel, "Footnote to a Satire: Salieri's *Prima la musica, poi le parole*," *Musical Times*, vol. 126 (January 1785), 21–24.

Schirlbauer, Anna, "Belvedere-Sommerkonzerte im Josephinischen Wien (1785–1787)," *Wiener Geschichtsblätter*, vol. 66 (2011), 189–211.

Schlitter, Hans, *Geheime Correspondenz Josefs II. mit seinem Minister in den Österreichischen Niederlanden Ferdinand Grafen Trauttmansdorff, 1787–1789*, Vienna: Holzhausen, 1902.

Schenk, Erich, *Mozart and His Times*, London: Secker & Warburg, 1960.

Schwob, Rainer J., "Partner oder Rivalen? Italienische Oper und deutsches Singspiel in der Ära Joseph II," in *Mozart und Salieri*, ed. Paolo Budroni, Vienna: Vienna University Press, 2008, 75–82.

Sommer-Mathis, Andrea, *"Tu felix Austria nube": Hochzeitsfeste der Habsburger im 18.Jahrhundert*, Vienna: Musikwissenschaftlicher Verlag, 1994.

Siniscalchi, Marina Maymone, *L'Ape Musicale di Lorenzo Da Ponte*, Rome: Il ventaglia, 1988.

Spaethling, Robert, *Mozart's Letters, Mozart's Life*, London: Norton, 2000.

Steptoe, Andrew, *The Mozart–Da Ponte Operas*, Oxford: Clarendon Press, 1988.

Swenson, Edward, "Prima la musica," *Analecta Musicologica*, vol. 9 (1970), 112–29.

Tyler, Linda, "Aria as Drama: A Sketch from Mozart's *Der Schauspieldirektor*," *Cambridge Opera Journal*, vol. 2 (1990), 251–67.

Tyson, Alan, *Mozart: Studies of the Autograph Scores*, Cambridge, Mass.: Harvard University Press, 1987.

Unverricht, Hubert, *Carl von Dittersdorf: Briefe, ausgewählte Urkunden und Akten*, *Studien zur Musikwissenschaft*, vol. 54 (2008).

Verti, Roberto, "The *Indice de' teatrali spettacoli*, Milan, Venice, Rome 1764–1823: Preliminary Research on a Source for the History of Italian Opera," *Periodica Musica*, vol. 3 (Spring 1985), 1–7.

Verti, Roberto, ed., *Un almanacco drammatico: Indice de' teatrali spettacoli* [facsimile], Pesaro: Fondazione Rossini, Italy, 1996.

Volek, Tomislav, and Ivan Bittner, *The Mozartiana of Czech and Moravian Archives*, Prague: Archives Dept., Czech Ministry of the Interior, 1991.

Warrack, John, *German Opera: From the Beginnings to Wagner*, Cambridge: Cambridge University Press, 2001.

Weidinger, Hans Ernst, "Il dissoluto punito. Untersuchungen zur äußeren und inneren Entstehungsgeschichte von Lorenzo da Pontes & Wolfgang Amadeus Mozarts Don Giovanni," Ph.D. diss., University of Vienna, 2002.

Weidinger, Hans Ernst, "The 'Dux Drafts,' Casanova's Contribution to Da Ponte's and Mozart's *Don Giovanni*," in *Maske und Kothurn, Internationale Beiträge zur Theater-, Film- und Medienwissenschaft*, vol. 52, no. 4, ed. Michael Hüttler, Vienna: Böhlau, 2007, 95–130.

Weyda, H., "Briefe an Erzherzog Franz (nachmals K. Franz II) von seiner ersten Gemahlin Elisabeth 1785–1789," *Archiv für Österreichische Geschichte*, vol. 44 (1871), 1–262.

Will, Richard, "The Ambivalence of Mozart's Countess," in *Music, Libraries, and the Academy: Essays in Honor of Leonore Coral*, ed. James P. Cassaro, Middleton: A-R Editions, 2007, 31–54.

Wolf, Adam, *Leopold II. und Marie Christine. Ihr Briefwechsel (1781–92)*, Vienna: Gerold, 1867.

Wolf, Adam, *Marie Christine, Erzherzogin von Oesterreich*, vol. 1, *1742–1788*, Vienna: Gerold, 1863.

Wolff, Christoph, *Mozart at the Gateway to His Fortune*, New York: Norton, 2012.

Wolff, Larry, *The Singing Turk: Ottoman Power and Operatic Emotions on the European Stage from the Siege of Vienna to the Age of Nations*, Stanford: Standford University Press, 2016.

Woodfield, Ian, "'Che soave zeffiretto' and the Structure of Act III of *Le nozze di Figaro*," *Journal of the Royal Musical Association*, vol. 143 (2018), 89–136.

Woodfield, Ian, "Christian Gottlob Neefe and the Early Reception of *Le nozze di Figaro* and *Don Giovanni*," *Newsletter of the Mozart Society of America*, vol. 20 (Spring 2016), 4–6.

Woodfield, Ian, "Fireworks and Wind Bands in 1780s Vienna: A Context for Mozart's 'Nacht Musique?,'" *Music & Letters*, vol. 98 (2017), 1–25.

Woodfield, Ian, *Mozart's Così fan tutte: A Compositional History*, Woodbridge: Boydell, 2008.

Woodfield, Ian, "Mozart's 'Jupiter': A Symphony of Light?," *Musical Times*, vol. 147 (Winter 2006), 25–46.

Woodfield, Ian, *Performing Operas for Mozart*, Cambridge: Cambridge University Press, 2012.

Woodfield, Ian, "Reflections on Mozart's 'Non so più cosa son, cosa faccio,'" *Eighteenth-Century Music*, vol. 3 (2006), 133–39.

Woodfield, Ian, "The Trouble with Cherubino . . . ," in *Mozart Studies 2*, ed. Simon Keefe, Cambridge: Cambridge University Press, 2015, 168–94.

Woodfield, Ian, *The Vienna Don Giovanni*, Woodbridge: Boydell, 2010.

Index